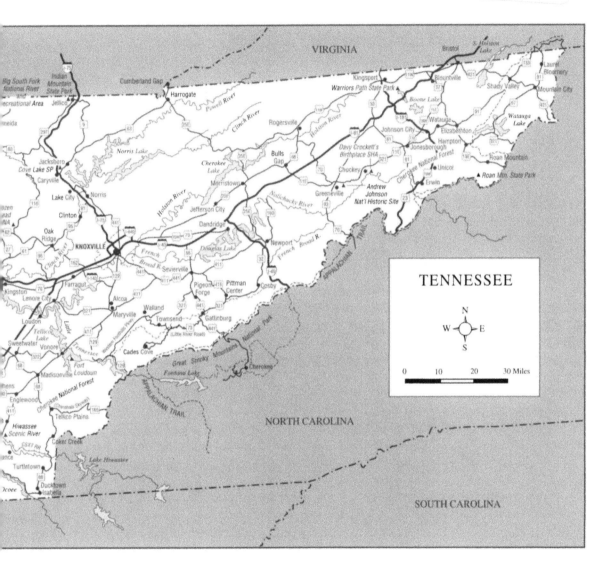

VIRGINIA

Big South Fork
National River
and
Recreational Area

Indian
Mountain
State Park

Cumberland Gap

Harrogate

Jellico

Oneida

Jacksboro
Cove Lake SP

Caryville

Lake City

Norris

Clinton

Oak
Ridge

KNOXVILLE

Kingston

Lenoir City

Loudon

Sweetwater

Vonore

Madisonville

Englewood

Turtletown

Ducktown
Isabella

Ocoee

Hiwassee
Scenic River

Tellico Plains

Cherokee National Forest

Fort
Loudoun

Tellico
Lake

Cades Cove

Fontana Lake

APPALACHIAN TRAIL

Lake Hiwassee

Little Tennessee

Vonore

Athens

Farragut

Alcoa

Maryville

Walland

Townsend

Gatlinburg

Pigeon
Forge

Pittman
Center

Cosby

Newport

Sevierville

French
Broad R.

Douglas Lake

Dandridge

Jefferson City

Morristown

Cherokee
Lake

Bulls
Gap

Rogersville

Powell River

Clinch River

Holston River

Norris Lake

Clinch River

Holston River

French Broad R.

Nolichucky River

Greeneville

Davy Crockett's
Birthplace SHA

Chuckey

Andrew
Johnson
Nat'l Historic Site

Cherokee National Forest

Erwin

Unicoi

Roan Mountain

Roan Mtn. State Park

Jonesborough

Johnson City

Elizabethton

Hampton

Watauga

Watauga
Lake

Mountain
City

Shady Valley

Laurel
Bloomery

Kingsport

Warriors Path State Park

Blountville

Bristol

S. Holston
Lake

Boone Lake

Great Smoky Mountains National Park

APPALACHIAN TRAIL

Cherokee

NORTH CAROLINA

SOUTH CAROLINA

TENNESSEE

N
W   E
S

0   10   20   30 Miles

Traveling Tennessee

A COMPLETE TOUR GUIDE TO THE VOLUNTEER STATE
FROM THE HIGHLANDS OF THE SMOKY MOUNTAINS
TO THE BANKS OF THE MISSISSIPPI RIVER

CATHY AND VERNON SUMMERLIN

RUTLEDGE HILL PRESS® ■ *Nashville, Tennessee*

Published in Nashville, Tennessee, by Rutledge Hill Press, Inc., 211 Seventh Avenue North, Nashville, Tennessee 37219. Distributed in Canada by H. B. Fenn & Company, Ltd., 34 Nixon Road, Bolton, Ontario L7E 1W2. Distributed in Australia by The Five Mile Press Pty., Ltd., 22 Summit Road, Noble Park, Victoria 3174. Distributed in New Zealand by Tandem Press, 2 Rugby Road, Birkenhead, Auckland 10. Distributed in the United Kingdom by Verulam Publishing, Ltd., 152a Park Street Lane, Park Street, St. Albans, Hertfordshire AL2 2AU.

Typography by Karen Phillips, Nashville, Tennessee
Design by Gore Studio, Inc., Nashville, Tennessee
Map by Parrot Graphics

All photographs are by the authors unless otherwise indicated.

Library of Congress Cataloging in Publication Data
Summerlin, Cathy, 1953–
    Traveling Tennessee : a complete tour guide to the Volunteer State
  from the highlands of the Smoky Mountains to the banks of the
  Mississippi River / Cathy and Vernon Summerlin
        p.   cm.
  Includes index.
  ISBN 1-55853-676-0 (pb)
    1. Tennessee--Tours. 2. Summerlin, Vernon, 1943– . I. Title.
F434.3.S86 1998
917.6804'53--dc21   983-41744

Printed in the United States of America

1 2 3 4 5 6 7 8 9 — 03 02 01 00 99

For Shell, Maria, and Ashley,
three of our favorite reasons
to come home

Contents

MIDDLE TENNESSEE

Loop 5

Loop 6

Nashville

Loop 7

Chattanooga

WEST TENNESSEE

Acknowledgments

EVERY DAY, as we traveled Tennessee, we met friendly, helpful people who eagerly shared their love of their favorite places with us. Though they'll have to remain nameless, we thank them for making our job such fun.

We also thank Larry Stone, president of Rutledge Hill Press, whose willingness to search for a creative solution when the page counts ran far too long makes us once again appreciate his faith in the project. Jennifer Greenstein has been wonderful in helping us sort through manuscripts and slides, displaying those chosen to best advantage. Peaches Scribner, one of our hardworking editors, is now enjoying life in Florida. John Reiman and Mike Towle added finishing touches.

The many writers who have shared their knowledge with us either in person or through their wonderful books include Jeff Bradley, Robert Brandt, Bill Hooks, Jimmy Jacobs, Ardi Lawrence, Lea Lawrence, Russ Manning, Doug Markham, Evan Means, Vicki Rozema, Carolyn Sakowski, Holly Sherwin, the writers of the Smoky Mountains Natural History Association, and the writers involved so long ago in the WPA Writers Project in Tennessee.

We thank all those who have so kindly opened their inns and businesses to us. A special thanks to those who opened their cities to us: Landon Howard of Chattanooga; Kay Powell and Bob Easton of Pigeon Forge; Barbara Parker, Carlynne Foster, and Lorene Lambert at Tennessee Tourism; and Barbara Stagg of Rugby. The local convention and visitor bureaus and chambers of commerce were especially helpful, but none more so than Lori Franklin of Byrdstown, Robin Plumlee and Linda Eaves of Townsend, and Randy McKeel of Memphis, whose tours left us with indelible impressions of the communities they represent.

The many rangers we've talked to through the years at the Great Smoky Mountains National Park represent a wealth of information and share it willingly. Nancy Gray was a wonderful help with last minute details. Ranger Howard Duncan and the rest of his crew at Big South Fork are always helpful and informative.

We also thank our friends and family, who served as models when we needed them, shared their favorite Tennessee spots, and understood what deadlines are all about. Thanks to Bobbie McAllister for her never-ending support and Kathie German for keeping an eye on the tribe.

Introduction

Tennessee, the sixteenth state admitted to the Union, is divided into three traditional divisions of East, Middle, and West Tennessee that are roughly defined by the meandering Tennessee River.

The topography ranges from rugged six-thousand-foot peaks in the Great Smoky Mountains in the east to the vast, flat, fertile floodplain along the Mississippi River at the western border. The climate, flora, and fauna in East Tennessee are similar to conditions found in New England. The rolling hills and basins of Middle Tennessee approximate the conditions in the Ohio Valley, while the rich, dark soil and warmer climate in West Tennessee are part of the Deep South.

Diverse cultures are represented in Tennessee. Between its borders you can explore the role of longhunters in the westward expansion of our young nation in East and Middle Tennessee. A tour of Tennessee's musical heritage takes you from the birthplace of country music in East Tennessee to today's lively country music scene in Nashville, before continuing to Memphis, the home of the " king" of rock 'n' roll and the father of the blues.

The stories of the proud Cherokee Nation and Tennessee's gold rush unfold in the foothills of the Smokies around the Cherokee National Forest near Tellico Plains. You may choose to learn more about Tennessee's utopian societies and the legacy of coal miners while visiting one of the popular state parks on the beautifully rugged Cumberland Plateau.

Among the earliest white settlers in the area that would become Tennessee were longhunters, men who left their frontier homes for long periods at a time in search of game. The longhunters followed game trails through the natural barriers created by the rugged peaks of the Allegheny Mountains, as the Appalachians were then known.

Frontiersmen like Daniel Boone and Davy Crockett captured the attention of the nation as they explored the lands that later became Tennessee. The discovery of the Cumberland Gap opened exploration and settlement of the land west of the original thirteen colonies as Tennessee became the gateway to the west.

Political diversity is a Tennessee hallmark. Tennessee was the last state to join the Confederacy and the first to rejoin the Union. The years that lay between these events turned neighbors into bitter enemies as 454 battles and innumerable skirmishes were fought on Tennessee soil. Only Virginia saw more battles take place within its boundaries.

In the midstate, the vast Nashville Basin lay

between the Tennessee River to the west and the western escarpment of the Cumberland Plateau to the east. This was traditional Indian hunting ground, but much of the fertile farmland was offered to Revolutionary War veterans as payment for service to the fledgling central government. Nashville quickly became the seat of government and civilization on the western frontier in the early 1800s when the Natchez Trace connected Nashville by land with the southern outposts of Natchez and New Orleans on the Mississippi River.

Middle Tennessee was the scene of several major Civil War battles and struggles for control of Nashville, Franklin, Murfreesboro, and Chattanooga as the Union and Confederate armies swept through the area repeatedly. Major Middle Tennessee battlefield sites include Stones River in Murfreesboro, Franklin, Shiloh, and Chattanooga.

In 1925 radio listeners heard the WSM *Barn Dance* on Saturday nights. It became the *Grand Ole Opry* and Nashville became Music City USA to millions of country music fans across the country and around the world who come for Saturday night shows and popular events like Fan Fair and Tin Pan South.

Like East Tennessee, today Middle Tennessee has many well-preserved communities with antique shopping, bed and breakfasts, and historic sites as well as popular state parks with lakes and rivers for water sports nearby.

At the western end of the state, the forces of the mighty Mississippi worked to create the broad flood plains and oxbow lakes found on Tennessee's last frontier.

Most of West Tennessee became Chickasaw territory. The Chickasaw were visited on the bluffs along the Mississippi by the Spaniard Hernando de Soto in 1541 who was in search of gold. The French came seeking trade with the Chickasaw in

1673. The British also wanted control of the Chickasaw Bluffs in order to control the Mississippi River. The three nations competed for influence and control for many years.

Early Nashville settlers played prominent roles in the establishment of Memphis. On the fourth Chickasaw Bluff on the east bank of the Mississippi, Gen. James Robertson of Nashville established a depot to conduct business with the Chickasaw in 1782. Twelve years later, John Overton established a trading post at Chickasaw Bluff. In 1819 Overton, Andrew Jackson, and Gen. James Winchester founded Memphis by marking out 362 lots on a high bluff overlooking the Mississippi at the mouth of the Wolf River.

The settlers of West Tennessee found rich soil prime for planting in the early to mid-1800s. Memphis became the most populated area and the cultural center of West Tennessee because it was a river town—shipping timber, cotton, and other products our growing country needed. Today West Tennessee leads the state in agricultural production.

Unlike the sustenance farms of East Tennessee, Memphis was surrounded by vast cotton plantations worked with slave labor brought up from New Orleans. Barges and flatboats made their way from Memphis to New Orleans and river trade flourished with the advent of steamboats. By 1850 Memphis was designated a port of customs and became one of the busiest ports in the United States.

Beale Street was the center of black culture in the South and Memphis was the home of Beale Street. W. C. Handy, Father of the Blues, lived and performed here, as did many other blues greats.

Sun Studios brought rock and roll to Memphis—and the world—with recordings of an unknown named Elvis Presley. Millions make the pilgrimage to Graceland, the home of the only "king" America ever produced.

Memphis is not only the home of a thriving Beale Street blues scene, but also of more attractions than you can visit in a week of steady sightseeing, including Graceland, Mud Island, the Pink Palace Museum and IMAX theater, the National Civil Rights Museum, the Pyramid, the Memphis Zoo, and the Brooks Museum of Art.

Tennessee is blessed with deep, clear lakes, rushing rivers, lush forests, and picturesque communities as well as sophisticated cities with much to offer, including Knoxville, the gateway to the Smokies; Chattanooga, the environmental city; Nashville, Music City USA, and Memphis, the birthplace of rock 'n' roll.

In *Traveling Tennessee*, we take you from the founding of the state in 1796 to the present, east to west, and north to south, in a series of loop tours designed to explore the best a particular region has to offer. Along the way you'll meet famous personages and everyday folks, explore some incredibly beautiful countryside, visit restaurants, museums, bed and breakfasts, antique malls, specialty shops, and historic sites.

We offer information on the social, political, and natural history of areas we visit, but we don't profess to be academic historians, geologists, or naturalists. We feel compelled to pass on intriguing bits of information that we find interesting and make reference to books by other authors we think you may find interesting.

We introduce you to TVA and U.S. Army Corps of Engineer lakes, state parks and wildlife management areas, national parks and forests, and the opportunities to enjoy Tennessee's great outdoors while hiking, biking, rafting, fishing, hunting, swimming, camping, wildlife watching, golfing, horseback riding, or canoeing.

Although we don't have room to take you to every community in our 42,022-square-mile state, we direct you to what we consider the best events and sites each region has to offer. We hope you'll find your time pleasantly spent in each of the communities we explore and look forward to hearing which you liked best.

We omitted individual addresses and phone numbers in each community for national motel/hotel franchises but made mention of their presence. The following toll free numbers may be used for reservations:

Best Western	800-528-1234
Budget Host	800-283-4678
Comfort Inn	800-228-5150
Clubhouse Inn	800-258-2466
Crowne Plaza	800-227-6963
Days Inn	800-325-2525
Doubletree	800-222-8733
Econo Lodge	800-553-2666
Family Inns of America	800-251-9752
Garden Plaza	800-342-7336
Hampton Inn	800-426-7866
Heritage Inn	800-762-7065
Hilton Inn	800-445-8667
HoJo Inn	800-446-4656
Holiday Inn	800-465-4329
Hyatt Regency	800-233-1234
Quality Inn	800-228-5151
Radisson	800-333-3333
Ramada Inn	800-272-6232
Red Carpet Inn	800-251-1962
Shoney's Inn	800-222-2222
Super 8	800-800-8000
Travel Lodge	800-578-7878

Cathy and Vernon Summerlin live quietly in the country near Leipers Fork, Tennessee.

Cathy, when she gets time away from performing duties as a registered nurse at Vanderbilt Medical Center, loves to travel and garden. She is a regular contributor to the travel sections of newspapers throughout the southeast. Her first two books, *Traveling the Trace*, and *Traveling the Southern Highlands*, were coauthored with Vernon.

Vernon is an award-winning outdoor writer, columnist, and photographer. He is the publisher and editor of *Tennessee Angler* magazine, producer of *Tennessee Angler Radio*, cohost of *Volunteer Sportsman Radio*, a freelance writer and photographer, and a television field host. His articles have appeared in many outdoor magazines, including *Field & Stream*, *Outdoor Life*, and *Bassmaster*. His first book was *Two Dozen Fishing Holes—A Guide to Middle Tennessee*. His next book, *The Compleat Tennessee Angler*, written with Doug Markham, was scheduled for a 1999 release.

Traveling Tennessee

Although East Tennessee's mountain vistas attract millions of visitors annually, it's still possible to find a private getaway.

EAST TENNESSEE

Visitors to East Tennessee enjoy visiting historic sites and traveling into the beautiful high country for outdoor recreation ranging from hiking to white-water rafting. We have divided East Tennessee into a series of loop tours originating along and returning to I-40, I-81, or Knoxville for ease of access.

The first East Tennessee tour begins on the Tennessee-Virginia state line in Bristol and proceeds to visit the first permanent settlement outside the original thirteen colonies, enjoys the beautiful high country nearby at Roan Mountain State Park, and experiences mountain hiking and camping in the Cherokee National Forest.

You will also visit historic Jonesborough, the oldest town in Tennessee, the home of President Andrew Johnson at Greeneville, and the oldest continually operating inn in Tennessee, the Hale Springs Inn in Rogersville.

Another loop explores the communities bordering the eastern and northern edge of the Great Smoky Mountains. As always, we direct you to outdoor recreation, including our favorite hiking trails and trout streams, bed and breakfasts, antiques shops, and our preferred restaurants while sharing with you some of the historic and cultural attractions of the area.

A third loop visits the quiet side of the Smokies at Townsend, the historic homeland of the Overhill Cherokee, and the southwestern portion of the Cherokee National Forest. This was the site of the legendary Cherokee capital, Chota, and later Tennessee's gold rush at Coker Creek. It's also home to one of the most scenic mountains byways in the Southeast, the Cherohala Skyway between Tellico Plains and Robbinsville, North Carolina. Both the Hiwassee and the Ocoee Rivers provide water sports for white-water enthusiasts and there are many miles of trout streams in the vicinity.

Another tour visits the historic Cumberland Gap and the Wilderness Road carved by Daniel Boone as well as the cities built by technology at Norris and Oak Ridge, the "Atomic City."

One entire chapter is devoted to the many good reasons to visit Knoxville, the gateway to the Smokies, including interesting museums, great restaurants, and the Old Town district.

Whether you spend a weekend or a week, visit the most-visited national park in the nation, or find a personal place of solitude, you'll find many reasons to enjoy your stay and to return to explore new horizons and retrace the footsteps of those who preceded us to this beautiful country.

ᔰ Loop I

I *Bristol*

A Tale of Two Cities

During the earliest colonial settlement of the area now known as Bristol, the French and British were engaged in an escalating struggle for dominance in America that began with the establishment of the British colony at Jamestown in 1607 and the French colony at Quebec in 1608.

The British victories at Montreal and Quebec paved the way for the Treaty of Paris in 1763 which gave the British sole dominion over Canada and the land east of the Mississippi. In an attempt to soothe the Indian populace west of the Allegheny Mountains, as the Appalachians were then known, George III prohibited settlement beyond the crest of the mountains from Maine to Georgia. Settlers already living there were to leave and private purchase of lands from the Indians was forbidden.

By 1772 there were about seventy farms belonging to settlers on land that had been obtained in a treaty negotiated with the Cherokee in the fall of 1770 that legitimized what had previously been squatter claims. Virginia governed these settlements north of the Holston River while North Carolina officiated at settlements farther south at Sycamore Shoals (*see* Elizabethton).

Bristol's earliest name was Big Meet Camp, the Cherokee name for the area of canebreaks that drew game to graze from nearby salt licks. With white settlement, other names for the future twin cities followed, including Sapling Grove and Shelby's Fort, named for early settler Evan Shelby who bought land and built a fort here in the 1770s. According to Carolyn Sakowski in *Touring the East Tennessee Backroads,* a hundred thousand immigrants passed through the fort during the 1780s on their way west.

Evan Shelby's son moved on to Kentucky and sold the family's East Tennessee land to Col. James King. The community on the Tennessee side became known as Kings Meadow with the Virginia side known as Goodson, named for another colonel who figured prominently in the development of the area.

By 1856 an economic boom was expected from the railroad line from Kings Meadow to Knoxville. The Virginia side of the town was incorporated as Goodson and the Tennessee side chartered as Bristol, named after the manufacturing center at Bristol, England, in anticipation of future industry. Locals chose to call both communities Bristol and in 1890, Goodson officially became Bristol, Virginia.

The dividing line between the states of Virginia and Tennessee was disputed until 1901 when it was established at its present location. State Street was established as the dividing line when Tennessee formally ceded the northern half of the street to Virginia in 1901, officially ending the dispute that began more than one hundred years earlier. In 1910 a brightly lit sign was erected over State Street that claims a Kodak moment as it promises "Bristol VA TN—A Good Place to Live."

Bristol claims the honor of being the birthplace of country music. In late July and early August 1927, Ralph Peer of the Victor Talking Machine Company came to town after advertising for local talent to record.

He used a temporary studio to record titles

that launched the career of Jimmie Rodgers, a former railroad brakeman who became country music's first big star with yodels heard 'round the world. He also recorded the Stonemans and the Carter family, A. P., Sara, and Maybelle.

A mural on the wall outside Lark Amusement Company at 824 State Street pays tribute to this part of Bristol's history.

Country music fans from near and far make the trek to the Carter Family Fold and Museum in nearby Hiltons, Virginia, at Maces Spring. There's now a museum in the store A. P. Carter came home to run after he and Sara retired.

This was the site of Saturday night performances in the midseventies that drew so many listeners they had to move to a new building called the Fold that holds nearly one thousand fans of the family-oriented traditional acoustic music played here.

A two-day festival is held the first weekend in August commemorating the 1927 recording sessions.

Bristol was also the birthplace and early child-hood home of country music legend Tennessee Ernie Ford. The unassuming frame house at 1223 Anderson Street also serves as the headquarters of the Bristol Historical Association.

As you drive along State Street you can't miss the grand marquee for the Paramount Theatre Center for the Arts, a renovated 1931 movie palace. The 756-seat venue offers Pickin' at the Paramount, an acoustic bluegrass and country music heritage performance one evening each month and shows ranging from country music headliners like Ricky Skaggs to Broadway musical revues. An assortment of bluegrass and traditional musicians play on Tuesday evenings.

Down the street a fifty-year bluegrass tradition continues at the Star Barber Shop where locals gather to pick and grin every Thursday morning. Visitors are welcome to listen or join in as they feel fit.

While you're downtown, visit the antique malls and shops on State Street including Heritage Antiques and Collectibles, Mary Ann Stone Antiques and Interiors, and Antiques Unlimited

Bristol is recognized as the birthplace of country music.

or turn north on Commonwealth Avenue to visit A Abe's or the Bristol Antique Mall.

The Troutdale Dining Room has developed a loyal following of Bristol diners. The historic structure lends itself to casual candlelit dining and their selections of fine wines and coffees invite you to relax. The Athens Steakhouse, the Vinyard Restaurant and Lounge, the Bristol Bagel and Bakery Company, and K. P. Duty Gourmet Shoppe and Cafe are also popular.

New Hope Bed and Breakfast is a two-story late Victorian with four rooms with queen- or king-sized beds and private baths. You may choose to take your breakfast in your room, in the dining room, or on the large wraparound porch.

Both Bristols and a fifty-mile vicinity swell with up to one hundred thousand eager auto racing fans making their way to the Bristol Motor Speedway, the world's fastest, i.e., shortest, steeply banked half-mile National Association for Stock Car Auto Racing (NASCAR) track. If NASCAR racing isn't your cup of tea, we suggest you steer clear of Bristol on its six "big" race weekends each year.

National franchises represented include Comfort Inn, Days Inn, Hampton Inn, HoJo Inn, Holiday Inn, and a KOA campground.

The two-thousand-acre Steele Creek Park is city operated and features a nine-hole golf course, paddleboat rentals, fishing, hiking trails, and a nature center.

Bristol Caverns off scenic US 421 are five miles southeast of town. The seventy-eight-acre cave is one of two caves of interest in the area and one of the largest caverns in the southern Appalachian region. You'll see formations here 200 million years old on three levels.

Continue on US 421 to visit South Holston Lake, a TVA impoundment of the South Fork of the Holston River which drains the Mount Rogers area of Virginia. The scenic twenty-four-mile-long lake is surrounded by sheer rock bluffs with the Holston Mountains towering above the southeastern shoreline.

The dam is a huge dirt-filled structure 285 feet high spanning 1,600 feet impounding 7,580 surface acres. Anglers seek a wide variety of fish, with smallmouth bass, walleye, catfish, and rainbow trout fisheries leading the lot. Record-sized brown trout have been taken from the tailwaters below the dam.

There are several commercial docks and marinas dotting the shoreline. RV camping is available at Friendship Marina, Painter Creek Dock, Sulli-

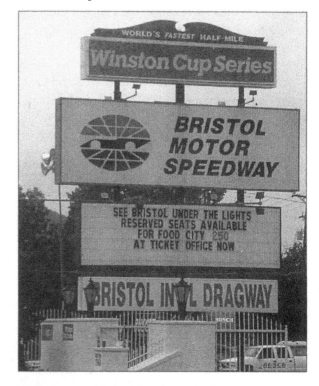

NASCAR fans attend races at Bristol Motor Speedway.

At Rocky Mount, between Bristol and Johnson City, visitors can view one of the oldest structures in the state.

van County Park, and Washington County (Virginia) Park while basic (no hookups) camping is available at the U.S. Forest Service campgrounds at Jacob's Creek Recreation Area and Little Oak Mountain Recreation Area.

The second cave in the vicinity is Appalachian Caverns off US 11E south of Bristol near the historic community of Blountville, named for Gov. William Blount. Operated by the nonprofit Appalachian Caverns Foundation, the caverns have nearly a mile of walkways in the regular tour and a three-to-four-hour "wild tour" for more adventuresome spelunkers.

The seat of Sullivan County, Blountville claims more original log structures than any other town in Tennessee. Stop by the two-story log cabin known as Anderson Townhouse for a walking tour map and information.

Smith Haven Bed and Breakfast was built between 1848 and 1851, but it has been modernized with bathrooms and air conditioning. The

house and guest rooms are filled with period antiques.

Farther southwest along US 11E toward Johnson City, Rocky Mount, one of the oldest structures in the state, is a two-story log structure built during 1770–1772 by William Cobb. The living area and bedrooms are separated from the dining area and kitchen by a covered porch known as a dogtrot.

When William Blount was appointed governor and superintendent of Indian Affairs of the Southwest Territory by George Washington in 1790, he came to live with the Cobb family at Rocky Mount for two years, making it the site of the first capitol of the Southwest Territory.

Rocky Mount is now the property of the state of Tennessee. The house, grounds, outbuildings, and the Massengill Museum of Overmountain History are open for viewing daily except weekends in January and February, Thanksgiving, and December 21–January 5 (*see* Elizabethton for more on overmountain men and Knoxville for more on William Blount.)

Continue on US 421 to visit South Holston Lake, Shady Valley, and Mountain City.

All of the following accommodations are Bristol, TN, with zip code 37620, and all telephone listings are area code 423, except where noted.

Accommodations:
Glencarin Manor, 224 Old Abingdon Hwy., Bristol, VA 24201; 800-484-5591 or 540-466-0224.
New Hope Bed and Breakfast, 822 Georgia Ave., 989-3343.
Smith Haven Bed and Breakfast, 2357 Hwy. 37, Blountville, 37617; 800-606-4833 or 323-0174.

Attractions:
Appalachian Caverns, 323-2337.
Bristol Caverns, 878-2011.
Bristol Motor Speedway, 764-8449 or 764-1161.
Carter Family Museum, Hiltons, VA; 540-386-6054.
Paramount Theatre Center for the Arts, 968-7456.
Rocky Mount Museum, Piney Flats, 37686; 538-7396.
Star Barber Shop, 540-466-8921.

Dining:
Athens Steakhouse, 652-2202 or 540-466-8271 (two locations).
Ridgewood Restaurant, 538-7543.
The Troutdale Dining Room, 968-9099.

Shopping:
A Abe's Antiques, Bristol, 423-466-6895.
Antiques Unlimited, Bristol, 423-764-4211.
Bristol Antique Mall, Bristol, 423-466-4064.
Heritage Antiques, Bristol, 423-669-0774.
Mary Ann Stone Antiques and Interiors, Bristol, 423-968-5181.

Special Events:
August–Carter Family Memorial Concert
September–Autumn Chase Festival

Camping:
Friendship Marina, 423-878-3128.
Jacob's Creek Recreation Area, Elizabethton, 423-542-2942.
Little Oak Mountain Recreation Area, Elizabethton, 423-542-2942.
Observation Knob at Sullivan County Park, 423-878-5561.
Washington County Park, Abingdon, VA, 540-628-9677.

For More Information:
Bristol Tennessee/Virginia Chamber of Commerce, 20 Volunteer Pkwy., P.O. Box 519, Bristol, VA 24203; 423-989-4850.

2 *Shady Valley, Mountain City, Laurel Bloomery*
Land Between Two States

Shady Valley, a lovely little community at the intersection of US 421 and TN 133, is surrounded by the Iron and Holston Mountains and the northern portion of the Cherokee National Forest.

The Cranberry Festival held in Shady Valley each October honors the Tennessee cranberries that grow along Beaver Dam Creek with food, music, dance, children's activities, and craft demonstrations.

Choices for accommodations in Shady Valley include Patton's Bed and Breakfast two miles north on TN 133 which has one room with a private bath and the Beaver Dam Creek Guest House. The Guest House is a two-bedroom, one-bath farmhouse that can accommodate up to eight people and provide trout fishing or tubing on a mountain stream.

The Cherokee National Forest campground at Backbone Rock Recreation Area has thirteen campsites that are generally open from April to October.

This unusual rock formation consists of a wall of sandstone nearly one hundred feet high and thirty feet thick jutting off of Holston Mountain. In 1901 a fourteen-foot-long railroad tunnel was blasted through the rock, which TN 133 passes through today. The area has two picnic shelters built by the Civilian Conservation Corps (CCC) in the 1930s. Beaverdam Creek, a scenic trout stream, flows through the recreation area if you're interested in wetting a line.

There are spring wildflowers along the creek

The Johnson County Welcome Center in Mountain City fronts a campground and picnic areas.

bottomland and hiking trails, including a short trail that goes over the top of Backbone Rock with the assistance of CCC-built rock steps. If you're traveling with children, this is an area requiring adult supervision.

Mountain City, the county seat of Johnson County, is situated at an altitude of 2,499 feet in a high valley surrounded by lofty peaks. It was originally called Taylorsville, but the name was changed to Mountain City in 1885 to reflect its status as the highest town in Tennessee.

The beautiful grounds of the Butler House Bed and Breakfast won't fail to attract your attention as you enter Mountain City. The two-story brick mansion was built in 1876 by Roderick Randon Butler, a lieutenant colonel in the Thirteenth Tennessee Cavalry during the Civil War, a state legislator, and U.S. congressman.

Owners Joan and Bill Trathen have filled the four guest rooms with antiques; they all have pri-

vate baths; and the library is well stocked. A full breakfast is served.

There's also a Days Inn franchise in town. Hidden Treasures and Mountain City Antiques and Collectibles give shoppers an antique alternative to the three discount outlets in town.

The Johnson County Welcome Center is in a new log cabin on US 421 south. Inside you'll find information and a museum. Behind the welcome center facility is a campground with picnic area and full hookups that is open all year.

Roan Valley Golf Estates and the Golf Course Restaurant are on your right as you continue on US 421 toward Boone, North Carolina. Seven cabins are available. Farther along US 421 south, Trade Days is held each June to celebrate the heritage of Tennessee's oldest unincorporated town.

Bluegrass and gospel music are performed on Friday nights at Davidson's Store in Laurel

The Italianate 1876 Butler House is now a bed and breakfast welcoming visitors to Mountain City.

Bloomery, a tiny community in a pretty valley northwest of Mountain City via TN 91. The picking starts around 7 P.M.; admission is free and everyone is welcome to drop by. The Old Mill Park features bluegrass and gospel on Sunday afternoons during the summer months and hosts an Old Time Fiddlers Convention the Saturday before Labor Day.

As you drive along US 91 you will notice Donnelly House Antiques on your right. The lovely old farmhouse is chock-full-to-overflowing with antiques and collectibles.

Gentry Creek Falls are off Sugar Creek Road about two miles outside Laurel Bloomery. A 4.6-mile roundtrip hike leads to the forty-foot falls. On the way you'll pass the Rogers Ridge Scenic Area and the 6.75-mile horse trail that eventually leads to the intersection with the Virginia state line after passing a series of grassy balds with grand views.

Continue on TN 67 to Watauga Lake, Roan Mountain State Park, and Elizabethton.

All of the following accommodations are Mountain City with zip code 37683, and all telephone listings are area code 423, except where noted.

Accommodations:
Beaver Dam Creek Guesthouse, 3771 Hwy. 33, Shady Valley; 888-304-7031 or 739-9360.
The Butler House Bed and Breakfast, 309 N. Church St. (Hwy. 91); 727-4119.
Creek Side Guest House, Rt. 4, Box 350; 727-6853.
Hidden Acres Farm Bed and Breakfast, Rt. 3, Box 39; 727-6564.
Mountain Empire Motel, US 421; 727-7777.
Newcombe's Place Bed and Breakfast, US 421; 727-5392.
Patton's Bed and Breakfast, Shady Valley, 739-3815.
Roan Valley Golf Estates, US 421S; 800-444-6615 or 727-5756.

Attractions:
Johnson County Welcome Center and Museum, Hwy. 421 south of Mountain City, 423-727-5800.
Shady Valley Music Park, 739-9393.

Dining:
Cooks Cafeteria, US 421; 727-7910.
Roan Valley Golf Course Restaurant, Hwy. 421S; 800-444-6615 or 727-8283.
Shady Valley Trading Company Restaurant, 739-9393.

Shopping:
Donnelly House and Antique Shop, 777-9005.
Mountain City Antiques and Collectibles.
Shady Valley Trading Company, Shady Valley, 739-9393.

Special Events:
June—Trade Days and Pow-Wow
August—Old Time Fiddlers' Convention, Laurel Bloomery; Mountain Heritage Days and Rodeo, Mountain City
October—Cranberry Festival, Shady Valley

Camping:
Johnson County Welcome Center Campground, Mountain City, 727-5800.
Shady Valley Trading Company, Shady Valley, 739-9393.

For More Information:
Welcome Center and Museum, P.O. Box 1, Hwy. 421, Mountain City, 37683; 727-5800. Open daily.
Cherokee National Forest, USDA Forest Service, Elizabethton, 37643; 423-542-2942.

3   Elizabethton, Roan Mountain, Watauga Lake
Land of the Overmountain Men

Elizabethton was founded on the site of a Cherokee village called the Watauga Old Fields near shoals in the Watauga River known as Sycamore Shoals.

Long hunters like Daniel Boone and William Bean were followed in 1770 to the Watauga Old Fields by North Carolinian James Robertson, a man who has been called the Father of Tennessee.

Robertson, according to Donald Davidson in *The Tennessee*, brought back a group of men and women to establish the first settlement west of the Appalachian Mountains in what they thought were parts of Virginia and North Carolina.

Finding themselves west of the mountains and beyond the law, they established a majority-rule government known as the Watauga Association in 1772, four years before the Declaration of Independence was signed. The rules created by the Watauga Association were considered the first constitution written by native-born Americans.

Sycamore Shoals was the site of the gathering of the "overmountain men" who went to meet British forces at Kings Mountain, South Carolina, on September 25, 1780. British Maj. Patrick Ferguson commanded eleven hundred British and Tories as a part of Lord Cornwallis's campaign through the Carolinas that began after Charleston fell in May 1780.

In one fateful day the ragtag overmountain men killed Ferguson and either killed or captured his entire command. It was a resounding defeat with fewer than thirty overmountain men lost. Many historians feel the defeat was the turning point of the Revolutionary War in the South.

Sycamore Shoals includes a reconstruction of Fort Watauga, a trail to the famous shoals, a museum, and interpretative programs including a film depicting early history in the area.

Carter County was named for Landon Carter, the son of John Carter, one of the great pioneer leaders of Tennessee. Elizabethton, the seat of Carter County was named for Landon Carter's wife, Elizabeth.

Built in 1882, the Doe River Covered Bridge is the oldest still in use in the state.

The 1770 Carter Mansion was the spot where the Watauga Association was formed. It has been preserved, although not restored, and is open to the public during the summer and by appointment through the Sycamore Shoals State Historic Area.

Descendants of Landon Carter Haynes, the brothers Robert and Alfred Taylor were colorful figures in Tennessee politics from the 1880s to the 1920s. The Taylors participated in the famous gubernatorial election of 1886 in which Alf was selected to run as the Republican candidate while younger brother, Bob, represented the Democrats. Wit and humor characterized the race that became known as the War of the Roses.

The Doe River Covered Bridge, known locally as the "kissing bridge," was hand built by craftsmen in 1882. The 134-foot white clapboard structure spans the Doe River and is believed to be the oldest covered bridge in use in Tennessee today. A weeklong Covered Bridge Celebration is held each June with concerts, craft show, an antique car show, and children's activities.

City Market is a classic restaurant with red-and-white checkered tablecloths and homemade desserts and soups.

Area accommodations include the Old Main Manor Bed and Breakfast and the Rhudy House in Elizabethton, General Wilder's Bed and Breakfast in Roan Mountain, and the Blue Heron Inn at Watauga. National franchises include Comfort Inn

The visitor center at Roan Mountain State Park overlooks a clear, cold stream.

and Days Inn. Appalachian Trail through hikers enjoy the hot showers at Laurel Creek Lodge Campground and Hostel on Dennis Cove Road. Mountain Lake Wilderness Resort in Butler about a mile from Watauga Lake has log cabins with tin roofs and front porch swings available daily or weekly.

Elizabethton is situated in Carter County in the midst of 84,500 acres of the Cherokee National Forest at the intersection of the Watauga and Doe Rivers.

The cool waters of the Doe offer stream fishing. The seventy-two-acre trout-filled Little Wilbur Lake below Watauga Dam is also very popular. Primitive campsites are available nearby with picnic tables, grills, and a bathhouse.

Watauga is a Tennessee Valley Authority lake, nestled among the surrounding mountain peaks like a jewel in a crown. With 6,430 surface acres and 106 miles of meandering shoreline with very little development, it offers outdoor enthusiasts ample opportunities for fishing, boating, swimming, and water skiing with plenty of elbow room.

There are several day-use recreation areas along the lake including Shook Branch and Watauga Point which both have swimming areas. Camping is available at the Carden's Bluff Campground. Short hiking trails follow the shoreline at Carden's Bluff and Watauga Point.

Watauga Lakeshore Resort and Marina has a motel, cottages, fishing, ski boat and pontoon boat rentals, a swimming pool, and the Captain's Table Restaurant.

About sixty miles of the Appalachian Trail are in Carter County, including portions that hug the shoreline of Watauga Lake and traverse the Roan High Knob at Roan Mountain State Park. The longest stretch of grassy balds in the southern Appalachians extends from Carvers Gap to Big Hump Mountain

Roan Mountain State Park has the only cross-country ski and snowshoe trails in Tennessee. (Courtesy of Tennessee Photographic Services.)

and vies for the distinction of being the prettiest part of the Appalachian Trail system.

Roan Mountain State Park is named for the 6,285-foot peak that towers above it. The mountains in the park are believed to be at least 650 million years old. Roan Mountain is one of the most beautiful and most popular parks in the upper East Tennessee region.

The 2,156-acre park has twenty cabins, two campgrounds with bathhouses, playgrounds, picnic tables, hiking, the only cross-country ski trails and snowshoe trails in Tennessee, and a swimming pool. No ski equipment is available for rent at the park.

One of the largest natural rhododendron gardens in the world is at the top of the Roan. The purplish-rose Catawba bloom tends to peak in the last half of June and it is an impressive show with six hundred acres of rhododendron flaming along the mountain peaks.

From Roan Mountain proceed to Unicoi and Erwin via TN 173 to TN 107. Turn west on TN 107 to intersect US 19/23 at Unicoi. A left turn takes you to Erwin.

From Elizabethton take US 321 to intersect US 19/23 and turn left to Erwin.

All of the following accommodations are Elizabethton with zip code 37643, and all telephone listings are area code 423, except where noted.

Accommodations:
Laurel Creek Lodge, Campgrounds and Hostel, 1511-A Dennis Cove Rd., Hampton, 37658; 725-5899.
Mountain Lake Wilderness Resort, P.O. Box 300, 166 Wilderness Trail, Butler, 37640; 800-381-6751 or 768-3030.
Old Main Manor, 708 N. Main, 543-6945.
Roan Mountain State Park, Rt. 1, Box 236, Roan Mountain; 800-250-8620 or 772-3303.
Watauga Lakeshore Resort, Rt. 2, Box 379, Hampton, 37658; 725-2201.

Attractions:
Doe River Covered Bridge, 543-2122.
Sycamore Shoals State Historic Area, 543-5808.
Watauga Lake and River, 587-5600.

Dining:
Captain's Table at Lakeshore Resort, Hampton, 725-2201.
City Market, 543-1751.
Classic Malt Shop, 543-7141.
Dino's, 542-5541.
Duck Goose Cafe, Duck Crossing Antique Mall.
O'Dellys, two locations, 543-3354 and 772-9490 or 772-4700.
Ridgewood Restaurant, 538-7543.
Southern, 542-5132.

Shopping:
A Touch of Time Past and Present, 543-0377.
Antique and Curio Corner, 542-0603.
Antiques on Elk, 542-3355.

Duck Crossing Antique Mall, 542-3055.
The Hack Line Shop, Roan Mountain, 772-3371.
Maude's Antiques, 543-1979.
Mountain Memories Antiques and Gifts, 772-3526.

Special Events:
Easter weekend—Peter's Hollow Egg Fight
May—Sycamore Shoals Craft Festival; Annual Roan Mountain Wildflower Tours and Birdwalks, Roan Mountain State Park
June—Slagle's Bluegrass Festival, Slagle's Pasture, Old Hwy. 19E, 542-8615
June—Covered Bridge Celebration
June—Rhododendron Festival

Camping:
Carden's Bluff Campground, Watauga Lake.
Pioneer Landing, Butler, 768-3164.
Roan Mountain State Park, Roan Mountain; 772-3303.

For More Information:
Elizabethton/Carter County Chamber of Commerce Tourism Council, 500 19E bypass, P.O. Box 190, 800-347-0208, 888-547-3852 or 547-3850.
TVA Dams, Watauga Lake; 542-2951.
Watauga Ranger District, Cherokee National Forest, Rt. 9, Box 2235, 542-2942.

4 Erwin
The Beauty Spot

As you enter Erwin, the beautiful high country of the Unaka Mountains and the Cherokee National Forest of Unicoi County surround you. Unaka (pronounced U nay kah) is the Indian word for "white," possibly referring to the white mist that often cloaks the upper slopes of the 5,189-foot Unaka Mountain.

Nearly half of Unicoi County's 118,400 acres lies within the Cherokee National Forest. A thirty-mile scenic automobile loop tour travels through the Unaka Scenic, Wilderness, and Primitive areas. A map is available from the Unaka Ranger District office in Erwin.

The auto loop through the Unaka Scenic Area winds its way peacefully along the slopes of Unaka Mountain outside Erwin.

along a steeply winding road to Indian Grave Gap where it crosses the Appalachian Trail (AT) at the North Carolina state line. Although the AT "runs the ridges" passing through forests and balds, the trip from south to north involves about two thousand feet more climbing than traveling the opposite direction.

The auto tour continues on Forest Service Road 230 to the first of three spectacular high country panoramas. The first is known as Beauty Spot, a grassy bald of unknown origins. Explanations for the existence of such balds found throughout the southern Appalachians include forest fires, Indian activity, grazing by buffalo herds in the seventeenth century, grazing by cattle in the eighteenth century, altitude, and timberline. Many of these theories are contradicted by Mount Mitchell in North Carolina which supports forest growth all the way to its 6,684-foot summit.

A journey five miles farther down the gravel road brings you to Beauty Spot Gap at an elevation of 4,500 feet. This is a good spot for spring wildflower viewing.

The road slowly climbs 1,000 feet in elevation in about 3.5 miles to the Unaka Mountain overlook, which has a parking lot on top. On a clear day, the view is spectacular.

The driving loop continues through spruce-fir forests past Red Fork Falls to TN 107. The turnout to Red Fork Falls is not marked on your map, but if you wish to visit the nearly one hundred-foot falls watch for a turnout on the left as you descend the mountain.

Longhunters from North Carolina were the first white men to enter this rugged area. Around 1772 permanent settlements were first located in a cove between Unicoi and the Nolichucky River known as Greasy Cove. Hunters killed bears

About three miles outside Erwin on TN 395, you'll pass Rock Creek Recreation Area, a camping, recreation, and picnic facility built by the Civilian Conservation Corps (CCC) in the 1930s. A 1.5-mile trail leads from the recreation area to Rock Creek Falls, a fifty-foot tiered cascade at the base of Unaka Mountain.

There's also a rock-walled spring-fed swimming pool in the recreation area that's guaranteed to cool you off on a hot summer day.

The auto loop continues about three miles

On a clear day, the view from the 5,500-foot crest of Unaka Mountain is spectacular.

inhabiting the area between Unicoi and the Nolichucky and rendered the grease in crude vats while camped in the cove.

Horse racing was a favorite frontier diversion and the half-mile semicircular track at Greasy Cove was well known when twenty-one-year-old Andrew Jackson came up from Jonesborough in 1788 to race his horse in a widely publicized contest against Col. Robert Love's prize racer. Jackson lost the race, and by all accounts, was a sore loser.

Unicoi is the spelling the Tennessee State Legislature adopted for the Cherokee pronunciation of Unaka which was "u-na-kaw." The county seat was first called Longmire, then Vanderbilt in hopes of attracting the attention of George Van-

derbilt who was looking for several thousand mountain acres for his estate.

Vanderbilt built his estate near Asheville and the town changed its name to Ervin. By some accounts, the post office made a mistake and changed the *V* to *W* and that's what it's been called ever since. Others claim the name was eventually changed to honor the first county court clerk, Jesse B. Erwin.

Much of Erwin's growth resulted from the railroad industry in the area. The need for a north-south rail line was talked about for years before the Charleston, Cincinnati, and Chicago Railway challenged the rugged terrain to build it in 1899.

The presence of the railroad brought a strange chapter to Erwin's history in 1916 when it became the town that executed an elephant. The bizarre tale began with a circus parade in Kingsport that featured the "world's largest elephant," who was named Mary.

For unclear reasons Mary tossed her hapless trainer to the ground and trampled him to death. The crowd was outraged and murderous Mary was condemned to death on the spot. They tried shooting and electrocuting her before the railroad at Erwin was called upon to carry out the sentence.

Officials decided against smashing her between two railroad cars and proceeded to hang her from a crane before a crowd of thousands. She was laid to rest at an unknown site. The Hanging Elephant Antique Mall reflects this part of Erwin's railroad history. The Main Street Mall is a couple of blocks down the street and has antiques and collectibles including Blue Ridge pottery.

Erwin was also the home of Southern Potteries, Inc., maker of the highly collectible hand-painted Blue Ridge pattern. Millions of pieces of the hugely popular Blue Ridge pottery were sold by large department stores throughout the country.

Although Southern Potteries went out of business in 1957, the colorful flower designs continue to grow in popularity with collectors. An excellent display of Blue Ridge pottery is open from May to October at the Unicoi County Heritage Museum at the National Fish Hatchery property, and there's a Blue Ridge Pottery Club Show and Sale during the Apple Festival each fall.

The Erwin National Fish Hatchery was established in 1897 to provide rainbow trout fingerlings. Operated by the U.S. Fish and Wildlife Service, the hatchery ships 15 million rainbow trout eggs all over the United States and supplies brood fish to other hatcheries. The visitor center and picnic pavilion are open year-round.

Next door, the former superintendent's residence, built in 1903, is now home to the Unicoi County Heritage Museum. In addition to the Blue Ridge pottery in the dining room, visitors find artifacts from prehistoric Indians to the twentieth century. The museum is open May–October and visitors are invited to also use the picnic pavilion and walk the self-guided nature trail on the thirty-acre property.

Local accommodations include the Tumbling Creek Bed and Breakfast south of Erwin with two rooms that share a bath, and a large balcony that invites you to linger and enjoy the sounds of Tumbling Creek. Between Erwin and Johnson City, the Buffalo Mountain Resort/Family Inns of America is nestled in the Unicoi Valley and features a swimming pool and a golf course in a pretty rural setting.

The owners of the Farmhouse Gallery and Gardens have created a wildflower and wildlife habitat on their seventy-acre property that they share with visitors. They offer wildlife art in an old log cabin studio and sell wildflower and herbal teas. The sign for the gallery is several miles past

The Unicoi Heritage Museum is located next door to the Erwin National Fish Hatchery.

the Tipton-Haynes Historic Site on the way to Erwin from Johnson City.

If you leave Erwin on TN 107 toward Greeneville, you'll be traveling along the historic Nolichucky River valley. As you follow along the river, you'll understand why the Indians called it "rushing waters."

Rapids are classified using an international scale with Class I rapids being for beginners and Class III/IV challenging for experienced canoeists. The upper Nolichucky has nearly a dozen such challenges.

The lower section is broader and much gentler with occasional Class II/III rapids and enough ripples to keep you interested. Cherokee Adventures is located one mile out of Erwin on TN 81/107 toward Jonesborough. They specialize in water sports along the Nolichucky, including the wild and scenic trips on the upper section and the gentler float trips through the lower section. They can also arrange bike rides.

Whether you're interested in hiking, automobile rides through spectacular scenery, or thrilling white-water rafting, Erwin has something for the nature lover in you.

From Erwin follow US 19/23 to Johnson City to visit the site of the battle for the state of Franklin.

All of the following accommodations are Erwin with zip code 37650, and all telephone listings are area code 423, except where noted.

Accommodations:
Tumbling Creek Bed and Breakfast, Rt. 2, Box 380A, 743-5308.
Buffalo Mountain Resort/Family Inns of America, Rt. 2, Hwy. 19/23, Unicoi, 37692; 743-6438.

Attractions:
Cherokee Adventures, Looking Glass Mountain, 743-7733.
Nantahala Outdoor Center, 743-7400.

Erwin National Fish Hatchery, 743-4712.
Farmhouse Gallery and Gardens, Unicoi, 800-952-6043 or 743-8799.
Unicoi County Heritage Museum, 743-9449.

Dining:
Clarence's Drive-In, Unicoi, 743-7200.
Country Kitchen, Flag Pond, 743-9534.
Elms Restaurant, 743-6181.

Shopping:
Farmhouse Gallery and Gardens, Unicoi, 800-952-6043 or 743-8799.
The Hanging Elephant Antique Mall, 743-9661.
Main Street Antique Mall, 743-7810.

Special Events:
April—April Garden Party at the Farmhouse Gallery and Gardens
May—Ramp Festival at Flag Pond
October—The Apple Festival; Autumn Jubilee and Open House at the Farmhouse Gallery and Gardens

Camping:
Rock Creek Recreation Area, USDA Forest Service; 743-4452.
Limestone Cove Recreation Area, USDA Forest Service; 743-4452.
North Indian Creek Campground, Unicoi, 743-4502.

For More Information:
Erwin/Unicoi Chamber of Commerce, P. O. Box 713, 100 S. Main St.; 743-3000.
Unaka Ranger District, USDA Forest Service, 1205 N. Main St.; 743-4452.

5 *Johnson City*
Battle for the State of Franklin

Johnson City was once known as the village of Green Meadows. It was renamed three times before it became Johnson City in 1869, named for Henry Johnson, according to the *WPA Guide to Tennessee.*

After the East Tennessee and Virginia Railroad built a water tank in the settlement known as Blue Plum in 1858, Johnson built a depot at his own expense and trains began to stop here. Johnson simultaneously served as the first postmaster, depot agent, merchant, magistrate, and hotelkeeper before being elected the first mayor. During the War Between the States, the town was called Haynesville in honor of Landon Carter Haynes whose estate, now known as the Tipton-Haynes Historic Site, is owned by the Tennessee Historical Commission, and is open to the public.

The Tipton-Haynes Historic Site south of town on South Roan is along an old buffalo trail that was visited by Woodland Indians and later by the Cherokee. The trail became part of the Stage Road and a log home was built along it in the 1780s by Col. John Tipton.

The dispute that took place here between Tipton, a North Carolina magistrate, and John Sevier, the governor of the wannabe state of Franklin, became known as the battle for the state of Franklin.

After North Carolina and Virginia were pressed to cede their vast western holdings to the impoverished central government to use in payment for service in the Revolutionary War, settlers in what is now upper East Tennessee formed the state of Franklin in 1784.

The Franklinites chose as their first governor John Sevier, Tennessee's first frontier hero and leader at the battle of Kings Mountain.

Franklin failed in its bid for statehood, but so popular was Sevier that he was also the first governor of Tennessee when it was admitted to the Union in 1796 although he had been arrested for treason by the state of North Carolina while serving as governor of the state of Franklin from 1784 to 1788.

John Tipton and John Sevier were bitter political and personal rivals. When news was received in the area that North Carolina had changed its mind

about governing what is now East Tennessee, the Franklinites refused North Carolina's demands that the state of Franklin be dissolved. During the winter of 1788, when Sevier refused to pay North Carolina taxes, slaves and other property belonging to him were seized by North Carolina Sheriff John Pugh of Jonesborough as payment for taxes.

Sheriff Pugh took the confiscated persons and property to the home of magistrate John Tipton, a North Carolina loyalist. Sevier returned to his home, discovered what had happened, and

The battle for the state of Franklin took place at the Tipton-Haynes Historic Site between Johnson City and Erwin.

Picnic tables offer a roadside respite at Buffalo Mountain Park.

promptly marched with a group of about 150 men to John Tipton's home and demanded the return of his property.

A contingent of about forty-five Tipton allies refused to surrender. Reinforcements were called for by Sheriff Pugh, a fight ensued, and in the melee Sheriff Pugh was killed and two of Sevier's sons were captured (*see* Greeneville for more on the state of Franklin).

David Haynes purchased the clapboarded log house from the grandchildren of John Tipton before the Civil War, as a wedding present for Landon Carter Haynes. The house has been restored to its appearance in Haynes's day.

The look of Johnson City has been greatly transformed by the urban renewal projects of the 1970s, the presence of 12,100 students at East Tennessee State University (ETSU), and a 1996 population of about 50,000 residents.

ETSU houses the B. Carroll Reece Museum which has a collection of frontier artifacts and antique musical items. The Ambrose Manning Collection is part of the Appalachian Archives, an extensive collection of music of the Appalachians, including many recordings available for research purposes.

The Quillen College of Medicine at ETSU is closely aligned with the Veterans Affairs Medical Center, known as Mountain Home. Since its founding in 1903, generations of visitors have shared the lovely 450-acre grounds with the resident vets.

The facility just north of ETSU continues to be a pleasant green oasis in the midst of increasing urban sprawl. In 1994 physician Abraham Verghese published *My Own Country,* a best-selling book about his experiences treating AIDS patients while practicing in Johnson City.

South of ETSU, the horizon is dominated by the thirty-five-hundred-foot Buffalo Mountain. Hiking trails and a park with picnic tables in a natural setting rewards those who venture to the top.

The area between Johnson City and Elizabethton is home to Milligan College, which was founded in 1867. Students included the Taylor brothers (*see* Elizabethton).

In addition to franchise motels like Comfort Inn, Days Inn, Hampton Inn, and Holiday Inn, the Hart House Bed and Breakfast welcomes visitors to three comfortable second-floor guest rooms with private baths. Queen-sized beds, color cable TVs, full breakfasts, and an exercise room round out the amenities in this 1910 Dutch Colonial home located within a few blocks of I-181.

The Antique Village, Memory Lane Antique Mall, and the Hands On! Museum are all downtown on Main Street. The Hands On! Museum offers over fifty exhibits and interactive displays ranging from tractors to airplanes and coal mines designed to appeal to children under age twelve for a memorable learning experience. The downtown antique malls have a good assortment of antique furniture and collectibles.

There are a slew of barbecue restaurants in town. For many years, the only spot with good pulled barbecue (for our tastes the only kind to consider since sliced and chopped 'cue are crimes against nature) was the Red Pig Barbecue, the granddaddy of them all. Newer contenders like the Dixie Barbecue Company, the Firehouse

Restaurant, and the House of Ribs continue to entice barbecue lovers of all persuasions.

The Peerless Steak House, a favorite of area diners since 1938, has a long tradition of serving delicious food. The Epicurean features European cuisine and a good wine list. Generations Bookstore/Cafe is a fine spot to browse for reading material and to enjoy lunch or dinner and a steaming cup of espresso. Poor Richard's Deli has great sandwiches and Sunny's Cafeteria offers tasty cafeteria-style dining in a simple setting, but the most popular cafeteria in the area is Picadilly at the mall.

For many years the Down Home Pickin' Parlor was the only place in town to hear topnotch bluegrass performers. These days Down Home features a bit broader range of musicians but retains its reputation for quality performances.

Boone Lake was constructed in 1952 by impounding the South Fork of the Holston and the Watauga Rivers. It has 4,310 surface acres and 130 miles of shoreline in a distinct *V* shape stretching between Johnson City and Kingsport. Largemouth bass are the predominant game fish species, although trophy-sized stripers and hybrids have come from Boone in recent years.

From Johnson City proceed to Kingsport via I-181 to visit Long Island, sacred land of the Cherokee.

All of the following accommodations are Johnson City with zip code 37601, and all telephone listings are area code 423, except where noted.

Accommodations:
Broadway Motel, 2608 N. Roan; 282-4011.
Hart House B&B, 207 E. Holston Ave; 926-3147.

Attractions:
Boone Lake Dam, TVA, Kingsport, 239-2000.
Buffalo Mountain Park; 283-5815.
Carroll Reece Museum, ETSU campus; 929-4392.
Center for Appalachian Studies and Services, ETSU, 439-5348.

The Hart House Bed and Breakfast welcomes visitors to three comfortable guest rooms in a convenient neighborhood location.

Down Home, 929-9822.
Hands On! Museum, 928-6508 or 928-6509.
Tipton-Haynes Historic Site, 926-3631.

Dining:
The Epicurean, 282-8196.
The Firehouse Restaurant, 929-7377.
Galloway's Restaurant, 926-1166.
Generations Bookstore and Cafe, 283-0912.
House of Ribs, 282-8077.
Peerless Steak House, 282-2351.
Picadilly Cafeteria at the Mall, 282-4327.
Poor Richard's Deli, 926-8611.
Red Pig Barbeque, 282-6585.
Sunny's Cafeteria, 926-7441.

Shopping:
Antique Village, 926-6996.
Antiques and Heirlooms, 928-8220.
Memory Lane Antique Mall, 929-3998.
Town Square Antiques, 929-3373.

For More Information:
Johnson City Convention and Visitors Bureau, 603 E. Market,
    P.O. Box 180, Johnson City, TN 37605; 800-852-3392 or
    461-8000.

6 *Kingsport*
Along the Great Warrior's Path

Kingsport was chartered as a model industrial center in 1907 and became home to industrial giant Eastman Chemical Company (formerly Kodak) long after it was known as Long Island by the Cherokee who regarded this spot along the confluence of the North and South Forks of the Holston River as sacred ground.

Long Island was strategically situated along the Warrior's Path, or the Great Indian War Trail, which traveled from Virginia through the Great Valley of East Tennessee north to the Cumberland Gap and south to the important Cherokee overhill settlements near Tellico Plains.

The Cherokee allowed traders to join the Long Island encampment as early as the mid 1700s. A peace treaty in 1761 gave permission for travelers going west to pass through the area and Fort Robinson was built in 1761 near a ford on Long Island.

So many settlers came by wagon to Long Island and built boats along the riverbank to continue their arduous westward journey by water that an area known as the Boat Yard developed on the shore of the Holston River.

The Boat Yard was a point of departure and commerce from 1768 to 1850. In 1775 Fort Patrick Henry was constructed on the former site of Fort Robinson. William King, who owned saltworks in nearby Virginia, built King's Boat Yard, a river port that eventually became known as Kingsport.

Representatives of northern Indian tribes urged the younger Cherokee braves to rise up against the invasion of their homelands by hoards of settlers. In 1776 settlers along the Holston, Watauga, and Nolichucky Rivers were warned of the attack by Nancy Ward, Cherokee leader and niece of Cherokee chief Attakullakulla, in the interest of peace between the Cherokee Nation and the white settlers.

Dragging Canoe, the nephew of Attakullakulla, led the Cherokee attack against Long Island, but he was wounded and the Cherokee were driven back by the militias of Tennessee and Virginia.

More battles with the settlers followed and the Cherokee were forced to cede the sacred ground at Long Island and extensive holdings in Tennessee and Alabama in 1806.

In 1976 a part of this island was returned to the Cherokee by the city of Kingsport. This was in

Warrior's Path State Park near Kingsport offers camping along the shores of Fort Patrick Henry Reservoir.

accordance with instructions of the Mead Company which owned Long Island at the time and donated a portion of it to the city.

To visit this site travel west on US 11W to the Netherland Inn Road. You will travel along the North Fork of the Holston River and enter the Boat Yard District, now a city park with jogging trails and picnic areas. Park and walk down the path to the swinging bridge to reach Long Island.

The Boat Yard District was the point of departure in December 1779 for John Donelson and his party of thirty flatboats carrying the women, children, servants, and household possessions of the settlers bound for the Cumberland Settlement (*see* Nashville for more on Donelson).

In addition to the river traffic, the Great Stage Road brought travelers through the area. Richard Netherland obtained a stage contract and established the Netherland Inn on property facing the Great Stage Road he had obtained from the estate of Boat Yard owner William King. The Federal-style inn and tavern became a popular coach stop in 1818 along the road from Washington City to Nashville.

The three-story inn hosted Tennessee Presidents Jackson, Johnson, and Polk and is now a museum. It has been restored and contains many of the original furnishings. The first-floor tavern, second-floor family quarters, and third-floor guest rooms appear much as they would have 150 years

DECEMBER 22 1779

Colonel John Donelson in his flatboat "Adventure", leading a flotilla of about 300 people in flatboats and canoes, departed from Fort Patrick Henry on that epic voyage to the Big Salt Lick on the Cumberland River (now Nashville). The voyagers were stopped by the fall of water on the shoals at the mouth of Reedy Creek, 600 yards upstream from here. They remained here for almost 2 months, repairing their boats and waiting for the water to rise. They arrived at their destination on April 24, 1780.

Kingsport's historic Boat Yard district now contains a city park with walking trails.

ago. Outbuildings include a log cabin that was Daniel Boone's home during 1773–1775 long before it was moved here to house a children's museum. The first weekend in May there's a big season-opening celebration.

The frontier homestead known as the Exchange Place, or the Gaines Preston Farm, was part of a nearly two-thousand-acre plantation that became a stagecoach relay station where teams of tired horses were exchanged for fresh ones and passengers could exchange their Tennessee and Virginia currencies.

The two-story log main house was built around 1820. Six of the eight buildings are original and were built before 1850.

A spring Festival and Herb Sale held here features traditional craft demonstrations and sales as well as the sale of hundreds of herbs. The Fall Folk Arts Festival and a special Christmas craft sale are also popular.

Kingsport's role as a model city emerged from the vision of Dr. John Nolen who planned industries along the river with residential areas on higher ground and commercial areas between the two. Kingsport continues its highly successful industrial programs and today Eastman Chemical Company is the largest private employer in the state with more than thirteen thousand employees.

The 870-acre Warrior's Path State Park is three miles southeast of Kingsport on the shores of TVA's Fort Patrick Henry Reservoir. Over 130 camping sites have tables and grills. Of these, 94 have water and electrical hookups. Picnic tables and grills dot the water's edge.

Paddle boats and small fishing boats are available for rent at the marina. There is no park fee for fishing, but you must have a valid Tennessee fishing license. Fort Patrick Henry Reservoir is known for good fishing, including large and smallmouth bass, white bass, crappie, bluegill, catfish, rainbow trout, muskie, and walleye.

Visitors will also find an eighteen-hole, par-72

golf course, an Olympic-sized pool and a water slide. Horseback riding is available through the park stables, and nine miles of hiking trails follow the bluffs along the Holston River.

Anglers also pursue largemouth bass, bluegill, crappie, hybrids, and stripers on Boone Lake, a TVA impoundment winding through high rock bluffs between Johnson City and Kingsport. Camping is also available at a KOA franchise.

Bays Mountain Park and Planetarium is a delightful three-thousand-acre city park, outdoor education center, and nature preserve with twenty-two miles of hiking trails and an active schedule of star watches. Guided barge rides around the forty-four-acre reservoir are very popular, so make arrangements as soon as you arrive. The river otter's pool is a favorite stop among the animal exhibits, but deer, wolves, and bobcats viewed in woodland habitats are popular as well.

You won't find snack bars, souvenir shops, or beaches for sunbathing, so bring a sack lunch and prepare to enjoy a delightful focus on nature.

C. J.'s Place is a two-story white frame house in town less than a block from Quebecor Press. Each of the four bedrooms has its own bath, telephone, and cable TV. Warrior's Rest sits amid sixty acres near Warriors Path State Park. The former farmhouse now boasts three rooms for bed and breakfast guests who want to enjoy the peaceful countryside. Fox Manor, minutes from downtown near Kingsport's Dobyns-Bennett High School, has four guest rooms and serves breakfast and high tea.

Certainly worth a mention is the 196-room Meadowview Conference Resort and Convention Center with its Craftsman-style furnishings, roughhewn beams, massive fieldstone fireplaces, eighteen-hole golf course, heated outdoor pool,

fitness center, whirlpool, and twenty-five-acre park and wetlands conservatory. National franchises include Comfort Inn, Days Inn, Holiday Inn, and Ramada Inn.

Kingsport has a half-dozen or more excellent antique malls along Broad Street including Colonial Antique Mall, the Haggle Shop, and Haggle Shop Antique Mall #2.

You might want to search out the Mezzanine Tea Room at Home Sweet Home if you're in the vicinity in early afternoon and treat yourself to an inspired dessert while you contemplate your purchases. Amanda's Antiques, Anchor Antiques, and Transportation Station offer more shopping.

Skoby's Restaurant has reigned as the best place for special outings and good food in Kingsport for fifty years. Amato's, Giuseppe's, and Motz's all serve Italian specialties along with American selections. Wright's Country Cuisine serves up down-home lunches and dinners while Sharon's Bar-B-Q and Burgers is reminiscent of a hangout for bobby soxers with duck tails.

Harmony Grocery features delicious Cajun

The 1802 Netherland Inn was a stop along the Great Stage Road from Washington to Nashville.

Woodland habitats have been created for wildlife viewing at Bays Mountain Park and Planetarium.

and Creole cooking, off I-181 between Kingsport and Jonesborough. The Olde West Dinner Theater between Kingsport and Johnson City offers professional theater along with evening and matinee meals.

If you visit during July, you'll have nine days of opportunities to participant in Fun Fest. This annual event features more than one hundred activities for all ages ranging from concerts to mountain biking, chili cook-offs to fireworks displays.

The First Night New Year's Eve celebration is a community-wide event to promote the arts in a drug-and-alcohol-free setting for all ages. Among the continuous activities starting about 6 P.M. are a 5K road race, parade, concerts, dancing, storytelling, games, food, and a midnight fireworks finale.

Travel US 11W from Kingsport to visit Rogersville, the first of three towns in East Tennessee's historic triangle.

All of the following accommodations are Kingsport with zip code 37660, and all telephone listings are area code 423, except where noted.

Accommodations:
C. J.'s Place, 634 Arch St., 378-3517.
Fox Manor Bed and Breakfast, 1612 Watauga St., 378-3844.
Meadowview Conference Resort and Convention Center, 1901 Meadowview Pkwy., 800-228-9290 or 578-6600.
Warrior's Rest Bed and Breakfast, 1000 Colonial Heights Dr., 239-8838.

Attractions:
Bays Mountain Park and Planetarium, 229-9447.
Boat Yard-Riverfront Park, 229-9457.
Exchange Place, Gaines Preston Farm, 288-6071.
Netherland Inn Historic House Museum, 246-6262.

Dining:
Amato's, 245-4043.
Giuseppe's Lounge, 288-5265.
Harmony Grocery Co., 348-6183.
Motz's Italian Restaurant, 239-9560.
Olde West Dinner Theater, 323-1468.
Skoby's, 245-2761.
Wright's Country Cuisine, 245-2565.

Shopping:
Anchor Antiques, 137 Broad St., 378-3188.
Colonial Antique Mall, 245 Broad St., 246-5559.
Haggle Shop Antique Mall #1, 146 Broad St., 246-8002.
Haggle Shop Antique Mall #2, 246-6588.
Home Sweet Home-Mezzanine Tearoom, 246-1331.

Special Events:
April—Exchange Place Spring Festival and Herb Sale
May—Netherland Inn's Season Opening Celebration
July—Funfest
September—Exchange Place Fall Folk Arts Festival
December—Christmas at Allandale Mansion; First Night

Camping:
Lakeview Marina, 323-1054.
Warrior's Path State Park, Kingsport, 239-8531 or TN Dept. of
    Conservation, 800-421-6683.

For More Information:
Kingsport Convention and Visitors Bureau, 151 E. Main St.,
    P.O. Box 1403; 800-743-5282 or 392-8820.

7 *Rogersville*
Member of East Tennessee's Historic Triangle

Settlements were seen in this area as early as 1772, but the town was named for a later arrival who married the daughter of early settler and wealthy landowner Thomas Amis (pronounced AIM-ee). Amis gave a wedding gift of land to his daughter Mary and her Irish husband, Joseph Rogers, in 1785. One year later the town of Rogersville was founded on a portion of this land situated along the Great Stage Road. Rogersville lay between the Holston River to the south and the Clinch Mountain Range on the north. Today it's at the northeastern end of the Tennessee Valley Authority's Cherokee Lake (*see* Morristown).

Rogersville competes with Dandridge for the honor of second-oldest town in Tennessee. Both towns have an abundance of well-preserved historic structures.

The Hale Springs Inn was built in 1824 by attorney John McKinney and claims to be the oldest continually operated inn in Tennessee. Originally known as McKinney's Tavern, the lovely old tavern has seen additions though the years and has undergone full restoration. All three Tennessee presidents stayed here on their travels between Washington and Tennessee.

The dining room was part of the original tavern and the antique mantel remains. Meals are served to guests of the inn and the public daily except Monday at the Carriage House Restaurant. Check out the romantic fireside and candlelit dinners. If you'd like wine, you should bring your own bottle.

All the large rooms have their own baths and are filled with antiques of museum quality but remain comfortable and inviting. The Andrew Jackson Suite is the actual room he used in 1832 and has a corner table dating from 1824 and a sofa from 1835.

The Victorian Railroad Depot Museum was deeded to the town by Southern Railway, renovated in 1989, and is now home to the Hawkins County Museum, the chamber of commerce, and the visitor center.

The Hawkins County Courthouse is one of a handful of pre-Civil War courthouses still in use in Tennessee. The 1836 handmade brick structure was one of the first buildings of Greek Revival design in the state.

Heritage Days is billed as a nineteenth-century harvest celebration. The town of about five thousand swells to forty thousand when visitors join the hometown crowd the second full weekend each October. Festivities begin with a children's parade, storytelling, singing, dancing,

Some of the furnishings at the Hale Springs Inn date to 1824, the year the inn was built.

and horse-drawn buggy rides around town. Folks pack lawn chairs and come early to enjoy the Sunday gospel singing.

The Rogersville Park and Recreation Building is home to the Music Junction, a totally unrehearsed show that is free to the public. Performances range from country and bluegrass to gospel and rock 'n' roll.

The town has about thirty historic buildings still in use. The Antique Emporium, Jane's Antiques, and Mountain Star Antique and Craft Mall satisfy the urge to explore for treasures.

Several springs in the vicinity were believed to possess medicinal properties, but the Ebbing and Flowing Spring is one of only two springs in the world to exhibit a peculiar tidal characteristic. Every two hours and forty-seven minutes the spring runs the full gamut from a tiny trickle to a flow of five hundred gallons per minute.

Such a phenomenon generated much speculation and the spring was credited with having

extraordinary powers in matters of the heart. Local legend claimed that any couple drinking from the spring at the peak of its flow would marry within the year. The spring is privately owned by descendants of Thomas Amis but is open to the public.

The community of Bulls Gap is about twelve miles southwest between Rogersville and Morristown. There you'll find several bed and breakfasts, Old Town, a National Register of Historic Places site, the Archie Campbell Tourism Complex, and the Railroad Museum.

A North Carolina gunsmith named John Bull received a land grant of fifty-five acres on Bays Mountain near a passageway through the mountains in 1792 that became known as Bulls Gap. Railroads from Virginia, East Tennessee, and Georgia met in the Bulls Gap area in 1858.

During the Civil War many battles were fought to gain control of the town with the Federals victorious most of the time. After the Civil

The Hawkins County Courthouse is one of six antebellum courthouses still in use in Tennessee.

Accommodations:
The Guest House, 272 Blevins Rd., 272-0816.
Hale Springs Inn, 110 W. Main St., 272-5171.
The Home Place Bed and Breakfast, 132 Church Ln., Moores-
    burg, 37811; 800-521-8424 or 921-8424.
Pittman's Country Inn, 842 Pleasant Hill Rd., Bulls Gap,
    37711; 235-2455.
Round Hill Farm Bed and Breakfast, 150 Noe Ln., Moores-
    burg, 37811; 921-9089.
Sandman Motor Lodge, 207 Hwy. 66, 272-6800.

Attractions:
Ebbing and Flowing Spring.
Hale Springs Inn, 272-5171.
Hawkins County Courthouse.
Rogersville Depot Museum, 272-1961.

Dining:
Big John's Restaurant, 272-3999.
Carriage House Restaurant at Hale Springs Inn.
Oh Henry's Restaurant, Main and Church, 272-0980.
Kathryn's Meat Shop and Country Deli, 272-6625.

Shopping:
Antique Emporium, 272-6891.
Jane's Antiques, 272-5573.
Mountain Star Antique and Craft Mall, 272-7800.

Special Events:
October—Heritage Days

Camping:
Cherokee Lake Campground, Mooresburg, 272-3333.

For More Information:
Rogersville/Hawkins County Chamber of Commerce, 301 E.
    Main St.; 272-2186.

War, Bulls Gap rebuilt and prospered as a railroad town. When passenger service was discontinued, the old town center went into decline. The depot and many of the old railroad buildings have been torn down.

Continue to Greeneville, the second town in the historic triangle and home of President Andrew Johnson, on TN 70.

All of the following accommodations are Rogersville with zip code 37857, and all telephone listings are area code 423, except where noted.

8 Greeneville
Home of President Andrew Johnson

Both Greeneville and Greene County were named for Gen. Nathanael Greene, a Revolutionary War veteran. Greeneville was the capital of the Lost State of Franklin from 1785 to 1787 (*see* Johnson City and Jonesborough for more on the state of Franklin).

Andrew Johnson National Historic Site tells the tale of Johnson's rise to the presidency.

President Andrew Johnson's home was in Greeneville. He came here from North Carolina with his parents in 1825 and worked as a tailor. When he was eighteen he married sixteen-year-old Eliza McCardle who taught him to read and write. Two years later he entered politics and served as alderman on the Democratic ticket prior to serving in the Congress for ten years from 1843 to 1853.

He was then elected governor of Tennessee from 1853 to 1857 and the appointed military governor during the Union occupation of most of the state during the Civil War.

He was called upon by President Lincoln in 1865 to serve as vice president in his second administration and succeeded to the presidency after Lincoln's assassination one month later as the Civil War was coming to an end.

The conquered South hated him because he was a Unionist. The Republicans dominated Congress and hated the Democratic Johnson so much that they tried to impeach him on the grounds that he had violated the Tenure of Office Act. They failed in the House of Representatives by a single vote.

His tailor shop and both homes are open to the public at the Andrew Johnson National Historic Site. The Andrew Johnson Presidential Library is located on the campus of Tusculum College a few miles east of Greeneville. In addition to the president's papers and books, there's a large collection of newspapers from across the country published during the Civil War.

The 1821 Dickson-Williams Mansion on Church Street is open for tours. Flamboyant Confederate Gen. John Hunt Morgan was surprised by Union forces and killed here on September 4, 1864.

The Nathanael Greene Museum tells the story of Greeneville's first one hundred years and its impact on Tennessee, the South, and the nation. If you have time to browse, Ye Olde Tourist Trappe is a cooperative of about 150 local craftsmen. The

Greeneville Antique Market is open daily for treasure hunters.

The General Morgan Inn is a landmark hotel in the National Register of Historic Places created from four interconnecting railroad hotels that were built in the 1800s.

The restoration of the General Morgan grew out of Greeneville's selection as one of the first towns in Tennessee to participate in the Main Street program designed by the National Trust for Historic Preservation to help communities vitalize their historic downtowns.

The result of public/private fundraising efforts centers around the four-star non-profit General Morgan Inn and Conference Center.

The lobby boasts thirty-eight-foot ceilings and extensive marble work. There are fifty-two elegant rooms and guest services befitting East Tennessee's premier historic hotel. The inn's restaurant, Brumley's, serves southern, Continental, and American cuisine.

The adjacent Madison Day Spa offers full body massage and body treatments with licensed therapists, bath and body products, and a full-service hair salon.

There are national franchises for Days Inn and Holiday Inn as well as several bed and breakfasts in Greeneville. The Big Spring Inn on North Main Street has six guest rooms, a swimming pool, and two acres of landscaped grounds within walking distance of downtown.

Nolichucky Bluffs on Kinser Park Lane offers four completely equipped two-bedroom cabins on seventeen acres set on one-hundred-foot bluffs overlooking the Nolichucky River. There's also a five-person hot tub in a screened gazebo with a great view and a bed and breakfast with three rooms, including one room with a queen-sized bed and whirlpool tub. Children are

welcome, pets are not.

One-half mile down the road, Kinser Park has campsites overlooking the Nolichucky River, a nine-hole golf course, swimming pool, water slide, tennis courts, bath houses, picnic tables, and a boat ramp.

Oak Hill Bed and Breakfast sits on a hilltop about three miles from town with views that seem

The General Morgan Inn is the heart of the National Trust for Historic Preservation's Main Street Program in Greeneville.

Picnicking is popular along the banks of the Nolichucky River near the birthplace of David Crockett.

to go on forever. There's a wide front porch with rocking chairs, a swimming pool, and a master suite with a king-sized bed, fireplace, whirlpool, and sitting area. Full breakfasts are served and dinner can be arranged with advance reservations.

Hilltop House Bed and Breakfast also has mountain views, a relaxing front porch, private verandas, and three rooms with private baths.

A bit farther from town are classic accommodations at the Snapp Inn Bed and Breakfast, an 1815 Federal-style home near Davy Crockett Birthplace State Park on the banks of the Nolichucky River. There are two rooms with private baths. Full breakfasts are served.

David Crockett was born on August 17, 1786, along the banks of the Nolichucky River. He became one of our country's best-loved historical figures, often portrayed as larger than life due to his skills as a teller of tall tales. Though he may not have "killed himself a bar when he was only three," his reputation as a hunter seems to have been well deserved.

He left his East Tennessee home for Middle Tennessee where he built and operated a grist mill and distillery on Shoal Creek until it was destroyed by a flood in 1821. The gregarious, five-foot-nine Crockett moved to West Tennessee where he was elected to Congress. There he boasted, "I can out look a panther and out stare a flash of lightning, tote a steamboat on my back and play rough and tumble with a lion."

But Crockett ran afoul of Andrew Jackson's political machine and lost his seat in Congress. He left Tennessee for Texas and the Alamo where legend has him playing his fiddle while waiting for Santa Anna's army to attack. All the Americans were killed or executed, including Crockett, who died on March 6, 1836, at the age of forty-nine.

Davy Crockett Birthplace State Park has seventy-three campground sites with hookups, a swimming pool, Nolichucky River access, a reconstruction of Crockett's birthplace, and a museum in the visitor center telling the story of the colorful frontiersman's life.

The tiny community of Chuckey has two bed and breakfasts. Harmony Hill Inn has two rooms with private baths in a 150-year-old farmhouse. Flintlock Inn and Stables has three rooms with antique furniture and private baths in a rustic home constructed from three 200-year-old log cabins. Three family-style meals are available.

Once you arrive at the Flintlock Inn, you can kick back in a rocker on the porch, curl up in front of a cozy stone fireplace, or head out for guided horseback adventures lasting from two hours to overnight.

One of the longer trips includes a trip to a hot spring via a scenic mountain trail. Other trips explore gently rolling farm land. Those of you having horses with negative Coggins tests can corral your mounts here and plan an unguided trip to the Cherokee National Forest with Gayle and Jimmy's advice if you prefer.

In addition to horseback riding, packages with golf, hiking, fishing, canoeing, rafting, and hunting may be arranged for a weekend getaway or a week-long escape to the great outdoors.

There are many opportunities for outdoor recreation in the Nolichucky District of the Cherokee National Forest. There's an excellent trail system, designated wilderness areas, and five camping sites. The Bald Mountain Scenic Area has sixteen trails. One of the shortest and most popular is the 0.7-mile trail to Marguerite Falls which begins off Horse Creek Road on Shelton Mission Road.

Horse Creek Recreation Area is 2.8 miles off TN 107 between Greeneville and Jonesborough. The scenic, densely forested area offers hiking, biking, fishing, swimming, hunting, and camping.

Continue on TN 107 to visit Jonesborough, the oldest town in Tennessee.

All of the following accommodations are Greeneville with zip

code 37743, and all telephone listings are area code 423, except where noted.

Accommodations:
Big Spring Inn, 315 N. Main St., 638-2917.
Flintlock Inn and Stables, 790 G'Fellers Rd., Chuckey, 37641; 257-2489.
General Morgan Inn and Conference Center, 111 N. Main St., 800-223-2679 or 787-1000.
Harmony Hill Inn, 85 Pleasant Hill Rd., Chuckey, 37641; 257-3893.
Hilltop House Bed and Breakfast, 6 Sanford Cir. off US 70, 639-8202.
Nolichucky Bluffs, 301 Kinser Park Ln., 800-842-4690 or 787-7947.
Oak Hill Farm Bed and Breakfast, 3035 Lonesome Pine Trl., 639-5253.
Snapp Inn Bed and Breakfast, 1990 Davy Crockett Park Rd., Limestone, 37861; 257-2482.

Attractions:
Andrew Johnson National Historic Site, 638-3551.
Dickson-Williams Mansion, 638-8144.
Doak House Museum, Tusculum College, 636-8554.
Nathanael Greene Museum, 636-1558.
President Andrew Johnson Museum and Library, Tusculum College, 636-7348.

Dining:
Augustino's, 639-1231.
Brumley's at the General Morgan Inn, 787-1100.
The Butcher's Block, 638-4485.
The Tannery, 638-2772.

Shopping:
Greeneville Antique Market, 638-2773.
Madison Day Spa, 638-4656.
Ye Olde Tourist Trap, 639-1567.

Special Events:
April—Iris Festival
May—Greenespring

Camping:
Davy Crockett Birthplace State Park, Limestone, 257-2061.
Horse Creek Recreation Area, Cherokee National Forest, 638-4109.
Kinser Park Golf Course/Campground, 639-5912.

For More Information:
Greeneville/Greene County Tourism Council, 115 Academy St., 638-4111.
Nolichucky Ranger District, Office of the Cherokee National Forest, 120 Austin Ave., 638-4109.

9 *Jonesborough*
Tennessee's Oldest Town

Jonesborough was established in 1779, which makes it the oldest town in the state of Tennessee. It was named for Willie Jones, a North Carolina politician who was supportive of the settlers beyond the Allegheny Mountains, as the southern Appalachians were then known. As is befitting a community of such historical significance, Jonesborough was the first town in Tennessee to be placed in the National Register of Historic Places.

At the time of Jonesborough's founding, North Carolina had authority over what is now East Tennessee. In 1775, North Carolina authorized the creation of a district to represent settlers along the Watauga and Nolichucky Rivers with authority to muster a militia and hold court.

The new district was named Washington in honor of George Washington and included all of what is now Tennessee.

In 1784 North Carolina ceded these western lands to the central government at the request of the Continental Congress. If North Carolina beyond the Allegheny Mountains had seemed a distant governing body, the central government was even more so.

Jonesborough, Tennessee's oldest town, is in the National Register of Historic Places.

Into the void stepped residents who decided their interests would best be served by creating their own state, to be named Franklin. Those supporting the state of Franklin, or Franklinites, elected John Sevier their one and only governor and chose Jonesborough as the state's first capital.

In 1785 the capital of the state of Franklin moved to Greeneville but after John Sevier's term as governor expired in the fall of 1787, support for the state of Franklin faltered. The state of Franklin quietly ceased to exist and was replaced by the Southwest Territory until the state of Tennessee was admitted as the sixteenth state in the Union in 1796.

Andrew Jackson was one of many young men making his way westward to Jonesborough in 1788. He was admitted to the bar and boarded for a time at the Christopher Taylor house, one of the oldest log houses in Tennessee and now relocated to the center of the historic district.

Tennessee presidents Jackson, Polk, and Johnson stayed at the Chester Inn on Main Street, which was built in 1797. It was a popular stop along the Great Stage Road between the central government at Washington City and Nashville. It is now owned by the state of Tennessee and is the home of the National Storytelling Center and the National Association for the Preservation and Perpetuation of Storytelling (NAPPS).

One of Tennessee's most controversial figures, William Gannaway "Parson" Brownlow, used a first-floor room at the Chester Inn as the office for his newspaper, the *Whig*.

Brownlow editorialized his hatred for the Confederate cause in his newspaper. He left Tennessee, returning April 5, 1865, as the soundly despised governor during Reconstruction.

The National Storytelling Festival is sponsored every October by NAPPS. Since 1972 it has been a beacon drawing storytellers from across the country to participate in the revival of this oral tradition.

The three-day Storytelling Festival brings thousands of visitors to the historic town of thirty-four hundred. The only accommodations in Jonesborough are bed and breakfast inns, so many visitors during the festival make arrangements to stay in neighboring Johnson City, Greeneville, Rogersville, Erwin, Elizabethton, Kingsport, or Bristol.

Main Street is dominated by the seventh of Washington County's courthouses, a neoclassical brick design completed in 1912. The historic street has benefited from a multimillion-dollar restoration program and is lined with brick sidewalks, old-fashioned street lamps, underground wiring, inviting antique shops, soda shops, restaurants, and specialty gift shops. The entire town has been in the National Register of Historic Places since 1969.

Many of Jonesborough's historic buildings are now specialty shops or bed and breakfasts.

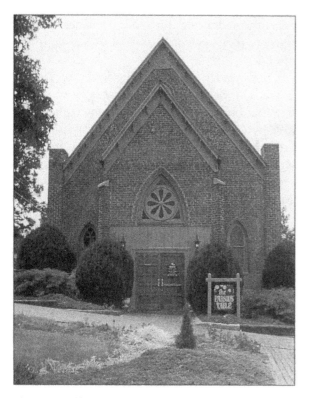

The Parson's Table is a favorite restaurant of many diners in Jonesborough.

There's a "new" visitor center, built in 1982, with the Jonesborough-Washington County History Museum inside. The museum displays tell the two-hundred-year-old story of Jonesborough. A walking tour brochure is available at the visitor center that briefly describes the history and architecture of many of Jonesborough's oldest structures, including the Mail Pouch Building, Sisters' Row, and the Salt House, which rationed salt to area residents during the Civil War.

You may want to inquire at the visitor center about various tours, including Jonesborough's Time and Tales Tour, a more thorough look inside historic homes and buildings peppered with anecdotes and interesting stories.

One of the historic markers along West Main Street describes the publication during 1819–1820 of the first periodicals in the United States devoted to the abolition of human slavery, the *Manumission Intelligencer* and the *Emancipator*.

The Jonesborough Antique Mart is one of our favorite stops. The Pig and Slipper also has antiques and collectibles.

There are several good lunch spots. In town try the Old Sweet Shop for sandwiches, salads, and ice cream treats. The Main Street Cafe across from the Chester Inn has soups, sandwiches, and salads.

The Parson's Table serves gourmet selections in a historic building that was formerly a church. You may prefer to drive out to the popular Harmony Grocery off TN 81N. for Cajun and Creole dinner selections. You may bring your own wine since no alcohol is served. Ditto for the Parson's Table.

Bed and breakfasts thrive in Jonesborough. The Hawley House is a 1793 log-and-stone dwelling believed to be the oldest building in Jonesborough. It has a comfortable wraparound porch, guest rooms with queen-sized poster beds, private baths, and air conditioning.

Down the street in the 1848 Shipley-Bledsoe House is Jonesborough Bed and Breakfast. The house on the hill across from the Parson's Table has a formal living room with antiques and a grand piano. Visitors may choose from three large bedrooms with poster beds and one with double canopy beds; all have central heat and air; some have TVs and phones. Bathrooms may be private or shared.

The Cunningham House is across from the

Christopher Taylor Log House and down an alley beside Main Street Cafe. Tours and bed and breakfast accommodations are available in the 1840 two-story home filled with period antiques.

The Aiken-Brow House is an 1850s Greek Revival structure on Third Avenue South. The three guest rooms have private baths.

The Woodrow House is a completely furnished private two-bedroom vacation cottage located in Jonesborough's historic district. The Old Yellow Vic has two rooms with private baths. The Bugaboo Bed and Breakfast is outside town on fifteen acres and offers two rooms with private baths.

The Wetlands Water Park has a giant water slide, lap pool, concessions, and a picnic area for family fun from May to September. Next door is the Home Federal Park, a forty-five-site year-round campground with full hookups.

Return to the starting point in Bristol via US 11E to complete the East Tennessee loop tour.

All of the following accommodations are Jonesborough with zip code 37659, and all telephone listings are area code 423, except where noted.

Accommodations:
Aiken-Brow House, 104 Third Ave. S., 753-9440.
Bugaboo B&B, 211 Semore Dr., 753-9345.
Cunningham House, 119 W. Main, 753-9292.
Hawley House B&B, 114 E. Woodrow Ave, 753-8869.
Jonesborough B&B, 100 Woodrow Ave, P.O. Box 722, 753-9223.
The Old Yellow Vic B&B, 411 W. Main St., 753-9558.

The Tea Room, 130 W. Main, 753-0660.
Woodrow House, inquire at Keene Gallery, 125 W. Main, 753-8234.

Attractions:
Discover Jonesborough's Times and Tales Tour, 753-1010.
Jonesborough/Washington County History Museum, 753-1015.
Wetlands Water Park, Jonesborough Parks and Recreation, 753-1553.

Dining:
The Harmony Grocery, 348-6183.
Main Street Cafe, 753-2460.
Old Sweet Shop, 753-8851.
The Parson's Table, 753-8002.

Shopping:
Jonesborough Antique Mart, 753-8301.
Nifong's Crafts and Wood Products, 753-4551.
Old Town Hall, 753-2095.
Pig and Slipper, 753-2141.
The Salt House, 753-5113.

Special Events:
April—Spring Doll Show
July—Historic Jonesborough Days
August—Quilt Fest
October—National Storytelling Festival
December—Christmas in Old Jonesborough (progressive dinner; contact the Jonesborough Civic Trust, 753-5281)

Camping:
Davy Crockett Birthplace State Park, Limestone, 257-2167.
Home Federal Park, 753-1555.

For More Information:
Historic Jonesborough Visitors Center, 117 Boone St., 800-400-4221 or 753-5961. Open daily.
Jonesborough Civic Trust, P.O. Box 451, 753-5281.
National Storytelling Association, P.O. Box 309, 800-525-4514 or 753-2171.

🪶 Loop 2

10 *Dandridge*
The Historic Town
Spared by TVA

Dandridge was initially settled on the northern bank of the French Broad River in 1783. It has the distinction of being the only city in the nation named in honor of Martha Dandridge Custis, the wife of George Washington. In 1793 it became the county seat of Jefferson County. Dandridge, the second-oldest town in Tennessee, was incorporated in 1843. Its antebellum courthouse is the oldest still in use in the state.

In addition to government offices, the Jefferson County Courthouse contains the Jefferson County Museum, which has a collection of display cases lining the hallways. Inside them you will find Indian artifacts, Civil War relics, a copper moonshine still, and the August 12, 1806, marriage bond of frontiersman David Crockett and Polly Finley.

The land around Dandridge is comprised of rich loam silt and red upland limestone, suitable for agriculture and capable of high crop yields. As a result, the area is surrounded by family farms. The farm of John Stokely was a remarkable example. According to Carolyn Sakowski in *Touring the East Tennessee Backroads*, John Stokely died in 1890, leaving a wife and nine children to farm their land along the French Broad near Dandridge.

By 1897 their efforts were so successful that they hit on the notion of canning some of their surplus tomatoes. They formed a partnership with a relative, Col. Alfred Swann, and the famous Stokely Brothers Company was born.

In the 1930s the Tennessee Valley Authority

Many fine historic structures line the streets of Dandridge, one of Tennessee's oldest towns.

(TVA) was busy planning to dam the French Broad River to create Douglas Lake. The project would have flooded thousands of acres of ultra-productive farmland and the historic community of Dandridge. A member of the Swann family, Frances Burnett Swann, came to the rescue with a flood of letters to U.S. senators and congressmen, even to Eleanor Roosevelt.

Although TVA was not known to be especially sensitive to displacement of citizens or the covering of communities by floodwaters in other projects, a presidential decree eventually established the dike that saved Dandridge. On the Dandridge side, the dike rises like a grassy knoll with no hint of the lake that lies beyond it. The earth and stone dike and a good view of the lake are visible from the small park on Church Street that overlooks the lake.

Douglas Lake stretches along the southern edge of Dandridge. It is 43.1 miles long with 31,600 surface acres and 555 miles of shoreline. Its waters yield good catches of black bass, sauger, walleye, crappie, and bluegill. Along its shores are campgrounds, marinas, and resorts to host visitors drawn to Dandridge for water sports. The annual sixty-foot draw down exposes extensive mud flats that attract wintering waterfowl.

West of town TVA's Douglas Headwater Campground has fifty-three sites adjacent to the beach and free public boat ramp. Rest rooms are available. The TVA Douglas Tailwater Campground has sixty sites, twenty with electric hookups. Both are first-come, first-serve and open on the honor system from April to October.

East of town Lake Cove Resort on Oak Grove Road has boat and cabin rentals, a dock with sandy beach, boat ramp and ninety campground sites with full hookups available year-round. A bit farther east the Baneberry Golf and Resort on Harrison Ferry Road overlooks Douglas Lake and

Many fine historic structures line the streets of Dandridge, one of Tennessee's oldest towns.

offers an eighteen-hole, par-72 golf course, driving range and putting green, tennis, boat ramp, water sports, and a restaurant/lounge. Baneberry offers packages for golfers with unlimited golf, lodging, breakfast buffet, and dinner from two nights to a week.

Everywhere you look in the small town of 1,575 there are historic structures. The police department is in the 1845 brick Hickman Tavern Coach House. The city hall is next door in the 1845 Hickman Tavern. Across the street is the

Revolutionary War cemetery. In 1972 Dandridge was declared a historic district containing the courthouse and twenty homes.

The Barrington Inn is owned by Vincent and Sharlene Barrington. Sharlene's a native of Ohio and Vincent was born in Great Britain. They had been living in the Bahamas and Florida where they ran a restaurant at Key West. They came to Dandridge, loved the area, and found that, as the chamber of commerce says, "It's a great place to visit, but a much better place to live."

They purchased twenty-four acres and discovered that the two-story farmhouse on it had originally been a pre-Civil War log cabin. Envisioning the elegant structure it could become, they added another story, exposed the logs, and opened up the back as a gourmet restaurant with an intimate ambiance that's been very well received. Each of the four guest bedrooms has a private bath and amenities like fireplaces and whirlpool tubs to choose from.

If you're a guest in the bed and breakfast, you can make arrangements for dinner during your stay; otherwise, the restaurant is open to the public Thursday, Friday, and Saturday evenings by reservation.

Don't be fooled by the New Market address, the Barrington has a Dandridge phone number and is located north of town about 2.5 miles from Interstate 40.

Also north of town is the Mill Dale Farm, owned by Lucy Franklin who started the bed and breakfast when she stopped operating the family farm. The nineteenth-century, two-story farmhouse is surrounded by well-kept grounds that create a relaxed country atmosphere. She serves a delicious farm breakfast to the guests staying in her three guest rooms with private baths.

West of town, the Mountain Harbor Inn overlooks Douglas Lake. The eleven rooms all have private baths. A complimentary breakfast encourages a leisurely start to a day on the lake. Boat launching and docking are available. Fishermen may want to arrange charters or guides to acquaint them with crappie hot spots and largemouth bass honey holes on Douglas.

The Mountain Harbor Restaurant is one of the few in the area serving broiled seafood selections along with prime rib and grilled chicken for dinner. Sandwiches, salads, and pasta dishes are offered for lunch Tuesday through Saturday. Just down the road you'll find Cowboy's Fish House serving popular fried fish selections.

The Dandridge Seafood Restaurant on East Meeting Street draws seafood lovers from near and far but also serves steak for lunch and dinner Tuesday through Sunday. The Wagon Wheel Restaurant and Anna Lee's Hearthside Restaurant near the interstate offer country cooking.

Travel south of Dandridge on TN 92 to intersect US 411. Turn west (right) on US 411 and travel along the base of English Mountain to Sevierville.

All of the following accommodations are Dandridge with zip code 37725, and all telephone listings are area code 423, except where noted.

Accommodations:
Baneberry Golf and Resort, 704 Harrison Ferry Rd., Baneberry; 800-951-4653 or 674-2500.
The Barrington Inn, 1174 McGuire Rd., New Market, 37820; 888-205-8482 or 397-3368.
Lake Cove Resort, 1889 Oak Grove Rd., 397-4080.
Mill Dale Farm B&B, 140 Mill Dale Rd., 800-767-3471 or 397-3470.
Mountain Harbor Inn, 1199 Hwy. 139, 397-3345.
Tennessee Mountain Inn, 531 Patriot Dr., P.O. Box 918, 800-235-9440 or 397-9437.

Attractions:
The Jefferson County Museum, Jefferson County Courthouse.
Douglas Lake.

Dining:
Anna Lee's Hearthside Restaurant, 397-9387.
The Barrington Inn, New Market, 888-205-8482 or 397-3368.
Cowboy's Fish House, 327-2529.
Dandridge Seafood Restaurant, 397-2315.
Mountain Harbor Restaurant, 397-3345.

Shopping:
Moore House Antiques, 397-3846.
Spirit of the Hand Gallery, 397-2914.

Special Events:
August—Peach Festival.

Camping:
Douglas Dam Campgrounds (Headwaters and Tailwaters),
     TVA, Morristown, 587-5600.
Fancher's Willow Branch Campground, 397-3510.
Lake Cove Resort, 397-4080.

For More Information:
Jefferson County Chamber of Commerce, 532 Patriot Dr., Jef-
     ferson City, TN 37760; 397-9642.

II *Sevierville*
Home of Dolly Parton

Sevierville was named to honor the first governor of Tennessee, John Sevier. Sevier was a prominent figure on the western frontier and was elected governor of the short-lived state of Franklin (*see* Johnson City, Jonesborough, and Greeneville). During the earliest settlement, frontier settlers in this area established an independent government, the Association of the South Holston and French Broad Rivers.

The need for such associations ended with Tennessee's statehood in 1796, but they were the providers of frontier law and order in the intervening years. The first court in Sevierville was held in a flea-infested barn that was a far cry from the lovely 1896 domed courthouse that dominates the town today.

The original Seth Thomas clock sounds on the half-hour and hour much as it has sounded since the turn of the century. There's a statue out front of country music artist Dolly Parton, pickin' and grinnin' in her girlhood. She was raised in Sevierville and members of her family still live here.

For those of you exiting I-40 at TN 66, shopping opportunities beckon from both sides of the busy four-lane highway. Even those who aren't knife aficionados stop at Smoky Mountain Knife Works to see the antique knife displays inside the

Dollywood Theme Park is named for Dolly Parton, country music megastar and Sevier County's best-known native.

Antique shops line TN 66, between Interstate 40 and Sevierville.

world's largest knife store. Antique shoppers are hard pressed to decide which mall to visit first. This is the largest collection of antique shops in the area and they're all chock full of varied and interesting stuff.

The Douglas Lake Dam is about three miles east of TN 66 on Douglas Dam Road. Camping facilities at Douglas Dam are open from April to Halloween. The forty-mile-long lake offers swimming, boating, fishing, and water skiing (*see* Dandridge).

As tourists migrate from I-40 to Gatlinburg, they often choose to make the one-block turn to downtown Sevierville, which manages to strike a pleasing balance between its rural roots and its need to welcome the millions of tourists who travel the US 441 Parkway to its neighbor, the Great Smoky Mountains National Park (GSMNP).

One block off US 441, Josev's has been a favorite stop of ours for several years. The food is good, the atmosphere pleasing, and the service prompt and friendly. No alcohol is served during lunch or dinner but you may bring your own. Sunday brunch is perennially popular.

Down the street you can get down to some country-style cooking at Virgil's 50's Restaurant where both the atmosphere and the food are classic fifties.

A bit farther down Bruce Street is the 131 Antique Mall. The last stop on Bruce Street is the Sevier County Heritage Museum. Take a right at the intersection with Parkway to rejoin US 441, heading south to Pigeon Forge.

On your way to Pigeon Forge, you'll pass the Applewood complex on Apple Valley Road. What started as a family-owned dairy farm on the banks of the Little Pigeon River in 1910 has been converted to an apple orchard, cider mill, bakery, gift shop with bins of fragrant fresh apples in season, a winery, and the Applewood Restaurant and the Applewood Farms Grill.

A bit farther down Apple Valley Road is Hidden Mountain Resorts with cabins and townhomes featuring fireplaces, cable TV, whirlpool tubs, fully equipped kitchens, and screened porches. Honey-moon cottages have private hot tubs.

National franchises include Best Western, Comfort Inn, Days Inn, Econo Lodge, Hampton Inn, and Ramada Inn.

If hot barbecue and a cold glass of beer sound good, head for Damon's, one of the rare restaurants in Sevierville or Pigeon Forge able to serve alcohol.

For an elegant evening meal, visit Five Oaks Restaurant on US 441 across from Apple Valley Road. The dim interior, crisp white linens, and sparkling goblets create a pleasant atmosphere for sampling chicken, beef, veal, and pasta entrees.

The eighteen-hundred-seat Lee Greenwood Theater features Greenwood in more than 250 shows per year between late March and December with special Christmas shows in November and December and a New Year's Eve gala on December 31 closing the season.

Sevierville, along with Pigeon Forge and Gatlinburg, hosts the annual WinterFest, a two-month series of events and outdoor lighting extravaganza that grows every year.

Follow US 411 (also known as Dolly Parton Parkway) and turn right (east) to Forbidden Caverns, a cave beneath English Mountain open to the public since 1967. The commercial cave is known for a running stream, unusual rock formations accented with special lighting and sound effects, and an usually large wall of cave onyx. The cave is open daily from April 1 through November.

Turn right on Middle Creek Road off US 411 to visit Blue Mountain Mist Country Inn and Cottages on Pullen Road. Each of the twelve guest rooms has its own bath, some with old-fashioned claw-foot tubs.

This modern "Victorian" is a peaceful retreat situated on sixty acres with a great view of Shields Mountain from the swimming pool or the wrap-around front porch. Behind the inn are five cottages, each with fireplace, bedside whirlpool tub, TV/VCR, and kitchenette. Continue about six miles on Middle Creek Road to Pigeon Forge.

Some of the bed and breakfasts with Sevierville addresses, including the Von Bryan Inn, Little Greenbrier Lodge, and the Wonderland

Five Oaks Restaurant is housed in an elegant two-story brick structure that once was the heart of a horse farm.

Hotel, are best reached from Pigeon Forge via Wears Valley Road and are discussed in more detail in that chapter.

To reach Gatlinburg the back way, proceed past the turnoff to Middle Creek Road on US 411 before turning right (south) on TN 416. Continue on TN 416 to Bird Creek Road and the Gatlinburg Arts and Crafts Community (*see* Gatlinburg for more). When you reach US 321 turn west to enter downtown Gatlinburg.

All of the following accommodations are Sevierville with zip code 37862, and all telephone listings are area code 423, except where noted.

Accommodations:
Blue Mountain Mist Country Inn, 1811 Pullen Rd., 800-497-2335 or 428-2335.
English Mountain Condo Resort, 1081 Cove Rd., 800-842-6415 or 453-1071.
Hidden Mountain Resorts, 475 Apple Valley Rd., 800-541-6837.
Little Greenbriar Lodge, 3685 Lyon Springs Rd., 800-277-8100 or 429-2500.
Place of the Blue Smoke, 3760 Cove Mountain Rd., 453-6355.
The Von Bryan Inn, 2402 Hatcher Mountain Rd., 800-633-1459 or 453-9832.
Wonderland Hotel, 3889 Wonderland Way, 800-428-0779 or 428-0779.

Attractions:
Eagle's Landing Golf Course, 429-4223.
Forbidden Caverns, 453-5972.
Lee Greenwood Theater, 800-769-1125 or 453-0777.
River Islands Golf Course, 933-0100.
Sevier County Heritage Museum, 453-4058.
Walden's Creek Horseback Riding, 429-0411.

Dining:
Applewood Farmhouse Restaurant and Applewood Farms Grill, 428-1222.
Damon's, 428-6200.
Five Oaks Beef and Seafood Restaurant, 453-5994.
Josev's, 428-0737.
Virgil's 50's Restaurant, 453-2782.

Shopping:
Action Antiques and Collectibles, 453-0052.
Antique Mall, 428-0001.

Apple Barn Cider Mill and General Store, 453-9319.
Ole Smoky Antique Mall, 429-0100.
Riverside Antique and Collectors Mall, 429-0100.
Smoky Mountain Knife Works, 453-5871.
Robert A. Tino Gallery, 453-6315.

Special Events:
Winterfest—November through February

Camping:
Douglas Dam Campground (Headwaters and Tailwaters), Morristown, 587-5600.
East Knoxville Dumplin Valley KOA; 933-6393.
River Plantation RV Park, 800-758-5267 or 429-5267.
Riverside Campground, 453-7299.

For More Information:
Sevierville Chamber of Commerce, 866 Winfield Dunn Pkwy., P.O. Box 4280; 800-255-6411, 453-6411. Open daily.

12 *Pigeon Forge*
Home of Wilderness Week

Although the town of Pigeon Forge was not incorporated until 1960, an unincorporated community existed here long before that. Settlers arrived in this isolated area as early as 1795. Originally named Fanshiers for one of these early arrivals, the community was renamed for an iron foundry on the Little Pigeon River that looked south toward Cove Mountain and the towering peaks of Mount Le Conte.

One of the few surviving man-made landmarks in Pigeon Forge from this era is the Old Mill, built in 1830 by William Love and his father, Isaac. The mill is in the National Register of Historic Places and continues to produce meal and flour, making it the oldest operating commercial water-powered mill in Tennessee. It's situated along the banks of the Little Pigeon River at a location in the heart of the burgeoning commercial district along US 441 approaching the north-ern entrance to the Great Smoky Mountains National Park (GSMNP).

Pigeon Forge grew slowly from the time GSMNP was dedicated in 1940. It took forty years for the boom to come. Today Pigeon Forge is a community of around thirty-two hundred year-round residents, but there are accommoda-tions for about thirty-five thousand vacationers in the vicinity.

Pigeon Forge is best known to many of us as a shopping mecca. The more than two hundred out-let malls here were voted the favorite shopping spot in the South in *Southern Living* magazine's Readers Choice Awards. The outlet malls are pop-ular year-round, but the activity really begins to hum around Thanksgiving.

If you *really* like to shop, you'll find your time well spent in Pigeon Forge when the supersales occur during the World's Largest Outlet Sale in December or the Winter Savings Fest in February when hotel rooms are plentiful and cheap.

Pigeon Forge is also a gateway to the eight-hundred-square-mile Great Smoky Mountains National Park, part of the largest wilderness area in the eastern United States. The young at heart are drawn to its fast-paced, action-packed laser arcades, bumper cars, go-cart racing, helicopter rides, indoor sky-diving, and bungee jumping.

It's also the home of Dollywood Theme Park,

The Old Mill in Pigeon Forge is a remnant of the community that thrived in the shadow of the Smokies in the 1830s.

The Day Dreams Country Inn welcomes visitors to Pigeon Forge.

a popular family destination with twenty-nine rides and attractions and forty live shows daily during peak season. Dollywood also hosts the Smoky Mountain Christmas Festival each November and December. Visitors are dazzled by 2 million twinkling lights and welcomed to restaurants with Christmas menus and gift shops filled with holiday ideas.

Winterfest activities continue from November through February and include our favorite, Wilderness Wildlife Week of Nature, referred to by most of us who insist on attending every year as Wilderness Week.

The free activities include more than forty walks led by area hikers and professional guides, more than sixty indoor lectures, panels, demonstrations, and slide shows by life-long residents, wildlife biologists, ornithologists, naturalists, botanists, professional photographers, park rangers, and university professors at the host facil-

ity, the Heartlander Country Resort.

In addition to the Heartlander, which has both indoor and outdoor pools, the Capri Motel offers a large pool and reasonable rates. The River Place Inn and Willow Brook Lodge offer in-room whirlpools, fireplace suites, and heated pools. Visitors also find national motel chains like Days Inn, Holiday Inn, Howard Johnson, Quality Inn, and Ramada Inn, as well as a KOA campground.

Bed and breakfasts waiting to welcome you include the Day Dreams Country Inn Bed and Breakfast, a two-story western cedar and hemlock log home with six large antique-filled bedrooms with private baths situated on three tranquil acres, protected from the bustle of Pigeon Forge by a couple of blocks and the bubbling Mill Creek. One bedroom has handicapped access. They prefer that you make special arrangements if your children are coming.

Hilton's Bluff Bed and Breakfast is also close to downtown Pigeon Forge, just off Wears Valley Road. This hilltop hideaway offers ten guest rooms with private baths and a full breakfast. Limited accommodations are available for children by special arrangement.

Other area favorites include the Von Bryan Inn on Hatcher Mountain Road about seven miles west of Pigeon Forge off Wears Valley Road. The inn features six rooms with private baths, a chalet for groups of four to six, and a spectacular 360-degree view. Children over ten may stay in the inn and younger visitors are welcome in the chalet. There's a hilltop swimming pool and a twelve-person hot tub.

On the opposite side of Wears Valley Road, the "new" Wonderland Hotel invokes the spirit of the "old" Wonderland Hotel at Elkmont. The new creation has rustic wood paneling in the simply furnished rooms and front porch rockers and swings that recreate a relaxed, down-home feel. The restaurant serves three meals daily and there's also a stable with horses for hire or facilities for your mount.

A favorite for generations, the Little Greenbrier Lodge on Lyon Springs Road sits on the side of Cove Mountain overlooking Wears Valley about one hundred yards from a national park trailhead. Built in 1939, the historic Little Greenbrier has eleven cozy, antique-filled rooms and all but three have private baths. A full country breakfast is served and guests with children should call ahead.

There are more than seventy restaurants in the area but our favorite is Chef Jock's Tastebuds Cafe on Wears Valley Road. This is, without doubt, the

More than 30,000 visitors are welcomed to Pigeon Forge by hotels, motels, and bed and breakfasts like Hilton's Bluff.

best source of gourmet dining to be found in Pigeon Forge or Gatlinburg. No alcohol is served, but you can bring wine to enjoy while you relax and wait, for this is good food, not fast food. You'd better get reservations; Jock stays busy regardless of the season.

Another favorite spot for a good, quick lunch or dinner is J&S Cafeteria near the Heartlander on Parkway. The Old Mill Cornflour Restaurant serves country comfort foods for breakfast, lunch, and dinner daily in a great setting overlooking the Little Pigeon River. Bennett's Pit Barbeque has a forty-item soup and salad bar in addition to barbecue selections.

The most unusual dinner setting in Pigeon Forge is the Dixie Stampede Dinner Theater. About one thousand diners are served while agile equestrians and their equally talented mounts put on a mock North vs. South rodeo complete with southern belles and bareback acrobats.

Many visitors choose to ride the Pigeon Forge Fun Time Trolley to over one hundred stops in Pigeon Forge. As pollution increasingly becomes an issue in the GSMNP, trolleys in Pigeon Forge and Gatlinburg may play an even larger role in transportation of visitors to the area. Continue on US 441 to Gatlinburg.

All of the following accommodations are Pigeon Forge with zip code 37863, and all telephone listings are area code 423, except where noted.

Accommodations:
Blue Mountain Mist Country Inn, 1811 Pullen Rd., Sevierville, 37862; 800-497-2335 and 428-2335.
Day Dreams Country Inn, 2720 Colonial Dr., 800-377-1469 or 428-0370.
Heartlander Country Resort, 2385 Pkwy., 800-843-6686 or 453-4106.
Hidden Mountain Resorts, 475 Apple Valley Rd., Sevierville, 37862; 800-943-9359 or 453-9850.

Hilton's Bluff Bed and Breakfast Inn, 2654 Valley Heights Dr., 800-441-4188 or 428-9765.
Little Greenbrier Lodge, 3685 Lyon Springs Rd., 800-277-8100 or 429-2500.
River Place Inn, 3223 Pkwy., 800-428-5590 or 453-0801.
Von Bryan Inn, 2402 Hatcher Mountain Rd., Sevierville, 37862; 800-633-1459 or 453-9832.
Willow Brook Lodge, 3035 Pkwy., 800-765-1380 or 453-5334.
Wonderland Hotel, 3889 Wonderland Way, Sevierville, 37862; 800-428-0779 or 428-0779.

Attractions:
Dixie Stampede Dinner Attraction, 800-356-1676 or 453-4400.
Dollywood, 800-DOLLYWOOD or 428-9488.
Five Oaks Stables, 428-9764.
Gatlinburg Municipal Golf Course.
Music Mansion Theater, 428-7469.
Ogle's Water Park, 453-8741.
The Old Mill, 453-4628.
Parkway Speedway, 428-0555.
Pigeon Forge Fun Time Trolley, 453-6444.
Smoky Mountain Jubilee, 428-01836.
Smoky Mountain Tours, 463-3471, 428-3014.

Dining:
Bennett's Pit Barbeque, 429-2200.
Cornflour Restaurant in the Old Mill Complex, 429-3463.
J&S Cafeteria, 429-3070.
Tastebuds Cafe, 428-9781.

Shopping:
Belz Factory Outlet World, 453-3503.
Pigeon Forge Factory Outlet Mall Office, 428-2828.
Tanger Factory Outlet Center, 428-7001.

Special Events:
November, December, January, February—Winterfest
January—Wilderness Week

Camping:
Creekstone Outdoor Resort, 800-848-8181 or 453-8181.
Fort Wear Campground, 800-452-9835 or 428-1951.

For More Information:
Pigeon Forge Welcome Center, 2450 Pkwy, P.O. Box 1390, 800-251-9100 or 453-8574.

13 *Gatlinburg*
Honeymoon Capital of the South

Gatlinburg is known by millions of visitors because of its location at the northern entrance to the Great Smoky Mountains National Park (GSMNP). It's also the unofficial honeymoon capital of the South to about ten thousand newlyweds each year and was voted the favorite mountain getaway of *Southern Living* magazine's Readers Choice Awards.

We prefer Gatlinburg and the Smokies in the winter and spring, not only because the number of visitors significantly declines but also to experience the wild winter beauty and the lovely Appalachian spring.

Gatlinburg began attracting tourists as early as 1916 when Andy Huff built the Mountain View Hotel. Initially built to house timber customers, the Mountain View was expanded to provide fine food and lodging for vacationers and later housing for employees of the National Park Service and Bureau of Roads. Some of the earliest resorts included the Gatlinburg Inn, the Buckhorn Inn, Le Conte Lodge, and the Wonderland Hotel in Elkmont (*see* GSMNP for more on Le Conte and the Wonderland).

The classic Gatlinburg Inn was built in 1937 by R. L. Maples and is still open from April 1 to November. 1. The dining room is closed but more than seventy rooms and suites are available.

The Buckhorn Inn was built in 1938 and has six guest rooms with private baths and four cot-

Gatlinburg is the northern gateway to the Smokies.

The 1930s Buckhorn Inn has four cottages and six guest rooms on forty acres.

tages on forty acres east of Gatlinburg on Tudor Mountain Road looking toward Mount Le Conte. The inn remains a gracious mountain retreat decorated with oriental rugs and antiques.

Full breakfasts are served for guests daily and gourmet dinners are available at 7 P.M. for the public if arrangements are made by early afternoon on the day you'd like to come. Diners are invited to bring wine for the evening.

Gatlinburg, a town with a permanent population of 3,816, is ringed by mountain peaks and streams, further concentrating the serious traffic problems faced during the peak summer and fall tourist seasons. The exhaust from the cars of millions of visitors is contributing to decreasing visibility and increasing acidity in the GSMNP.

Fortunately, an excellent trolley system is in place that allows visitors to relax and enjoy the sights while someone else watches the road. The routes are color coded to help newcomers find the right trolley. For example, the red route runs to Pigeon Forge, Dollywood, and the Gatlinburg golf

course while the yellow route runs to the Great Smoky Arts and Crafts Community.

Located on Glades Road and Buckhorn Road off US 321 three miles east of Gatlinburg, the Great Smoky Arts and Crafts Community showcases eighty local artists and craftsmen working in galleries along an eight-mile auto loop that is the largest group of independent artists and craftsmen in the United States.

Reservations are a good idea at the rustic Wild Plum Tearoom, a favored lunch spot along the crafts loop that's open from 11:30 to 3:00 Monday through Saturday. Several restaurants and popular bed and breakfasts are located in or near the crafts community, including the Buckhorn Inn, the Colonel's Lady, and Hippensteal's Mountain View Inn, an eight-bedroom modern Victorian inn with all rooms opening onto large porches facing views of Greenbriar Pinnacle, Mount Le Conte and Mount Harrison. Each room has a fireplace, queen-sized beds, private bath, and whirlpool tub.

The Colonel's Lady sits nearby on Big Ridge

Mountain and has mountain views, hot tubs, and eight rooms with private baths. Gourmet breakfasts and afternoon refreshments are served.

Another source of high-quality crafts from the entire southern Appalachian region is found at the Arrowcraft Shop, which was founded in 1926 and is operated by the Southern Highlands Guild. Arrowcraft is next door to Arrowmont School which has a craft instruction program that includes spring and summer week-long workshops with room and board, evening sessions for area residents, and Elderhostel programs in subjects ranging from stone sculpture to basketry. The school is nationally known for its woodturning program.

In addition to arts and crafts, Gatlinburg has more than four hundred specialty shops decked out in alpine trim offering items from Belgian lace to stuffed black bears.

Outdoor enthusiasts of all kinds will want to visit Beneath the Smoke, a shop offering a large selection of books, calendars, and photography. Located on the Parkway, it's owned by award-winning photographer Ken Jenkins.

Old Smoky Outfitters down the street at 511 Parkway offers guided fly-fishing for trout during full or half-day trips. Other outings include bass fishing, nature hikes, history tours, and seasonal small and big-game hunts.

Hikers will want to stop at Tom Brosch's shop, the Happy Hiker, near the Sugarlands entrance to GSMNP in the Burning Bush Plaza at traffic light number 10 for warm, lightweight hiking gear, trail guides, topo maps, and advice.

If you're not interested in shopping or hiking, Gatlinburg offers lots of other ways to spend your time. One of the oldest attractions in town is Christus Gardens. There are interior gardens, but the focus here is on the dramatically lit, life-sized figures depicting the life of Christ, which have been seen by zillions of tour groups and vacationing families.

Hippensteal's Mountain View Inn has a bird's eye view of the Smokies.

Some visitors prefer those "amazing" museums, Guinness World Records and Ripley's Believe It or Not. Others choose to ride elevators into the Space Needle or take the Sky Lift up Crockett Mountain. Ride the aerial tram to Ober Gatlinburg, a popular spot for winter snow skiing on one of eight slopes or ice skating at an indoor arena, but there's also a restaurant with live entertainment, a bungee tower, water rides, a go-cart track, and Kiddie-Land with kiddie rides and a playground for warm weather entertainment for the younger set.

If you've worked up an appetite, choices range from candy kitchens to steak and seafood houses. For breakfast, take a seat in the glass-enclosed atrium at the Burning Bush Restaurant between 8 A.M. and 2 P.M., select the Bountiful Breakfast (which lives up to its name), and enjoy the birds at the feeder in front of the park boundary line. They also serve lunch and dinner daily and reservations are a good idea.

The Park Grill across the street serves dinner in a lovely setting. The massive timbers overhead, accompanied by copper accents and unusual touches like the massive carved wooden doors, create the feel of a high country lodge. Maxwell's does not accept reservations, but you can call ahead to check seating availability. The Peddler on River Road does not accept reservations for dinner, but you can relax in the bar overlooking the river if there's a wait. Steaks are the specialty here, but chicken and seafood are also offered.

Bennett's Pit Barbeque is open for breakfast, lunch, and dinner. Ogle's Buffet has been serving breakfast, lunch, and dinner for more than fifty years. The Pancake Pantry serves breakfast all day.

The Greenbrier Restaurant in a historic log cabin on Newman Road off US 321 about 1.5 miles east of Gatlinburg is known for its seafood and beef dishes.

The woodturning program at Arrowmont School offers intensive week-long instruction. (Photo courtesy of Arrowmont School)

Mountain Laurel Chalets on Ski Mountain Road has more than one hundred chalets designed in a variety of styles ranging from one to eleven bedrooms. All have woodburning or gas log fireplaces, cable TV, and fully equipped kitchens. Some chalets have whirlpools, hot tubs, stereos, VCRs, and game tables.

The Olde English Tudor Inn is situated one block off Parkway on West Holly Ridge Drive, placing it within walking distance of many of Gatlinburg's downtown attractions, shops, and restaurants. Each of the seven guest rooms has queen- or king-sized beds, private bath, and cable TV/HBO. A full breakfast is served, children are welcome, and the English garden and waterfall are outstanding.

The Brevard Inn is also on West Holly Ridge. The inn has three rooms with private baths, cable TV, and fireplaces. The Butcher House in the Mountains has five rooms with private baths and a deck with awesome views. Evening desserts and gourmet brunch are served.

Eight Gables Inn has a big wraparound porch,

ten guest rooms with private baths, and a secluded Honeymoon Suite with a whirlpool tub. A four-course breakfast is served daily. Eight Gables is about a mile outside Gatlinburg on North Mountain Trail near the visitor center between Pigeon Forge and Gatlinburg and welcomes children to this four-diamond AAA inn.

The 7th Heaven Log Inn sits on the seventh green, but you don't have to be a golfer to enjoy your stay at this modern log home with swimming and tennis available. There's a pool table in the game room, a stone fireplace to gaze into, a hot tub to soak in, and four bedrooms with private baths.

Among the ninety-one hotels and motels in Gatlinburg are national franchises for Best Western, Comfort Inn, Holiday Inn, Quality Inn, Ramada Inn, and Travel Lodge.

Smoky Mountain Tours will pick you up at your motel or the Gatlinburg Chamber of Commerce for tours ranging from two and one-half hours to seven and one-half hours that include trips to Cherokee with tickets to *Unto These Hills* outdoor drama or special hayride tours to Cades Cove.

Depart Gatlinburg on US 321 to visit Cosby or continue on US 441 to visit the GSMNP.

All of the following accommodations are Gatlinburg with zip code 37738, and all telephone listings are area code 423, except where noted.

Accommodations:
Buckhorn Inn, 2140 Tudor Mountain Rd., 436-4668.
Butcher House in the Mountains, 1520 Garrett Ln., 436-9457.
The Colonel's Lady, 1120 Tanrac Trl., 800-515-5432 or 436-5432.
Eight Gables Inn, 219 Mountain Trl., 800-279-5716 or 430-3344.
The Gatlinburg Inn, 755 Pkwy., 436-5133.
Hippensteal's Mountain View Inn, Grassy Branch Rd., 800-527-8110 or 436-5761.
Le Conte Lodge, mailing address 250 Apple Valley Rd., Sevierville, 37862; 429-5704.
Mountain Laurel Chalets, 440 Ski Mountain Rd., 800-626-3431 or 436-5277.
Oak Square at Gatlinburg, River Rd., 800-423-5182 or 436-7582.
Olde English Tudor Inn, 135 W. Holly Ridge Rd., 800-541-3798 or 436-7760.

The Park Grill serves diners in an outstanding setting of native stone and massive logs.

River Terrace Resort, 240 River Rd., 800-251-2040 or 436-5161.

Rocky Waters Motor Inn, 333 Pkwy., 800-824-1111 or 436-7861.

7th Heaven Log Inn, 3944 Castle Rd., 800-248-2923 or 430-5000.

Tennessee Ridge Inn, 507 Campbell Lead, 800-737-7369 or 436-4068.

Timber Rose English Lodge, 1106 Tanrac Trl., 436-5852.

Attractions:
Arrowmont School of Arts and Crafts Gallery, 436-5860.
Bent Creek Golf Resort, 800-251-9336 or 436-2875.
Christus Gardens, 436-5155.
Gatlinburg Sky Lift, 436-4307.
Gatlinburg Space Needle and Arcade, 436-4629.
Gatlinburg Welcome Center, 436-0519.
Great Smoky Arts and Crafts Community, 671-3504.
Guinness World Records Museum, 436-9100.
McCarter's Riding Stables, 436-5354.
Ober Gatlinburg Ski Resort and Amusement Park, 436-5423.
Old Smoky Outfitters, 430-1936.
Ripley's Believe It or Not Museum, 436-5096.
Smoky Mountain Tours, 436-3471.
Smoky Mountain Winery, 436-7551.

Dining:
Bennett's Pit Barbeque, 436-2400.
The Burning Bush, 436-4168.
The Greenbrier Restaurant, 436-6318.
Maxwell's Beef and Seafood, 436-3738.
Ogle's Buffet Restaurant, 436-4157.
The Pancake Pantry, 436-4724.
The Park Grill, 436-2300.
The Peddler, 436-5794.
Ruby Tuesday, 436-9251.
Wild Plum Tearoom, 436-3808.

Shopping:
Arrowcraft Shop, 426-4604.
Beneath the Smoke, 436-3460.
Great Smoky Arts and Crafts Community, 671-3504.
The Happy Hiker, 800-HIKER01 or 436-6000.

Special Events:
April—Spring Arts Festival; Annual Easter Craft Show, Easter weekend; Wildflower Pilgrimage
May—Scottish Festival and Games
November—Annual Christmas Craft Show, Thanksgiving weekend
November–February—WinterFest
December—Annual Twelve Days of Christmas Craft Show

Camping:
Smokemont Campground, GSMNP, 800-365-2267 or 436-1293.

Dudley Creek Travel Trailer Park and Log Cabins, 800-922-6799 or 436-5053.

Twin Creek RV Resort, 800-252-8077 or 436-7081.

For More Information:
Gatlinburg Visitors and Convention Bureau, 234 Airport Rd.; P.O. Box 530, 800-343-1475 or 436-4178.
Gatlinburg Chamber of Commerce, 800-568-4748 or 430-4148.
Gatlinburg Welcome Center, US 441 south, 436-0519. Open daily.
GSMNP, 107 Park Headquarters Rd., 436-1200.
GSMNP Sugarlands Visitor Center, 436-1293.

14 Great Smoky Mountains National Park
The Nation's Most-Visited National Park

The Great Smoky Mountains are the oldest existing mountains in the world. Called Shaconage ("place of the blue smoke") by the Cherokee, the Smokies are part of the larger Appalachian Mountain chain. The range of the Great Smoky Mountains stretches on a northeast-southwest axis more than fifty miles. Within this area sixteen peaks crest at more than 6,000 feet including Clingman's Dome, the second highest peak in the eastern United States at 6,643 feet.

One widely accepted theory postulates the Smokies resulted from tremendous geologic forces generated by the widening of the bottom of the Atlantic Ocean. During the Ice Age nearly two million years ago, glacial cycles came within one hundred miles. As the glaciers retreated, cold-loving plants were limited to higher elevations.

Spruce-fir forests crown the lofty peaks above five thousand feet and create a pleasing outline

The Smokies are filled with boulder-strewn, clear, cascading streams.

Of the park's 520,197 acres, nearly 400,000 acres consist of lush second-growth forests supported by fifty inches of annual rainfall in Gatlinburg and more than eighty inches of annual rainfall on Clingman's Dome. More than sixty kinds of fish live in two thousand miles of streams cascading through the Smokies in forty-five watersheds that flow northwestward into the Tennessee, Little Tennessee, or French Broad Rivers, eventually winding up in the Gulf of Mexico.

GSMNP harbors more than fifteen hundred kinds of flowering plants, two hundred species of birds, and seventy mammal species. The GSMNP has been designated an International Biosphere Reserve by the United Nations because of the significant biodiversity found here. The climate ranges within the Smokies compare to the vast area from northern Georgia to Maine. In general, temperature decreases by two to three degrees Fahrenheit for every one thousand feet of elevation.

The historic territory of the Cherokee included the Smokies and extended beyond them to include much of what is now Tennessee, North Carolina, and north Georgia. They formulated a rich belief in magical creatures living in the lush, mysterious mountains.

The earliest white men to enter the Smokies were fur traders following game trails through this remote Cherokee country. They arrived as early as 1673 and by 1690 had established trading posts. Early surveyors establishing the boundary of North Carolina called the peaks we now know as the Great Smoky Mountains the Iron Mountains.

In 1901 Col. W. B. Townsend purchased eighty-six thousand acres for lumbering that stretched from Tuckaleechee Cove in present-day Townsend to Clingman's Dome. In 1910 Parsons Pulp and Lumber Company purchased twenty-five thousand acres from the Eastern Band of the

against the smoky mist that often bathes them. The hardwoods gradually replace the coniferous forests at elevations from thirty-five hundred to five thousand feet.

The Appalachian cove forest is a mixture of deciduous hardwoods and evergreens, foresting slopes at two thousand to four thousand feet with an understory of redbud, dogwood, fringebush, and serviceberry, or "sarvis" as it's locally known, along with mountain laurel and rhododendron. Wildflowers also thrive in this shady, moist environment.

Wildflowers, like this trout-lily, thrive in moist hardwood forests.

Cherokee. In 1916 Champion Fiber and Paper Company purchased ninety-two thousand acres including twenty-five thousand acres in Greenbrier Cove. Logging threatened to decimate the Smokies.

William P. Davis, a Knoxville businessman, and his wife helped organize the Smoky Mountain Conservation Association in 1923 with the intent of promoting the development of a national park in the Smoky Mountains similar to the ones in the west. Although about 75 percent of the Smokies' forests had been logged by this time, at least one hundred thousand acres of old-growth forests remained, the largest such area remaining in the eastern United States.

A bill creating the park was signed by President Calvin Coolidge in 1926. Parks in the west had been created from lands already owned by the federal government, often on land that was uninhabited. The land planned for GSMNP was owned by hundreds of families and a few large timber and paper companies.

The 1926 legislation did not include funding for purchase of privately held lands, so fundraising became the dominant issue. Nationwide campaigns were undertaken that raised $1 million, including the nickels and dimes of school children. The Tennessee and North Carolina legislatures appropriated $1.5 million and $2 million respectively, but all sources totaled only about half the amount needed.

Arno B. Cammerer, associate director of the National Park Service, was able to convince John D. Rockefeller Jr. to match the amount raised. The federal government came to the rescue with the remaining funds to handle the rising costs of land.

Leases were granted on a short-term basis, but leaseholders couldn't cut timber, hunt, or trap. A lease was given to Jack Huff for a lodge accessible only by trail on top of Mount Le Conte. Le Conte Lodge remains the only lodging available within the Great Smoky Mountains National Park.

Le Conte Lodge was founded in 1926 and continues to fill its beds the 247 nights per year it's open. First-time visitors get a shot at the formidable telephone reservation system each year on October 1. This process involves a lot of activity with the redial button on your phone.

Although the accommodations are Spartan, most consider them delightful. There's no electricity in the cabins, bunk beds are the order of the day, and in addition to the roommates you've planned, you may have a few field mice if you keep food in your cabin.

Other leaseholders were located in Cades Cove, but the highest concentration was within the resort area known as Elkmont in privately owned cottages and the Wonderland Hotel, which saw its last visitor in 1992.

Removal of evidence of logging operations,

construction of new facilities including many of the stone bridges and structures in the park like the Mount Cammerer Fire Tower, and restoration of buildings were accomplished by members of the Civilian Conservation Corps (CCC). The CCC was an agency of the federal government created to provide jobs for unemployed young men during the Great Depression. CCC programs began in 1933 and continued until 1942, when World War II closed the program.

The Great Smoky Mountains National Park (GSMNP) was officially dedicated by Franklin Delano Roosevelt on Labor Day 1940, with an audience of ten thousand visitors. Since that time, the GSMNP has grown to become our nation's most visited national park with nearly 10 million annual visitors.

Self-guided nature trails like those at Sugarlands Visitor Center, Clingman's Dome, Laurel Falls, Elkmont Campground, Cades Cove, and the Noah "Bud" Ogle Trail on Cherokee Orchard Road are generally casual outings of relatively

The Sugarlands Visitor Center at the northern entrance to the GSMNP near Gatlinburg offers a wealth of information about the park.

short duration designed to introduce visitors to natural and man-made points of interest.

The longer, more strenuous hikes require comfortable, broken-in, waterproof hiking shoes, an extra pair of socks, and some moleskin. It's a good idea to layer your clothes to allow for changing weather conditions, and carry at least one quart of fresh water with you. A lunch or trail snack is also welcome.

When hiking with children it's a good idea to keep everyone within sight, especially until children learn to match their abilities and the outdoor terrain accurately.

Good practices to ensure a fun and safe outing include staying on the trail and remembering rocks near streams are always slick.

You'll need a permit if you're going to camp overnight. You should use precautions to prevent being raided for food by bears. In general, if a bear approaches, it's a good idea to beat a quick retreat and give it plenty of space.

More than one thousand improved campsites, one hundred primitive campsites, and eight hundred miles of trails welcome visitors to the park. In addition to the sixty-eight-mile section of the Appalachian Trail, most of the Tennessee trails can be roughly divided into five general sections according to trailhead location.

Sugarlands/US 441

Located at the northern entrance to the park near Gatlinburg, Sugarlands Visitor Center is the central source of information for park visitors. There are displays, maps, rest rooms, rangers with information, and lots of publications about the area. Two easy hikes in the immediate vicinity offer quick trips into the Smokies.

The 3.4-mile roundtrip Gatlinburg Trail wanders through rhododendrons along the West Prong

Clingman's Dome is the highest peak in the Smokies.

of the Little Pigeon River. There's a nice 0.5-mile side trip to the forty-foot-high Cataract Falls.

Sugarlands Valley Trail is a three-thousand-foot paved loop trail designed for visitors with disabilities that begins off US 441 one-fourth mile south of the visitor center.

The park is bisected by US 441, which passes from the Sugarlands Visitor Center near Gatlinburg between two of the highest peaks in the Smokies, Clingman's Dome and Mount Le Conte, on the way to Cherokee, North Carolina, via Newfound Gap.

Visible to the west (right) on US 441 headed south are the twin peaks known to the Cherokee as the Gap of the Forked Antler and to the American settlers as Chimney Tops. A strenuous four-mile roundtrip hike leads to the Chimney Tops from the trailhead which is off US 441 about two

miles from the Chimneys Picnic Area.

The next must-see landmark is Clingman's Dome, the highest peak in the GSMNP. After a seven-mile drive up Clingman's Dome Road, a steep 0.5-mile paved trail climbs the final 330 feet to the summit. From the observation tower on top, you'll see Fraser firs, under attack from the deadly balsam woolly adelgids. This tiny European insect was accidentally introduced to the United States in the early 1900s.

Andrews Bald is a moderate 4.2-mile roundtrip on Forney Ridge Trail that starts near the parking lot at Clingman's Dome. Although the first part of the trail is tough because it's rocky, Andrews Bald is the easiest of the balds to reach. It has a fine display of flame azalea and Catawba rhododendron in June and great views from spring to late fall.

The Boulevard Trail is accessible by the Appalachian Trail at Newfound Gap on US 441 at the North Carolina state line. The Boulevard climbs 1,545 feet making it strenuous by most standards, but it's easily the most popular trail to Le Conte.

The summit of Mount Le Conte is covered by a spruce and fir forest. Trails are cut through the dense growth of mountain laurel and Catawba rhododendron to heath balds at either end of the crest line. Cliff Top, to the north, is the site of frequent gatherings to watch the sun slip behind the towering peaks. Myrtle Point, to the east, is named for the sandmyrtle, a member of the heath family, that cloaks it. It offers spectacular sunrises on clear mornings for those willing to face the prospect of a chilly dawn.

Other routes to Le Conte include the steep 5.5-mile Alum Cave Trail which begins on Newfound Gap Road about nine miles from the Sugarlands Visitor Center. This hike usually takes us about five hours but can probably be done in four.

US 441 continues into the North Carolina portion of the GSMNP on its way to Smokemont Campground, Oconaluftee Visitor Center, Mingus Mill, and Cherokee, North Carolina, home of the Eastern Band of the Cherokee.

Little River Road/Elkmont/Metcalf Bottoms

As you leave Sugarlands Visitor Center, turn west (right) on Little River Road to visit Laurel Falls, an easy 2.6-mile paved roundtrip hike from the trailhead. This paved trail climbs only two hundred feet and is easy enough for preschoolers, but it can be treacherous in winter when ice covers the trail and the falls.

Much of the forest you see along Little River Road is second-growth forest that has reclaimed the virtually denuded slopes since lumber cutting ceased in 1938. In fact, the roadway you're driving was built on the bed of the tracks of Little River Railroad.

Today there's a nice, shady campground at Elkmont with 220 sites, water, and rest rooms but no hookups. Unless budget cutbacks have become dramatic, the campground is open year-round

Hikers walk the roads formerly traveled by members of the resort community at Elkmont on their way to Saturday-night dances held at the Wonderland Hotel in the 1920s.

Henwallow Falls is a popular hike on the northeast side of the GSMNP.

with some sections closed during the winter months.

Some of the historic buildings like the Wonderland Hotel remain at Elkmont, but they are not restored, not open to the public, and not likely to be.

Little River, Cucumber Gap, and Jakes Creek Trails combine to make a 5.1-mile roundtrip loop that begins about one mile above the Elkmont

campground. Short spurs on the left lead down to fishing spots, and wildflowers are abundant.

A trail leads from the Metcalf Bottoms Picnic Area off Little River Road to the rustic, log Little Greenbrier School on the way to the Walker Sister's Farmstead. Openings along the way provide views of Wears Valley and wildflowers line the trail.

Cades Cove

Cades Cove is the most-visited area in the most-visited national park in the United States. The scenic cove is a limestone basin one mile wide and four miles long, ringed by mountains. Picturesque log cabins, a grist mill, two churches, and lovely old cantilevered barns have been restored.

There's a visitor center at Cable Mill with information, a gift shop and rest rooms and 161 campsites with thirty-five trailer spaces, water and picnic tables, horse stable, and bicycle rentals available at the Cades Cove Campground.

Try to avoid the crowds by visiting Cades Cove on weekdays if you're driving. The cove is closed to automobiles on Wednesday and Saturday summer mornings between sunrise and 10 A.M., which means if you're scooting the eleven-mile, one-way paved loop on a bicycle, you'll have a much nicer ride with lots of opportunities for wildlife viewing along the way.

GSMNP is believed to have a population of four hundred to six hundred black bears. Males may reach six feet in length and weigh four hundred pounds as adults. Black bears usually have a period of extended inactivity from December to March or April.

According to Doug Markham in *Boxes, Rockets and Pens, a History of Wildlife Recovery in Tennessee*, during this time the mother gives birth to her cubs numbering from one to five but commonly born in pairs of eight-ounce newborns. When food supplies are scant, fewer cubs will be born.

The five-mile roundtrip moderate hike to Abrams Falls rewards you with twenty-foot falls that form a broad pool more than one hundred feet across during high-water periods. Be very careful on the slippery rocks around the falls and the pool.

The trail is enjoyed by adults and school-age children and accessed by taking a right turn off the Cades Cove loop road after crossing Abrams Creek before you reach the Cable Mill Visitor Center.

Gregory Bald, named for Russell Gregory who was killed by Confederates in 1864, is known for its June display of flame azalea. This broad meadow is accessed from a trail that travels 4.5

miles one-way from the trailhead on Parsons Branch Road, one of the two gravel roads leading out of Cades Cove.

The pink lady's slipper may be seen along the Cades Cove Vista Nature Trail.

Bud Ogle's / Cherokee Orchard / Roaring Fork

Only 3.5 miles from traffic light number eight in downtown Gatlinburg are the Noah "Bud" Ogle Place, Cherokee Orchard, and Roaring Fork Motor Nature Trail. A self-guiding pamphlet is available at the beginning of the three-quarter-mile loop to Bud Ogle's 1800s home and barn. Spring wildflowers are especially plentiful along this trail.

Nearby is Roaring Fork Motor Trail, a wind-

Many stream crossings occur at lower elevations in the Smokies.

ing 5.5-mile auto loop open spring through fall that is also known for its wildflower displays. The largest and best known of the organized wildflower walks in Tennessee is the Wildflower Pilgrimage in the Great Smoky Mountains National Park, usually held on a late April weekend.

The three-mile roundtrip hike to Grotto Falls is a favorite. When the Roaring Fork Motor Nature Trail is open, you can skip the first 2.4 miles and join the trail at the Grotto Falls parking lot near post number five, an easy hike that rises only five hundred feet in 1.5 miles.

During the winter when the gate is locked, hike 2.4 miles along Trillium Gap Trail from the trailhead at the Rainbow Falls parking area at Cherokee Orchard. Trillium Gap is the route taken by the llamas on Mondays, Wednesdays, and Fridays to carry provisions to Le Conte Lodge. Llama pack trains are used because their padded feet have far less impact on the trails than horses' hooves, but sometimes Trillium Gap is still muddy in spots.

Rainbow Falls and Bull Head Trails also originate at the Rainbow Falls parking area. Rainbow Falls Trail is 6.7 miles to the summit of Le Conte, but the waterfall is 2.7 miles from the trailhead. Many hikers choose to hike up Rainbow Falls to Le Conte and return via the Bull Head Trail.

Greenbrier/Cosby

Popular choices in the Greenbrier/Cosby area east of Gatlinburg on US 321 include the eight-mile roundtrip to Ramsay Cascades and Henwallow Falls, a 4.4-mile roundtrip with several stream crossings on the moderate 520-foot climb to the falls.

The area around Cosby on the northeastern side of the park also offers the Mount Cammerer trail. The restored fire tower at the top of Mount Cammerer was built by the CCC in the 1930s and is the only one of its type surviving east of the Mississippi.

Karen Wade, the thirteenth superintendent of GSMNP, says the park is "open space used for restoration of the spirit and nourishment for the soul." In our visits to the park since the 1950s, we've found this to be the case. It offers opportunities for enrichment of visitors of all ages and physical abilities and we hope you will each find a special, peaceful spot of your own within it.

For More Information:
Great Smoky Mountains National Park Headquarters, 423-436-1200; 800-365-CAMP for campground reservations.
Great Smoky Mountain Natural History Association, 115 Park Headquarters Rd., Gatlinburg, 37738; 423-436-7318.
Le Conte Lodge, 250 Apple Valley Rd., Sevierville, 37862; 423-429-5704.

15 Cosby and Newport
Former Moonshine Capital of the World

Cosby was first settled in 1783 and named for Dr. James Cosby. It sits in a small, relatively flat area at the northeastern corner of what is now the Great Smoky Mountains National Park (GSMNP). The area of Cocke County around Cosby was known locally for many years as the moonshine capital of the world and corn squeezings were the primary cash crop. Apples are now an important crop, but it's the infamous ramp that is Cosby's claim to fame.

Considered by some to be the most noxious of vegetables, the ramp is a native product of the Appalachians. It is similar to a wild onion, but the odor of a ramp is much stronger and stays with you longer.

Mountaineers, figuring anything that smelled so vile must be good for you, believed it had curative powers when ingested each spring. Tiny, unincorporated Cosby welcomes thousands of visitors who are dedicated to the proposition of eating ramps by the bushel at the annual Ramp Festival the first Sunday in May.

The other attraction in town is the Schilling Family Folk Life Center on TN 32. The family makes dulcimers, including hammered dulcimers, releases recordings of mountain music, publishes books, and sells crafts produced by residents. They also host festivals with mountain music and traditional dancing throughout the year. Most are on holiday weekends but the Dulcimer and Harp Festival begins on the otherwise uneventful second Friday in June.

There's a campground of the Great Smoky Mountain National Park at Cosby with 175 campsites and restrooms but no hookups south of the US 321/TN 32 junction. It is open from mid-April to October on a first-come-first-serve basis and tends to be one of the more underutilized campgrounds in GSMNP.

The Cosby Barbecue Pit in "downtown" Cosby is open daily in season, but only on weekends December through March. Although much of Cosby shuts down or cuts back on hours of operation for the winter, the Front Porch Restaurant on US 321 between Cosby and Newport has good Mexican food, and local bluegrass musicians perform on Friday and Saturday nights year-round. The Front Porch is open Friday, Saturday, and Sunday for lunch and dinner.

Cocke County was once a national center for illegal distilling, the art better known as moonshining.

Intrepid adventure seekers should consider making the trek to the locally infamous restaurant known as Fort Marx. The owners have created a restaurant/bar of sorts at one end of their double-wide mobile home to serve loyal patrons of a former restaurant they owned closer to town.

The art of distilling was brought to Cocke County by European settlers. The term *moonshine* may be derived from the old British word *moonlighter* which referred to the nocturnal practice of smuggling brandy from the continent to the British coast.

When Prohibition went into effect in 1919, whiskey distilling suddenly became a lucrative proposition for mountaineers searching for a way to support their families in the depressed post-World War I rural economy. The rugged topography lent itself to the secretive industry that developed here based on corn liquor, or moonshine as it came to be known.

The equipment used in corn liquor production consists of a furnace to generate heat, a metal cylinder called a still where the corn mash ferments and is heated, and a pipe, called a horse's head, which carries steam to a keg for collection. Coils of copper, known as a worm, begin to condense the steam. The worm is encased in a barrel of cold water so the alcohol will condense.

During the 1920s thousands of gallons of moonshine left Cocke County in nightly runs to markets as far away as Detroit.

During the 1960s, agents of the Department of Tobacco, Alcohol and Firearms, known as "revenuers," finally managed to seize and destroy the more than two hundred operating stills in Cocke County, effectively putting an end to the moonshine industry.

The Eastern Foothills Parkway connects to I-40 a few miles north of Cosby while TN 32 pro-

ceeds to Newport. Eleven miles north of Cosby along TN 32 you'll see a left turn onto English Mountain Road which takes you to the turn for Christopher Place Country Inn on top of Pinnacles Way.

The ten tasteful rooms feature private baths and amenities that range from hot tubs to fireplaces. The inn has over two hundred acres for guests to explore, a swimming pool, sauna, tennis court, and exercise room.

Breathtaking views, antique furnishings including a grand piano in the parlor, a fireside library, and a billiard and game room create a quiet elegance that makes a stay here a memorable visit to a country estate.

Newport is the county seat of Cocke County. According to *Tennessee Historical Markers*, a publication of the Tennessee Historical Commission, "the new port" was established in 1799 near a ford on the French Broad River. The town grew as the center of flatboat navigation on the French Broad and by many accounts was known for its lawlessness long before moonshining became a local industry. Today, Cocke County is the largest producer of apples in Tennessee and you'll see several orchards.

James Stokely, son of the founder of the Stokely Company, married Tennessee state historian and author Wilma Dykeman. The graduate of Northwestern University was appointed state historian by Governor Lamar Alexander on January 17, 1981, and has received many honors in her long and distinguished career. Her books provide an enlightening perspective on many areas and eras in Tennessee's colorful history.

The Cocke County Museum is located in the community center on US 321. Inside you'll find information about Cocke County and prominent citizens. In addition to permanent collections, special exhibits are sponsored each year including an annual quilt show. The museum is open Saturday from 9 A.M. to 4 P.M. and by appointment on weekdays.

One of Cocke County's most famous visitors has had her story told to millions of readers and television viewers. *Christy* is the story of a young schoolteacher who came to teach in a mountain mission school at Cutter's Gap, which is in Cocke County near Del Rio.

The historic Mimosa Manor Bed and Breakfast is conveniently located in downtown Newport. The gracious four-square brick is filled with lovely antiques. Choices for accommodations include the Seahorn Suite which has its own parlor with a fireplace, queen canopy bed, and private bath. A full breakfast is served in the formal dining room. National franchises include Best Western, Holiday Inn, and a KOA campground.

The Cherokee National Forest has three recreation areas in Cocke County. The recreation area along the French Broad River has boating access and fishing while the Houston Valley and Round Mountain sites near Del Rio have campgrounds with drinking water and sanitary facilities.

The Appalachian Trail runs from the northeastern edge of the GSMNP along the southern edge of the county. Both the French Broad and Pigeon Rivers have white-water commercial outfitters providing equipment, river guides, or both.

Daniel Jennette of Smoky Mountain Outdoors Unlimited in Hartford provides exciting trips down the Big Pigeon River that encounter forty-three Class I and II rapids, 14 Class IIIs, and four Class IVs in the 6.5-mile float. For the fainthearted, Jennette offers lower Pigeon and French Broad River trips as well as guided fishing and hiking trips. English Mountain Llama Treks offers backcountry trips in the Pisgah National Forest

ranging from one-day trips with picnic lunches to three days or more.

Visit C. J. Papadops on Briar Thicket Road for steaks as well as Greek and Mediterranean food that get rave reviews from locals and visitors alike. Continue on US 25/70 to I-40 near Dandridge to complete this loop.

All of the following accommodations are Cosby with zip code 37722, and all telephone listings are area code 423, except where noted.

Accommodations:
Christopher Place Country Inn, Newport, 800-595-9441 or 623-6555.
Mimosa Manor Bed and Breakfast, Newport, 37821; 623-4228.
Williams Log Cabins,487-2646.

Attractions:
Cocke County Museum, Newport.
Folklife Center of the Smokies, 487-5543.
Newport/Cocke County Museum, Newport.
Smoky Mountain Outdoors Unlimited, Hartford, 800-771-7238.
The Whitewater Company, Hartford, 800-723-8420.

Dining:
C. J. Papadops, Bybee.
Cosby Barbecue Pit, 487-5438.
Fort Marx, 487-2112.
The Front Porch, 487-2875.

Shopping:
Carver's Orchard, 487-2419.
Folk Life Center of the Smokies, 487-5543.
Halloways, 487-3866.

Special Events:
May—The Ramp Festival

Camping:
GSMNP, Cosby Campground.
Fox Den Campground, 888-FOX-DEN1.
TMC Campground, Newport, 37821; 625-0433.

For More Information:
Newport/Cocke County Tourism Council, 360 E. Main St., Suite 141, Newport, 37821; 625-9675.
Newport/Cocke County Chamber of Commerce, 803 Prospect St., Newport, 623-7201.

Loop 3

16 *Maryville and Townsend*
Western Foothills of the
Great Smoky Mountains

Maryville was named for Mary Grainger Blount, the wife of William Blount. Blount was the only governor of the Southwest Territory and one of the first U.S. senators from Tennessee (*see* Knoxville).

Maryville, the county seat of Blount County, grew up around Fort Craig. The fort was built along Pistol Creek by John Craig in 1785 and served as a refuge for hundreds of settlers during periods of Indian unrest. Visitors will find a monument commemorating the fort in Greenbelt Park, which has a 2.5-mile walking trail along Pistol Creek.

Sam Houston arrived in Blount County in 1807 at the age of fourteen with his eight brothers and widowed mother, Elizabeth. Young Sam did not take to farm life. He didn't take to clerking in a store in Maryville and didn't much care for school either, although he was reportedly fond of the classics and later was something of a self-taught frontier scholar.

He found kindred spirits among the Cherokee Indians living nearby and ran away to live with Cherokee Chief John Jolly on Hiwassee Island where the Hiwassee River joins the Tennessee near present-day Dayton. Although his brothers found him, he remained as the adopted son of Chief Jolly, known as *Colonneh*, meaning "the Raven," for three years before returning to Maryville.

After his return, Houston taught in a one-room log schoolhouse that is the oldest school in Tennessee. The Sam Houston Schoolhouse, museum, and gift shop are open to visitors daily about five miles northeast of Maryville.

After the war, Houston was appointed Indian agent to the Cherokees at Fort Southwest Point near Kingston and served in this capacity until he moved to Middle Tennessee.

He was elected to two terms in Congress and became governor of Tennessee in 1827. At thirty-four, the sitting governor married twenty-year-old Eliza Allen, the daughter of a prosperous Middle Tennessee plantation owner, on a cold January day.

In less than three months, Eliza left him. Controversy whirled about him as endless speculation persisted. Both Houston and Eliza refused to offer any explanation during their lifetimes, and Houston resigned the governorship.

Alcoa is considered Maryville's "sister city." Named for the Aluminum Company of America, Alcoa was designed by the company to house the workers involved in aluminum production and the construction of dams on the Little Tennessee River.

As you follow US 321 from Maryville toward Townsend you'll pass through the tiny community of Walland and the entrance to the Western Foothills Parkway about 5.5 miles north of Townsend. This national park service scenic parkway will ultimately be seventy-two miles long and parallel the northwestern boundary of the GSMNP.

There are several scenic overlooks with views of the Smokies, the Tennessee Valley, and the Cumberland escarpment along the seventeen-mile western section that travels between Walland and US 129 at Chilhowee Lake. A paved 0.5-mile hike to the vista at Look Rock Observation Tower begins at the overlook and is well worth a stop on a clear day.

According to *The Tennessee Wildlife Viewing Guide,* it is common to see one thousand raptors on a single autumn day with the aid of binoculars and spotting scopes. Mid-September may bring large concentrations of monarch butterflies.

A turnoff on West Miller's Cove Road off Highway 321 southbound leads to the Inn at Blackberry Farm at Walland. In the 1930s Florida and Dave Lasier found this lovely spot and built the original nine-bedroom house of native mountain stone.

Fifty years later Kreis and Sandy Beall bought the eleven-hundred-acre estate and transformed it into an inn that has been named one of the top country house hotels in the United States by readers of *Southern Living* and *Condé Nast's Traveler.*

All of its elegant rooms are beautifully decorated and create the classic ambiance of an English country inn. Guests are provided with everything from snacks and picnic lunches to robes and binoculars, but they should bring their own choice of alcoholic beverages. TVs and phones are available on request. Generally, children under ten are not suitable guests at Blackberry Farm.

The hefty tariff includes three meals prepared daily by executive chef John Fleer, the creator of an award-winning "foothills cuisine." A heated swimming pool with an outstanding view of the mountains, four tennis courts, Schwinn ten-speed mountain bikes, a pond stocked with bass and bream, a trout pond, and a creek to test your angling skills provide plenty of recreation.

The Mill House Restaurant specializes in fine dining across the road from the Little River east of US 321 on Melrose Station Road. Take the turn near the Walland Post Office to dine on Fridays and Saturdays.

An outstanding view and elegant accommodations greet visitors to the Inn at Blackberry Farm. (Photo courtesy of Inn at Blackberry Farm)

Now known as the quiet side of the Smokies and the gateway to Cades Cove, Townsend was originally called Tuckaleechee Cove. It was renamed for Col. W. B. Townsend, president of the Little River Lumber Company and the Little River Railroad.

According to Ronald G. Schmidt and William S. Hooks in *Whistle Over the Mountain,* Townsend grew up in the first area on the Little River that was flat enough and wide enough for the facilities needed to harvest the forty thousand acres of standing timber purchased by the Little River Lumber Company in 1901.

As the lumber industry in Townsend moved from labor intensive horse and wagon transportation to the more efficient steam engine, more extensive logging took place. In a period of less than forty years most of the forest was logged. Under the stewardship of the National Park Service, the denuded slopes now support a lush green forest that makes it almost impossible to imagine the clear cutting that took place. The Little River Railroad Lumber Company Museum does a good job of showing us what the area looked like then and telling the story of the community, the railroad, and the lumber company operations from early settlers to W. B. Townsend.

The engine sitting out front is old No. 2147, a Shay engine once used to haul men and logs down the steep mountain grades. The Shay was a geared steam engine locomotive developed by Michigan sawmill owner Ephraim Shay. It was a small locomotive that was very good for handling steep grades with sharp curves, uneven track, and heavy loads.

Stop by the log cabin Smoky Mountain Visitors Bureau for brochures on area businesses, bicycle routes, hiking in the GSMNP, and calendars of events.

There are about twenty motels and inns and thirty businesses offering nearly three hundred cabins, bed and breakfasts, and cottages in Townsend. National franchises include Best Western, Days Inn, and Hampton Inn. We strongly suggest you call ahead for reservations, especially

on weekends and in the fall.

The Richmont Inn was inspired by cantilevered barns built in Blount and Sevier Counties during the nineteenth century. This style of barn may have been inspired by frontier blockhouses as the second-floor loft overhangs the first-floor crib.

Within Richmont's unique design, you'll find ten large rooms with private baths. Our favorite was the third-floor Chief Attakullakulla Room with skylights over a king-sized bed, a double-sized tub for star gazing in style, a private balcony, and a wood-burning fireplace. There is one handicapped-accessible room on the first floor.

Innkeepers Susan and Jim Hind pamper their guests with award-winning desserts served by candlelight each evening in the romantic glass-walled, slate-floored dining area. Susan is a graduate of the Culinary Institute of New York and prepares daily breakfast specials.

Golf privileges are extended to guests at the neighboring eighteen-hole Laurel Valley Country Club. Golfers may also arrange tee times at one of four other area golf courses.

Twin Valley Bed and Breakfast Horse Ranch

The story of logging in the Smokies is told at the Little River Railroad Lumber Company Museum in Townsend.

Swimming holes along the Little River are especially popular on warm summer days.

has something for every taste. The main lodge is a bed and breakfast. There's also a private cabin and wilderness shelters for those doing backcountry horseback rides.

Pioneer Cabins has seven log cabins with porches, fireplaces, and hot tubs on forty-three peaceful acres with a fishing pond and trails through the woods. Hideaway Cottages allows well-behaved children and pets in their thirty-acre mountain hollow. Gilbertson's Lazy Horse Retreat has cabins with fireplaces, VCRs and color TVs, and a stable with box stalls or outdoor paddocks for your horses.

In addition to the Cades Cove Campground, campers may choose Tremont Hills, Mountaineer, or Lazy Daze Campgrounds on the Little River. Tuckaleechee Campground and Horse Camp offers RV hookups, horse camp sites with a twenty-eight-stall covered horse shelter, and tent camping.

For water sports, check out the Y, a well-known swimming hole on Little River before the turn off Little River Road to go to Cades Cove.

Those of you looking for outdoor recreation can opt for some time in the saddle at Cades Cove Riding Stable or Davy Crockett Riding Stable off TN 73 near the GSMNP boundary.

If the three-mile Townsend Bicycle Trail whets your appetite for cycling, ask for a copy of *Bicycle Routes in Blount County* at the Smoky Mountain Visitors Bureau.

For those of you interested in learning more about the Smokies, the Smoky Mountains Institute at Tremont offers year-round programs for individuals and school groups on geology, flora, and fauna of the Smokies. Lodging and family-style meals are available for reasonable rates.

The Carriage House Restaurant has served Townsend residents and visitors for nearly thirty years. You may order from the menu or choose the nightly buffet. House specialties include fried chicken and country ham, a Friday night seafood buffet, and a Sunday buffet with chicken pot pie.

Earthtide Gallery offers juried local arts and

Amid a lovely woodland setting, Lee Roberson's log cabin gallery is filled with prints of Smoky Mountain scenes.

crafts and semiannual demonstrations days. The Old Rose and Silver Tearoom next door offers afternoon tea and gift ideas. Other area craftsmen are represented at the Nawger Nob Craft Settlement on US 321 where you'll find an assortment of baskets, pottery, jellies, and jams. Yoder's Deck and Lawn Furniture stocks functional pressure-treated pine Amish love seats and chairs. The River View Antique Mall has an assortment of collectibles and antiques.

Lee Roberson's Studio/Gallery is an idyllic log cabin retreat with beautiful grounds complete with babbling brook. The lovely getaway is open to the public off Wears Valley Road a couple of miles outside Townsend on the way to Pigeon Forge. Roberson's traditional prints feature picturesque Smoky Mountain scenes and his gallery is filled with framed and unframed prints. You'll find

rocking chairs to relax in while you make up your mind about your purchase.

If you're visiting Townsend between March 15 and November 15, stop by Tuckaleechee Caverns off US 321 on Dry Valley Road. The Big Room is the largest cavern open to the public in the eastern United States. It's an easy walk beginning with stairs to see the sixty-thousand-square-foot room and its dramatically illuminated formations.

Townsend holds a Spring Festival and Wildflower Celebration in April. This is also a perfect time to visit Hedgewood Gardens, the result of one woman's love of nature and her daughter's desire to honor that legacy.

Townsend Heritage Festival and Old Timer's Day is held in late September and features lots of bluegrass music, food and beverages, antique engine and tractor shows, and vintage music displays. You're advised to bring along a lawn chair and your favorite instrument for some pickin' and grinnin' Townsend style. Old Timer's Day in Cades Cove usually coincides with the Townsend Festival.

Return to US 411 to visit the land of the Overhill Cherokee.

All of the following accommodations are Townsend with zip code 37882, and all telephone listings are area code 423, except where noted.

Accommodations:
Gilbertson's Lazy Horse Retreat, 938 Schoolhouse Gap Rd., 448-6810.
Hideaway Cottages, off US 321, 984-1700.
Highland Manor Motel, 7766 E. Lamar Alexander Pkwy., 800-213-9452 or 448-2211.
The Inn at Blackberry Farm, 1471 W. Millers Cove Rd., Walland, 37886; 984-9850.
Pioneer Cabins and Guest Farm, 253 Boat Gunnel Rd., 800-621-9751 or 448-6100.
Richmont Inn, 220 Winterberry Ln., 448-6751.
Talley Ho Inn, 8314 TN 73, 800-448-2465 or 448-2465.
Twin Valley Bed and Breakfast and Horse Ranch, 2848 Old Chilhowee Rd., Walland, 37886; 800-872-2235 or 984-0980.
Wayside Manor Bed and Breakfast, 4009 Old Knoxville Hwy., Rockford, 37853; 800-675-4823 or 970-4823.

Attractions:
Cades Cove Riding Stable, Walland, 448-6286.
Davy Crockett Riding Stable, 448-6411.
Hedgewood Gardens, 984-2052.
Little River Railroad & Lumber Company Museum, 448-2211.
Sam Houston Schoolhouse, Maryville, 983-1550.
Tuckaleechee Caverns, 448-2274.

Dining:
The Carriage House Restaurant, 448-2263.
Laurel Valley Country Club, 448-9534.
The Mill House, Walland, 982-5726.
The Timbers Restaurant, 448-6838.

Shopping:
Antiques and Uniques, 448-1033.
Earthtide Gallery, 448-1106.
Nawger Nob Craft Settlement, 448-2259.
Lee Roberson's Studio/Gallery, 800-423-7341 or 448-2365.

Special Events:
April—Spring Festival and Wildflower Pilgrimage
June—Arts and Crafts Fair

September—Old Timers Day, Townsend and Cades Cove
October—Maryville College Harvest Crafts Festival

Camping:
Cades Cove Campground, 800-365-CAMP.
Lazy Daze Campground and Motel, 448-6061.
Little River Village Campground, 448-2241.
Mountaineer Campground, 448-6421 Apr.–Oct.; 448-2386, Nov.–Mar.
Tremont Hills Campground, 448-6363.
Tuckaleechee Campground and Horse Camp, 448-9608.

For More Information:
Smoky Mountain Visitors Bureau at the Townsend Visitor Center, 7906 E. Lamar Alexander Pkwy., 800-525-6834 or 448-6134.

17 *Vonore, Madisonville, Tellico Plains, Coker Creek*
Land of the Overhill Cherokee

This part of Tennessee was once known as the Overhill Country of the Cherokee because of its location over the Appalachian Mountains from the Carolina settlements.

Very little evidence has been found of Paleo-Indian occupation, but that may be due to flooding that took place along the rivers where these very early sites (10,000–8000 B.C.) were most likely to be found. Evidence does support Native-American occupation as early as the Archaic Period, a span of time from 8000 to 1000 B.C.

White traders visited the area in 1673, but Eleazar Wiggin, the first English trader to live among the Overhill Cherokee, did not arrive until 1711. The Cherokee traded up to fifty thousand deerskins per year in exchange for guns, ammunition, tools, trade beads, mirrors, and clothing.

The completion of the TVA impoundment of the Little Tennessee River at Tellico in the fall of

1979 covered Tanasi, the capital of the Cherokee Nation between 1721 and 1730. It was this town that gave its name to the river nearby and eventually to the state.

By 1750 Tanasi was overshadowed by the neighboring village of Chota, or Echota as it is sometimes called. This was the beloved Cherokee capital and a town of refuge and peace. According to Jefferson Chapman in *Tellico Archaeology*, Chota remained the political center of the Overhill Cherokee for most of the eighteenth century.

Most of the physical remains of these areas were covered by Tellico Lake following extensive excavation, but the Tellico Blockhouse and a small part of Chota remain.

The Tellico Dam project was marked by controversy, partly due to the irreplaceable Cherokee archaeological sites. The loss of rich farmland and one of Tennessee's legendary trout rivers was also hard to accept. For a time, it seemed the discovery of the snail darter would be the eleventh-hour savior of the conservationists, but a last-minute congressional action exempted the project from the Endangered Species Act and the waters rose behind the 105-foot dam.

Although it has no electrical generating capacity, a canal connects Tellico Lake to Fort Loudoun Lake and the hydroelectric turbines at that dam. At full pool the lake covers 16,500 surface acres and it does not have a dramatic fall drawdown.

Along its shoreline you'll find facilities that include boat ramps, recreation areas, marinas, and campgrounds. Tellico is an excellent brown and rainbow trout fishery but bass are common as well. Sailboating is popular and the canal connection to Fort Loudoun Lake makes long-distance cruising feasible.

Begin your tour at Vonore by following US 411 to TN 360. The first stop will be Fort

The Fort Loudoun Visitors Center sits along the shores of Tellico Lake, which now covers the Cherokee capital town of Chota.

Loudoun State Historic Area along the shores of Tellico Lake. The fort was built by the British in 1756 in exchange for support by the Cherokee during the French and Indian War. It was named for the Earl of Loudoun, the commander in chief of British forces in North America.

The fort was intended to protect Cherokee women and children while the warriors were away fighting for the British. In a strange series of misadventures, the alliance was strained by cultural differences and miscommunication.

Fort Loudoun has been partially reconstructed on a site created with landfill along the shores of Tellico Lake above the original location. The visitor center has a bookstore and a museum that features a film discussing the history of the site. There are also picnic and swimming areas.

Vonore is familiar to students of Cherokee history as the birthplace of George Gist, better known as Sequoyah, the man responsible for giving the Cherokee the power of the written word with his Cherokee syllabary.

Sequoyah Birthplace Museum is owned and

operated by the Eastern Band of the Cherokee and the site is about 0.5 miles from Fort Loudoun State Historic Area. The museum not only tells Sequoyah's story but contains some of the artifacts recovered before the lake was formed. It's a short walk from the museum to the Cherokee Memorial, a mound containing nearly two hundred bodies recovered during archaeological excavations.

The Chota Memorial is on a narrow peninsula in the Tellico Lake Wildlife Management Area and Refuge off TN 360. Eight stone pillars mark the support posts of the central townhouse which was large enough to hold five hundred people.

Near the Fort Loudoun site, the Tellico Blockhouse, built in 1794 by the Southwest Territory governor, William Blount, was intended to protect the Cherokee from the advancing tide of white encroachment. It was used as a meeting place to conduct business between the United States and the Cherokee until 1807.

Madisonville was named for James Madison. It is the county seat of Monroe County, which was named for the fifth president of the United States. Once a mule trading center, it's now the crossroads of US 411 and TN 68. Hog Heaven BBQ is on US 411, if you're interested in "cue," or Donna's Ole Towne Cafe on College Street will serve you breakfast, lunch, or dinner daily. The Motor Inns of America offers overnight accommodations.

The Orr Mountain Winery on TN 68 is a family-owned vineyard and winery known for its award-winning Mountain River series. Treat yourself to a free tour before you visit the tasting room. If you come during the August grape harvest, check out the "picking and stomping."

Tellico Plains is on the site of one of the most important Overhill towns, Talequah or Telliquo. It was at a meeting in Talequah in 1730 that a Briton, Sir Alexander Cumming, convinced Cherokee leader Moytoy to send seven chiefs, including Attakullakulla, to London where they renewed a treaty binding them to England. This alliance would eventually place the Cherokee in opposition to the fledgling American nation.

Today visitors to Tellico Plains enjoy easy access to fishing, hunting, kayaking, hiking, and sightseeing. We stopped by the Tellicafe for dinner one evening after a drive on the Cherohala Skyway from Robbinsville. We enjoyed the friendly folks, good service, and good food.

Overnight guests are welcomed to a twentieth-century boarding house turned bed and breakfast known simply as the Hotel. Ten rooms with an old-fashioned feel and antique furniture are available at the Hotel for adults and children over twelve. There's a private bath in the downstairs suite which boasts a sitting room and a claw-foot tub. The upstairs rooms share two modern bathrooms.

Sina Mae Cole serves a full breakfast to her guests and will arrange one- and two-day fishing packages complete with lunch and a guide. Bring your own equipment or you may make arrangements for rods to be provided. They suggest you bring waders, a 7-foot, 5 weight rod or 7-foot, 6-inch to 8-foot, 5 weight rod and a selection of wet and dry flies.

The Magnolia House Bed and Breakfast has two modern guest rooms with king-sized beds, central heat and air, and refrigerators that share the two-story white frame "farmhouse" with Tellico Plains Realty downstairs. A third room has two single beds and the common area has TV and phone.

Several companies in the area offer cabin and chalet rentals including Arrowhead River Lodge

Coker Creek was the site of Tennessee's gold rush.

on the banks of the Tellico River along TN 68 at the edge of Cherokee National Forest. Each log chalet sleeps up to five and has a fully equipped kitchenette, bath, cable TV, central heat and air.

From Tellico Plains proceed west on TN 165 to Cherohala Skyway, a fifty-one-mile stretch of mountain majesty. The dream of former Tellico Plains mayor Charles Hall, the Cherohala Skyway grew from an annual wagon train trek over the mountains that began in 1958.

It was dedicated in 1996, its name being derived from its route through the *CHERO*kee National Forest in Tennessee (twenty-four miles) and the Nanta*HALA* National Forest in North Carolina (twenty-seven miles). The Skyway is over a mile high at points and passes through outstanding scenery on its route to Robbinsville, North Carolina. You should make sure you have plenty of gas and that your brakes are in good condition before setting out on this delightful outing.

The Cherokee National Forest offers many outdoor activities. Stop by the ranger station off TN 165 for information about activities, including a visit to the one-hundred-foot Bald River Falls.

There's a fishing area for children and handicapped citizens a short distance beyond Green Cove Motel. The motel is open from March to November. Children especially enjoy a visit to see the large brood trout at Pheasant Fields Trout Rearing Station a short distance from Green Cove.

North of Cherohala Skyway, Indian Boundary Recreation Area has campsites for one hundred people, a lake, swimming area, and fishing piers near the Citico Creek Wilderness Area which adjoins North Carolina's Joyce Kilmer/Slickrock Creek Wilderness Area.

About ten miles south of Tellico Plains on TN 68, you'll see Coker Creek, the site of the second U.S. gold rush, the first being near Dahlonega, Georgia, in 1828.

Nearly twenty-five years before the California gold rush, legend tells us a soldier noticed a large gold nugget worn by an Indian woman. He was told the nugget came from Coqua Creek and whites soon began to illegally work gold fields on Indian lands at a spot they called Coker Creek. Gold mines were dug and the creek was panned until the Civil War interrupted the efforts of nearly one thousand miners.

Coker Creek Village has the Old Country Store which offers for sale the work of more than twenty-five local artists and craftsmen.

The campground has one hundred primitive sites and twenty-five sites with hookups, a shower house, and dump station. The Village Inn Restaurant serves a country-style buffet on Saturday evening and Sunday afternoon from April to October.

If you catch gold fever, Coker Creek Village has instruction and equipment for rent or sale. The two-day Autumn Gold Festival held here each October features traditional mountain arts, crafts, foods, and music.

The Mountain Garden Inn has two suites and two bedrooms with private baths. Wraparound porches, rockers, and a stone fireplace in the great room assure comfortable, relaxing evenings year-round. A full breakfast is served and children are welcome.

East Tennessee Riding Stables offers the chance to experience the Cherokee National Forest on horseback year-round.

Our next stop on this loop tour continues south on TN 68 to the area known as the Copper Basin in the extreme southeastern corner of Tennessee.

All of the following accommodations are Tellico Plains with zip code 37385, and all telephone listings are area code 423, except where noted.

Accommodations:
Arrowhead River Lodge, Rafter Rd., 800-251-9568.
Coker Creek Village, 12528 Hwy. 68, 800-448-9580 or 261-2310.
Fort Loudoun Motel, Vonore, 884-6363.
Green Cove Motel, River Rd., 253-2069.
The Hotel Bed and Breakfast, TN 165, 253-7439.
Magnolia House Bed and Breakfast, P.O. Box 269, 305 TN 165, 800-323-4750 or 253-3446.
Motor Inns of America, Madisonville, 442-9045.
Mountain Garden Inn, P.O. Box 171, TN 68, Coker Creek, 37314; 261-2689.
Tellico Riverside Resort, 222 Rafter Rd., 253-7360.
Town and Country Motel, Madisonville, 442-2084.

Attractions:
Coker Creek Village, 800-448-9580.
Fort Loudoun State Historical Area, 884-6217.
Orr Mountain Winery, Madisonville, 442-5340.
Sequoyah Birthplace Museum, Vonore, 884-6246.

Dining:
Donna's Ole Towne Restaurant, Madisonville, 442-3304.
Hog Heaven BBQ, Madisonville, 442-5279.
Town Square Cafe and Bakery, 253-2200.
Tellicafe, 253-2880.
The Village Inn, 261-2310.

Shopping:
Benton's Smoky Mountain Country Hams, Madisonville, 442-5003.
Coker Creek Gallery, Coker Creek, 261-2157.
Coker Creek Village, Coker Creek, 261-2310.
H&W Frontier Willowcraft, Coker Creek, 261-2516.
Orr Mountain Winery, Madisonville, 442-5340.

Special Events:
May—Memorial Day Encampment at Fort Loudoun
September—Fort Loudoun Trade Fair; Cherokee Arts and Crafts Festival, Sequoyah Birthplace Museum
October—Autumn Gold Festival, Coker Creek
December—Christmas at Fort Loudoun

Camping:
Cherokee Campground, 253-3094.
Cherokee National Forest, 253-2520.

For More Information:
Monroe County Chamber of Commerce, P.O. Box 37, Madisonville, 37354; 800-245-5428 or 442-9147.
Tennessee Overhill Heritage Association, P.O. Box 143, Etowah, 37331; 263-7232.

18 Ducktown, Ocoee, Hiwassee, Etowah, Athens
Land of Beloved Scars and Rushing Rivers

The three communities of Isabella, Copperhill, and Ducktown are situated in the extreme southeastern corner of Tennessee in an area known as the Copper Basin. At the time of the Cherokee Indian removal in 1838, the area was land no one wanted until copper was discovered here by whites in 1843. A boom followed the completion of the Copper Road from Cleveland to the Copper Basin in 1853. In some areas copper was mined to a depth of nearly one-fourth of a mile.

More than fifty square miles of the surrounding hillsides were deforested to fuel open-pit smelting. Huge heaps of raw ore were slowly burned to lower the sulfur content. Unfortunately, this released large amounts of sulfur dioxide into the air.

By 1876 the surrounding forest was exhausted. The erosion and acid rain eventually created a man-made biological desert. The high concentration of heavy metals washed from the steep hillsides by more than fifty inches of annual rainfall completely destroyed aquatic life in some sections of the Ocoee. Eventually this barren "moonscape" became the only memory residents had of the once lush landscape.

After mining millions of tons of copper ore, mining halted temporarily in 1878 until the Tennessee Copper Company opened the Burra Burra mine in 1899. During the early 1900s, new developments in mining technology allowed the sulfur dioxide gas to be reclaimed as sulfuric acid, which was used by the fertilizer industry.

Now lushly carpeted with acid-resistant pines, devastation like this tiny remnant once surrounded Ducktown as far as the eye could see.

More than 16 million trees, acid-tolerant grasses, and legume seeds have been planted in an effort to complete the reclamation by the year 2000. Today some sections of the Ocoee remain sterile, as yet unable to recover sufficiently to support aquatic life.

Visitors can get an idea of the devastation that once existed here at a three-hundred-acre portion of the "beloved scar," the name given by residents to the formerly blighted landscape. This land has been set aside as a memorial at the Burra Burra Historic Mine Site. The Ducktown Museum on the mine site has exhibits on early settlers, mining and environmental law.

The two-story Victorian house at 104 Main Street is home to the White House Bed and Breakfast. Three bedrooms have shared or private bath and a full country breakfast is served. The Company House at 125 Main was built in 1826 and has six rooms with private baths. A full country breakfast is served. Julia's Kitchen on US 64 serves country cooking every day. You'll also find a Best Western franchise here.

From Ducktown, follow US 68 south to Copper Hill, where Maloof's Bed and Breakfast, a couple of antique shops, and the delightful El Rio Restaurant await you. You may also choose to head west on US 64 toward Lake Ocoee on the Ocoee Scenic Byway along parts of the Old Copper Road once used to haul wagonloads of rich copper ore from Ducktown and Copper Hill to Cleveland.

The Ocoee Scenic Byway travels through the Ocoee River Gorge, one of the top ten white-water rivers in the United States, past the site of the 1996 Olympic canoe and kayak competition below Ocoee Dam No. 3.

The first of the hydroelectric dams created beautiful Parksville, or Ocoee Lake, tucked between Sugar Loaf and Bean Mountains. Parksville Campground has forty-one campsites, water, electric hookups, showers, and picnic tables. Some of the sites may be reserved between May and October and camping is available year-round.

Two additional dams harness the power of the Ocoee, which is now controlled by the Tennessee Valley Authority (TVA). The TVA provides a regular schedule of 106 water releases per year for white-water sports. In return, fees collected by commercial outfitters repay the TVA power system for the loss of revenue when the generators are idle.

With rapids earning names like Double Trouble and Hell's Hole, it's a good thing US 64 runs alongside the river in case you decide to abandon the river and walk to your vehicle. The water level

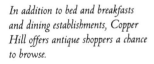

In addition to bed and breakfasts and dining establishments, Copper Hill offers antique shoppers a chance to browse.

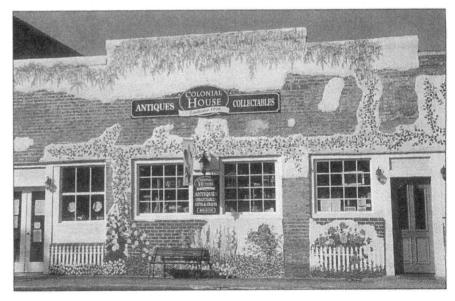

The Ocoee Whitewater Center is situated along the Old Copper Road, or US 64, between Ducktown and Cleveland.

fluctuates dramatically according to the generation schedule so be sure to check the TVA information line listed at the end of this section before you put in. Several outfitters offer thrilling guided raft trips.

The Ocoee Whitewater Center was built by the US Forest Service for the 1996 Olympics below Ocoee Dam No. 3 and is now a visitor information center for both land- and water-based recreation in the area.

The Chilhowee Recreation Area on top of Chilhowee Mountain offers eighty-eight campsites, a swimming area, nine hiking trails, watchable wildlife areas, fishing and boating on the seven-acre McCamy Lake. The sixty-five-foot Benton Falls is a 1.5-mile hike from the dam at McCamy Lake. To reach the recreation area, continue on US 64 past TN 30 and the Ocoee District ranger's office; turn on Forest Service Road (FR) 77 and follow the winding paved road about seven miles.

There are several roads heading north from US 64 west of Ducktown toward the Hiwassee River. The scenic Hiwassee River is not only prettier, it's much more forgiving than the Ocoee. In fact, it's the training river for the Tennessee Scenic Rivers Association (TSRA) summer canoe schools. Hiwassee Outfitters, like many others in the area, offers river rafting, guided fly- and spin-fishing in McKenzie drift boats for rainbow and brown trout along with camping facilities and cabins.

The 18.8-mile John Muir Trail follows the Hiwassee River from Childers Creek near Reliance to TN 68. Webb Brothers Store, a local landmark, offers snacks as well as a float service.

A bit farther west, US 411 turns north toward Benton, the county seat of Polk County.

The lower section of the Hiwassee begins at the US 411 bridge and is a leisurely Class I float used for family canoe trips and fishermen plying the clear, clean water.

The grave of the Cherokee ghiahau or "beloved woman" Nancy Ward is 7.5 miles south of Benton on US 411.

This amazing woman managed to fulfill her duties as leader of the clan council of Cherokee women with a voting voice in the ruling tribal council, yet she remained a consistent friend of early white settlers in her efforts to keep peace between the two cultures.

Nancy Ward remained an important Cherokee leader until the Cherokee left their capital at Chota. She then moved to operate an inn near Benton until her death in 1822.

The log blockhouse of Fort Marr is on the right a little more than a mile north of Nancy Ward's grave before you reach Benton. The blockhouse was one of the corners of the stockade that enclosed the 1814 Fort Marr, a source of protection for white settlers and also built to protect Cherokee women and children from warring Creeks. Fort Marr later served as a stockade to hold the Cherokee assembled in this area before their departure on the Trail of Tears in 1838.

Stop by Remember When Antiques on US 411 next to Benton Discount Drugs. Two blocks from the courthouse on US 411, the Ocoee Artists' Association features local arts and crafts. Tinsley's Restaurant serves barbecue beef, pork, chicken, and ribs in addition to a breakfast and lunch menu. R & Y Diner on US 411 specializes in country cooking with a buffet on weekdays and also short orders and dinners from the menu.

Built in 1916, Southern Memories Country Inn has four bedrooms with queen-sized beds and private baths and two Victorian cottages about five miles north of town on US 411.

From Benton continue on US 411 past the Hiwassee River and the turnoff to Chilhowee Gliderport to the railroad town of Etowah. The town was created when officials of the Louisville and Nashville Railroad announced their intention to build a new rail line between Cincinnati and Atlanta.

Accordingly, L&N bought land from twelve farmers, built a rail center, and planned a town.

The restored 1906 L&N Depot is at the corner of Tennessee (US 411) and Eighth Avenues. The fifteen-room building was once the headquarters for the Atlanta Division of the L&N Railroad.

Today it is home to the Etowah Chamber of Commerce, the Tennessee Overhill office, the Etowah Arts Commission, and the Cultural Arts Museum. The depot museum exhibits artifacts and photographs that tell the story of a town dominated by the railroad. An arts and crafts festival is held here each October. The area around the depot has a shaded walking trail.

The Etowah Antique Mall on Tennessee

The grave of beloved Cherokee leader Nancy Ward is on a high hill overlooking US 411.

Avenue has three floors of antiques and collectibles open daily.

The Hiwassee Ranger Station is located about two miles east of Etowah on TN 310. This is a good stop for those interested in floating the Hiwassee River, camping in the Gee Creek Wilderness, or hiking the John Muir National Recreation Trail, named for the famous naturalist who passed this way in 1867.

From Etowah follow TN 30 nine miles to Athens, the largest town on this loop with a population of more than fifteen thousand. The downtown area has antique shops, gift shops, and restaurants. Lunch at the Backstage Coffee House, On the Square Restaurant and Deli, Papaw Dan's Downtown Smokehouse, Jenkins' Restaurant and Deli, or Burkett's Pit Bar-B-Q. The Country Patch on South White Street offers healthy home cooking using canola oils and fresh ingredients, regular and sugar free desserts, and decaf tea.

Visit the McMinn County Living Heritage Museum in a former school building where Washington Street (TN 30) meets Madison Avenue for three floors of exhibits on early Tennessee and Cherokee Indian history as well as displays on the Civil War and early-twentieth-century farm and industrial life. The museum has a good collection of nineteenth- and twentieth-century quilts and is host to a national quilt show each spring. Fall brings a hand-woven coverlet show and dolls take the stage in December.

Construction began on Woodlawn, an antebellum Greek Revival home in 1858. The two-story brick home was used as a Union hospital and its original wooden columns were burned for firewood by Union troops. The renovated National Register of Historic Places property is an antique-filled bed and breakfast featuring four rooms with private baths. A full breakfast is served. National franchises include Days Inn, Holiday Inn, and a KOA campground.

Mayfield Dairy has a visitor center offering a film about the dairy, a tour of the milk and ice cream producing plant, and of course a tasting

The L&N Depot in Etowah sits across the street from a host of antique shops.

room to sample the finished product. The Swift Air Museum displays vintage Globe and Temco Swift aircraft and hosts an annual Swift owners convention on Memorial Day weekend. Knox Park has picnic pavilions and a small lake while Sunset Park has a pretty fountain, picnic areas, and a walking trail.

From Athens, proceed on US 11 to Sweetwater, home of the Lost Sea.

All of the following accommodations are Ducktown with zip code 37326, and all telephone listings are area code 423, except where noted.

Accommodations:
The Company House, 125 Main St., 800-343-2909 or Etowah Motel, 330 N. Tennessee Ave., Etowah, 37331; 263-7618.
Hideaway Cabins at Campbell Cove Lake, Rt. 1, Box 951A, Turtletown, 37391; 800-390-8888 or 496-4631.
Holiday Terrace Motel, 324 N.Tennessee Ave., Etowah, 37331; 263-7618.
Lake Ocoee Inn & Cabins, Rt. 1, Box 347, Benton, 37307; 800-272-7238 or 338-2064.
Maloof Building Bed and Breakfast, Copper Hill, 37326; 800-475-2016 or 492-2016.
Southern Memories Country Inn, US 411 North, Benton, 37307; 338-4351.
The White House Bed and Breakfast, 104 Main St., 800-775-4166 or 496-4166.
Woodlawn Bed and Breakfast, 110 Keith Ln., Athens, 800-745-8213 or 745-8211.

Attractions:
Adventures Unlimited, Nashville, 800-662-0667 or 615-662-0661.
Copper Basin Golf and Country Club, Copper Hill, 496-3579.
Ducktown Basin Museum, Burra Burra Hill, 496-5778.
Gem Theater, Seventh and Tennessee, Etowah, 263-7840.
High Country Adventures, Ocoee, 800-233-8594.
Hiwassee Outfitters, Reliance, 800-338-8133 or 338-8115.
L&N Depot/Railroad Museum, Etowah, 263-7840 or 263-2228.
Mayfield Visitors Center, Athens, 745-2151.
McMinn County Living Heritage Museum, Athens, 37303; 745-0329.
Nantahala Outdoor Center, Ocoee, 800-232-7238.
Ocoee Inn Rafting, Benton, 800-221-7238 or 338-2064.
Ocoee Outdoors, Ocoee, 800-533-7767 or 338-2438.
Ocoee Rafting, 496-3388.
Swift Aircraft Museum, Athens, 745-9547.

Nancy Ward Gravesite, US 411 near Benton.
Webb Bros. Float Service, Reliance, 338-2373.

Dining:
Backstage Coffee House, Athens, 745-9747.
Burkett's Pit Bar-B-Q, Athens, 745-9791.
Country Patch, Athens, 745-6104 or 745-3100, ext. 1200, for menu line.
El Rio Mexican Restaurant and Cantina, Copper Hill, 496-1826.
Julia's Kitchen, 496-5382.
Papaw Dan's Downtown Smokehouse, Athens, 745-5003.
Jenkins Restaurant & Deli, Athens, 745-7671.
Lake Ocoee Inn Restaurant, 338-2064.
On the Square Restaurant and Deli, Athens, 745-2622.
R & Y Diner, Benton, 338-2185.
The River Cafe, Ocoee, 338-1915.

Shopping:
Artists Alcove, Athens, 745-7312.
C&J Antiques and Collectibles, Ocoee, 338-8572.
The Cottage Antiques and Collectibles, Athens, 745-8528.
Cozy Corner Gift Shoppe, 496-3399.
Ducktown Collectibles, 496-2630.
Etowah Antique Mall, Etowah, 263-5312.
Ocoee Artists' Association, Benton, 338-4502.
Remember When Antiques, Benton, 338-5565.

Special Events:
March—Cousin Jake Memorial Bluegrass Festival, Etowah
April—Ramp Tramp Festival, Benton
April–May—Annual Quilt Show, Athens
May—Memorial Day Weekend, Athens, Swift Air Show. Free.
July 4 weekend—Miners Homecoming, Copper Basin
October—3rd weekend, Heritage Festival, Copper Basin; Ocoee Whitewater Rodeo
November–December—Annual Doll Show, Athens

Camping:
Gee Creek Campground, Delano, 338-4133.
Lost Creek Recreation Area (USFS), Etowah, 263-5486.
Quinn Springs Recreation Area, Etowah, 263-5486.
Tumbling Creek Campground, Benton, 476-9700.

For More Information:
Athens Area Chamber of Commerce, 13 N. Jackson St., Athens, 37303; 745-0334.
Cherokee National Forest: Ocoee Ranger District, 338-5201; Hiwassee Ranger District, 263-5486.
Copper Basin Area Chamber of Commerce, P.O. Box 428, Copperhill, 37317; 496-9000.
Etowah Area Chamber of Commerce, P.O. Box 458/ L&N Depot, Etowah, 37331; 263-2228.
Ocoee/Hiwassee Tourist Info., P.O. Box 241, Ocoee, 37361; 888-733-6263.
Polk County Chamber of Commerce, Benton; 338-5040.

Tennessee Overhill Heritage Association, L&N Depot, Etowah,
    37331; 263-7232.
Tennessee Scenic Rivers Association, P.O. Box 159041,
    Nashville, 37215.
TVA Information Line, 800-238-2264.

19 Sweetwater, Loudon, Lenoir City, Farragut

In the Great Valley
of East Tennessee

Sweetwater, a community of about six thousand, was named for a local creek known to the Cherokee as *culla saga*, or "sweet water." It is known to thousands of tourists as the home of the Lost Sea, "America's largest underground lake." Declared a National Landmark in 1976, the Lost Sea is located between Sweetwater and Madisonville about six miles from the I-75 exit.

It's familiar to thousands who have never visited because it's advertised on highway billboards throughout Tennessee. The Lost Sea is deep within the Craighead Cavern system which was named for Cherokee Chief Craighead who once owned the land in this area.

The Lost Sea earned its name as a result of unusual weather conditions that prevailed during the summer of 1905. Although portions of the cave had been used for Cherokee council meetings in the early 1800s, as a source of nitrates and phosphates for gun powder during the Civil War, as a source of red pigment for barn painting by farmers, and as a hideout for moonshiners, it took a drought and a boy with time on his hands to rediscover the "lost" sea.

The 1905 drought dropped the water level in the cave and exposed a forty-foot-long passageway to the giant lake room. When the boy convinced his father to return with him the next year, the water level had risen and once again covered the three-foot-high entry through the rock. Portions of the cave were opened commercially in 1915, but the sea remained "lost" until the 1960s when a tunnel was blasted through to the chamber containing the 4.5-acre lake.

The one-hour tour includes a land tour through the cavern on wide sloping walkways and a ride around the lake in a glass-bottomed boat. In addition to spiky white anthodite or cave flower formations, you'll see large "rooms," a waterfall, and a population of huge, friendly resident rainbow trout.

A cafe on the grounds serves pit barbecue and has outdoor picnic tables and nature trails to enjoy.

There are several national franchises represented here including Budget Host Inn, Comfort Inn, Days Inn, and Red Carpet Inn. One of the largest overnight accommodations in the area is the Sweetwater Hotel and Convention Center on TN 68 which has a restaurant and lounge. The Sweetwater Valley KOA campground is open year-round while the Tennessee Valley Authority's Hornsby Hollow Campground is open from April to October.

Continue on US 11 to Loudon and Lenoir City. Both were once river towns along the banks of the Tennessee. Today this part of East Tennessee calls itself "the Lakeway to the Smokies."

With a population slightly less than five thousand, Loudon is the county seat of Loudon County. Loudon, like Fort Loudoun, was named for the Earl of Loudoun, commander of the British forces in America during the French and Indian War. The town grew from Blair's Ferry on the north side of the Tennessee River.

The Lost Sea tour includes a ride around the underground lake on a glass-bottomed boat. (Photo courtesy of Tennessee Tourist Development)

Begin your tour of Loudon at the Loudon County Visitors Center at the historic Carmichael Inn. Here's where you can pick up a walking tour of Loudon brochure as well as information about the Carmichael Inn, an 1810 stagecoach inn for travelers from Knoxville, Chattanooga, and Nashville. Guests were ferried across the Tennessee River to spend the night before continuing their journey.

Now the home of the Loudon County Museum, the log inn is two stories tall and one room deep with a central chimney and a two-story porch running the length of the house. Inside you'll find period furnishings and artifacts along with a gift shop with handmade items produced by area artisans.

The museum is located at 501 Poplar Street beside the Loudon County Courthouse, a lovely brick Italianate structure on TN 11 that still looks much as it would have when completed in the fall of 1872. Across the street, there's a pretty fountain in a small triangle that was once part of the courthouse lawn where horses and mules were tied to hitching rails while business was conducted.

There are enough stops around town to keep you occupied for a leisurely afternoon. Mulberry Street began as a farm path, but in 1928 it was widened and paved into the famed Dixie Highway. Today you'll find the General Store offering antiques and contemporary folk art and the Brickbox and Antiques Cafe featuring fine coffees, homebaked breads, and pastries along with antiques and folk art. Sweet Memories has glassware, furniture, vintage clothing, and pottery. West End Cafe and Warehouse Antiques, Collectibles and Gifts are down the street.

Townson's Cafe on the courthouse square has an old-fashioned soda fountain and serves all three meals for weekday patrons. Weekends try the cafe for breakfast or lunch. Catino's Restaurant and Pizzeria serves homemade soups and desserts in addition to hot pizza and cold beer. Mountain

View Restaurant features catfish dinners Tuesday through Saturday.

The Mason Place Bed and Breakfast is located on Commerce Street in an 1865 home started by riverboat captain Thomas Jefferson Mason. This home, in the National Register of Historic Places, offers five beautiful guest rooms furnished with antiques. Each room has a private bath and gas fireplace. For a little different bed and breakfast experience, try the Smokehouse Suite near the pool. Three acres of manicured grounds offer a Grecian swimming pool, gazebo, and wisteria arbor.

The Loudon Valley Vineyards overlooks the Tennessee River and has picnic facilities available. In addition to wines that have taken regional and international awards, it has a snack shop offering bread, cheeses, and other treats to complete your picnic outing.

Continue north on US 11 about five miles along the upper edge of Watts Bar Lake to Lenoir City which sits across from Tellico Dam and Lake and downriver from Fort Loudoun Dam and Lake. As you would expect from a location like this, you'll find several stops along the lakefront including the Captain's Retreat, a waterfront bed and breakfast with four guest rooms with private baths and whirlpools overlooking a seventy-five-foot restored antique sternwheel riverboat that is the owners' residence.

You can fish from the boardwalk or paddle around the cove in a canoe. If your idea of recreation leans toward dry land, Cedar Hills Golf Course is less than a mile away. The par-70, eighteen-hole course is open to the public, but tee times are required for weekends and holidays.

Many of the area campgrounds offer fishing and boating including Crosseyed Cricket which has its own three-acre catfish lake and half-acre trout pond. They will fry or broil your fresh catch

at the restaurant. Other waterfront campgrounds include Lotterdale Cove on Tellico Lake, Melton Hill Dam Campground and Yarberry Campground, which is about two miles from Fort Loudoun Dam.

Fort Loudoun Marina rents twenty-five-foot pontoon boats for whole or half days if you'd like to get out on the water. The marina is next to Lenoir City Park on Fort Loudoun Lake.

The area that became Lenoir City was received by Gen. William Lenoir in a five-thousand-acre land grant for payment for service in the Revolutionary War. The property remained in the Lenoir family until 1876 when it was sold to developers.

In 1890 the Lenoir City Company established streets and parceled lots. Homes from this era are located between First and Fourth Avenues from Hill Street to B Street. The Old Lenoir City Hall Museum at 205 E. Broadway is filled with artifacts from Lenoir's early days. It's open Wednesday, Saturday, and Sunday afternoons from one to four o'clock.

Allen's Antiques and Used Furniture, John Farmer Sales, and Victoria's Antique and Craft Mall are also on Broadway.

If you've gotten a late start, Bob and Marty's Restaurant on A Street at Depot serves breakfast all day. Melton Hill Restaurant has daily homecooked specials. The Dinner Bell Restaurant is also open daily with a casual menu ranging from country ham, sawmill gravy, and beans to cornbread, catfish, and flounder. Gerald's Smokehouse serves everything from barbecue bologna (don't knock it until you try it) to prime rib. The waterfront location and bar make Calhoun's at the marina on City Park Drive a good choice for a relaxing evening.

Continuing along US 11 north, you'll reach Farragut which was named for David Glasgow Farragut who has come down through the years since the Civil War as the originator of the pithy quote, "Damn the torpedoes, full speed ahead!"

Born near present-day Knoxville, the boy who would become the first-ever admiral in the American navy moved to New Orleans with his parents when he was six. The rest, as they say, is history and you can learn about it at the Farragut Folklife Museum.

In addition to local history, displays include an extensive collection of Admiral Farragut's personal memorabilia. Follow US 11 into Knoxville where it joins Kingston Pike to return to Knoxville and complete the loop.

All of the following accommodations are Sweetwater with zip code 37874, and all telephone listings are area code 423, except where noted.

Accommodations:
The Captain's Retreat, 3534 Lakeside Dr., Lenoir City, 37772; 986-7421.
Mason Place Bed and Breakfast, 600 Commerce St., Loudon, 37774; 458-3921.
Sweetwater Hotel and Convention Center, I-75 at TN 68, 337-3511.

Attractions:
Carmichael Inn Museum, Loudon, 458-1442 or 458-9020.
Cedar Hills Golf Course, Lenoir City, 986-6521.
Farragut Folklife Museum, Farragut, 966-7057.
Fort Loudoun Dock and Dam, Lenoir City, 986-3737.
Fort Loudoun Marina, Lenoir City, 986-5536.
The Lost Sea, 337-6616.
Loudon Valley Vineyards, Loudon, 986-8736.

Dining:
Bob & Marty's Restaurant, Lenoir City, 986-5393.
Brickbox and Antiques Cafe, Loudon, 458-0850.
Catino's Restaurant and Pizzeria, Loudon, 458-1000.
Davis' Restaurant, 337-5651.
Dinner Bell Restaurant and General Store, Lenoir City, 986-9958.
Gerald's Smokehouse, Lenoir City, 986-6159.
Hartman's Corner Cafe, 337-9912.
Melton Hill Restaurant, Lenoir City, 986-0772.
Mountain View Restaurant, Loudon, 458-9121.
Townson's Cafe, Loudon, 458-9340.
West End Cafe, Loudon, 458-5157.

Shopping:
Allen's Antiques and Used Furniture, Lenoir City, 986-2724.
Brickbox and Antiques Cafe, Loudon, 458-0850.
The General Store, Loudon, 458-6433.
Goodwin's Antiques, Lenoir City, 986-3396.
Sweet Memories, Loudon, 458-2331.
Twin Lakes Antiques, Lenoir City.
Victoria's Antique and Craft Mall, Lenoir City, 988-7957.
Warehouse Antiques, Collectibles & Gifts, Loudon, 458-3412.

Special Events:
June—Lenoir City Arts and Crafts Festival
August—Smoky Mountain Fiddler's Convention and Arts and Crafts Show, Loudon; Memories on Mulberry Antique and Quilt Show, Loudon

Camping:
Crosseyed Cricket, Lenoir City, 986-5435.
Lotterdale Cove, Greenback, 856-3832.
Melton Hill Dam Campground, Lenoir City, 986-8329 or 632-3791.
Yarberry Peninsula Campground, Lenoir City, 986-7420.

For More Information:
Farragut Chamber of Commerce, Box 22461, Farragut, 37933; 675-7057.
Loudon County Visitors Bureau, 1062 TN 321N, Lenoir City, 37771; 888-LOUDONC or 986-6822.
Monroe County Tourism Council, 800-245-5428.

✺ Knoxville

20 *Knoxville*
Where Nature and Technology Meet

Knoxville is a crossroads between the rugged natural beauty of the ancient Smoky Mountains and the ultramodern technology at Oak Ridge.

Although the Great Smoky Mountains are visible to the south, Knoxville is actually situated in the Great Valley of East Tennessee, a westward continuation of the Shenandoah Valley of Virginia.

According to Edward Luther in *Our Restless Earth*, the Great Valley of Tennessee is about forty-five miles wide with its eastern edge buried by the Great Smoky Mountains. Its floor consists of a series of undulating ridges that resulted from the compression from the southeast (*see* the Great Smoky Mountains chapter for more geological information).

Knoxville evolved from a crossroads settlement known as White's Fort about four miles from the confluence of the Holston and French Broad Rivers which join to form the Tennessee River. The land grant for White's Fort was given to James White of North Carolina in 1785 as payment for military service in the Revolutionary War.

The White homestead was a convenient stopping point for settlers traveling west. The settlement on the hill soon expanded to include three log guest houses and a stockade for protection from the Cherokee beyond the river.

Today the James White Fort is open for tours of the great house and kitchen, guest house, smoke house, a small museum, and the blacksmith shop in downtown Knoxville.

In the fall of 1791, the city was officially founded and named for Gen. Henry Knox, President Washington's secretary of war. The first and only governor of the "Territory South of the River Ohio," William Blount, moved his capital from Rocky Mount between present-day Bristol and Johnson City to White's Fort in 1792. Legend has it that Blount's wife, Mary Grainger, refused to move to the Tennessee wilderness until he built her a proper house.

Construction began around 1792 on the Blount Mansion, the finest of its kind and possibly the first frame house built west of the Appalachian Mountains. It is said that the Cherokee called this National Historic Landmark "the house with many eyes" because of its glass windows.

Inside the Georgian Colonial mansion visitors tour an extensive collection of late-eighteenth-century furnishings. According to Mary French Caldwell in *Tennessee: The Dangerous Example*, William Blount became a U.S. senator after Tennessee was admitted to the Union in 1796. Claims that he was engaged in a conspiracy with England, swindling the Indians, and trying to discredit the president surfaced in Washington with the appearance of a letter supposedly written by Blount. According to Jack Neely in *Knoxville's Secret History*, Blount's goal was to protect free access to the Mississippi River with an alliance of British, Cherokee, and frontiersmen who would seize Louisiana from the Spanish before the increasingly aggressive French could.

Blount was charged with treason, but it was never proven that Blount wrote the letter and the charges were dismissed. Blount was elected without opposition to serve in the Tennessee legislature by loyal supporters.

Knoxville, the third-largest city in Tennessee, has an active waterfront.

In the late 1700s and early 1800s, Knoxville was a rowdy frontier town along the Wilderness Road frequented by travelers heading west. The county seat of Knox County became the first capital of Tennessee in 1796 and remained so until 1812 when the capital was moved to Nashville.

Several historic sites are of interest to visitors, including Marble Springs, the only remaining home of legendary frontiersman and six-term Tennessee governor John Sevier. Sevier first won fame in the Revolutionary War at Kings Mountain, South Carolina (*see* Elizabethton). His reputation as an Indian fighter was unsurpassed. He lived at Marble Springs with his second wife, Catherine Sherrill, who was known as Bonnie Kate, from 1790 to 1815 (*see* Johnson City for more about Sevier).

Another of Knoxville's historic homes, Crescent Bend, is located on Kingston Pike, one of Knoxville's main east-west thoroughfares. Crescent Bend was built in 1834 near the bend of the same name in the Tennessee River.

Down the road from Crescent Bend, Confederate Memorial Hall was known as Bleak House by its builder, Robert Houston Armstrong. It became the headquarters of Gen. James Longstreet during the Civil War siege of Knoxville.

In order to protect the East Tennessee and Georgia Railroad in Knoxville, about ten thousand Confederates under Gen. Felix Zollicoffer occupied the city from 1861 to 1863. The Confederates withdrew to Chattanooga in August 1863 and were quickly replaced by twenty thousand troops commanded by Union Gen. Ambrose Burnside.

In 1863, an army of fifteen thousand Confederates attempted to retake the city by siege from November 17 to December 2. Confederate Gen. James Longstreet and his staff occupied Bleak House overlooking the river during this effort.

Knoxville withstood the siege, with Union sympathizers bringing provisions in via the river under cover of darkness, but the city suffered extensive damage. According to Michael J. McDonald and William Bruce Wheeler in *Knoxville, Tennessee,* the town welcomed Union occupation because business activities could resume and food and clothing shortages could be remedied.

After the war ended, Knoxville quickly rebuilt its damaged railroad and public and private buildings. Many Union soldiers who were mustered out in Knoxville remained here. The population tripled between 1860 and 1870 and both sides sought to put the conflict behind them.

The rise of merchants and businessmen in Knoxville paralleled similar changes taking place throughout the New South. Dramatic population shifts took place and large numbers of blacks and rural whites moved into the city in search of employment in furniture factories, cloth mills, wholesale houses, the Knoxville Iron Company (which was founded by a former Union officer), and railroad shops.

The University of Tennessee was established in 1794 as Blount College. The campus was moved to its present location in 1826. Records indicate it may have been the first college in the country to educate women. Barbara Blount, daughter of William Blount, was among its early graduates.

In 1807 Blount College became East Tennessee College and policies denied women admission until 1893. By this time it was known as the University of Tennessee.

The Tennessee Valley Authority (TVA) arrived in the 1930s, bringing with it jobs and hydroelectric power to fuel the race to develop atomic energy at nearby Oak Ridge. A series of dams and reservoirs were built creating new

The Blount Mansion was the finest frame home west of the Appalachians in the late 1700s.

opportunities for industry, navigation, and flood control for the forty thousand square miles drained by the Tennessee River. The TVA head-quarters tower above the north end of Market Square Mall and overlook Krutch Park (*see* Norris for more on TVA).

In the mid-1970s, community leaders sought a means to revitalize what had become a decaying urban landscape. The Boeing Corporation had planners in the area anticipating the completion of the Tellico Dam project by the TVA. Knoxville mayor Kyle Testerman persuaded Boeing to have the planners take a look at Knoxville at no cost to the city.

The seeds for Knoxville's present appearance were planted with the plan proposed by Boeing and adopted by the city in 1972, which recommended eliminating the dilapidated housing around the old Southern Railway yard and in the process reconnecting the downtown area with UT to the west.

In the mid-1970s, the Boeing plan was merged with the notion of hosting a World's Fair in Knoxville with the theme "Energy Turns the World." The site selected for the 1982 fairgrounds was the precise area targeted by the Boeing study ten years earlier. The results are impressive.

Using the World's Fair Park as the starting point, most destinations of interest to visitors in Knoxville tend to be clustered. To the east are downtown, Market Square Mall, and Old Town. To the west are the University of Tennessee, historic sites, and restaurants along Kingston Pike. To the south are the exciting new developments and restaurants along the riverfront.

Dominating the skyline is the huge golden Sunsphere, a nearly three-hundred-foot-tall landmark seen by ten million visitors during the 1982 World's Fair, on Henley Street at the World's Fair

Marble Springs was once the home of Governor John Sevier.

Park. This is a good place to start your exploration of Knoxville since it is home to a visitor center filled with information about the area.

A short walk across the pedestrian bridge is the Candy Factory which continues an 1889 tradition initiated by the Littlefield and Steere Company. In addition to gourmet chocolates and candies that are sold fresh and shipped all over the country, there are rest rooms, gift shops, and galleries in the building with nice selections.

Next door is the modern rectangular Tennessee pink marble building that is the home of the Knoxville Museum of Art. You can enjoy permanent and traveling collections in five galleries.

The Victorian houses along 11th and Laurel at the western edge of the park house several galleries, studios, antique and specialty shops. Fort Kid playground is across from the Knoxville Museum of Art. It was built by volunteers and has swings and wooden structures for kids to clamber over. There are also a snack shop and picnic tables for your enjoyment.

Henley intersects with Cumberland Avenue, which becomes Kingston Pike as it runs west

The University of Tennessee is home to twenty-six thousand students and is a vital part of Knoxville's cultural life.

alongside the UT campus. The 102,000-seat football stadium is on Neyland Drive which follows along the river roughly parallel to Cumberland Avenue. Watch out for unbelievable traffic congestion in this area on UT football weekends.

The McClung Museum on campus may be accessed by Kingston Pike or Neyland Drive. This museum is filled with collections in archaeology, art, and local history that are well worth visiting.

It houses one of the largest collections of prehistoric Indian artifacts in the Southeast and exhibits on the geology and fossil history of Tennessee with many rock samples.

Try Calhoun's for casual dining and good ribs on the river. The Tennessee Riverboat Company offers buffet dinner cruises and sightseeing aboard the authentic sternwheeler riverboat Star of Knoxville. Boarding takes place at Neyland Drive, east of Gay Street.

The area along the river is part of Knoxville's newest revitalization, known as Volunteer Landing. One of the main attractions at Volunteer Landing is the Southern Highlands Nature and Technology Visitors Center, a partnership between the City of Knoxville, the National Park Service, the Department of Energy, and Lockheed Martin Corporation which welcomes visitors to the entire region.

As befits the home of the national champion UT women's basketball team, the Women's Basketball Hall of Fame will be located next to Volunteer Landing and is expected to be the spiritual home of women's basketball in the United States.

Other popular attractions include the Beck Cultural Exchange Center, which preserves and displays the story of Knoxville's black men and women from the early 1800s. The Mabry-Hazen House has artifacts and furnishings from the Civil War and Victorian eras. More than two thousand Civil War soldiers are buried nearby at Bethel Cemetery.

Knoxville was the home of James Agee. Foremost among Tennessee's authors, the Pulitzer Prize-winning Agee was a poet, author, film critic, and journalist. He may be best known for *A Death in the Family*, which became a Broadway play and a Hollywood motion picture. Although little physical evidence remains in Knoxville of Agee or other members of its colorful literary society, many writers sojourned here or had close family ties.

There are several good restaurants along Kingston Pike including the Orangery, Knoxville's only four-star restaurant and an excellent choice for a really special evening. We were pleasantly surprised by the elegant country French decor and sophisticated menu.

In addition to a long tradition of delicious food, they're rightfully proud of their extensive wine list. The luncheon menu features several items under ten dollars and is a good choice if you need to watch your budget but want to enjoy the savory selections and wonderful atmosphere.

Naples Italian Restaurant next door is also a top contender with many Knoxville diners for its romantic atmosphere and delicious traditional northern Italian cuisine. Down the road you'll find one of Knoxville's most entertaining restaurants in the Baker Peters Jazz Club. The Copper Cellar is popular for lunch, dinner, and Sunday brunch.

The Maple Grove Inn is a lovely 1799 Georgian–style home west of downtown on Westland Drive off Kingston Pike. Visitors may choose from bedrooms and suites with amenities like fireplaces, whirlpool tubs, and saunas. Its gracious fifteen acres include an outdoor pool and tennis court. The Maple Grove serves dinner by reservation only in an elegant five-table dining room.

If you want to stay overnight downtown, there's a Holiday Inn beside the Sunsphere. The Radisson Summit Hill, Hyatt Regency on Hill Avenue overlooking the river, and Hotel St. Oliver in an 1883 building in the National Register of Historic Places located on Union Street are also considered downtown locations. Other national franchises include Best Western, Comfort Inn, Days Inn, Hampton Inn, Hilton, and Ramada Inn.

Head back downtown and turn east on Main Street and north on South Central to visit the Old City District. This was a bustling warehouse

The Maple Grove Inn is situated on fifteen acres off Kingston Pike. (Photo courtesy of Maple Grove Inn)

The revitalized Old City warehouse district is home to specialty shops and restaurants.

district of the nineteenth century complete with speakeasies and bordellos. In the 1980s the Old City was given new life as businessmen and women with vision reclaimed building after building. Today a nice assortment of restaurants, nightclubs, microbreweries, antique malls, art galleries, and specialty shops make the Old City enjoyable to visit.

Regas has been serving award-winning food since 1919. We were pleased with the quietly elegant setting, non-smoking areas, seafood, and aged beef.

Two streets over on Gay is the historic 1909 Bijou Theatre which hosts music, dance, and theater. Down the street you'll spot the Tennessee Theatre, a renovated rococo-style movie palace that started showing films in 1928 to the accompaniment of a "mighty Wurlitzer" organ. Today films and occasional musical concerts top the bill and the sounds of the Wurlitzer frequently fill the

air before the show.

Harold's Deli on Gay Street serves hefty kosher sandwiches. Sam and Andy's across from UT serves delicious steamed deli sandwiches.

Market Square Mall is a tree-lined outdoor mall that was once an open-air farmers' market surrounded by buildings with boarding houses on the second floor offering all-you-can-eat noonday meals. Today two restaurants carry on the tradition of fresh food on Market Square. Tomato Head has great pizza, salads, and sandwiches and walls lined with changing displays of various artists. The Soup Kitchen has excellent soups and delicious fresh breads and is a big favorite of the lunch crowd.

Market Square Mall is the scene of many of the activities associated with the Dogwood Arts Festival held each April. The citywide celebration includes art exhibits, crafts, music, food, and numerous auto tours when the city's lovely dogwood trees are in bloom.

Krutch Park at the southern end of the mall is across the street from the East Tennessee Historical Center in the historic Customs Building. Exhibits inside concentrate on regional history from pioneers to statehood, through the Civil War and Reconstruction to moonshiners, the TVA, and Oak Ridge during World War II.

The Ijams Nature Center, an eighty-acre bird sanctuary on the Tennessee River across the Gay Street Bridge, has more than 3.5 miles of trails through woodlands, pond, and gardens. One trail is paved and handicapped-accessible. There's a boardwalk around the pond. A museum in a refitted 1910 house has nature displays.

Sharp's Ridge Memorial Park is located at the highest elevation in Knoxville. It is a favorite bird-watching site during spring and fall migrations when more than 133 species have been sighted. Picnic tables and shelters are available and the park is reached via Fairfax Street off Broadway.

About three miles east of town off I-40 East, the 130-acre Knoxville Zoo is home to more than one thousand creatures from around the world. The zoo is known for its big cats including snow leopards, lions, Bengal tigers, cheetahs, and pumas.

The Discovery Center is located in Chilhowee Park, next to the Knoxville Zoo. This museum presents children with fun learning experiences involving computers, lasers, microscopes, plasma balls, and holograms, birds, butterflies, dinosaurs, and a planetarium.

Knoxville has lots of antique shops and malls. We always stop at Campbell's Station Antique Mall. It's easy to reach from exit 373 off I-40 west of Knoxville if you're driving through and want to take a break to treasure hunt. If you're really serious about antiques, you'll want to make sure you're here on the third weekend of the month for the Knoxville Flea Market, also east of Knoxville and one of the area's biggest and best.

With a present-day population of nearly 170,000 in addition to the 26,000 students at UT, Knoxville is a growing, vital city. It is the largest town in East Tennessee, the third largest city in Tennessee, and has lots to offer visitors headed to the Great Smoky Mountains.

All of the following accommodations are Knoxville with zip code 37902, and all telephone listings are area code 423, except where noted.

Accommodations:
Hotel St. Oliver, 407 Union Ave., 521-0050.
Maple Grove Inn, 8800 Westland Dr., 690-9565.

Dining:
Baker Peters Jazz Club, 690-8110.
Copper Cellar (two locations), 673-3411 or 673-3422.
Harold's Deli, 523-5318.
JFG Coffeeshop, 525-0012.
Naples Italian Restaurant, 584-5033.
The Orangery, 588-2964.
Regas Restaurant, 637-9805.
Sam and Andy's Deli (two locations), 524-9527 or 675-4242.
Soup Kitchen (two locations), 546-4212 and 539-6500.
Spaghetti Warehouse, 637-9706.
Sullivan's, 522-4511.
Tomato Head, 637-4067.
Ye Old Steak House, 577-9328.

Shopping:
Barnes and Noble Booksellers, 670-0773.
Book Eddy, 637-3339.
Candy Factory and Victorian Houses Shops and Galleries, 546-5707.
Campbell Station Antique Mall, 966-4348.
Davis-Kidd Booksellers, 690-0136.
East Towne Mall.
Farmers' Market, 524-FARM.
Jackson Antique Marketplace, 521-6704.
The Museum Shops of Knoxville at the Candy Factory.
Old City Bookshop, 546-8837.
Susan Key Antiques, 584-1513.
West Town Mall, 693-0292.
Old City District, Jackson and Central.

Attractions:
Armstrong-Lockett House, 637-3163.
Bijou Theatre, 522-0832.
Beck Cultural Exchange Center, 524-8461.
Blount Mansion, 525-2375.
Ijams Nature Center, 577-4717.
Confederate Memorial Hall, 522-2371.
James White Fort, 525-6514.
Knoxville Museum of Art, 525-6101.
Knoxville Zoo, 637-5331.
McClung Museum of the University of Tennessee, 974-2144.
John Sevier Home, 575-5508.
Sharp's Ridge Memorial Park, 521-2090.
Tennessee Theatre, 525-1840.

Special Events:
April—Dogwood Arts Festival, beginning second Friday, lasting 17 days
September—Tennessee Valley Fair, Chilhowee Park, beginning Friday after Labor Day, lasting 9 days; 637-5840.
Esau's Antiques and Collectibles, third weekend every month; 423-588-1233, I-40 East, Rutledge Pk. exit.

For More Information:
Knoxville Convention and Visitors Bureau, P.O. Box 15012, 37901; 800-727-8045 or 523-7263.
University of Tennessee Sports Information Office; 800-332-8657 or 974-2491.

❧Loop 4

21 *Morristown, Jefferson City, Bean Station*
At the Crossroads of the Frontier

Morristown grew from the crossroads of the main road from Knoxville to Washington (US 11E) and the Buffalo Trail (US 25E) from Cumberland Gap to become a community of more than twenty-two thousand today.

America's famous frontiersman Davy Crockett left his Nolichucky River birthplace as a seven-year-old boy to move to Morristown with his parents, John and Rebecca. They established Crockett Tavern as a resting point for pioneers moving west in this productive valley ringed by the Clinch Mountains.

A reconstruction on the site of the original log tavern is filled with authentic colonial furnishings. Expensive metal cookpots had to be hauled over the rough mountain roads, but the quality of food served from them was important to the success of a frontier tavern. One of young Davy's (actually he was called David by his contemporaries) responsibilities was putting game on the table for the tavern. Crockett's hunting skills are legendary and stories are handed down of Crockett's hunting on a ridge west of the tavern, which is now called Crockett's Ridge (*see* Greeneville for more on Crockett).

The arrival of the Southern Railroad in the mid-1800s ensured growth. Named for an early settler, Absalom Morris, Morristown was officially incorporated in 1855.

The Civil War brought conflicts to Morristown because of its rail access that resulted in the town being held by each army at some time during the war.

The area around Morristown supported large crops of burley tobacco that were brought to one of six warehouses each fall. In the 1950s and 1960s, the overhead sidewalks that are such a prominent feature on downtown streets were developed.

Rose Center is the area's cultural and community center. The elaborate 1892 brick building is in the National Register of Historic Places and houses the Heritage Museum with historic exhibits about the history of Morristown.

Morristown is home to Walters State Community College, a two-year nonresidential college serving about fifty-five hundred students. Cultural activities are supported by groups like the Morristown Chamber Music Society which brings the Knoxville Chamber Orchestra to town for several concerts each year.

Crockett Tavern was established by the parents of the legendary frontiersman David Crockett.

The 1,435-acre Panther Creek State Park is about five miles out of Morristown on US 11E. It has camping, a swimming pool, hiking trails, and a boat launch ramp along the shore of Cherokee Lake, another in the TVA chain of "Great Lakes of the South." Cherokee is well known for large-mouth bass, smallmouth bass, crappie, white bass, and stripers.

Bird watchers and hikers occasionally spot albino deer in the white-tailed herd that inhabits the area around the park. A steep drive through thick woods leads to an awe-inspiring overlook.

Cherokee Park, a 178-acre county park north of Morristown on Cherokee Lake, has fifty-two campsites, ball field, volleyball court, playgrounds, and a children's wading pool.

National franchises include Comfort Suites, Days Inn, Holiday Inn, and Ramada Inn.

The Little Dutch Restaurant at 115 South Cumberland has served Morristown since 1939. Although you wouldn't guess it from the name, its menu includes Greek selections along with "Dutch" fare like charbroiled chicken breasts, calf liver smothered with onions, and pork chops as well as a savory collection of steaks and seafood.

Angelo's Fine Dining at 3614 West Andrew Johnson Highway, combines traditional Greek foods with a variety of beef and seafood dishes. At this writing, guest memberships cost five dollars and allow you to qualify as a member of a private club and therefore be eligible to be served alcoholic beverages in an otherwise dry county.

Cora's Corner at 701 West Third North Street serves hearty breakfasts and country cooking for lunch weekdays. There are two popular restaurants in franchise motels in town, Rebecca's at the Ramada Inn and Partners at the Holiday Inn.

Several antique shops offer shopping opportunities including Dianne's Place Antiques and Farm House Antiques, which adds Indian and Civil War relics to the usual antiques and collectibles collection. The Old Towne Antique Mall has more than fifteen thousand square feet of booth space. Bacons Antiques and Collectibles specializes in

Cherokee Lake is a TVA impound-ment popular with fishermen and water-sports enthusiasts.

Hoosier and Sellers cabinets and Alpha Antique Mall is open daily for antiques and specialty items.

Jefferson City was originally named Mossy Creek for the stream flowing nearby that had large amounts of moss floating on its surface and lining its banks. Mossy Creek also attracted a factory for spinning cotton and a woolen mill. The railroad arrived in 1858, connecting Mossy Creek with markets throughout the United States.

By this time the foundation had been laid for the liberal arts college known today as Carson-Newman College. Owned by the Tennessee Baptist Convention, Carson-Newman offers more than forty major fields of study and contributes to the cultural life of Jefferson City's residents.

The Glenmore Mansion, an 1868 five-story Victorian mansion with twenty-seven rooms, is maintained by the Association for the Preservation of Tennessee Antiquities.

The Branner-Hicks House offers bed and breakfast accommodations to Jefferson City visitors in one of three bedrooms with private baths in an antebellum home.

Bean Station grew up at the intersection of several important trade routes, including the intersection of the Great Indian Warpath and the Daniel Boone Trail. It was named for the Bean brothers, Jesse, William, Robert, and George, frontiersmen who erected a fort here to protect settlers from Indians in 1787.

In 1801 Bean Station became the home of the famous Whiteside Inn, a popular stop on the Baltimore to New Orleans Highway, or Lee Highway as it later came to be known. Today this historic route is known as US 11W. Bean Station was also a stop on the Kentucky Stock Road, once part of the Louisville-Charleston Turnpike and now US 25E. It was visited by westbound settlers and eastbound stock drovers.

The first Whiteside Inn was replaced with a grander three-story brick structure with ballrooms and room for two hundred. Most of the inn was destroyed by fire in the late 1800s but lived on as part of the Old Colonial Inn until the original site of Bean Station was flooded when Cherokee Lake was impounded.

From Morristown and Bean Station follow 25E to Harrogate and Cumberland Gap.

All of the following accommodations are Morristown with zip code 37814, and all telephone listings are area code 423, except where noted.

Accommodations:
Arrow Hill Bed and Breakfast, 6622 W. Andrew Johnson Hwy., Talbot, 37877; 585-5777.
Branner-Hicks House, 1169 N. Chuckey Pk., Jefferson City, 37760.
The Home Place, 132 Church Ln., Mooresburg, 37811; 921-8424.
Parkview Cabins, 3643 Brights Pk., 586-5096.
Round Hill Farm Bed and Breakfast, 150 Noe Ln., Mooresburg, 37811; 921-9089.

Attractions:
Baneberry Golf and Resort, 674-2500.
Clinchview Golf and Country Club, 993-2892.
Crockett Tavern and Museum, 587-9900.
Glenmore Mansion, Jefferson City, 475-7643.
Millstone Golf Club, 586-4000.
Morristown Golf and Country Club, 586-9953.
Panther Creek State Park, 587-7046.
Rose Center Heritage Museum, 581-4330.

Dining:
Angelo's Fine Dining, 581-4882.
The Attic, 475-3508.
Little Dutch Restaurant, 581-1441.
The Mustard Seed Cafe, 587-5118.
Partners Restaurant, 581-8700.
Rebecca's Restaurant and Catering, 587-2400.

Shopping:
Alpha Antique Mall, 581-2371.
Bacons Antiques and Collectibles, 581-7420.
Dianne's Place Antiques, 318-0700.
Farm House Antiques, 581-1527.
Johnny's Antiques, 587-4750.
Olde Towne Antique Mall, 581-6423.
Pickers Paradise Antique Mall, New Market, 475-5055.

Radio Center Antiques, 586-4337.
Rose Arbour Antiques and More, 921-8222.
Yesterday's Antiques and Uniques, 586-9273.

Special Events:
October—Mountain Makins at the Rose Center

Camping:
Cherokee Dam Campground, Muscle Shoals, AL, 205-386-
  2006.
Cherokee Park, 586-0260; park office, 586-5232.
Panther Creek State Recreational Park, 587-7046.

For More Information:
Jefferson City/County Chamber of Commerce, 532 Patriot Dr.
  Jefferson City, 37760; 397-9642.
Morristown Area Chamber of Commerce, P.O. Box 9, 825 W.
  First North St., 586-6382.

22 Cumberland Gap and Harrogate
Land of the Trailblazers

During the early years of American colonization,
settlers were prevented from expanding westward
by the wall of mountains that stretched diagonally
from Maine to Georgia, known collectively as the
Allegheny or Appalachian Mountains. Long
before white men sought a passage through the
mountains where present-day Kentucky, Virginia,
and Tennessee meet, buffalo and deer established a
trail through a gap in what we know as the
Appalachians to the fertile valleys to the west.

This gap was also a part of the famed Warrior's Path (*see* Kingsport) that led from the
Potomac River to the Ohio River. The lack of
archaeological evidence of ancient Indian settlements in the area supports the theory that the area
known as the Cumberland Gap was largely used as
a travel route.

The gap was first seen by a white man, Dr.
Thomas Walker, on Good Friday 1750, but it
remained part of Cherokee lands until the treaty
of Sycamore Shoals (*see* Elizabethton) was signed
twenty-five years later. Walker and five companions
set out from Albemarle County, Virginia, to find a
proper place to locate an 800,000-acre land grant
for the Loyal Land Company.

Frontiersman Daniel Boone heard about Cumberland Gap from John Finley. In 1769 Boone,
Finley, and four other men set out for the gap. In
1773 Boone led a party of settlers toward the gap,
but his son was killed in an Indian attack before
they reached it and the party turned back. In 1774
Col. James Harrod and forty men laid out a town,
but Indians forced them to flee also.

After the 1775 treaty of Sycamore Shoals
transferred ownership of twenty million acres to
the Transylvania Land Company, Daniel Boone
was hired to blaze a trail through the Cumberland
Gap into Kentucky. He and his crew of thirty
backwoodsmen marked and roughly hacked a 208-
mile trail from Long Island at Kingsport to Cumberland Gap in less than three weeks during the
spring of 1775. The first settlers founded Boones-
borough a few weeks later.

In 1796 the road was widened to support
wagons. While other portions of the Alleghenies
had individual gaps, they were quickly followed by
the next group of impenetrable ridges in the chain.
Cumberland Gap was unique in that four geographic features combine to create a gateway
through the entire range.

At one time Yellow Creek flowed south into
the Powell River and as it did so, cut a notch, or
gap, in Cumberland Mountain. Cumberland
Mountain continued to rise faster than the creek
could wear it down and the creek was diverted
northward into the Cumberland River. Beyond the

gap is a large flat area, known as the Middlesboro Basin. As Yellow Creek flowed out of the basin, it created a valley leading to a second gap that crossed Pine Mountain and led to the rolling hills of the bluegrass region of Kentucky.

The rugged trail evolved into the Wilderness Road, the safest passage for settlement in the territory south of the Ohio River.

By the end of the Revolutionary War, more than twelve thousand settlers had passed through the gap into the land known as "Kan Tuc Ke." In 1792 Kentucky was admitted as the fifteenth state in the Union with a population of more than one hundred thousand.

As westward expansion began to use railroads and steamboats in the 1820s and 1830s, Cumberland Gap lost its importance. That was to change when it was viewed as the "Gibralter of America" by U. S. Grant during the Civil War.

Though no major battles were fought here, the gap changed hands four times during the Civil War. Both the Union and the Confederacy felt it held strategic importance. Both sides had difficulties mounting an adequate defense of the gap and control was relinquished in a series of evacuations and retreats that culminated in the surrender by Confederates in 1863 with Federal control established for the remainder of the war.

Tucked in a hollow at an altitude of 1,304 feet on the Tennessee side of the southwestern edge of Cumberland Mountain is the town of Cumberland Gap, population about 210. The town was built by British entrepreneur Col. A. A. Arthur's American Association, Ltd., to house laborers working on a railroad tunnel through the mountains.

A new four-lane tunnel opened in fall 1996. It reroutes US 25E away from the gap, bypassing the town in order to allow the Wilderness Road to be restored to its appearance in Boone's day. It's well worth the short detour into the historic Tennessee town on your way to the 20,271-acre Cumberland Gap National Historical Park (CGNHP) just across the Kentucky line in Middlesboro.

Today Cumberland Gap is an old-fashioned town that's cultivating a modern tourist appeal. Nowhere is this mix more apparent than in the two restaurants that sit on opposite corners of Colwyn Avenue. Many locals tend to gravitate to one or the other; tourists love the mix.

Webb's Country Kitchen has gingham checked curtains, a menu that leans toward home-style cooking, and a Friday night all-you-can-eat catfish special accompanied by "pickin' in the Gap," a spontaneous song swappin' good time with music ranging from traditional mountain string music to a cappella gospel. No alcohol of any type is served at Webb's.

Across the street behind lace curtains is Ye Olde Towne Tea and Coffee Shoppe. We're told it can seat four hundred in a combination of venues

The town of Cumberland Gap grew up along the Wilderness Road originally blazed by Daniel Boone in 1775.

that include the fern-bar "garden side" and the elegant "bank side" complete with antique accents like a Victorian settee in the small waiting area that looks like a parlor.

The lunch menu includes salads, sandwiches, beef, chicken, pork, and pasta dishes. The dinner menu expands to include grilled seafood. They serve beer or you may bring your own choice of alcoholic beverages. There's additional outdoor seating in season.

Follow your nose to the delicious aromas wafting out of the building on Pennlyn Avenue next to the picturesque Cumberland Gap Wedding Chapel on the corner of Colwyn and Pennlyn. The Cookie Cabin and Cake Box offers a variety of tasty, aromatic cookies, candy, breads, and cakes that are a perfect accompaniment for a walk on the Wilderness Road that begins at the Iron Furnace, a historic site down the street.

This iron furnace began operation in the 1820s, a typical representative of an industry made practical in areas with an abundance of ore, limestone, and timber. It required two hundred bushels of charcoal, five hundred pounds of limestone, and two tons of ore to produce one ton of ore. At full capacity this furnace could produce up to six tons of 150-pound ingots, or "pigs." A waterwheel powered the bellows and a giant five-hundred-pound hammer pounded the pigs into shape. In its heyday this furnace shipped iron as far away as Chattanooga. By 1880, more efficient means of smelting made furnaces like this one obsolete.

To the left of the furnace, the Wilderness Road Trail begins its nearly four-hundred-foot climb along the original route of the Wilderness Road to the Cumberland Gap and the old roadway for US 25E, which is now closed to vehicles.

Cumberland Gap has an old-fashioned feel that contrasts with the new four-lane tunnel leading across the Kentucky line to CGNHP.

CGNHP plans to rip up the concrete roadway and restore it to a semblance of the Wilderness Road. Several hiking trails are accessed along the old roadbed including the Tri-State Trail.

There are two motels in town. The Holiday Inn is up on the hill by the "new" road. The Cumberland Gap Inn is downtown in the hollow. There are also two rooms with private baths available in the Cumberland Gap Bed and Breakfast upstairs in the Victorian structure that houses Cumberland Gap Historical Art on Colwyn Avenue.

Cumberland Gap has a variety of annual events including Crazy Aunt Sadie Day, a city-wide yard sale, and Wild West Wagon Days, which features mule barrel racing, potato racing, horse-shoeing demonstrations, live music, a bonfire, and weenie roast. Cruisin' the Gap features a classic car show and parade while Scot-Irish-English Days

The Wilderness Road trail begins at the remains of this historic iron furnace.

highlight traditional activities like clogging, bag-pipe music, storytelling, and moonshine still demonstrations.

The Cumberland Gap Folk Festival focuses on craftspeople who spin wool into yarn, make soap, weave baskets, forge black iron into Civil War–style tableware, and make apple butter. Also featured are Native Americans and longhunters in period costumes and old-time music makers.

Just across the Kentucky line, the CGNHP attracts 1.25 million visitors each year. It's a good idea to begin your visit to the park with a stop at the visitor center where you can pick up maps and tour the excellent museum that tells the story of Cumberland Gap and Kentucky settlement in displays and film. Ask the rangers about such demonstrations as firing a smooth bore black powder rifle and historic programs and reenactments. The visitor center is open 8 A.M. to 5 P.M. daily except Christmas.

A steep, curving road leads from the visitor center to Pinnacle Point, a 2,440-foot overlook on the Kentucky-Virginia line that's reached by a paved, handicapped-accessible trail from the parking lot.

CGNHP is primarily known as a historic site, but it offers outdoor recreation with more than fifty miles of trails for hiking, as well as camping and picnic facilities.

The park requires a free backcountry permit for overnight camping in designated campsites. Horseback riding is available on many of the trails and at the Hensley Settlement area which has a corral and a camp. Horses may be rented from the livery at Cumberland Mountain Outdoor Adventures.

The trails at Little Pinnacle, where park property meets Lincoln Memorial University (LMU) in Harrogate about two miles south of Cumberland Gap, are also popular.

Pinnacle Point offers handicapped-access to sweeping vistas. (Photo courtesy of Cumberland Gap National Historical Park)

Harrogate was established as a resort town in 1892 with the seven-hundred-room Four Seasons Hotel expected to draw visitors to enjoy the healthful climate and mineral waters. Unfortunately for the investors in the project, the expected visitation did not materialize and three years later the hotel was torn down. Rev. and Mrs. A. A. Meyers wanted the hotel property for their Harrow School for the education of local children which had been established at Cumberland Gap in 1890. In 1897 the successor to the Harrow School, LMU, was chartered, and it opened in 1899 on the site of the Four Seasons Hotel as a living memorial to Abraham Lincoln, whose parents probably traveled through Cumberland Gap on their way to Kentucky.

The Abraham Lincoln Museum at LMU is visible from US 25E. Inside the modern structure is one of the largest collections of "Lincolnabilia" in the country. Displays, photographs, and artifacts tell Lincoln's story from his railsplitting, riverboating days to Lincoln the lawyer, congressman, husband, father, and president.

Canoeing the scenic, clear, Class I Powell River a few miles south of Harrogate is also popular. Float trips up to thirty miles may be arranged through outfitters, with prices beginning as low as twenty dollars per canoe for short trips. According to paddler Holly Sherwin in Canoeing in Tennessee, a good put-in for a 10.6-mile float is on US 25E 2.2 miles south of the intersection with TN 63 on Powell River Road with a shuttle take-out on Gap Creek Road off TN 63 about 3.3 miles from the intersection with US 25E.

From Cumberland Gap and Harrogate follow TN 63 to LaFollette, Jacksboro, and Caryville.

All of the following accommodations are Cumberland Gap with zip code 37724, and all telephone listings are area code 423, except where noted.

Accommodations:
Cumberland Gap Bed and Breakfast, 511 Colwyn Ave., 869-2282 daytime or 869-8243 evening.
Cumberland Gap Inn, 630 Brooklyn St., 888-408-0127 or 869-9172.

Attractions:
Abraham Lincoln Museum, Harrogate, 869-6235.
Cumberland Gap Museum, 896-3860.
Cumberland Gap National Historical Park, Middlesboro, KY, 606-248-2817.
Cumberland Gap Outfitters, 869-2999.
Cumberland Mountain Outdoor Adventures, Harrogate, 800-208-4273 or 869-2217.

Dining:
Ye Olde Tea and Coffee Shoppe Restaurant, 800-899-4844 or 869-4844.
Webb's Country Kitchen, 869-5877.

Shopping:
Cumberland Gap Historical Art, 869-8243.
The Depot Gift Shoppe, 869-9031.
Cumberland Gap General Store, 869-2282.
Nail Keg Craft Shoppe, 869-2608.
Past Times in the Gap, 869-2850.

Special Events:
April—Crazy Aunt Sadie Day
May—Wild West Wagon Days
June—Cumberland Gap Folk Festival
July—Cruisin' in the Gap
September—Fall Bluegrass Jam
October—Scot-Irish-English Days, last Sat.
December—Victorian Christmas

Camping:
Cumberland Gap National Historical Park, 606-248-2817.

For More Information:
Cumberland Gap Towne Hall, P.O. Box 78 GAP, 869-3860. Open Mon.–Fri., 8–4.
Cumberland Gap National Historical Park, 606-248-2817. Open daily except Christmas.

23 LaFollette, Jacksboro, Caryville
Lake Country

LaFollette was originally known as Big Creek, a town that grew up in the late 1700s around the development of the area's coal and iron reserves. The Court of Pleas and Quarter Sessions was held here in December 1806 with an old wagon bed constituting the first courthouse. Iron production had been established here prior to that time.

Coal was discovered in the area in 1853, but the mines closed during the Civil War and remained closed until the railroads arrived in 1897.

There are several large resorts with LaFollette addresses along the eight-hundred-mile Norris Lake shoreline. Walleye, sauger, white bass, crappie, catfish, bluegill, largemouth bass, smallmouth bass, spotted bass, and trophy stripers on Norris are waiting for fishermen in the secluded coves created by this flooded ridge and valley impoundment.

A variety of wildlife thrives near the clear blue-green water. It's not uncommon to spot a bald eagle. Visitors are reminded that it is unlawful to approach or disturb a nest, and they are asked to report any such sightings to wildlife officials.

Osprey are also majestic fishermen, but not quite as large as the eagle. They dive, rather than swoop, but land the catch of the day with their talons as eagles do. Wild turkey and white-tailed deer also populate the valleys and low ridges.

Deerfield Resort is situated on a nine-hundred-acre peninsula on the Powell River arm of the lake, across from the Chuck Swan Wildlife Management Area. Deerfield is a highly developed

Lovely Cove Lake State Recreational Area has nature trails, bike paths, camping, swimming, wildlife viewing, and fishing.

vacation destination that offers water sports, an eighteen-hole golf course and a three-thousand-foot private airstrip. Golf packages include luxury condominiums or homes, golf, dinner at the Deerfield Restaurant (which is quite good), and limousine transfers for those arriving by commercial flight at Knoxville.

Big Ridge State Park is on the Clinch River arm of the Norris Lake twelve miles east of I-75 via TN 61 (*see* Lake City-Norris-Clinton for more information on camping, cabins, etc., at Big Ridge).

Jacksboro was laid out during 1808–9 and a stone jail and courthouse were built. This original courthouse was replaced in 1855 by a building that burned in 1894. The third courthouse was decimated by yet another fire in 1926, which destroyed most of the business district.

US 25W between Jacksboro and LaFollette is slowly becoming an interurban commercial route of the kind that occurs when a town of about seventy-five hundred reaches with steady determination toward its nearest neighbors and the closest interstate. This means you'll find strip malls and small shopping centers, gas stations and fast food stops concentrated along this corridor.

Caryville was known as Wheeler's Gap when it was first settled in 1806. It was named for the three Wheeler brothers, Benjamin, Richard, and Thomas who collectively owned more than three thousand acres at the southern end of the "big valley" nestled between the eastern edge of the Cumberland escarpment and the Appalachian Mountains. When the Knoxville-Ohio railroad came to town in 1867, the town became known as Wheeler's Station. It changed its name for the last time around 1880, when citizens desired something more metropolitan sounding and chose Caryville in honor of yet another early family in the area.

Today Caryville is best known to visitors as the home of the 667-acre Cove Lake State Recreational Area on Cove Creek at the western end of Norris Lake.

In the spirit of innovation that was present during the Roosevelt administration of the 1930s, a triad of recreation demonstration areas was established by the Tennessee Valley Authority (TVA), the National Park Service (NPS), and the Civilian Conservation Corps (CCC) in the region northwest of Knoxville. All three, including Norris, Big Ridge, and Cove Lake, are on Norris Lake and the tributaries that feed it.

Cove Lake is located in a pretty valley encompassed by peaks of the Cumberland Mountains. It was created by an auxiliary dam in Caryville and deeded to the state of Tennessee by the U.S. government in 1950.

More than 300 million years ago, this area contained marshes and swamps that created the fossil beds that became coal, which is still mined in the area. Evidence of prehistoric Indians known as Mound Builders at the Cove Lake area indicates habitation from A.D. 1000 to 1200.

At present, much of the Cove Lake area has become marshy, creating the perfect habitat for migrating waterfowl including approximately four hundred wintering Canada geese. Viewing the geese is a popular pastime in winter. You may spot a great blue heron, as there's a heron rookery about two miles up Cove Creek from Norris Dam.

Anglers fish for bass, bluegill, and crappie on the 210-acre lake with a valid Tennessee fishing license. No personally owned boats or motors break the stillness, but you may hear the occasional slap of a pair of oars propelling a rented rowboat. It's a very pretty place, hidden from the eastern edge of I-75, but quickly and easily accessible via US 25W. Caryville also has a Hampton Inn and a Holiday Inn.

Another demonstration project resulted in reclamation of former strip-mined land at Jellico, about thirty miles north of Caryville. Jellico derived its name from angelica root, a member of the parsley family with clusters of white flowers that early settlers used to concoct an intoxicating brew called "jelca" or "gelca." The original settlement was known by the less colorful name of Smithburg until 1883 when it was given the title of Jellico.

Within the present city limits of Jellico, Indian Mountain State Park is on land that was once operated as a surface, or strip, mine. This was one of the first demonstration projects in the Southeast to reclaim abandoned strip mines and show how the altered terrain can be restructured. In the case of Indian Mountain, a camping park offering boating, biking, and hiking nature trails has evolved through support from the U.S. government, the state of Tennessee, the Appalachian Regional Commission, and the Tennessee Wildlife Resources Agency. Jellico has Best Western and Days Inn franchises.

Continue on 25 W to Lake City from Caryville or take I-75 from Jellico to Lake City to continue the loop tour north of Knoxville.

All of the following accommodations are LaFollette with zip code 37766, and all telephone listings are area code 423, except where noted.

Accommodations:
Blue Moon Bed and Breakfast, Rt. 2, Box 236, G-3, 800-340-8455 or 566-1550.
Deerfield Resort, 403 E. Central Ave., 800-458-8455 or 566-0040.
Dogwood Acres Bed and Breakfast and Country Inn, Alder Springs Rd., 566-1207.
Shanghai Resort, Rt. 2, Box 337, exit 134, I-75, Caryville, 37714; 800-245-7651 or 562-7651.

Attractions:
Cove Lake State Recreation Area, Caryville, 566-9701.
Indian River Marina, Jacksboro, 562-5290.

Dining:
Cove Lake State Park Restaurant, Caryville.
Deerfield Restaurant, Deerfield Resort, 800-458-8455 or 566-0040.

Shopping:
Antiques, Etc., Jacksboro, 562-1077.
Limited Editions Antiques and Crafts, 562-4569.
The Attic Window, 562-8220.

Special Events:
August—Annual Coal Miners' Rescue Contest, Cove Lake State Park, Caryville

September—Gospel Singing at Indian Mountain State Park, Jellico

December—Christmas in the Park, Cove Lake State Park, Caryville; Christmas in the Park, Indian Mountain State Park, Jellico

Camping:
Cove Lake State Recreational Area, Caryville, 566-9701.
Indian Mountain State Park, Jellico, 784-7958.
Powell Valley Resort and Marina, 562-5975 or 562-9731.
Shanghai Resort on Norris Lake, 800-245-7651 or 562-7651.

For More Information:
Campbell County Chamber of Commerce, P.O. Box 305, Jacksboro, 37757; 566-0329.
Jellico Tourism, Suite 1, 849 Fifth St., Jellico, 37762; 784-3275.

24 *Lake City, Norris, Clinton*

Along the Shores of Norris Lake

This eighteenth-century gristmill still sells cornmeal at Norris Dam State Park. (Photo courtesy of Tennessee Photographic Services)

Lake City was originally known as Coal Creek when it was founded in the early 1800s after the 1798 treaty of Tellico opened much of the area to settlement. The area was strongly pro-Union and many men joined the Union army despite being branded traitors by fellow Tennesseans.

Coal mining dominated the area after the Civil War when the railroads arrived. The mines were worked by Scots-Irish settlers in the area and miners who came from Pennsylvania seeking work. By 1870 Coal Creek was a boom town with ten businesses including three saloons but the history of coal mining here is tumultuous.

The state of Tennessee passed a law in 1865 that allowed prison laborers to work in the coal mines to pay for their upkeep. Unfortunately, this arrangement put the miners in an even worse bargaining position in trying to obtain reforms like payment in cash rather than scrip, or credit. Scrip was redeemable only at the mine-owned general store, which often increased prices substantially to its captive customers. They also sought improved working conditions including adequate ventilation.

Tensions and frustrations grew until the miners took action and sent the convicts and their guards packing on the train to Knoxville in the summer of 1891. The governor called out the state militia. The miners called on other miners from East Tennessee and the convicts were again escorted out of town.

The third time the convicts were returned to the mines, a crowd of fifteen hundred released the convicts and newspapers around the country began to carry accounts of the "East Tennessee War," and the people of Coal Creek were labeled anarchists. Soldiers arrested more than three hundred members of the community but they refused to name participants. Things bumped along until 1896, when the legislation allowing prison labor in the mines expired.

Two terrible mine disasters claimed the lives of hundreds in the Coal Creek area. In 1902 everyone working in the Fraterville Mine died in an early morning explosion. Many of them died slowly from suffocation due to inadequate ventilation. The community was devastated by the loss. Today Lake City is an interstate town and the mining communities have all but disappeared.

Much like Oak Ridge, Norris was chosen as a site for a town by a federal agency, the Tennessee Valley Authority. TVA was developed from a program introduced by U.S. Sen. George Norris of Nebraska to harness the power of an entire river system for flood control, power production, and navigation.

Norris, a Republican, introduced bills proposing the project on the Clinch River that were vetoed by Presidents Coolidge and Hoover before Roosevelt supported the project in 1933. The Roosevelt Administration in Washington supported programs like the TVA in order to bring economic revitalization to a nation reeling from the ravages of the Great Depression.

Taking its name from the seven-state area drained by the Tennessee River, TVA was an independent government corporation with regional authority that transcended state lines in the interest of flood control, navigation, national defense, and generation and sale of surplus electricity.

TVA's first reservoir, the Norris Dam project, underwent construction beginning in fall 1933. The process involved the condemnation and purchase of more than 150,000 acres. TVA's power of condemnation coupled with a policy of no price bargaining forced citizens to forsake their homeplaces without benefit of negotiation.

Carolyn Sakowski, author of *Touring the East Tennessee Backroads*, discusses the flooding of all of the most desirable farmland and forcing farm owners to move to less productive lands. No assistance of any kind was offered to the tenant farmers who comprised a majority of the families forced to move. Sakowski quotes the general solicitor for TVA as saying, TVA could not risk "being turned into a relief and charitable agency."

Older people with deeper ties to the communities being washed away by the project had more trouble accepting the change. Six families out of three thousand had to be forcibly evicted. Emigrants disinterred their dead and took them on the exodus. Many were forced to forsake a rural way of life as well as their farms. The many "heritage" festivals held in this region celebrate the days and ways that disappeared with the coming of the dam.

But the TVA had its mission and a town was needed to house the twenty-eight hundred workers involved in the construction of a dam containing a million cubic yards of concrete. Rather than house them in temporary camps, a model town was created in 1934, which used a variety of home designs with ultramodern electric appliances and heating equipment. The design included parks and the green belt concept that is so popular in communities across the United States today.

With the completion of the dam in the spring of 1936, water filled the valleys of the Clinch and Powell Rivers. The dam is 1,860 feet long, 265 feet high from its lowest point, and 208 feet thick at the base. The resulting reservoir has a surface area of 34,200 acres, extending

Strutting peacocks put on a show at the Museum of Appalachia.

seventy-two miles up the Clinch and sixty-five miles up the Powell.

TVA has retained a continuous shoreline strip dedicated to public recreation. Along the shores of Norris are state parks, marinas, and resorts as well as numerous boat launch sites and two wildlife management areas.

The 4,038-acre Norris Dam State Park spreads along the shoreline from Norris Dam for more than 400 acres. Facilities include thirty completely equipped cabins, a marina, two camping areas, picnic areas, and an Olympic-sized pool. Visitors will also find a crafts shop with selections reflecting the cultural heritage of the area.

East of the dam, you'll see an eighteenth-century gristmill and the Lenoir Pioneer Museum. The gristmill still grinds corn and sells the meal in the summer.

Trail maps are available at the information center at the dam. The Edge Path, a quarter-mile paved trail that's handicapped accessible, starts at the dam. It meets the Songbird Trail on the east side of the Clinch. As the name implies, the Songbird Trail is of interest to bird watchers. Wildflower enthusiasts will want to take the 3.2-mile River Bluff Trail to see two members of the poppy family, Dutchman's breeches and wood poppy, blooming from March to May, as well as the delicate trout lily which is in bloom from April to June.

There's a pleasant thirteen-mile float trip that begins at the dam and continues toward Oak Ridge. It is a favorite of canoeists during generation periods and popular with fishermen year-round. According to Holly Sherwin in *Canoeing in Tennessee*, you must portage around a TVA weir dam within a mile of putting in at the Songbird Canoe Access. During nongeneration periods, you can put in above the dam at Big Ridge State Park and paddle the coves of Norris Lake. This is a really beautiful trip during the spectacular fall foliage display.

Big Ridge State Park, on the southern shore of Norris Lake on State Highway 61, twelve miles east of I-75, is a heavily forested 3,642-acre rustic park that has fifty-six fully equipped campsites and nineteen rustic cabins adjacent to the lakeshore. In addition to thirty-five miles of shoreline along Norris Lake, Big Ridge has fifteen miles of hiking trails and a forty-nine-acre man-made lake with a sandy beach and canoe, paddle-boat, and flat-bottomed rowboat rentals.

The park is on the south side of the Chuck Swan Wildlife Management Area, a peninsula that encompasses 24,300 acres between the Powell and Clinch River arms of Norris. It's good for wildlife viewing, with white-tailed deer frequently seen feeding along the shoreline at dusk.

The annual Fall Homecoming at the Museum of Appalachia unites crafts-men, musicians, country cooking, and Appalachian heritage.

Our favorite museum dealing with Appalachian culture is the Museum of Appalachia on TN 61 about a mile off I-75 at exit 122 in Norris. This terrific collection is the result of John Rice Irwin's desire to preserve the remnants of a rapidly disappearing way of life.

A native of the hills around Norris, Rice's family had twice been forced to leave their home to make way for government-sponsored projects that dramatically and irreversibly affected everyday living—Norris Dam and Oak Ridge.

The split-rail fence leads to a museum that is special, not just because Irwin managed to collect over 250,000 relics, but for the care he has taken in preserving the history of the items "they made, used, mended, loved, and passed on," including where they came from, what they were used for, and who used them.

There's a collection of thirty authentic structures filled with more artifacts on the sixty-five-acre living history museum including the family cabin of Mark Twain, a log schoolhouse, gristmill, broom and rope house, and church. The grounds are alive with grazing sheep with lambs at their sides, peacocks that strut their stuff, and chicks and ducklings struggling to keep up with their mothers.

The Appalachian Hall of Fame contains an extensive Indian artifact collection that includes fourteen-thousand-year-old Sandia points, effigy pipes and bowls, chunky stones, game balls, stone gorgets, trade beads, and pipes.

Music displays feature many regional musicians in addition to the nationally known Carter Family, Bill Monroe, and Uncle Dave Macon. The collection of musical instruments includes banjos made out of ham cans and hubcaps, fiddles, mandolins, guitars, dobros, and dulcimers.

It'll take several hours to take a quick peek at

everything, but you may want to plan to spend a few days here in October at the Tennessee Fall Homecoming. In addition to heritage demonstrations, about 250 musicians perform during the three-day event. Some are famous professionals like John Hartford and members of the Carter Family, but many play only for the pure joy of the mountain music-making. Festivities begin at 9 A.M. and continue until dark but there's no overnight camping, so make plans to stay nearby.

The hills on the northwestern rim of the Great Valley around Clinton were visited by Indians in the 1400s. Longhunters explored this part of the area known by geologists as the valley and ridge province in 1761. It was originally named Burrville, but the name was changed in 1809 after Aaron Burr's disgrace to honor George Clinton, who was vice president during Thomas Jefferson's administration.

Slaveholders here were in the minority when the issue brought the country to Civil War and residents were deeply divided. After the Civil War, coal mining became a strong factor in the region's economy.

At an altitude of 850 feet, the seat of Anderson County has a population of ninety-four hundred. Clinton had most of its historic structures burned in fires in the early 1900s. A Best Western and a Super 8 Motel welcome visitors.

From 1895 to 1936, Clinton was the home of a thriving pearl industry based on the pearl-producing mussels in the Clinch River. The impoundment of Norris Lake eliminated the mussel habitat but its construction also created thousands of jobs for residents.

The Eagle Bend Fish Hatchery is a one-hundred-acre site operated by the Tennessee Wildlife Resources Agency (TWRA) along the Clinch River that produces walleye, striped bass, bluegill, and largemouth bass.

Bull Run Steam Plant is one of the world's largest and most efficient coal-fired generating plants thanks to the installation of scrubbers on the smokestacks by TVA.

Continue on TN 61 and TN 95 to visit Oak Ridge before completing this tour.

All of the following accommodations are Norris with zip code 37828, and all telephone listings are area code 423, except where noted.

Accommodations:
Brick House Bed and Breakfast, 200 Howard St., Clinton, 37717; 463-8254.
Lamb's Inn Motel and Restaurant, 602 N. Main, Lake City, 37769; 800-638-5720 or 426-2126.
Norris Dam State Park, Box 27, 426-7461.

Attractions:
Bull Run Steam Plant, Clinton, 945-3480.
Eagle Bend Fish Hatchery, Clinton, 457-5135.
Lenoir Museum, Lake City, 494-9688.
Museum of Appalachia, 494-7680 or 494-0514.
Norris Dam Marina, Lake City, 494-8138.
Norris Dam State Park, 426-7461.
Rice Grist Mill, 494-0720.
TVA Norris Dam Reservation, 632-1539.

Shopping:
Clinton Antique Mall, 457-3110.
Market Place Antiques, 463-8635.
Twin Gables Antique Mall, 494-8078.
Valley Antiques, Lake City, 426-9445.

Special Events:
Easter—Redbud Festival, Oliver Springs
May—Mayfest, Oak Ridge
October—Appalachian Homecoming, Norris

Camping:
Big Ridge State Park, 992-5523.
Loyston Point, 632-1500.
Mountain Lake Marina and Campground, 426-6510.
Norris Dam State Park, 426-7461.

For More Information:
Anderson County Tourism Council, P.O. Box 147, 1196 Blockhouse Valley Rd., Clinton; 800-524-3602 or 457-4542.
Anderson County Chamber of Commerce, 457-2559.

25 *Oak Ridge*
The City with a Secret

With a current population around twenty-eight thousand, Oak Ridge did not exist until 1942. At least it didn't exist for anyone except a local farmer named John Hendrix who told his friends and neighbors around the turn of the century he'd "seen" a town located on Black Oak Ridge, complete with railroad lines and factories.

As America stood at the threshold of war with the Japanese during World War II, President Roosevelt received a letter from Albert Einstein explaining that uranium atoms could be split, releasing huge amounts of energy with tremendous military potential. It was known that the Germans had succeeded in splitting uranium atoms in 1939 and it was presumed they were trying to construct an atomic weapon.

Following the Japanese attack on Pearl Harbor, December 7, 1941, and Germany's formal declaration of war on the United States, Gen. Leslie Groves directed an effort authorized by the War Department to construct a top-secret facility devoted to development of the atomic bomb on the sixty-thousand-acre site John Hendrix had "seen" on Black Oak Ridge nearly a half-century earlier.

The land was condemned under eminent domain and the one thousand affected families were given ninety days to move. The facilities at Oak Ridge were developed under the direction of the Manhattan Corps of Engineers which had been formed in June 1942 to oversee the development of atomic energy.

The finest scientists and engineers were recruited from across the country. In 1943 they began to move their families to the remote area in the hills of East Tennessee about seventeen miles

The American Museum of Science and Industry tells the story of the secret city.

west of Knoxville without knowing exactly where they would live or what duties they would perform.

Although originally planned for thirteen thousand inhabitants, Oak Ridge grew to seventy-five thousand becoming Tennessee's fifth largest city in less than three years.

Housing consisted of about six thousand trailers, ninety-eight dormitories, and more than eighty-seven hundred prefabricated single family dwellings that were produced at a rate of one house every thirty minutes at the height of development. Construction workers worked a seventy-hour week or more.

A cyclone fence and a cloak of secrecy surrounded the city. No one over twelve entered or left Oak Ridge without producing identification at one of seven guarded gates leading into the eighty-square-mile compound.

Massive plants known by their wartime code names Y-12 and K-25 were built to separate the uranium 235 isotope from natural uranium producing a fissionable material for atomic weapons. At X-10 was a pilot graphite-moderated nuclear reactor that demonstrated the methods used to create the full-scale plant in Hanford, Washington, that produced the plutonium used for the bomb dropped on Hiroshima on August 6, 1945.

When the Japanese refused to surrender, a second bomb was dropped on Nagasaki three days later. On August 14 the Japanese surrendered. Most members of the Oak Ridge community had no idea that the heart of the project that had so absorbed them was the production of the bomb.

The Atomic Energy Commission (AEC) assumed management of Oak Ridge in 1947 and opened the gates to the public for the first time in 1949. The New Bethel Church Interpretive Center is open to visitors daily. The 1924 church served

as a wartime meeting room for scientists and engineers at Oak Ridge.

In 1948 the X-10 area became the Oak Ridge National Laboratory (ORNL) of the Department of Energy, an internationally recognized non-weapons multiprogram research center for basic sciences, genetics, energy systems, fusion, energy conservation, global climate change, and nuclear safety. A free, self-guided tour is offered Monday through Saturday. A marked overlook on Bethel Valley Road offers a panoramic view of ORNL.

The graphite reactor was decommissioned in 1963 after producing the world's first electricity from nuclear energy. It was the world's foremost source of radioisotopes for medicine, agriculture, and industry for many years and has been designated a National Historic Landmark.

A self-guided motor tour brochure of Oak Ridge available from the visitor center takes you farther along Bethel Valley Road past the graphite reactor to intersect TN 95, the Oak Ridge Turnpike.

The American Museum of Science and Energy (AMSE) on Tulane Avenue is a terrific place to start learning about the Oak Ridge story. Its mission is to personalize science by demonstrating the influences science and society have on each other. A twelve-minute film is helpful to view before entering the museum. You should allow at least an hour for the self-guided tour.

These museums and tours are free, with support provided by the Department of Energy. The Oak Ridge Convention and Visitors Bureau next door to AMSE, offers a variety of self-guided motor tours and maps of area attractions. The visitor center is east off TN 62 and south off the Oak Ridge Turnpike on Tulane Avenue.

Oak Ridge boasts unusual amenities for a town its size including a good variety of ethnic restaurants, the oldest performing symphony orchestra in Tennessee, a civic ballet, and a museum of fine arts.

The Jackson Square Historic Park is the original Oak Ridge townsite. It now has a fountain, gardens, and historic displays surrounded by a retail district. Jackson Square is north of the Oak Ridge Turnpike between New York Avenue and Georgia Avenue. Accommodations include Comfort Inn, Days Inn, Garden Plaza Hotel, Hampton Inn, and a Super 8 Motel.

Outdoor recreational opportunities include water sports at the TVA's Melton Hill Lake. This 5,690-surface-acre impoundment of the Clinch River is fed by the icy waters emerging from Norris Dam. This means cool water species like northern pike are found here along with crappie, bream, large and smallmouth bass, rockfish, and hybrids. Completed in 1963, Melton Hill is forty-four miles long and has 173 miles of shoreline. Unlike Norris which can experience drawdowns of seventy-five feet, Melton Hill has minimal drawdowns that generally don't exceed six feet.

The four-mile flatwater Haw Ridge Canoe Trail along the meandering shoreline of the Clinch River/Melton Hill Reservoir begins at Solway Park on Edgemoor Road. A ramp for fishing boats is available at Haw Ridge Park and Oak Ridge Marina. The marina is east of town about two miles south of the Oak Ridge Turnpike on Melton Lake Drive.

The hiking trails at the University of Tennessee Arboretum range from 0.5 miles to 4.0 miles with color-coded trail markers and interpretative signs along the way. The grounds are open for walking daily from 8 A.M. to sunset. Hikers also enjoy the 7.5-mile North Ridge Trail which passes through city-owned greenbelt land. The trail is marked with white trail markers and the eight access trails are designated with blue trail markers. A trail map is available at the Oak Ridge Convention and Visitors Bureau.

Return to Knoxville via TN 62 to complete this loop or proceed to Harriman on TN 61 to begin the next loop tour on the Cumberland Plateau.

All of the following accommodations are Oak Ridge with zip code 37830, and all telephone listings are area code 423, except where noted.

Accommodations:
Oak Ridge Inn, 420 S. Illinois Ave., 483-4371.

Attractions:
American Museum of Science and Industry, 356-3200.
Children's Museum of Oak Ridge, 482-1074.
Historic Graphite Reactor, 574-4160.
Jackson Square Historic Park, 482-8450.
New Bethel Church Museum, 574-4160.
Oak Ridge Art Center, 482-1442.
University of Tennessee Arboretum, 483-3571.

Dining:
Atomic Cafe and Catering Co., 483-4363.
Ayala, 482-6397.
Big Ed's Pizza, 482-4885.
Ham'N'Goody's, 483-7083.
Jefferson Fountain/Restaurant, 482-1141.
Mustard Seed Cafe, in Oak Ridge Mall, 482-9952.
Riverwatch, 481-3200.
The Bleu Hound Grille, 481-6101.
The Daily Grind, 483-9200.
The Soup Kitchen, 482-3525.
Village Restaurant, 483-1675.

Shopping:
Antiques and Attractions, 482-1257.
Larry's Antiques, 482-0046.
Out House Antiques, 482-7466.

For More Information:
Oak Ridge Convention and Visitors Bureau, 302 S. Tulane Ave., 800-887-3429 or 482-7821.
Anderson County Tourism Council, 800-524-3602.

The Battle Above the Clouds took place in 1863, on the sides of Lookout Mountain overlooking Chattanooga.

MIDDLE TENNESSEE

Although we begin Middle Tennessee's loop tours on the lovely, rugged Cumberland Plateau visiting utopian societies, scenic wonders, and historic sites, travelers to Middle Tennessee often come to visit Nashville, the state capital and the second largest city in the state.

Nashville has a thriving country music industry that invites fans to annual events like Fan Fair and Tin Pan South, but also offers regular entertainment in a variety of venues ranging from intimate seating at the Bluebird Cafe to live Grand Ole Opry shows every weekend and genres from country to classical, blues to Broadway. Of course, there's always the opportunity for informal "star gazing" in neighborhood restaurants and shops.

In Nashville you also encounter the home of President Andrew Jackson and the Natchez Trace Parkway, a scenic corridor maintained by the National Park Service extending 450 miles from Nashville to Natchez, Mississippi. Along the way, interpretive markers at points of interest, picnic areas, waterfalls, and historic sites invite visitors to experience the beautiful, historic Natchez Trace.

Nashville is also home to the fabulous Opryland Hotel, a host of fine dining establishments, the lively Second Avenue historic district which includes the Wildhorse Saloon, Planet Hollywood, and the Hard Rock Cafe and a large antiques shopping district, in addition to National Football League and National Hockey League franchises. So even if you're not a country music fan, you'll find plenty to keep you entertained.

The Middle Tennessee loops orient to Nashville, I-40, I-24, I-65, and Chattanooga. The rolling hills of Middle Tennessee surrounding Nashville are home to Civil War battlefields and antebellum homes, charming communities built around traditional courthouse squares lined with antique and specialty shops, as well as bed and breakfasts and restaurants serving down-home-style meat-and-threes. Here you'll find canoe liveries, lakes for water sports, the final resting place of Strolling Jim, champion Tennessee Walking Horse, the home of the poet laureate of Tennessee, and the distillery known by most of the country as the producer of Tennessee's finest sippin' whiskey, Jack Daniel's.

As you continue south, the South Cumberland Recreation Area welcomes outdoors enthusiasts. Altamont, Tracy City, Monteagle with its historic assembly grounds, and the lovely campus of the University of the South at Sewanee offer other good reasons to visit.

Chattanooga, Tennessee's environmental city, welcomes visitors to the Tennessee Aquarium, the Chattanooga Choo Choo, the Incline Railway, Ruby Falls, and as all those painted barns proclaim, no trip is complete without taking the children to see Rock City.

 Loop 5

26 *Kingston*
Gateway to the
Cumberland Plateau

Settlement began in what is now Kingston in 1792 when a military post known as Southwest Point was established. Gen. John Sevier commanded the territorial militia strategically stationed here on a hill near several fords across the Tennessee and Clinch Rivers.

Southwest Point was a noted place on the western frontier. Many travelers from Knoxville to Nashville journeyed over the Cumberland Road accompanied by militiamen from Southwest Point.

In 1795 the first important road connecting Knoxville and Nashville, known as the Avery Trace, was completed. As travel to the west increased, the population around the fort grew and the community known as Kingston developed. In 1796 Tennessee became the sixteenth state admitted to the Union. By 1797 the militia had been replaced with federal troops who were charged with keeping the peace by preventing illegal settlement on remaining Cherokee lands in Tennessee. From 1801 to 1807, Southwest Point was the headquarters of the principal agent to the Cherokee Nation. Sam Houston was the Indian subagent at Fort Southwest Point long before he became governor of Tennessee in 1827.

Fort Southwest Point has been partially reconstructed on its original foundations. The site presently includes a welcome center, the Fort

Southwest Point Museum, a barracks, a blockhouse, and 250 feet of palisade walls. The museum is open daily April 1–December 15. A walking trail follows the lake near the Fort.

Chartered in 1799, Kingston was a thriving town strategically located at the junction of southeastern overland and river trade routes.

On September 21, 1807, Kingston was the site of a one-day session of the Tennessee state legislature that was the technical fulfillment of terms in a treaty with the Cherokee by establishing the Tennessee capital at Kingston, though only for one day.

Today Kingston sits between I-40 and the north shore of Watts Bar Lake, a TVA project fed by the Tennessee, Clinch, and Emory Rivers. The skyline to the north is dominated by the towering smoke stacks of the Kingston Fossil Fuel Plant. If you take the thirty-minute tour offered weekdays, you'll learn they're over one thousand feet high. Fishermen and gamefish are drawn to the fertile warm waters in the vicinity of the "steam" plant.

The Pennybacker House offers good soups, salads, and a chicken salad that's widely recommended.

Another of Tennessee's remaining antebellum courthouses, the old Roane County Courthouse now houses the Roane County Museum of History.

The antebellum Pennybacker House Bed and Breakfast has a restaurant on the premises that serves lunch for the public. Handee Burger serves three meals daily. Mama Mia's serves Italian dishes, sandwiches, and freshly made pizzas. National franchises include Comfort Inn, Days Inn, and Family Inn.

The Roane County Museum of History is in the 1856 Greek Revival courthouse. Inside you'll find artifacts and displays of Roane County and Tennessee history. The new Roane County Courthouse, built in 1975, is down the street.

With thirty-nine thousand surface acres, Watts Bar Lake is the largest TVA impoundment in East Tennessee. It is 96 miles long with 771 miles of shoreline. Commercial docks and more than sixty public boat ramps ensure good accessibility. Fishermen eagerly seek bluegill, crappie, large and smallmouth bass as well as big striper, hybrids, and cats. A city park hugs the northern shoreline.

Long Island Marina is open daily while Watts Bar Campground and Marina is open from mid-March to mid-November with forty-five RV sites and a swimming pool. Blue Springs Marina offers the Ship and Shore Restaurant and four cabins with kitchens and cable TV. Four Seasons RV Park, as you would guess, has forty-five sites available year-round with a swimming pool for summer enjoyment.

A visit to the Whitestone Country Inn also lets you enjoy Watts Bar Lake. Whitestone is the culmination of thirty years of observations by Paul and Jean Cowell as they visited resorts in the United States and Europe.

The result is a delightful 14,500-square-foot country estate on 275 acres with seven thousand feet of lake frontage surrounded by the Paint Rock Wildlife Waterfowl Refuge.

The Whitestone Country Inn sits high on a hill overlooking Watts Bar Lake.

Nearly three thousand feet of decks and porches invite visitors to relax and enjoy the view of Watts Bar Lake accented by the towering peaks of the Great Smoky Mountains rising beyond. Canoes and paddleboats are available for guests. Six miles of walking trails invite you to explore the grounds.

Each extra large guest room or suite has a big, comfortable bed; fireplace; bath with whirlpool tub; and TV and VCR. The rooms have individual heating and air-conditioning units, ceiling fans, and controls for the central sound system.

A sunny breakfast room toward the back of the house lets guests enjoy the view along with a big country breakfast. The dining room is used for lunch and dinner, available by reservation. It's a great place to enjoy some well-deserved peace and quiet.

If you can tear yourself away, Harriman, the town temperance built, is the next stop on the Upper Cumberland loop tour via I-40 or US 70 to TN 29.

All of the following accommodations are Kingston with zip code 37763, and all telephone listings are area code 423, except where noted.

Accommodations:
Blue Springs Marina, 3952 River Rd., 376-7298.
Whitestone Country Inn, 1200 Paint Rock Rd., 888-247-2464 or 376-0113.

Attractions:
Fort Southwest Point and Museum, 376-3641.
Kingston Fossil Fuel Plant, 376-9826.
Roane County Museum of History and Art, 376-9211.
Watts Bar Lake, 376-1356.

Dining:
Handee Burger, 376-2186.
Mama Mia's Pizzeria and Restaurant, 376-5050.
The Pennybacker House of Fine Food, 717-3706.
Ship and Shore Restaurant, Blue Springs Marina, 376-7298.

Shopping:
The Cottage Antiques and Collectibles, 376-1926.

Special Events:
June—First Fridays at the Fort
October—Kingston Country Fair
December—Kingston Christmas Home Tours

Camping:
Four Seasons Campground, 376-4568.
Riley Creek Campground, Muscle Shoals, AL, 205-386-2006.
Soaring Eagle Campground, W. Lenoir City, 376-9017.
Watts Bar Lake Campground and Marina, 376-8847.

For More Information:
Roane County Visitors Bureau, N. Kentucky St., P.O. Box 1033, Kingston, 37763; 800-386-4686 or 376-4201.

27 *Harriman*
The Utopia of Temperance

The town of Harriman was envisioned by Col. Robert King Byrd in 1845, when he established a plantation here on large holdings he'd purchased. Unfortunately, Byrd who served as a first lieutenant in the Mexican War and colonel of First Tennessee Infantry, USA, died five years before a city was founded at the site he believed "nature had ordained a town should be."

In 1889 the East Tennessee Land Company bought 10,000 acres of his land. The company platted 343 acres and advertised the establishment of a town of social temperance across the country. Thousands came to the Great Land Sale of 1890. On February 26, 1890, the first 574 lots were sold at auction. The community was named for Union Gen. Walter Harriman.

According to Tennessee Historical Markers published by the Tennessee Historical Commission, in 1891 the movement to found the city was led by Union Gen. Clinton B. Fisk, founder of Fisk University and Prohibition candidate for the presidency of the United States in 1888.

Harriman was incorporated to be "an ideal industrial city, an object lesson for thrift, sobriety, superior intelligence and exalted character, where workers would be uncorrupted by Demon Rum."

The *WPA Guide to Tennessee* indicates the Women's Christian Temperance Union had a strong influence on the development of the town. The first office building of the East Tennessee Land Company became the home of the American Temperance University, founded in 1893. This three-story building now houses the Harriman Heritage Museum on Roane Street, which tells the story of the "City that temperance built" with artifacts, photos, and memorabilia.

Bushrod Hall Bed and Breakfast is listed in the National Register of Historic Places. The 1892 Victorian home on the hill was built using the finest imported components for its massive oak staircase. Situated in the ten-block Cornstalk Heights Historic District, the former Bushrod W. James Hall of Domestic Science for Young Ladies, has been lovingly restored by Nancy and Bob

This impressive Victorian structure now houses the Harriman Heritage Museum.

Ward. A variety of rooms, all with private baths, are available. Gourmet breakfasts are served and, best of all, Nancy conducts "junking tours" for her guests to area flea markets and antique shops every third weekend. National franchises include Best Western, Holiday Inn, and Scottish Inn.

Dixie's Restaurant has a long tradition of serving home-style cooking. It's also the site of popular Friday night gospel singing. The Harriman Antique Auction is scheduled for Sundays at two, but you should call for dates. If there's no auction and you're looking for antiques, check Harriman Antique Mall, Cornstalk Heights Antiques and Collectibles, Out of the Past Antiques or Wright's Antiques. The last time we visited, there was a good selection of antique furniture at Out of the Past.

Continue on TN 328 to the junction of US 27 to Wartburg.

All of the following accommodations are Harriman with zip code 37748, and all telephone listings are area code 423, except where noted.

Accommodations:
Bushrod Hall Bed and Breakfast, 422 Cumberland St. NE, 888-880-8406 or 882-8406.

Attractions:
Harriman Heritage Museum, 882-0335.

Special Events:
September—Street Festival

Dining:
Dixie's Restaurant, 882-1802.

Shopping:
Harriman Antique Auction, 882-2756 or 376-7758.
Out of the Past Antiques, 882-9756.
Wright's Antiques, 882-6060.

For More Information:
Roane County Visitors Bureau, N. Kentucky St., P.O. Box 1033, Kingston, 37763; 800-386-4686 or 376-4201.

28 *Wartburg*
Germanic Dreams on the Cumberland Plateau

Wartburg was settled in 1845 by Swiss and German immigrants who had read about it in a book written in 1834 by a fellow German who described the area favorably.

According to the *WPA Guide to Tennessee*, it was named for Wartburg, Germany. On the other hand, Carolyn Sakowski in *Touring East Tennessee Backroads* says it was named for the castle in Thuringia, Germany, where Martin Luther translated the Bible into German. At any rate, more than 170,000 acres were purchased by the East Tennessee Colonization Company with the intent of promoting colonization. Agents met German immigrants arriving in U.S. port cities and recruited colonists in Germany and Switzerland as well.

In 1845 the first fifty settlers arrived and many stayed at one of the first buildings in town, known as the Immigration House, until land could be cleared and dwellings built. Most chose to move to outlying farm lands rather than build houses in town.

Dissension arose because the settlement's only minister, a Lutheran pastor, refused to preach or serve communion to the Swiss Reformed members of the community, which inflamed them considerably, causing many to abandon their dreams of life on the Cumberland Plateau.

The community endured, and by 1870 Wartburg had been established as the county seat of Morgan County, named for Gen. Daniel Morgan, a Revolutionary War veteran.

Nearby, on TN 62 at the intersection of Court and Maiden Streets is the headquarters of

Frozen Head State Park Visitor Center is open daily.

the Obed Wild and Scenic River, one of only three Wild and Scenic Rivers in the Southeast. The visitor center offers information about difficulty ratings for various sections of the river system. It is considered one of the premier white-water areas in the eastern United States from December to April.

The Obed passes through portions of the Catoosa Wildlife Management Area, a rugged landscape with spectacular gorges up to five hundred feet deep. Approximately 1.5 miles out of Wartburg you'll find the forty-five-foot-high Potter's Falls on Crooked Fork Creek.

Frozen Head State Park is about five miles out of Wartburg off TN 62 and is reached by passing through Morgan County Regional Correctional Facility, the former Brushy Mountain State Honor Farm where convicts raised produce and farm animals. The top of Frozen Head Mountain, at 3,324 feet, is often covered in ice and snow in winter, which gives this landmark its name. More than

fifty miles of trails ranging from easy to strenuous crisscross the ten-thousand-acre Frozen Head State Park and Natural Area. Trail maps and information about backcountry camping permits are available at the visitor center. There's also a primitive campground with bathhouses and restrooms but no water or electrical hookups.

About 12.5 miles out of Wartburg is the old community of Oakdale which was home to a small colony of dark-skinned people known as Melungeons. Whites discovered the dark-skinned, fine-featured Melungeons as they advanced through the mountains toward the west.

Mystery shrouds the origins of these people who were found only in the mountainous regions of eastern Tennessee and North Carolina. One theory postulated that they were the descendants of the "lost colony." The Melungeons themselves believed they were "port-ghee," but had no knowledge of when and how their ancestors arrived from Portugal.

Proceed north on US 27 to visit historic Rugby and the Big South Fork National River and Recreation Area.

All of the following accommodations are Wartburg with zip code 37887, and all telephone listings are area code 423, except where noted.

Accommodations:
Clear Creek Retreat, 487 Ridge Rd., Lancing, 37770; 573-4089.

Attractions:
Obed National Wild and Scenic River, 346-6294.
Frozen Head State Natural Area, 346-3318.

Special Events:
April—Frozen Head State Park and Natural Area Wildflower Pilgrimage
August—Folklife Festival

Camping:
Frozen Head State Park and Natural Area, 346-3318.

For More Information:
County Executive Office, P.O. Box 387, 346-6288.
Catoosa Wildlife Management Area, 216 E. Penfield, Crossville, 38555; 800-262-6704 or 931-484-9571.
Frozen Head State Park and Natural Area, Rt. 2, Box 321, 346-3318.

29 *Rugby, Jamestown, Pall Mall*

Land of Heroes and Dreams

Rugby was founded in 1880 by a group of English investors and a visionary novelist, statesman, philanthropist, and social reformer named Thomas Hughes. Hughes envisioned a utopian community where the disenfranchised younger sons of British aristocrats could use their natural talents without social restrictions in business, trade, or manual arts.

In October 1880 the town officially opened and Hughes's speech talked of "this lovely corner of God's earth" and treating it "lovingly and reverently."

Among the first organizations formed was the Library and Reading Room Society. More than five thousand volumes were donated to the colony in honor of Hughes by various publishing houses and private individuals. Seven thousand volumes published between 1687 and 1899 remain in the original library building, which continues to shelter one of the finest collections of Victorian literature in America.

Today more than twenty historic structures remain in Rugby and several are open for tours including the Thomas Hughes Library, the Schoolhouse Visitor Centre, Christ Church Episcopal, and Kingstone Lisle, Hughes's Gothic cottage. Tours are available daily February through

The Thomas Hughes Library at Rugby has a fine collection of Victorian literature.

December and by appointment in January beginning at the Schoolhouse Visitor Centre.

As we walked through the buildings that are the remnants of the splendor that men sought to create here, it was bittersweet to imagine the hope with which they looked upon this Cumberland Plateau settlement. We certainly fell under its spell and believe you will as well.

The Harrow Road Cafe serves sandwiches, salads, and hot platters. You can shop for gifts ranging from handcrafted library chairs and quilts to British Isles products from the Commissary.

Seasonal events include Christmas at Rugby with visits to seven historic and reconstructed buildings decorated with holly, ivy, and other evergreens, costumed actors playing early Rugby personages, carolers at historic Christ Church Episcopal, and a four-course Christmas dinner served at the Harrow Road Cafe. Dinner tickets must be purchased in advance by mail or phone.

Reservations are available for lodging year-round in historic bed and breakfasts like the Newbury House and the Pioneer Cottage. The Newbury House has enough modern amenities to keep you comfortable but retains its Victorian furnishings and a wood burning fireplace in the parlor just right for curling up in front of. There are five bedrooms, most with private baths, and breakfast at the Harrow Road Cafe is included in the room rate.

Grey Gables Bed and Breakfast Inn is about a mile west of Rugby. Although it is of modern construction, its eight bedrooms are filled with antiques and country furniture collected by the innkeepers, Rugby natives Bill and Linda Brooks Jones who promise you'll receive a "hearty welcome, a restful bed, and a full table."

Fare at Grey Gables includes lodging, evening

Christ Church Episcopal is one of Rugby's historic buildings open for tours.

meal, and country breakfast. Special dinners with a variety of entertainments are offered throughout the year including Thanksgiving, Christmas High Tea Dinner complete with Madrigal singers, and Valentine Candlelight dining.

If you're ready to leave Rugby, you have two choices. The first option is to return to US 27 and travel north to Oneida, where you turn west on TN 297 to enter the Big South Fork National River and Recreation Area (BSFNRRA). The other option is to continue west on TN 52 to

The Newberry House retains its cozy Victorian parlor but offers modern conveniences for overnight guests.

visit Northrup Falls, Allardt, and Jamestown.

Oneida is on the eastern end of the BSFN-RRA about five miles from one of the most dramatic overlooks in the park at the East Rim. The spectacular view is only a five-minute walk from the parking lot off TN 297—if you take your time!

Although Oneida has historically been a shipping point for timber, coal, farm products, and livestock, it draws an increasing number of visitors because of the availability of outdoors recreation at its sprawling neighbor, the BSFNRRA. Each fall the Steam Train Autumn Festival sponsors music, arts and crafts, and a steam train that runs from Chattanooga to Oneida.

The BSFNRRA gets its name from the south fork of the Cumberland River which cut through the hard capstone layer of rock and created deep dramatic gorges of five hundred feet or more in the softer sandstone layers beneath.

As early as 1881 the Army Corps of Engineers was looking for ways to improve the useful-ness of the Big South Fork. Initially, improvements in navigation were considered, followed in the 1950s and 1960s by proposals for a dam at Devils Jump.

In 1966 the Tennessee Citizens for Wilderness Planning set out to find a permanent solution that would protect the scenic river gorge. They tried a variety of options and finally found a solution with the help of then-Tennessee Sen. Howard Baker, who drafted legislation creating the Big South Fork National River and Recreation Area.

The bill specified that the Army Corps of Engineers would plan and develop the park, but the National Park Service would ultimately take over its management and preservation. The result is 123,000 acres of multiple-use areas that include camping, fishing, hunting, hiking, horseback riding, mountain biking, white-water rafting, and canoeing.

A stop at the Bandywood Visitor Center will get you detailed information about hiking trails, camping permits, and special activities conducted by the park naturalists.

Charit Creek Lodge offers the only accommodations inside BSFNRRA. It is accessible only by horseback or on foot via one of several trails.

The lodge is situated in a lovely pasture ringed by bluffs at the confluence of Charit Creek and Station Camp Creek. The log cabin built here in 1817 by a white hunter named Jonathan Blevins is now part of Charit Creek Lodge.

Charit Creek Lodge offers hikers and horseback riders accommodations and hearty meals in rooms or group cabins. There's a stable for horses. As required by Tennessee law, all horses must have proof of current, negative Coggins test before being stabled. Whether you ride or hike in, it's a worthwhile adventure. You'll receive detailed directions after making your reservation.

BSFNRRA trails lead past many outstanding geologic features including Indian Rockhouses and Twin Arches (two of the largest arches in the eastern United State), waterfalls, and spectacular overlooks.

The Kentucky portion of BSFNRRA includes the Blue Heron Outdoor Historical Museum. Interpretive exhibits, audio tapes, and reconstructed buildings tell the stories of coal mining and logging in the area. You may also ride the Big South Fork Scenic Railway from Stearns, Kentucky, to Blue Heron.

If you decide to exercise the second option, and forego the BSFNRRA on your way to Allardt, watch for the small sign indicating the turn off TN 52 to visit Colditz Cove Natural Area and Northrup Falls. A one-mile loop trail takes you to the pristine sixty-foot-high Northrup Falls.

Allardt was founded by Germans at about the same time the British were settling Rugby. German land agent Bruno Gernt envisioned a self-sufficient model city on the Cumberland Plateau. He sold nine thousand acres in parcels of twenty-five, fifty, and two hundred acres at four dollars per acre the first year. The town was laid out geometrically and named for Gernt's partner, M. H. Allardt, who died before settlement began.

Gernt recruited skilled craftsmen and professionals from Germany and soon Allardt led the region in production of hay, fruits, and vegetables.

The south fork of the Cumberland River cuts five-hundred-foot gorges in the upper Cumberland Plateau.

For more than fifty years, Gernt never ceased his efforts to have Allardt be all he dreamed it could be.

Lodging is available at the Old Allardt Schoolhouse and East Fork Stables, a twelve-thousand-acre family-owned horseback facility that was created when descendants of Bruno Gernt decided to make their scenic property available to the public. It offers a sixty-three-stall horse barn and more than one hundred miles of horse trails, a full hookup campground, primitive campsites, and fully equipped cabins and cottages, including the restored National Register of Historic Places farmhouse of Bruno Gernt.

Continue west on TN 52 to Jamestown, the county seat of Fentress County. It was built upon the site of a Cherokee camp known to whites as Sand Springs. Jamestown was home for several years to John M. Clemens, father of Samuel L. (Mark Twain). Once the holder of large land grants in this county, the elder Clemens drew the plans for the first courthouse and jail, which were completed in 1827.

From the sequence of events, it appears unde-niable that Samuel, although born in Missouri five months after the family left Jamestown, was conceived in Fentress County. The Mark Twain Spring Park is named to honor this fact, as is the Mark Twain Restaurant. Jamestown appears in Mark Twain's novel *The Gilded Age* as "Obedstown."

Jamestown is headquarters for what is billed as "The World's Longest Yard Sale" in mid-August every year along the US 127 corridor. This route roughly parallels I-75 for 450 miles from just south of Cincinnati, Ohio, at Covington, Kentucky, to Chattanooga where it merges with the Lookout Mountain Parkway to Gadsden, Alabama.

South of Jamestown on US 127 visit the Cumberland Mountain General Store, A&M Cafe and Soda Fountain, and Antique Alley at Clarkrange. At the Mennonite community at Muddy Pond on TN 62 west of Clarkrange, a number of family-owned businesses offer baked goods, sorghum molasses, and other products. The Muddy Pond General Store features hand-made quilts, pottery, and a variety of crafts and

Large Indian rockhouses found in and near the BSFNRRA once sheltered men and livestock.

furniture. Although sorghum is shipped by the Guenther Family year-round, September and October bring sorghum-making to Muddy Pond and the public is invited to watch the process.

Highland Manor, the oldest winery in Tennessee, offers free tours to observe the wine-making process and tastings of varieties including Chardonnay, cabernet sauvignon, and Riesling, daily except Sunday. They continue to win awards for their fine wines, and their nonvintage white table wine has been praised by wine critic Coleman Andrews in his book, *Wines of America.* Their muscadine wine is so popular that there's usually a long waiting list. They also produce muscadine champagne.

US 127 travels through spectacular scenery, historic sites, and recreational areas with antiques, arts and crafts, and food to be sampled along the way. The Quilt Country Inn Bed and Breakfast, four miles north of Jamestown on US 127, has five large antique-furnished bedrooms and serves a large buffet-style breakfast.

Seven miles northwest of town on US 127 is the Alvin C. York State Historic Area. The York family was well known in Fentress County. The first deed conveying land in Fentress County in the fall of 1800 was made to Conrad Pile, the great-great grandfather of the reluctant World War I hero.

York's religious beliefs led him to apply for conscientious objector status, but his application was rejected and he left the Wolf River Valley for two years of military service.

In a strange twist of fate, during a legendary firefight in the Argonne Forest in France on October 18, 1918, armed with a rifle, a Colt .45 pistol, and the marksmanship he'd acquired as a backwoods hunter on the Cumberland Plateau, he shot 25 Germans who were manning "a machine gun

Northrup Falls, in the Colditz Cove Natural Area, offers a cool respite on hot summer days.

nest which was pouring deadly and incessant fire upon his platoon," according to the citation for his Congressional Medal of Honor. After a rush of 7 German soldiers failed when York took aim and felled them one by one, 132 Germans including 4 officers, surrendered to Corporal York and the surviving 7 men in his squadron.

He became America's most decorated World War I soldier and found himself the subject of

Both the home of World War I hero Alvin York and the family gristmill on the Wolf River are open to the public.

numerous newspaper and magazine articles. He returned to the United States in May 1919 to a New York ticker-tape parade, a banquet at the Waldorf-Astoria hotel, and a visit to the White House.

Upon his return, York quickly made his way home to his beloved Wolf Valley and his long-time sweetheart, Gracie Williams. They were married one week after his homecoming and moved into a handsome frame house on a 385-acre farm which grate-

ful Tennesseans had raised money to purchase.

The Yorks had ten children, all named for famous Americans including Betsy Ross and Thomas Jefferson. One of their sons, Andrew Jackson York, is the park ranger. Having Andy here to greet visitors with stories about his famous father adds an extra charm to this spot. Both the home and York family gristmill are open to the public. There's also a nice picnic area alongside the Wolf.

Granny's Guesthouse nearby welcomes overnight visitors to this lovely, peaceful valley. Hosts Billy and Pat Conaster say it's like a bed and breakfast but without the breakfast. On a working farm, the turn-of-the-century house has three bedrooms and one bath and a fully equipped kitchen where you can fix your favorite breakfast, as long as you brought along some provisions.

The Valley of The Three Forks Antique and Gift Shop, across from the Grist Mill Park, has picnic supplies, freshly baked goods, and mountain music tapes in addition to antiques, hand-spun yarns, and Susanne Wheeler's woven creations.

While visiting Pall Mall keep an eye out for Possum Trot Antiques. They're open daily with antique furniture, glassware, books, toys, and dolls.

A bit farther down the road toward Byrdstown, Forbus General Store was founded in 1892. Proprietor Joe Sells is a friendly sort who offers snippets of local history to visitors who stop by for local products like sorghum molasses, jams and jellies from Muddy Pond, baskets, and cured country hams found among items like kerosene lamps, galvanized tubs, hammer handles, jeans, nails, and food for area residents.

Twelve miles northeast of Jamestown on TN 154, the 11,752-acre Pickett State Rustic Park was Tennessee's first state park, developed by the Civilian Conservation Corps on land obtained from the Stearns Coal and Lumber Company. Within the surrounding forest are unusual rock formations, like Indian rock houses and natural bridges, numerous caves, and botanical diversity second only to the Great Smoky Mountains National Park.

Stop at the park office for maps of more than 58 miles of hiking trails, including scenic loop trails of as little as 0.5 miles, which are lined with rhododendron and wildflowers. A 0.25-mile trail leads to Hazard Cave where stone artifacts found in the cave indicate occupation by prehistoric Indians. At night glowworms in the cave provide a memorable sight.

On the opposite side of the road from the Hazard Cave parking area is the 0.2-mile trail to Indian Rockhouse, a massive rock overhang that gives you a good idea of what hiking in Pickett is all about. Some trails, like Hidden Passage Trail, connect with trails in BSFNRRA. Swimming and fishing are popular activities on the picturesque Arch Lake as long as you get there before the lake is drained after the fall foliage color change each year.

Canoes and fishing boats are rented for as little as $4.50 per half day. No personally owned boat motors are allowed to break the peacefulness. You must have a valid Tennessee fishing license to pursue bream, black bass, and rainbow trout. Hunting in-season is allowed at Pickett, except in safety zones around the park.

In addition to campsites for tent and trailer camping, Pickett has rustic stone cabins with fireplace, kitchen, bath, and screened porch; chalets with bedroom, bath, fireplace, and spiral staircase; and rustic villas with fireplace, three bedrooms, and two baths.

From Pall Mall, follow TN 325 to Byrdstown.

All of the following accommodations are Jamestown with zip code 38556, and all telephone listings are area code 931, except where noted. Be aware that both the area code and the time zone change on this portion of the loop tour, so you will move in and out of area codes and time zones as you travel.

Accommodations:
Big South Fork Wilderness Resorts, Station Camp Rd., Oneida, 37841; 423-569-9125.
Charit Creek Lodge, Reservation office, 250 Apple Valley Rd., Sevierville, 37362; 423-429-5704.
Clear Fork Farm Bed and Breakfast, 328 Shirley Ford Rd., Robbins, 37852; 423-628-2967.
East Fork Stables, P.O. Box 156, Allardt, 38504; 800-97TRAIL or 879-1176.
Galloway Inn, 299 Galloway Dr., Hwy. 27S., Oneida, 37841; 423-569-8835.
Granny's Guesthouse, Pall Mall, 38577; 879-5218.
Grey Gables Bed and Breakfast Inn, Hwy. 52, P.O. Box 52, 800-347-5252 or 423-628-5252.
Holiday Inn Big South Fork, Junction Hwys. 27 and 63, Helenwood, 37755; 423-663-4100.
Log Cabin Rentals, Allardt, 800-771-8940.
Newbury House at Historic Rugby, Hwy. 52, 423-628-2430 or 423-628-2441.
Pickett State Rustic Park, Rock Creek Route, Box 174, TN 154, 879-5821.
Quilt Country Inn, 1457 N. York Hwy. 127, 879-2001 or 879-1033.
School House Bed and Breakfast, Hwy. 296, Allardt, 38504; 879-9517 or 879-8056.
Wildwood Lodge Bed and Breakfast, Box 160, HC 61, Rock Creek Rt., 879-9454.

Attractions:
Alvin C. York State Historic Area, Pall Mall, 879-4026.
Big South Fork National River and Recreation Area, 879-3625.
Colditz Cove/Northrup Falls.
East Fork Stables, 800-97-TRAIL.
Highland Manor Winery Inc., 879-9519.
Muddy Pond Sorghum Mill, Monterey, 445-3357.
Historic Rugby Schoolhouse Visitor Center, Rugby, 423-628-2441.

Dining:
Allardt Restaurant, Allardt, 879-8051.
Beggar's Castle, Allardt, 879-8993.
Harrow Road Cafe, Rugby, 423-628-2269.

The Loft, Oneida, 423-569-4158.
The Mark Twain Restaurant, Jamestown, 879-2811.
Ruth's Family Restaurant, Jamestown, 879-8182.
Tobe's Restaurant, Oneida, 423-569-4689.

Shopping:
Allardt Haus Antiques, Allardt, 879-1399.
The Country Peddler, 879-8292.
Cumberland Mt. General Store, 873-3880.
Forbus General Store, 879-5427.
Mulberry Tree, 879-1395.
Mountaineer Craft Center, Jamestown, 879-4603.
Muddy Pond General Store, 445-7829.
Rugby Commissary.
Valley of Three Forks Antique and Gift Shop, Pall Mall, 879-1262.

Special Events:
May—Rugby Annual Festival of British and Appalachian Culture
September–October—Muddy Pond Sorghum Making
October—Allardt Pumpkin Festival and Weigh-off; Rugby Annual Pilgrimage
November—Rugby Thanksgiving Marketplace
December—Rugby Annual Holiday Tour

Camping:
Big South Fork National River and Recreation Area, Oneida, 879-4890.
East Fork Stables, 800-97-TRAIL.
Laurel Creek Travel Park, 800-484-8987 or 879-7696.
Pickett State Rustic Park, 879-5821.
Saddle Valley Campground, 423-984-0668.

For More Information:
Jamestown/Fentress County Chamber of Commerce, P.O. Box 1294, Courthouse Square, 879-9948.
Scott County Chamber of Commerce, P.O. Box 442, 800-645-6905 or 423-569-6900.

30 *Byrdstown*
Birthplace of the "Father" of the United Nations

Byrdstown, the seat of Pickett County, was established in 1879 near the Tennessee-Kentucky border. The reconstructed log cabin birthplace of Cordell Hull, "the father of the United Nations," is a popular attraction for visitors.

In addition to the cabin, there's a museum filled with personal memorabilia. For special events they proudly display his Nobel Peace Prize.

According to the *WPA Guide to Tennessee,* Cordell Hull's father, William, was a farmer when Cordell was born on September 30, 1871. William erected a small building for a school and hired a teacher to teach his son and the children of neighboring families.

When Cordell was four, the family moved to Celina. He became a skilled pilot of log rafts used to convey timber from the vast Cumberland Plateau forests. Although he was modest and somewhat shy in his youth, the values he learned growing up on the Cumberland Plateau would serve him and our nation well.

He served as a captain in the Spanish-American War and was a congressman from the fourth Tennessee district to the U.S. House of Representatives for twenty-three years. He served as U.S. senator from Tennessee from 1931 to 1933, championing the cause of the small farmer and fighting for the interests of everyday people against those of wealthy eastern industrialists.

He resigned from the Senate to become a member of Franklin Roosevelt's cabinet, serving as secretary of state from 1933 to 1944.

According to Robert Brandt, in *Touring the Middle Tennessee Backroads,* Hull's father once said, "Cord wasn't set enough to be a school teacher, wasn't rough enough to be a lumberman, wasn't sociable enough to be a doctor and couldn't holler loud enough to be a preacher. But Cord was a right thorough thinker."

Thorough indeed. He was fundamental in

The clear, cool water of Dale Hollow Lake draws visitors to the upper Cumberland Plateau.

guiding the United States toward cooperation in international relations, is widely considered the "father" of the United Nations, and was awarded the Nobel Peace Prize in 1945 in recognition of his efforts.

Byrdstown hasn't been greatly altered by tourism yet, but it is certainly eligible since nearby Dale Hollow is one of Tennessee's prettiest, most pristine lakes. Completed in 1943, Dale Hollow has more than six hundred miles of shoreline and thirty thousand surface acres for water sports.

Several excellent resorts hug the eastern shorelines at Byrdstown including Eagle Cove Resort which has five cabins and two gorgeous chalets with fireplaces, hot tubs, and three levels of bedrooms attractively furnished, in addition to fully equipped houseboats that sleep eight to fourteen. They also offer fishing and ski boat rentals.

Sunset Marina is conveniently located adjacent to the Obey River bridge on TN 42 next to the U.S. Army Corps of Engineers (USACE)

Obey River Recreation Area. In addition to comfortable lakeshore cedar cottages, luxury houseboat, pontoon and ski boat rentals, Sunset has a full service marina and well-stocked ship's store and a beautiful floating restaurant with good food and great views of the lake. The Obey River Recreation Area has 132 camping sites with hookups, five bath houses, a public swimming beach, picnic areas, and two boat ramps. Between them, Sunset and the recreation area have everything you need for a great getaway.

According to Holly Sherwin in *Canoeing in Tennessee*, the U.S. Army Corps of Engineers has mapped out a fifty-five-mile canoe trail suitable for paddlers of all abilities that begins on the Obey River at Eastport Marina upstream from Sunset and ends at the dam on the western end of the lake.

Dale Hollow Lake is the winter home of a population of bald eagles. The USACE conducts an eagle watch in January. Star Point Resort also has cabins, a lodge, condominiums, houseboat and ski boat rentals, and a restaurant that serves good food.

The Bob Cat Den Restaurant on TN 111 bypass specializes in freshly prepared, home-style cooking. The Dixie Cafe on the square offers a country buffet for visitors who have been shopping for crafts at Chanute Gift Shop and antiques at Crawford & Son Antiques, Ole Time Traditions, and Red Barn Antiques.

Although activity on the lake peaks between Memorial Day and Labor Day, good catches of large and smallmouth bass, Kentucky bass, walleye, muskie, catfish, bluegill, and crappie—in addition to the beautiful location—are making Dale Hollow popular year-round.

Follow TN 42 to Livingston, a delightful upper Cumberland community with great antique malls.

All of the following accommodations are Byrdstown with zip code 38549, and all telephone listings are area code 931, except where noted.

Accommodations:
East Port Marina and Resort, Star Rt., Box 147, Alpine, 38543; 879-7511.
Eagle Cove Resort, 5899 Eagle Cove Rd., 800-346-2622 or 864-3456.
Sportsman's Lodge Motel, Rt.1, Box 31, TN 42/111 S., 864-3349.
Star Point Resort, Rt. 1, Box 278, 4490 Star Point Rd., 864-3115.
Sunset Marina and Resort, Inc., 2040 Sunset Dock Rd., 800-760-8550 or 864-3146.

Attractions:
Cordell Hull Birthplace and Museum, 864-3247 or 864-3511.

Dining:
Bob Cat Den Restaurant, 864-3125.
Dixie Cafe, 864-6535.
Sunset Marina Restaurant, 864-3146.
Star Point Marina Restaurant, 864-3115.

Shopping:
Chanute Craft Shop, 864-6104.

Crawford & Son Antiques, 864-3125 or 864-6411.
Ole Time Traditions, 864-7237.
Red Barn Antiques, 864-3862.

Special Events:
January—Bald Eagle Watch on Dale Hollow Lake
June—Gospel Singing
July—Down Home Festival
September—Cordell Hull Folk Festival

Camping:
USACE Obey River Recreation Area, off TN 42 at Sunset Dock Rd., 864-6388.

For More Information:
Byrdstown-Pickett County Chamber of Commerce, P.O. Box 447, 864-7195.

31 *Livingston*
Standing Stones and Rolley Holes

Once known as Overton, Livingston was renamed for Edgar Livingston, the secretary of state during Andrew Jackson's presidency.

According to Robert Brandt in *Touring the Middle Tennessee Backroads*, Livingston's courthouse was burned during the Civil War by a band of guerrillas. Although no major battles were fought here, the region suffered the outrages of marauding bands of guerrillas working secretly for both Union and Confederate causes, pitting brother against brother and often cruelly targeting the families of men known to be away fighting in the war.

During the 1920s Tennessee seized the attention of suffragettes of the nation as the Nineteenth Amendment was poised for ratification. A native of Livingston, A. H. Roberts, was governor of Tennessee when the proposed amendment was awaiting the crucial vote of the thirty-sixth and final state needed for ratification. Roberts called a joint session of the Tennessee legislature to debate ratification and forces pro and con descended upon Nashville.

After heated debates and political maneuvering, the legislature was so divided that the measure passed in the House by a single vote. The measure was signed by Governor Roberts on August 24, 1920, ratifying the Nineteenth Amendment, establishing the right of women all over the United States to vote.

The Overton County Courthouse is surrounded by a town square lined with antiques and specialty shops.

The present brick Federal-style Overton County Courthouse was built in 1869 and dominates the charming, old-fashioned town square. There are several antiques shops on or near the square. The Antique Market has fifty booths of collectibles and antiques. Nearby, the Court Square Emporium has some antiques and collectibles and represents about forty regional and area craftsmen with offerings ranging from baskets and pottery to quilts.

A Different Drummer has six rooms of antiques and collectibles. Helen's Now and Then Antiques and Collectibles on East Main has lots of glassware. If you're looking for some good reading material, check out The Paper Place on Court Square.

At lunch time, look no farther than the Apple Dish next door to the Antique Market. Everything they serve, including bread and desserts, is freshly prepared. They're also open Thursday, Friday, and Saturday nights.

The square is filled with country and bluegrass music each July when the three-day Pioneer Days festival is held.

A couple of blocks off the square, you'll find Cornucopia Bed and Breakfast, one of the oldest homes in Livingston, lovingly restored, and filled with antiques. All guest rooms have private baths and you may choose a continental or full breakfast in the sky-lit dining room or the plant-filled sun room.

Guests are invited to enjoy the homemade cookies from the old-fashioned kitchen while enjoying a lazy afternoon in an easy chair on the side porch, wandering through the perennial gardens, or reading in the front parlor. Reading materials, a video library, cable TV and VCR are provided.

The Cornucopia Bed and Breakfast is located just off Court Square in Livingston.

Other choices for accommodations include the twenty-two cabins at Standing Stone State Rustic Park a few miles north of Livingston. The park is named for an eight-foot rock that once stood upright on a sandstone ledge, the legendary boundary marker between Cherokee and Shawnee territory. The remnant of this stone is preserved in Monterey where a Standing Stone Celebration of Native American Heritage is held each October.

Covering nearly eleven thousand acres, the park is known for its spring wildflowers, spectacular scenery, fishing for bass and bluegill on the sixty-nine-acre Standing Stone Lake, and the annual Rolley Hole (a marble game played in the area for generations) National Championship held each September.

In addition to the tournament, the Rolley Hole Festival features displays of marble making, marble trading, and mountain music makin'. There are rowboats for rent, campsites, picnic sites, an outdoor swimming pool, about ten miles of hiking trails, and tennis courts for those not interested in marbles.

From Livingston, continue on TN 54 to Monterey where you can visit Wilson's North American Wildlife Museum and the Garden Inn at Bee Rock before continuing to Crossville on US 70N.

All of the following accommodations are Livingston with zip code 38570, and all telephone listings are area code 931, except where noted.

Accommodations:
Cornucopia Bed and Breakfast, 303 Mofield St., 823-7522.
The Garden Inn at Bee Rock, 1400 Bee Rock Rd., Monterey, 38574; 839-1400.
Overton Motel, East Main St., 823-2075.
Standing Stone State Rustic Park, off TN. 52 between Livingston and Celina, 823-6347.

Attractions:
Standing Stone State Rustic Park, 823-6347.
Wilson's North American Wildlife Museum, Monterey.

Dining:
The Apple Dish, 823-3222.
The Overton Motel Restaurant, 823-2075.

Shopping:
The Antique Market, 823-4943.
Court Square Emporium, 823-6741.
A Different Drummer, 823-5856.
Helen's Now and Then, 823-1626.
The Paper Place, 823-2218.

Special Events:
July—Pioneer Days
September—Rolley Hole National Championship and Festival

Camping:
Deep Valley Park and Trout Farm, Allons, 823-6053.
Standing Stone State Rustic Park, 823-6347.

For More Information:
Livingston and Overton County Chamber of Commerce, P.O.
    Box 354, 823-6421.

32 Crossville
The Crossroads of the Cumberland Plateau

The Homestead Tower tells the story of a grand experiment conducted here during the Great Depression.

The area that is now Crossville was opened to settlement after 1805. As in most of the Cumberland Plateau, early settlers were Revolutionary War veterans who received land grants in lieu of cash payment for their military service.

Crossville, the county seat of Cumberland County, received its name around 1856 because of its location at the intersection of the old Nashville-Knoxville Road and the Kentucky-Chattanooga Stock Road. The Stock Road brought as many as one thousand head of horses and mules a day through Crossville on drives from Alabama and Kentucky to Virginia, much like the legendary cattle drives in western states.

In recent years Crossville has become a popular location for large resorts like the 12,700-acre Fairfield Glade, 9,000-acre Cumberland Gardens, and 5,000-acre Lake Tansi Village. Fairfield Glade is a Mobil four-star resort with twelve lakes, a marina for boating and fishing, four golf courses, including one that was named the number one public golf course in Tennessee in 1995 by *Golf Digest*, horseback riding trails, indoor and outdoor tennis courts, three restaurants, and a one-hundred-room lodge for overnight guests.

Cumberland Gardens has a golf course given a four-star rating by *Golf Digest* and, as the name indicates, outstanding gardens. Lake Tansi Village boasts a 550-acre lake for fishing, boating, sailing, and water skiing and an eighteen-hole golf course.

The lovely arched bridge at Cumberland Mountain State Park was built by the CCC. (Photo courtesy of Tennessee Photographic Services).

National franchises in Crossville include Best Western, Hampton Inn, and Ramada Inn.

As you drive into the older part of Crossville, you'll see many buildings constructed of a locally quarried mottled sandstone with unusually high silica content known as Crab Orchard stone.

Crab Orchard stone was used for the chapel at Scarritt College in Nashville in 1925 and later at Rockefeller Center in New York. Even Elvis Presley's pool at Graceland was ringed with Crab Orchard stone.

The coloring of the stone depends on the amounts of iron, titanium, and magnesium and shades range from tan and buff to gray, blue-gray, and rose. Many houses in Cumberland County were built using Crab Orchard stone along with public structures like the historic Homestead Tower and the beautiful arched Civilian Conservation Corps (CCC) dam at Cumberland Mountain State Park.

Modern technology makes it easier to harvest layers of the highly desirable stone that was once destined for the scrap heap, creating a multimillion-dollar industry for the region. Crab Orchard stone quarries are visible along US 70E between Crossville and Crab Orchard.

On US 70W, a couple of miles out of town, the Cumberland County Playhouse has the distinction of being designated a "major cultural resource" by the Tennessee Arts Commission. The seed for the playhouse was planted when television writer and theater director Paul Crabtree and his wife moved their family to Crossville in the summer of 1963.

Although there were no professional theaters in Tennessee and only four in the south, the community launched a fundraising effort that opened the doors of the playhouse two years later. Eighty percent of all revenues are generated by ticket sales to more than three hundred performances and concerts on two indoor stages and a seasonal outdoor stage from February through mid-December.

South of Crossville at the intersection of TN 68 and US 127/TN 28, the Homestead Tower

Museum tells the story of a depression-era program designed to rehabilitate 251 "stranded families" of unemployed miners, timber workers, and farmers.

Franklin Roosevelt's administration developed the Division of Subsistence Homesteads program that purchased ten thousand acres with the intention of putting these folks back on their feet, in decent housing and on their way to new occupations.

Beginning in 1934 the homesteaders cleared thirty-five-acre tracts, logged the timber, quarried the Crab Orchard stone for building materials, built modest stone houses, and developed cooperative enterprises, all of which were owned by the nonprofit Cumberland Homesteaders' Cooperative Association.

After five years of this grand experiment, the homesteaders were offered the opportunity to buy their land and houses. They did so, and in a very real sense reached the goal of the program by ending it.

Across the road from the tower is the Cumberland General Store, a popular destination for functional items and ole-timey oddities that you won't want to leave without.

A short distance down US 127/TN 28 from the Homestead Tower is the lovely seven-arch dam at the 1,720-acre Cumberland Mountain State Park, a major Kodak moment.

The dam actually serves as the bridge leading into the park. You drive across it to reach the Cumberland Mountain Restaurant which has good food, a nice view of Byrd Lake and the dam, and serves lunches and dinners daily except during the Christmas holidays. There's a wide path along the lake behind the restaurant that's perfect for a leisurely stroll.

The park has 147 campsites available first-come first-served with electric and water hookups, a group lodge and thirty-seven cabins ranging from rustic to modern with reservations taken up to one year in advance.

Rowboats, paddleboats, and canoes are available for rent and fishing from the bank is a popular pastime if you have a valid Tennessee fishing license. There's also an Olympic-sized pool, tennis courts, playgrounds, and several day-use hiking and nature trails as well as a ten-mile overnight backpacking trail.

At Crossville is the home office for the 79,740-acre Catoosa Wildlife Management Area, the largest WMA in the Tennessee Wildlife Resource Agency's domain. Like most of the plateau, the topography in Catoosa is rugged, wild country. It is popular with hunters seeking white-tailed deer, wild turkey, ruffed grouse, quail, rabbit, squirrel, and wild boar.

That's right, wild boar, as nasty-looking a creature as you're ever likely to see with a face not even a mother could love and ferocious-looking tusks jutting out from the sides of its mouth. The Russian wild boar was introduced in Tennessee in 1912 by wealthy British sportsmen. It mixed with the hardy southern "razorback" and multiplied, getting meaner all the while.

If you're not quite up to tackling a wild boar, Crossville is home to the headwaters of the Obed Wild and Scenic River which cuts through portions of the Catoosa like a roller coaster. Make sure you're really prepared before venturing down rapids that have earned names like Ohmigod! and the Widowmaker. According to Bob Sehlinger and Bob Lantz in *A Canoeing and Kayaking Guide to the Streams of Tennessee*, this wild and wooly river has been known to eat white-water canoes and leave paddlers to scale the bluffs or worse.

If you're not up for wild boar or white-water, it's still a great area for hiking, wildlife viewing, and photography. Catoosa is closed February 1 to March 27 to allow nonhuman residents some undisturbed time.

Tennessee's oldest hunting lodge, Caryonah, is located near Crossville. As you would expect, their most sought after game is the boar.

For those interested in less strenuous outdoor pursuits, the Garden Inn at Bee Rock at Monterey sits on fifteen acres overlooking Stamps Hollow one thousand feet below. The property includes hiking trails and natural formations ranging from stone bridges to caves. The property is named for bee rock, where the Cherokee collected honey. The eighty-six-hundred-square-foot facility has ten large guest rooms with handcrafted furnishings and private baths. All have views of the mountains or the gardens. A full breakfast is served and gourmet dinners are available by reservation on Saturday evenings.

Return to Kingston via I-40E or US 70 to complete this tour, or continue to Cookeville via I-40W or US 70 to begin the next loop.

All of the following accommodations are Crossville with zip code 38555, and all telephone listings are area code 931, except where noted.

Accommodations:
An-Jen Bed and Breakfast and Fantasy Wedding Chapel, Rt. 1, Box 594, US 127N, 456-0515.

Betty's Bed and Breakfast, Peavine Rd., 484-8827.
Caryonah Hunting Lodge, Rt. 10, Box 264, 277-3113.
Cumberland Gardens Resort, US 70E, Crab Orchard, 37723; 484-5285.
Cumberland Mountain State Park, Rt. 8, Box 322, 484-6138.
Fairfield Glade Resort, Peavine Rd., Fairfield Glade, 38557; 484-7521.
The Garden Inn at Bee Rock, 1400 Bee Rock Rd., P.O. Box 445, Monterey, 38574; 839-1400.
Holiday Hills Resort, US 70S, 484-9566.
Lake Tansi Village, Dunbar Rd., 788-6724.

Attractions:
Cumberland County Playhouse, 484-5000.
Cumberland General Store, 484-8481.
Cumberland Mountain State Park, 484-6138.
Homestead Tower Museum, 456-9663.

Dining:
The Bean Pot, 484-4633.
Cumberland Mountain State Park Restaurant, 484-7186.
Talavera De La Reina, 277-3749.
Traditions, 484-3454.
Vegas Steak House and Bar, 456-2850.

Shopping:
Crossville Collectibles, 456-7641.
Cumberland General Store, 484-8481.
Grandma's Attic, 456-5699.
The Great Upper Cumberland Trading Company, Ltd., 456-6270.
The Raspberry Briar, 707-9146.

Camping:
Cumberland Mountain State Park, 484-6138.

For More Information:
Greater Cumberland County Chamber of Commerce, 108 S. Main St., 484-8444.
Manager, Catoosa Wildlife Management Area, 216 E. Penfield, 800-262-6704 or 484-9571.

ᕙ Loop 6

33 *Cookeville*
A Highland Rim Railroad Town

Cookeville and Putnam County are relative new-comers by Tennessee standards. Enough settlers stopped here on their way to Middle Tennessee to petition for their own county in 1842. A dozen years later Putnam County was created. The county seat was laid out at the current site of Cookeville and named for state senator Richard Cooke, a supporter of the creation of Putnam County.

In 1890 the railroad from Nashville reached Cookeville. That event opened commerce between Cookeville and the rest of the country. It also moved "down town" to the train depot which was about a half-mile west of the town square that had formerly been the hub of the town's commerce. In time Cookeville became a trade center for the upper Cumberland region.

In 1916 Cookeville was selected by the state of Tennessee as the home of the Tennessee Poly-technic Institute (TPI). Today TPI is known as Tennessee Technological University, a comprehensive state university.

The population of Cookeville, the seat of Putnam County, is about twenty-six thousand, making it the largest town in the upper Cumberland area. It was recently ranked one of America's Top Ten Retirement Places by Rand McNally.

Because it is also the home of Tennessee Tech, it has cultural resources beyond expectation for a town its size. The Bryan Fine Arts Center on the campus of Tennessee Tech is also the home of the 500-seat Wattenbarger Auditorium which is used as a venue for a variety of concerts and recitals. The Cookeville Drama Center seats 474 and is used primarily for plays, concerts, and recitals.

The distinctive pagoda-roofed 1909 Cookeville Depot Museum is in the National Register of Historic Places. It has been totally renovated and now contains four rooms of exhibits that include artifacts of the Tennessee Central Railroad and old photos of railroading in Putnam County. Two cabooses outside contain additional exhibits.

There are several opportunities for outdoor recreation in or near Cookeville. The 260-acre Cane Creek Regional Park is a municipal park. It has a 56-acre lake with small fishing piers, paddle-boat rentals, biking and hiking trails, playgrounds, and picnic shelters.

The 40-acre City Lake Natural Area has a hiking trail to a waterfall overlook and fishing at the site of a 1920s water treatment facility on Bridgeway Road.

Burgess Falls, located about eight miles south of Cookeville, is a 130-foot three-tiered cascade created by three falls on the aptly named Falling Water River on its way to Center Hill Lake. A fairly easy 0.7-mile trail goes to the top falls; another trail splits to visit the middle, or take a steep descent down a metal stairway to the lower falls. Burgess Falls State Natural Area has a picnic shelter, a playground, and restrooms. From March to November, it's a great place to spend an afternoon.

When Arda Lee's uncle bought Hidden Hollow in 1952, Arda thought it was the most beautiful spot in the world—and he still does. After twenty-two years as an engineer for Lockheed, he was offered the chance to purchase the 86 acres and he jumped at it.

The Cookeville Depot Museum contains artifacts of the Tennessee Central Railroad.

A mill, waterfalls, lakes, canals, and picnicking spots join the bevy of ducks, rabbits, squirrels, geese, and deer that call the hollow home. Arda spends two months putting up zillions of Christmas lights. Best of all, he invites you to share a small petting zoo with your children and enjoy opportunities for hiking, fishing, and swimming. He's also built a bed and breakfast with two rooms and private baths.

The Scarecrow Country Inn is a rustic log building with stained-glass windows, four guest rooms with private baths, and a restaurant that takes reservations for gourmet lunches and dinners.

Several antique malls and popular restaurants are worth stopping for if you're driving along I-40 and in need of a break from the drive. Cookeville Antique Mall is parallel to the interstate; the Attic Window Antique Shop has antiques and collectibles; and J. J. Jax Gift Shop has some attractive jewelry as well as other gift ideas. Diana's serves soups, salads, and sandwiches in a lovely old Victorian house.

National franchise motels include Best Western, Comfort Inn, Days Inn, Hampton Inn, Holiday Inn, Howard Johnson, Quality Inn, Ramada Inn, and Super 8. Fast food restaurants proliferate along South Jefferson Street at exit 287 off I-40.

From Cookeville, follow TN 137 north to Celina.

All of the following accommodations are Cookeville with zip code 38501, and all telephone listings are area code 931, except where noted.

Accommodations:
Arda Lee's Hidden Hollow Park, 1901 Mt. Pleasant Rd., 526-4038.
Hummingbird Hill Bed and Breakfast, Rt.2, Box 161 A4, Baxter, 38544; 858-2598.
Little Bit O'Heaven Bed and Breakfast, 148B Dunn Ridge Rd., Baxter, 38544; 858-6388.
The Scarecrow Country Inn, 644 Whitson Chapel Rd., 800-304-5109 or 526-3431.

Attractions:
Bryan Fine Arts Center, 372-3161.
Burgess Falls State Natural Area, 432-5312.
Cookeville Depot Museum, 526-9591, ext. 296.
Ironwood Golf Course, 528-2331.

Southern Hills Golf Course and Country Club, 432-5147.
Tennessee Technological University, 372-3101.
White Plains Golf Course, 537-6397.

Dining:
Diana's, 256-6967.
Mama Rosa's Restaurant, 372-6694.
Nick's Restaurant and Lounge, 528-1434.
The Scarecrow Country Inn, 526-3431.
Spankies, 528-1050.

For More Information:
Cookeville/Putnam County Chamber of Commerce, 302 S.
   Jefferson Ave., 800-264-5541 or 526-2211.

34 Celina and Dale Hollow Lake
Home of the Bronzebacks

Celina, the seat of Clay County, was named for the daughter of Moses Fisk, a pioneer educator. According to Robert Brandt in *Touring the Middle Tennessee Backroads*, Celina grew up around a ferry that operated here in the early 1800s.

Its location at the confluence of the Obey and Cumberland Rivers made it an important part of the timber commerce that dominated the area after the Civil War until the Great Depression. Employment during this time was primarily associated with logging and transporting logs from area logging camps to Nashville for milling.

Skilled pilots led a crew of five along the treacherous route to Nashville, piloting huge rafts up to three hundred feet long. Even Nobel Prize-winner Cordell Hull took pride in the hard-won skills he'd acquired as a pilot.

Like many Tennessee towns, Celina had to be rebuilt after the ravages of the Civil War, but its original 1872 courthouse remains a landmark.

Among other items depicting the area's history, the Clay County Museum is home to an antique steam engine recovered from the bottom of Dale Hollow Lake in 1987.

In 1943 Dale Hollow Dam, one of the first flood control dams designed by the U.S. Army Corps of Engineers in the Nashville District, impounded the waters of the Obey and Wolf Rivers to create a highland reservoir with steep, heavily wooded slopes. It is situated on the Cumberland Plateau about halfway between Knoxville and Nashville.

In Tennessee, Celina is the closest town to the western end of the dam, while Byrdstown is closest to the eastern end. Although largely situated in Tennessee, part of Dale Hollow is located in Kentucky, home of Dale Hollow State Park.

Dale Hollow's topography minimizes siltation and makes it very clear with deep, cold water, a perfect habitat for smallmouth bass. Bronzeback trophy hunters concentrate their efforts in the lake's midsection on long shale points from Mitchell Creek to the junction of the Wolf and Obey Rivers. Cold-water species like lake trout and rainbow trout are also popular, but most freshwater gamefish species are represented here. Rainbow trout are sought by eager anglers along the tailrace below the dam, one of the most popular trout fishing locales in Middle Tennessee.

The U.S. Fish and Wildlife Service operates the southernmost trout hatchery in the U.S. on the banks of the Obey. You can view the operations and see fish in trout raceways and in an aquarium at the visitor center daily.

The prevalence of clear water attracts scuba divers to the area as well, while its cleanliness makes it popular with recreational boaters and water-skiers.

Dale Hollow has the second largest wintering eagle population in the state of Tennessee. An annual eagle watch is held on a Saturday (usually the third) in January. Participants are transported by boat to remote areas of the lake to view wintering eagles.

Pleasant Grove Recreation Area near the dam has a swinging bridge connecting it to Pleasant Grove Island. The island has the distinction of having a picnic site inside a cave. Red Oak Trail is a hiking and horse riding trail with places to swim, water your horse, and camp with hitching posts, a shelter, and pit toilets.

Fifteen docks and thirty-eight concrete boat ramps provide access along Dale Hollow's 620 miles of shoreline. A scenic fifty-five-mile flatwater canoe trail has been mapped from Eastport Dock at the eastern end on the Obey River to the dam, near Celina. Marinas and resorts offer cabin and houseboat rentals, fishing boat rentals, and fishing guide services.

Candle Lit Manor Bed and Breakfast has restored log cabins, welcomes children, and serves a full breakfast. Friday and Saturday night dining is available by reservation. Dale Hollow Marina has fourteen cabins; Cedar Hill has twenty-six cabins and a ten-unit motel as well as a restaurant. Holly Creek has a sixteen-unit motel. Pet policies vary.

From Celina, continue west on TN 52 to Red Boiling Springs.

All of the following accommodations are Celina with zip code 38551, and all telephone listings are area code 931, except where noted.

Accommodations:
Candle Lit Manor Bed and Breakfast, 1022 Jimmy Reneay Rd., 243-3281.
Cedar Hill Resort, 2371 Cedar Hill Rd., 800-872-8393 or 243-3201.

Dale Hollow Marina, 99 Arlon Webb Dr., 800-321-1669 or 243-2211.
Dale Hollow State Park and Dock, 6371 State Park Rd., Bow, KY, 42714; 502-433-7431.
Holly Creek Resort, 7855 Holly Creek Rd., 800-337-1780.
Horse Creek Resort, 1150 Horse Creek Rd., 243-2125.

Attractions:
Celina-Clay County Museum, 243-3338.
Dale Hollow National Fish Hatchery, 243-2443.

Dining:
Kat's Cafe, 243-9302.
New Day Subs, 243-4001.
Twin Rivers Restaurant, 243-3333.

Special Events:
January—Eagle Watch at Dale Hollow Lake

Camping:
Butlers Landing Campground, 243-4360.
Dale Hollow Dam USACE Recreation Area, 243-3554.
Pleasant Grove USACE Recreation Area, 243-3555.
Roaring Rivers Campground, 268-2540.

For More Information:
Dale Hollow/Clay County Chamber of Commerce, 805 Brown St., 243-3338.
Resource Manager, Dale Hollow Lake, Rt. 1, 243-3136.

35 *Red Boiling Springs*
Where the Healing Waters Flow

Red Boiling Springs was first settled by Edmund Jennings in 1830 after he'd located a salt lick and plentiful game in the area. Ten years later, a settler named Shepherd Kirby arrived and discovered the therapeutic properties of the water with red sediment that emerged from a bubbling spring. It seems Kirby had a painful eye infection that was relieved, and finally cured, after bathing his eyes in the "red boiling spring."

As the news spread, the quiet community on the edge of the Highland Rim began to receive increasing numbers of visitors. The town became the premier mineral springs resort in Tennessee, famous for its five types of mineral water: black, which contained hydrogen sulfide, iron oxides, and magnesium; red, with higher concentrations of the iron oxides giving it a reddish color; white, a milder mineral water named for the color a dime turned after sitting in it overnight; free stone, which tastes as if it's mineral-free; and, the most potent of all, double and twist, which made you do just that if you drank it!

You can barely walk a hundred yards in any direction before encountering an old-fashioned hand pump. Lots of folks bring jugs to fill up at the Arlington Red well near the edge of town.

Curative properties for conditions ranging from gout to kidney stones were attributed to the waters. The magnesium-containing black water was recommended for gastrointestinal troubles long before Milk of Magnesia became a household name. The red sulphur water was used as a diuretic and urinary analgesic. Double and twist was used for soaks in the bathhouses.

During its boom between 1890 and 1930, Red Boiling Springs had eight hotels and more than a dozen boarding houses to accommodate the summer visitors who came by railroad and horse-drawn wagons to "take the waters," rest and relax, play croquet on the manicured lawns of the large hotels, swim, play tennis, bowl, and dance to orchestras performing under the stars.

Three of the original hotels survive and welcome guests to Red Boiling Springs. Built in 1924, Armour's Red Boiling Springs Hotel is a two-story brick owned by lifelong Red Boiling Springs residents, Brenda and Bobby Thomas. There are no phones or televisions in the twenty-six guest rooms, but they all have private baths and one room has a large garden tub. There are even two honeymoon suites. If you've

just got to check in with the outside world, there's a telephone and a TV in the downstairs lobby. Some of the downstairs rooms are handicapped accessible.

The furnishings are old fashioned and comfortable, in keeping with the flavor of the hotel. The food is home cooked and there is no end to

The mineral water found at Red Boiling Springs was widely believed to have curative powers by summer visitors in the 1890s. (Photo courtesy of Tennessee Photographic Services)

Lick Creek meanders past a covered bridge in the middle of Red Boiling Springs.

it until you push back from the family-style dining table.

Those not staying at the hotel can sample the dining room fare with reservations. Children are welcome, smoking is allowed, and pets are not allowed inside.

Armour's is the only hotel in Red Boiling Springs offering mineral baths. We can't claim to be observably healthier after our baths and massage, but we sure were relaxed.

The Donoho Hotel, built in 1914, is a rambling two-story frame with a long white-colonnaded porch filled with rocking chairs and wicker furniture. Its thirty-two guest rooms have private baths and many have outside entrances. The dinner bell rings three times a day summoning guests and visitors with reservations to airy, antique-filled dining rooms for a family-style, all-you-can-eat menu very similar to Armour's. Children are fine, but call ahead if your pet is traveling with you. Nonsmoking rooms are available.

Sitting high on a hill at the opposite end of town, the Thomas House was rebuilt around the turn of the century when a fire destroyed the old Cloyd Hotel, as it was then known. The new brick structure had elaborate brickwork and an arched portico leading to a grand gathering area.

The rooms have European-style water closets, an unusual arrangement that involves a small watertight closet in which the shower and commode shared the space. As in days gone by, the swimming pool is open to the public. Three meals are served daily by reservation. Children are welcome, but pets are not. Smoking is permitted.

Two popular festivals draw a deluge of visitors to the community of about one thousand residents. The Folk Medicine Festival has grown to be a three-day summer celebration of the healing arts, with speakers, folk heritage demonstrations, arts and crafts, and food booths.

October heralds the arrival of the Heritage Days and Sorghum Festival in Palace Park. In addition to sorghum making, expect to see heritage craft demonstrations like shingle making, quilting, rope making, and displays of antique engines used to press cane.

A devastating flood in 1969 forced the community to reevaluate the use of the land along Salt Lick Creek which flows through the center of town. The result is a picturesque park stretching from one end of town to the other along the creek with meandering paths past the ever-present hand pumps, across covered bridges (there are two downtown) and past picnic pavilions and gazebos.

There are gift shops in the three hotels and a couple of shops in town. The Village Gift Shoppe and Sewing Basket has gifts and locally crafted items. The Little House Crafts and Gifts is across from the Donoho and has custom-made wooden gingerbread trim and white oak baskets in addition to other items crafted locally. Mineral Springs Arts is an art and craft cooperative featuring original paintings and prints as well as traditional crafts like quilts, pottery, and woodworking.

There are three ponds on the outskirts of Red Boiling Springs stocked with rainbow trout that are so used to being fed that we watched a fellow feed them literally out of his hand. Needless to say, these pampered "pet" trout have never had to fend for a meal or be molested by a fish hook—it'd be like chowing down on a family friend.

For those of you with piscatorial pursuits of another type in mind, there are three lakes near Red Boiling Springs. Cordell Hull Lake (*see* Carthage) is fifteen miles from town, Dale Hollow is twenty-five miles (*see* Celina) and Center Hill (*see* McMinnville) is thirty-five miles. You may not have them eating out of your hands, but all three have great fishing!

From Red Boiling Springs, follow TN 52 west through Lafayette to Hartsville where you'll take historic TN 25 to Castalian Springs and Gallatin.

All of the following accommodations are Red Boiling Springs with zip code 37150, and all telephone listings are area code 615, except where noted.

Accommodations:
Armour's Red Boiling Springs Hotel, 321 E. Main St., 699-2180.
Donoho Hotel, 500 E. Main St., P.O. Box 36, 699-3141.
The Thomas House, 520 E. Main St., 699-3006.

Dining:
Armour's Red Boiling Springs Hotel, 699-2180.
Donoho Hotel, 699-3141.
The Thomas House, 699-3006.

Shopping:
Little House Crafts, 699-2345.
Mineral Springs Arts, 699-2422.
Newberry and Sons Chairs, 699-3755.
Village Gift Shoppe and Sewing Basket, 699-3783.

Special Events:
May—Folk Medicine Festival
October—Heritage Days and Sorghum Festival

For More Information:
Call one of the three hotels.

36 Gallatin and Castalian Springs
Along the Historic Avery Trace

Gallatin was founded in 1802 and named for the U.S. secretary of the treasury, Albert Gallatin. The area around Gallatin and its neighbor Castalian Springs was very important in the history of the Cumberland settlement, or the Mero District, as early Middle Tennessee was known. Many signs of early settlement and several imposing homes from this period are open to the public.

The Hancock House Bed and Breakfast Inn was formerly a pre-1878 stagecoach stop and toll gate house known as Avondale Station. Today the fifteen-room inn has seven bedrooms with private baths, fireplaces, period antiques, telephones, and TVs. Full or continental breakfast is served to guests. Brunch, lunch, and dinner are available by reservation.

TN 25 follows the historic Avery Trace that connected Nashville and Knoxville until travel moved south of the Cumberland River in the 1830s.

Two blocks west of the Gallatin Public Square off TN 25, Trousdale Place was built around 1813. In 1822, it was purchased by William Trousdale, a soldier, politician, and statesman.

The two-story Flemish bond-brick house was deeded to the Clark Chapter of the United Daughters of the Confederacy in 1899 after the death of Trousdale's granddaughter, his last direct descendant. It is open to the public Wednesday through Sunday.

The Sumner County Museum is on the Trousdale Place property. There are more than 250,000 Sumner County artifacts exhibited in the ten-thousand-square-foot, three-level museum open daily from April to October.

Antiques on Main is a good stop while you're in town. It has nearly two hundred dealers offering antique furniture, collectibles, paintings, glassware, books, dolls, and Civil War artifacts.

If you've worked up an appetite, check out Franklin Station. Lunch is served daily except Sunday in the Victorian-era fire station. Dinner is served Thursday through Sunday.

Archaeological evidence suggests the presence of Paleo-Indians around 15,000 B.C. along the section of TN 25 from Gallatin to Castalian Springs. Later, Woodland Indians lived in a fortified village north of Bledsoe's Lick. The principal mound is visible on the northeast side of the intersection of TN 25 and Rock Springs Road.

Watch for the sign to the 164-acre Bledsoe Creek State Park south of TN 25 on Zeigler Fort Road, even if you're not camping because it's a good spot for spring wildflowers and wildlife viewing. Visitors find restrooms, 126 camping sites with electric hookup, hiking and nature trails along Old Hickory Lake, and a public boat-launching site. Bledsoe Creek participates in the horse-mounted ranger program and the Tennessee Walking horse assigned to the ranger is the only horse allowed in the park.

The creek is named for longhunters Isaac and Anthony Bledsoe. The brothers first visited the area around 1769. Isaac came upon a salt lick in 1772 attracting such a great herd of buffalo that he was afraid he'd be trampled if he got off his horse. After this tale circulated awhile, the lick became known as Bledsoe's Lick and the nearby creek came to be called Bledsoe Creek (for more on longhunters see Goodlettsville).

Both Isaac and his brother Anthony were killed by Indians in separate incidents five years apart.

Once a stagecoach inn, Wynnewood is one of many historic homes open to the public in Middle Tennessee.

On the north side of TN 25 high atop a rocky bluff about 3.5 miles from Bledsoe Creek State Park, the Georgian Colonial limestone home known as Cragfont was built in 1802 by Gen. James Winchester. Winchester, along with Andrew Jackson and Judge John Overton, laid out the plans for Memphis in 1818.

The next stop along the way is Wynnewood, the largest log structure standing in Tennessee. Built in 1828 by A. R. Wynne, William Cage, and Stephen Roberts as a stagecoach inn and mineral springs resort, the main house is 142 feet long with logs up to 32 feet long of oak, walnut, and ash.

There's an open hallway through the center known as a dogtrot and a log cabin attached to the rear of the inn built by Isaac Bledsoe between 1772 and 1780 that may be the oldest log cabin in the state. Wynne bought out his partners and Wynnewood became a family residence in 1834.

It remained in the family until 1971 when Wynne's grandson conveyed it to the State of Tennessee. This handsome structure is now open to the public.

There's a stone monument east of the entrance to Wynnewood marking the giant hollow sycamore that housed the first white settler in Middle Tennessee, longhunter Thomas Sharp Spencer, during the winter of 1778–79. According to Robert Brandt in *Touring the Middle Tennessee Backroads,* Spencer was a physically large man whose frontier skills became the subject of larger-than-life tall tales.

All of the following accommodations are Gallatin with zip code 37066, and all telephone listings are area code 615, except where noted.

Accommodations:
The Hancock House Bed and Breakfast Inn, 2144 Nashville Pk., 452-8431.

Attractions:
Bledsoe's Fort Historical Park.
Cragfont, 452-7070.
The Hancock House, 452-8431.
Key Park Log House, Lafayette, 666-5885.
Sumner County Museum, 451-3738.
Trousdale Place, 452-5648.
Wynnewood, 452-5463.

Dining:
Franklin Station, 451-9544.

Shopping:
Touch of Class Antiques and Collectibles, Lafayette, 666-2793.
Piccadilly Square, 451-1375.
Antiques on Main, 451-0426.
Red Chief Orchard and Cider Barn, 452-1516.

Special Events:
April—Historic Cragfont Tour of Homes
April–October—The Path of the Longhunter, tour of four historic homesteads
June—Wynnewood Summer Celebration; Hillbilly Days, Lafayette
October—Main Street Festival; Wynnewood Autumn Harvest Celebration
December—Christmas Tour of Historic Sites (Cragfont, Rosemont, Trousdale Place)

Camping:
Bledsoe Creek State Park, 452-3706.
Cages Bend Campground, 824-4989.
Shady Cove Resort, Castalian Springs, 452-8010.

For More Information:
Sumner County Tourism, P.O. Box 957, 230-8474.
Gallatin Chamber of Commerce, 118 W. Main St., 452-4000.

37 *Hendersonville*
Along the Shores of Old Hickory Lake

Hendersonville was named for Revolutionary War veteran William Henderson. Settlement began in the area during the late 1700s and consisted largely of scattered farms. The fertile rolling hills lent themselves to farming and animal husbandry.

Hendersonville was strategically situated midway along the Nashville-Gallatin Turnpike; but it grew slowly, although large farms in the area were the heart of Tennessee's Thoroughbred horse-breeding activities. Later an electric railway ran through Hendersonville from Nashville to Gallatin in the early 1900s.

Hendersonville was transformed from a largely rural community by the construction of Old Hickory Lock and Dam by the U.S. Army Corps of Engineers (USACE) on the Cumberland River between January 1952 and June 1954. The project was designed for flood control and energy production, but the recreational uses of Old Hickory Lake were soon apparent to all.

Twenty-six miles of the lake's 440-mile shoreline are in the city limits of Hendersonville. The lake is ringed by marinas, USACE Recreational Areas, and city, county, and state parks.

The USACE Visitor Center at Rockland Recreational Area has interactive museum displays on the history of the lake and its lock and dam system. Intrepid boaters can actually travel all the way from Hendersonville to the Gulf of Mexico by water through a series of locks and connecting tributaries. There are two boat ramps at Rockland, along with fishing and picnic areas.

Hendersonville is home to many country music stars and some of them have built showplaces on the lake. Trinity Music City, USA, is on the grounds of the original estate of Conway Twitty.

In addition to the mansion Twitty lived in, facilities seen on free tours of the thirty-acre property include recording studios for television programs and an auditorium that was the home of Country Music Television.

Trinity City presents free weekly live TV broadcasts and specially scheduled ticketed events. A virtual reality theater presents a movie about Jesus and a walk through a recreated street in old Jerusalem. During November and December, Trinity City blazes with more than one million lights until 9 P.M. every day except Christmas Day.

If water sports, star-gazing, and Trinity City aren't your style, consider visiting Rock Castle, the home of Gen. Daniel Smith that was begun in 1784 but not finished until 1791 due to Indian attacks.

Smith received a land grant that included the site of Rock Castle as payment for his services as a surveyor in what is now Middle Tennessee. He produced the first map of Tennessee and is credited with suggesting its name.

Since his job often kept him away from home, his wife, Sarah, was left to care for their two children and supervise the construction of the first stone masonry house in the Cumberland settlements while overseeing the management of the 3,140-acre plantation and fending off the Indians who were unhappy with the arrival of settlers in the area.

The family continued to prosper after Smith became a U.S. senator in 1798. Their daughter married the brother of Rachel Jackson and one of her sons became Andrew Jackson's private secretary at the White House.

Spring Haven, another of the early homes, is now a bed and breakfast inn. Situated on three manicured acres a block or two off East Main Street, the 1825 Federal-style inn offers four guest rooms with private baths, period antiques, and sitting areas with color TV and VCR.

Three rooms have king-sized beds, while the fourth has a double bed and a private entrance.

Evening desserts and full country gourmet breakfasts are served. Picnic lunches and candlelight dinners are available by special request.

Lakeview Bed and Breakfast features a variety of arrangements for visitors ranging from one room, to one floor, to the entire house. There's a honeymoon suite downstairs with a guest kitchen, living room with fireplace, and patio. Other choices include king- or queen-sized canopied rice beds with private baths.

Morning Star Bed and Breakfast looks like a Victorian farmhouse in a vision of yellow and white overlooking the Nashville skyline in the distance. It looks like vintage country but is actually a modern construction, which means it's the best of both.

There are four-poster king beds to lounge on and restored claw-foot tubs to soak in. There are a couple of practice tees for golfers, and breakfast can be served in the gazebo if you'd like.

If you're up for a full day on the links, visit Country Hills Golf Course, an eighteen-hole, par-70 public course or Bluegrass Yacht and Country Club's eighteen-hole PGA Championship course. There's also a Holiday Inn in town.

Dining choices range from "meat and three" at Mallard's or the Mason Jar, to combinations of toppings named for showbiz personalities at Hollywood Pizza. Steaks and seafood are the fare at Creekwood Bar and Grill and Tony's Lake House Grill. Center Point Barbecue has served delicious 'cue to loyal customers for more than thirty years. Take a few of their delicious fried fruit pies along for snacks later.

The arts are represented in Hendersonville by the Hendersonville Art Council's gallery in the historic Bradford-Berry House. The Bell Cove Club on the lake offers a venue for musicians ranging from bluegrass to rock.

From Hendersonville, take 31E to Old Hickory Boulevard and follow TN 45 to its intersection with US 70. US 70 leads to Lebanon, our next stop on this tour.

All of the following accommodations are Hendersonville with zip code 37077, and all telephone listings are area code 615, except where noted.

Accommodations:
LakeView Bed and Breakfast, 118 Venlee Dr., 824-0257.
Morning Star Bed and Breakfast, 460 Jones Ln., 264-2614.
Spring Haven Bed and Breakfast, 545 E. Main St., 826-1825.

Attractions:
Bell Cove Club, 822-7074.
Bluegrasss Yacht and Country Club, 824-6528.
Country Hills Golf Course, 824-1100.
Hendersonville Arts Council and Gallery Gifts, 822-0789.
Rock Castle, 824-0502.
Trinity Music City, 826-9191.
USACE Visitor Center, 822-4846.

Dining:
Center Point Barbecue, 824-9330.
Creekwood Bar and Grill, 826-0207.
Hollywood Pizza, 822-7723.
Irene's Frontier Kitchen, 824-9826.
Loco Lupe's Mexican Restaurant and Cantina, 826-8339.
Mallard's Restaurant, 822-4668.
Mason Jar Restaurant, 822-0288.
Tony's Lake House Grille, 826-9696.

Shopping:
Antique Gallery, 824-0930.
Hendersonville Antique Mall, 824-5850.
Sunflowers Antique Gallery, 824-2311.
Treasure Hut Antiques, 824-0930.
Tuttle Brothers Antiques, 824-7222.

Special Events:
April—Cedar Lane Festival, at the Bradford-Berry House

Camping:
Lakeshore Campground, 639 Walton Ferry Rd., 822-6638. 27 sites.

For More Information:
Hendersonville Area Chamber of Commerce, 101 Wessington Pl., 824-2818.

38 *Lebanon and Watertown*
Antiques Capital of
Middle Tennessee

There are a couple of stops you might be interested in along US 70W between Mount Juliet and Lebanon. Rice and Sons Old Country Ham Store has county-fair-winning hams on order months in advance by patrons who appreciate the end results of a ten-month aging process.

Ed Rice Jr. is the fourth generation to use the old-fashioned way of coaxing peak flavor while losing grease. Breeden's Orchard, Pie Kitchen and Cider Mill produces apples, honey, peaches, pears, pumpkins, sorghum, and cider on Beckwith Road off US 70.

The Natureview Inn sits on a hill overlooking horses grazing in pasture. There are four rooms with private baths and a swimming pool to relax in. Guests have a choice of a Tennessee country breakfast or New Mexico southwestern-style fare. Children are welcome and dogs are too. Stalls are available for horses.

Revolutionary War veteran Ned Jacobs built the first house in the area in 1780 near a spring. His wife, Layula, a member of a North Carolina Indian tribe, is credited with saving victims of a cholera epidemic in 1835 by using herbal medicines. Today the spring that drew Jacobs here is beneath the Public Square of Lebanon, which has one of the largest concentrations of antique shops and malls in Tennessee. You can easily spend an afternoon browsing and if you come on a flea market weekend there are even more treasures in town.

Around the corner, you'll find the New City Cafe serving meat and three, sandwiches, soups, salads, and fresh desserts for lunch weekdays.

You can stop in for an espresso for breakfast if you're getting an early start or try a sandwich, cup of cappuccino, and a sweet treat for lunch at the Perfect Cup Coffeehouse just down the street from the square on North Maple.

The selections expand to include steaks and seafood for lunch and dinner every day at Meacham's Cafe. Elaine's Country Restaurant will serve you a hot breakfast at the crack of dawn or country cooking plus steaks and seafood for

Lebanon's town square is one of Middle Tennessee's highlights for antiques shoppers.

lunch. You'll have to catch them on Friday night if you want frog legs for dinner—it's the only night they're open.

Lebanon was laid out in 1802 and chartered in 1819. Sam Houston practiced law here in a little red courthouse that stood in the center of Public Square. Andrew Jackson had a store on the south side of Public Square here for a time. According to some accounts, many of the buildings and homes in Lebanon were burned during a Civil War battle that took place on the square in 1862. Lebanon was suspected of being a stronghold for Confederate spies.

As a result of the rebuilding, many of the homes and buildings are Victorian in appearance rather than antebellum. One of the older houses in the area is the Fite-Fessenden House. Built in 1852, it is now the home of the Wilson County Museum.

Public Square was once the scene of gigantic mule sales. Now it's the home of several celebrations including Cedarfest, a gathering of buck dancers, fiddlers, artists, checker players, food vendors, and craftsmen the third week in July. In late November the streets are transformed to a Victorian Christmas with carolers, carriage rides, home tours, and bags of roasted chestnuts.

The square has been refurbished with old-fashioned street lights, attractive comfortable benches, and barrels with bright flowers spilling out of them. It's a nice place to visit.

The Hamblen House Bed and Breakfast is an early 1900s bungalow near Cumberland University about six blocks from Public Square. There are three antique-filled bedrooms with private or shared bath. A full country breakfast is served. National franchises include Best Western, Days Inn, Hampton Inn, and Holiday Inn.

Lebanon was named for the biblical cedars of

Hiking Trails offer visitors the opportunity to explore areas featuring limestone caves once used by moonshiners.

Lebanon. The vast cedar forests early settlers found here produced wood that was much sought after for its resistance to rot and relatively light weight.

By 1910 the cedar forests were nearly gone. South of town the Cedars of Lebanon State Park is part of an area of more than nine thousand acres including the adjacent forest that comprises one of the largest remaining cedar forests in the United States.

The Civilian Conservation Corps hired local workers to plant the trees you see today. Rather than true cedars, the Corps planted a very similar tree, the juniper, in an effort to reforest an area that had become desolate. Within this area are deep limestone caves like Hidden Spring Cave which was used by moonshiners. The name given to such a formation with numerous caves and sinkholes is Karst topography. Water with a lower pH after being combined with decaying organic material and carbon dioxide seeps into gaps in limestone and slowly dissolves it, eventually creating caves.

There are also cedar glades, or rocky clearings, that harbor unique plant communities able to tolerate the higher temperatures found in the thin-soiled rocky glades. The rare Tennessee coneflower finds a home in this somewhat harsh environment as do about 350 additional species of plants. Several wildflower species including coneflowers are seen along Hidden Springs Trail.

The park has nine two-bedroom cabins, 117 campsites with electric and water hookups, three shower houses, picnic tables and shelters, an outdoor swimming pool, and eight miles of hiking trails. There are also ball fields, tennis courts, playgrounds, and a Frisbee golf course.

The park does not rent horses but stables may be reserved for overnight guests wanting to take their mounts on the six miles of horseback-riding trails inside the park. There are additional hiking and horseback-riding trails in the state forest. Dogs are welcome but must be well-mannered and kept on a leash.

The James E. Ward Agricultural Center is home to the annual Wilson County Fair and to a permanent exhibit collectively called Fiddlers Grove. More than twenty original buildings donated by individuals, families, and businesses in the area have been reconstructed to recreate an old-time village at Fiddlers Grove.

Watertown is Lebanon's historic neighbor. Located in the Round Lick Creek valley it was originally named Three Forks because the three forks of the creek joined here.

Three Forks was renamed to honor a prominent citizen, Wilson Lawrence Waters. According to Robert Brandt in *Touring Middle Tennessee Backroads,* Waters was a Republican who freed his slaves prior to the Civil War. He attended the 1860 convention that supported Lincoln's candidacy. He also helped bring the Tennessee Central Railroad to Watertown.

Each April an excursion train sponsored by the Tennessee Central Railway Museum travels seventy-six miles roundtrip from Nashville to Watertown to shop A Mile-Long Yard Sale, visit at the antique and craft shops on the square, and sample some country-cooking area restaurants.

The Watertown Bed and Breakfast offers five rooms with private baths for visitors to the former 1898 Railroad Hotel. It's furnished with antiques

and you're invited to curl up with a good book from their generous library or ride the tandem bike they loan guests around town if you'd prefer. A full breakfast is served but you may want to venture out to the Barn for country cooking at lunch. The Depot Junction Restaurant is open every day. You can watch the model train while you wait for your meal to be prepared at breakfast, lunch, or dinner most days. From Lebanon, take US 70N to Carthage.

All of the following accommodations are Lebanon with zip code 37087, and all telephone listings are area code 615, except where noted.

Accommodations:
Cedars of Lebanon State Park, 328 Cedar Forest Rd., 800-421-6683 or 443-2769.
The Hamblen House Bed and Breakfast, 126 Tarver, 443-0327.
Natureview Inn, 3354 Old Lebanon Dirt Rd., Mount Juliet, 37122; 800-758-7972 or 758-4439.
Watertown Bed and Breakfast, 116 Depot Ave., Watertown, 37184; 237-9999.

The Watertown Bed and Breakfast is located in the old Railroad Hotel.

Attractions:
Cedars of Lebanon State Park, 443-2769.
Cumberland University, 800-467-0562 or 444-2562.
Fiddler's Grove Historical Village, 443-2626.
Wilson County Museum, 444-9127.

Dining:
The Barn, Watertown, 237-3008.
Depot Junction Restaurant, Watertown, 237-3976.
The Perfect Cup, 444-8037.
New City Cafe, 444-7117.
Sunset Restaurant, 444-9530.

Shopping:
Breeden's Orchard, Pie Kitchen and Cider Mill, Mount Juliet, 449-2880.
Cuz's Antiques, 444-8070.
Denise's Timeless Treasures, 443-4996.
Downtown Antique Mall, 443-3133.
The Emporium, 449-9601.
Heartbreak Ridge, 449-5993.
The Main Exchange, 449-6889.
Ophelia's Antiques, 443-0783.
Rice and Sons Old Country Ham Store, Mount Juliet, 758-2362.
Southern Rose Antiques, 444-3308.

Special Events:
April—Watertown Mile Long Yard Sale
July—Cedarfest
October—Moonlight Madness on the Square
November—Victorian Christmas

Camping:
Cedars of Lebanon State Park, 443-2769.

For More Information:
Lebanon/Wilson County Chamber of Commerce, 800-789-1327.

39 *Carthage*
Motorcades and Watersports

William Walton chose a spot on Tennessee's Eastern Highland Rim to redeem his land grant and moved his family here from Mansker's Station sometime after 1795. The Eastern Highland Rim is located between the fertile Nashville Basin to the west and the Cumberland Plateau to the east and is generally about three hundred feet higher than the basin and one thousand feet lower than the plateau.

For many years Walton operated a ferry at the confluence of the Caney Fork and Cumberland Rivers. He played an important role in the early settlement of the lands on and beyond the Cumberland Plateau by cutting a new road from present-day Cookeville to the mouth of the Caney Fork at present-day Carthage around 1801. The primary road between Knoxville and Nashville came to be known as the Walton Road. Today US 70N and I-40 follow this route across the Cumberland Plateau east of Carthage.

Three years later Walton's Ferry, as the community that grew up here was known, was chosen as the county seat of Smith County and renamed Carthage. A brick courthouse was erected in 1805 but the present Second Empire-style Smith County Courthouse was built in 1879.

The first steamboat made its way to Carthage from Nashville around 1829. Supplies arrived by this route and goods were taken back to markets downriver, so the arrival of the boats, or packets as they were called, generated lots of activity in the small towns up the Cumberland from Nashville, like Carthage and Celina. River traffic continued to dominate commerce in the remote upper Cumberland area long after railroads had captured substantial markets in other areas.

While you're visiting, you may spot motorcades bringing Vice President Al Gore home to visit his family. Carthage was once home to Cordell Hull, secretary of state under Franklin Roosevelt and "father of the United Nations."

Cordell Hull Lake is an impoundment of the Cumberland River. The construction of the dam began in 1963 and the project was completed for full use in 1973. The dam is about five miles upstream from Carthage, creating a 72-mile-long riverine lake with 381 shoreline miles. It has only two commercial marinas, Defeated Creek Marina at Carthage and Granville Marina in the lake's midsection. Both have cabin rentals, restrooms, and campgrounds.

There are eight U.S. Army Corps of Engineer (USACE) recreation areas. Five have campgrounds, most have ramps. The visitor center at the resource manager's office near the dam has exhibits about wildlife in Middle Tennessee and the generation of hydroelectric power.

The Bearwaller Gap Trail near the Cordell Hull Lock and Dam extends six miles bordering the lake along the outside of Horseshoe Bend. The Cordell Hull Horse Trail near Granville loops along Hollemans Bend to the Fort Blount Historic Site. According to Holly Sherwin in *Canoeing in Tennessee,* the most scenic part of the lake for canoeing is from Celina to Granville.

The fishing is good here with species ranging from bass, bluegill, and catfish to stripe, walleye, and sauger. Carthage Antique Mall on Third Avenue, Flower Basket Antiques, and Windy Hill Antiques have antiques and collectibles.

There are several other shops outside town including West Antiques, Massey's Country Antiques on Defeated Creek, Heavenly Treasures, and Pa's Antiques in Gordonsville. They welcome browsers and adore buyers.

The Gibbs Landing Bed and Breakfast sits at the end of the road facing the Caney Fork River as it joins the Cumberland River. Flower gardens, nature trails, and views from the riverfront bedrooms invite you to relax. There are private baths, an outdoor hot tub, and screened porches for enjoying the sounds of the river. You can arrange for a candlelight dinner on Fridays and Saturdays.

The Smith County Fall Heritage Festival is held on the town square. Arts and crafts, food booths, and heritage craft demonstrations are offered.

Return to Crossville on US 70 to complete this loop tour or rejoin I-40 and travel to Nashville.

All of the following accommodations are Carthage with zip code 37030, and all telephone listings are area code 615, except where noted.

Accommodations:
Cordell Hull Motel, Hwy. 25, 735-1300.
Defeated Creek Marina, 156 Marina Ln., 774-3131.
Gibbs Landing Bed and Breakfast, 136 Gibbs Landing, 735-2198.
Hospitality House Bed and Breakfast, 703 Main St., 735-3369.
Pride Hollow Bed and Breakfast, 52 Grant Hwy., Gordonsville, 38565; 683-6396 or 237-3540.

Dining:
B and B Drive-In, Elmwood, 735-9657.
City Cafeteria, 735-9990.
David's, 735-9990.
La Villa, 735-1331.
O. J.'s Family Restaurant, Gordonsville, 683-6441.
Watson's Bar-B-Que, 735-1575.

Shopping:
Carthage Antique Mall, 735-1590.
Creekside Antiques, 735-3190.
Flower Basket Antiques, 735-9585.
Massey's Country Antiques, 774-3146.
Pa's Antiques, Gordonsville, 683-6711.
West Antiques, 735-9658.
Windy Hill Antiques, 735-2561.

Special Events:
June—Gordonsville Fun Festival; Defeated Creek Country and Bluegrass Jamboree
October—Smith County Fall Heritage Festival

Camping:
Defeated Creek Campground, 774-3141.

For More Information:
Smith County Chamber of Commerce, P.O. Box 70; 735-1622.
Resource Manager, Cordell Hull Lake, Rt. 1, Box 62; 735-1034.

⨯⟲Nashville

40 *Nashville*
Music City USA

Nashville/Davidson County has a present population of about one-half million and is one of the fastest growing cities in the nation. It welcomes visitors daily from all over the world to a city whose skyline is pierced with skyscrapers, yet its friendly people still smile when they pass you on the street.

Some visitors are drawn to its antebellum mansions, museums, great restaurants, and many opportunities for outdoor recreation, but it remains one of the best destinations in the world if you're a music lover.

Although country music dominates the musical scene in Nashville with the Grand Ole Opry on Friday and Saturday nights, Tin Pan South, a showcase of Nashville's finest songwriters in April, and the International Country Music Fan Fair each June, you'll also be able to enjoy blues, jazz, classical, gospel, opera, Broadway musicals, and rock 'n' roll performances in a variety of settings ranging from the intimate Bluebird Cafe to the Tennessee Performing Arts Center (TPAC) and Starwood Amphitheater.

One of Nashville's newest attractions is the National Football League's Tennessee Titans, formerly known as the Houston Oilers. The team's new stadium in downtown Nashville along the east bank of the Cumberland River is scheduled for completion in fall 1999 and is eagerly welcomed by football fans.

The east bank of the Cumberland had a much different appearance when two separate parties of nearly five hundred settlers departed from East Tennessee in the fall of 1779. James Robertson led most of the men and boys across the overland route so they could drive the horses, cows, and sheep needed by the new settlement. They crossed the frozen Cumberland River on Christmas Day 1779.

The second party set out from the Boatyard at Long Island on the Holston River near present-day Kingsport. This group was led by Col. John Donelson and consisted of the women and children of thirty families traveling on flatboats with about thirty men to work the boats and defend them against the Indians.

They certainly had their work cut out for them on the one-thousand-mile river journey. They ran aground on uncharted shoals, repelled Indian attacks, and endured a smallpox outbreak along the way, but the group arrived the following spring with the household goods considered essential for frontier life, joining Robertson's group on April 24, 1780.

The new Cumberland settlement quickly established seven stations or forts along the Cumberland River to offer protection for the settlers from the hostile actions of Indians, including a renegade branch of the Cherokee known as the Chickamauga.

The central station at French Lick became known as Fort Nashborough, named for Gen. Francis Nash, a Revolutionary War veteran. Fort Nashborough prospered and was renamed Nashville in 1784 to eliminate the English-sounding *borough*. Originally part of North Carolina, Nashville became part of the sixteenth state in the Union in 1796 and the capital of the state thirty years later.

Nashville's skyline overlooks the Cumberland River. (David Wright photo courtesy of Nashville Convention and Visitors Bureau)

In the early 1800s Nashville was on the edge of the "new" western frontier. An overland route between Nashville and Natchez, Mississippi, known as the Natchez Trace, played an important part in maintaining communication between the young central government in Washington and the territory to the west.

Many of the leaders of our nation came from Nashville including Andrew Jackson who was elected president of the United States in 1828.

Following the election of Abraham Lincoln, South Carolina, Georgia, and Alabama seceded from the Union. The Confederacy was established and Jefferson Davis was elected as its president in 1861. Nashville, along with the rest of Tennessee, threw itself reluctantly into the fray on the side of the Confederacy.

After the Federals captured Fort Donelson seventy miles down the Cumberland from Nashville, the Union Army occupied Nashville until the end of the war, with Andrew Johnson the military governor.

During Reconstruction the city struggled for economic recovery. Nashville encountered additional hardships during two cholera epidemics, the first in 1866 followed by another in 1873. A few years later, the town had recovered and a business boom cycle was under way that culminated in the

Second Avenue is the heart of a collection of restaurants, night spots, specialty shops, and historic sites known collectively as the District.

Centennial Exposition which opened in 1897 on the land now called Centennial Park.

The construction of the world's only full-size replica of the Parthenon for this exhibition and the presence of sixteen institutions of higher learning, six graduate schools, two law schools, and two medical schools gave rise to one of Nashville's nicknames, "Athens of the South."

In addition to hosting sports events, the Nashville Arena on Broadway has become a favorite venue for up to twenty thousand concert goers queuing up for the likes of Amy Grant, LeAnn Rimes, and Jimmy Buffet.

The City Walk tour begins at Fort Nashborough on First Avenue North, a 1962 reconstruction of the original Cumberland River settlement. The contiguous 7.5-acre Riverfront Park is the site of free Dancin' in the District outdoor concerts every Thursday night in the summer, as well as other concerts with admission fees throughout the summer season.

As you continue the City Walk, you'll visit historic Second Avenue which is part of the area

also containing lower Broadway and Printer's Alley known as the District.

The District is a hotspot of urban revitalization of Nashville landmarks like the Ryman Auditorium and new arrivals including the Hard Rock Cafe, the Wildhorse Saloon, and Planet Hollywood.

The Ryman Auditorium was built after riverboat magnate Tom Ryman heard the preaching of famous evangelist Samuel Jones, one of the most important revivalists of his day. Capt. Thomas Green Ryman, owned thirty-five steamboats, "some of which were floating dens of iniquity." The news of Ryman's conversion flew through the city like wildfire. Ryman envisioned a huge tabernacle to continue the revival and to serve as a Nashville home for Sam Jones. The Union Gospel Tabernacle was built between 1889 and 1892. After Ryman's death, it was renamed the Ryman Auditorium in his honor and welcomed performers like Enrico Caruso and Sarah Bernhardt before it became the "mother church" of country music.

The National Life and Accident Insurance Company's (L&C) WSM Barn Dance began its radio broadcasts in the WSM studios in 1925. Two years later announcer George Hay facetiously dubbed it the "Grand Ole Opry" after it followed an opera broadcast.

Early performers included Vanderbilt University physician Dr. Humphrey Bate's string band and Uncle Dave Macon. The performers featured on the Opry had to be available for Saturday night performances so many of them found that living in or near Nashville was convenient and the industry slowly took shape.

After performing in several Nashville locations, the Opry saw its crowds continue to grow, and in 1943 it moved to the Ryman Auditorium.

During this time the music evolved from folk music to bluegrass to the Nashville Sound as country music found its way into the homes of mainstream America and an international audience.

Although the Ryman is no longer the home of the Grand Ole Opry, which moved to Opryland in 1974, it has become a performing arts center hosting performers ranging from Mary Chapin-Carpenter and Garrison Keillor to Bruce Springsteen and Alison Krauss. The Ryman is also the site of special musical productions highlighting the lives and works of country legends like Hank Williams and Patsy Cline. In addition, self-guided tours and exhibits on the main floor with photographs, videos, and memorabilia are well worth a visit for country music lovers.

Printers Alley, situated between Third and Fourth Avenues and bounded by Church and Union Streets, evolved from a haven for newspaper printers to speakeasies on its way to becoming the center of Nashville's nightlife in the 1940s. It remains a popular tourist attraction. The Bourbon Street Blues and Boogie Bar has live blues per-

Ryman Auditorium was the home of WSM's Grand Ole Opry for more than thirty years. (Donnie Beauchamp photo courtesy of Nashville Convention and Visitors Bureau)

formances nightly and Barbara's is popular with Music City musicians. In its heyday, Tootsie's Orchid Lounge on Broadway was a haven for singers and songwriters who dropped in for a break between sets at the Opry across the alley or a small loan to tide them over.

At the Nashville Hard Rock Cafe on Broadway, you may browse for free among walls filled with rock 'n' roll memorabilia from Elvis to Springsteen or sample a menu that tends toward burgers, 'cue, salads, pasta, and blue-plate specials for lunch and dinner.

Planet Hollywood is also on Broadway. You can't miss its revolving planet outside and won't want to miss the movie memorabilia inside. Like the Hard Rock, it's a fun spot to grab a burger or a sandwich.

The Wildhorse Saloon is a huge country music club owned by Gaylord Entertainment which also owns the Ryman Auditorium and Opryland Hotel. You'll find live country music performances by house bands here every night as well as concerts by headliners throughout the year. There's a cover charge that varies depending on the evening's entertainment. The Nashville Network (TNN) tapings happen every Tuesday and Wednesday.

There's a three-thousand-square-foot dance floor ringed with seats on two levels. Line dance classes are featured some nights for beginners. Replenish yourself with soups, salads, barbecue, and grilled sandwiches. Food is served from 11 A.M. to 10 P.M. and the dancing continues until 2 A.M. You may also visit one of the three bars on two levels. Children are welcome but must be accompanied by an adult.

Hatch Show Print on Broadway has produced promotional handbills for acts ranging from vaudeville to Grand Ole Opry stars since 1879. There's no formal tour, but you're welcome to walk around inside. Admission is free and you can purchase one of their posters if you'd like.

There are lots of specialty shops and restaurants in the District. One of the more unusual is the Broadway Dinner Train. Departing at the foot of Broadway at 6:30 P.M., it includes a thirty-five-mile train ride and a four-course dinner. The Melting Pot, a fondue restaurant, is a nice place to go for a long, relaxing meal accompanied by good conversation or a lively group of friends.

Mere Bulles has an upscale lounge with live entertainment as well as dining rooms overlooking the Cumberland and one of the best wine lists in town. On the other end of the scale, but at the same end of the street, the Spaghetti Factory provides a fun evening out if you need to watch your budget.

San Antonio Taco on Commerce isn't fancy but the chicken fajitas and cold beer are tough to beat and the price is right. Also on Commerce,

Demos' Steak and Spaghetti House has lots of pasta dishes along with reasonably priced steaks, salads, and weekday lunch specials.

Cafe Milano on Third Avenue North is a wonderful restaurant with live entertainment ranging from classical to big band sounds every night but Sunday. It can seat more than two hundred and the music sounds great because of the excellent acoustics.

The Merchants Restaurant on Broadway offers lunch and dinner if you're interested in fine dining and a romantic atmosphere. In the evening, the first-floor menu is a little more casual and prices go up significantly as you ascend to the second floor with its signature dishes.

Still in the downtown area, but several blocks from the District, the Tennessee Performing Arts Center (TPAC) on Deaderick is the home of the Nashville Symphony. Ballet, opera, repertory theater, and traveling Broadway musical series are also welcomed to TPAC. You may enjoy your choice of

The Tennessee State Capitol overlooks the Bicentennial Capitol Mall Park.

This replica of the Parthenon in Nashville's Centennial Park was originally constructed of temporary materials for the 1896 Exposition. (Photo courtesy of Nashville Convention and Visitors Bureau)

beverage from champagne to cappucino at TPAC, so it's a good idea to get there a little early for ease in parking and a little relaxation before the evening's performance.

The Tennessee State Museum is in the same building as TPAC. There's no charge for visiting exhibits on Tennessee history from prehistoric and historic Indian cultures to the Civil War, Prohibition, Civil Rights, and women's suffrage. The museum has a Military History Branch in the War Memorial Building across the street to the west. Both museums are closed Mondays.

Northwest of TPAC, the Tennessee State Capitol sits atop the highest hill in the area. Constructed in 1859, the antebellum structure was used by Union forces during Nashville's occupation. In addition to the tomb of the architect, William Strickland, at the northeast corner, the capitol grounds contain the graves of President and Mrs. James K. Polk and statues of Sam Davis, "boy hero of the Confederacy," (*see* Smyrna and

Pulaski) and World War I hero, Alvin C. York (*see* Byrdstown). The building is open to visitors weekdays and the legislature may be viewed from the visitors gallery when it's in session. Self-guided walking brochures are available at the information desk on the first floor.

The capitol and the War Memorial Plaza across the street bustle with booksellers, authors, and their readers during the Southern Festival of Books in October. The three-day event draws nearly two hundred authors for readings, panel discussions, and signings attended by thirty thousand bibliophiles.

The capitol overlooks Tennessee's newest state park to the north, the Bicentennial Capitol Mall State Park. Built in 1996, this park is open from 6 A.M. to midnight. Nashville Architect Kem Hinton designed a two-hundred-foot granite map of the state, thirty-one water fountains, and a Wall of History to commemorate the bicentennial.

The Nashville Farmers' Market was renovated

from creaky wooden stalls to the gleaming structure you see today when the park was built. Inside you'll find the same great selection of plants and produce as well as specialty and deli markets.

Two blocks away the Mad Platter has an intimate dining room with crisp white linens, fresh flowers on the table, and great food. Next door, Monell's serves southern food family style for lunch and dinner, which puts you in mind of Sundays at Grandma's house.

Most of the downtown accommodations recommend booking in advance since more than nine million visitors arrive in Nashville annually. The summer tourist season is busiest during Fan Fair in June, but rooms are booked far in advance for Country Music Week in October as well.

On Broadway you'll find the Clubhouse Inn and Suites and Union Station, a bustling railroad station in 1900 that has been restored and converted to elegant quarters for your stay in Nashville. From the beautiful stained-glass ceiling vaulting sixty-five feet above the lobby to the 124 tastefully decorated guest rooms, this National Historic Landmark provides luxurious accommodations. Downstairs, Arthur's restaurant features upscale Continental cuisine for dinner, while McKinley's serves a buffet breakfast, and the Broadway Bistro serves lunch, dinner, and cocktails.

Union Street near the capitol and TPAC offers the five-story no-frills Days Inn Downtown and Crowne Plaza Nashville, a twenty-eight-floor, 473-room hotel with a landmark revolving rooftop restaurant named the Pinnacle that offers a spectacular view of Nashville at night.

South of TPAC and the Tennessee State Museum, the Hermitage Suite Hotel on Sixth Avenue North was the site of the struggle for women's suffrage in 1920, the year Tennessee

became the thirty-sixth state to ratify the Nineteenth Amendment to the Constitution, reaching the majority needed to give women the right to vote all across the United States (see Livingston). It is Nashville's only remaining historic hotel. Built in 1910 in the elaborate beaux-arts style, a recent $4 million renovation updated its luxurious one- and two-bedroom suites. The Capitol Grille is reputed to be one of the best restaurants in the country and it serves lunch and dinner daily.

Other downtown hotels include the Doubletree on Fourth Avenue and the Renaissance Nashville on Commerce, which adjoins the Nashville Convention Center and is also convenient to the attractions in the District.

From Broadway turn south on Fourth Avenue and watch for the sign on your right at Oak Street to visit the Cumberland Science Museum and Sudekum Planetarium on Fort Negley Boulevard. Children and adults will find hands-on exhibits designed to explore technology, the environment, physics, and health.

The Country Music Hall of Fame will be located on Music Row until late 1999.

The Hillsboro House Bed and Breakfast is conveniently located for all Music Row/Vanderbilt activities.

Take Eighth Avenue South to visit Nashville's largest antiques district. Most of the shops are in the first few blocks south of the intersection with Wedgewood Avenue. Others are on Wedgewood east of Eighth Avenue on the way to the Tennessee State Fairground, the site of the Nashville Flea Market the fourth weekend of most months.

Nearby you'll find Douglas Corner Cafe, a small neighborhood bar on Eighth Avenue that showcases top songwriters and rising performers.

Travel west on Broadway, crossing over Interstate 40, to the *Y* split and follow the left side of the intersection to visit Music Row, Vanderbilt Medical Center, Hillsboro Village, and Green Hills.

The right side of this *Y* becomes West End Avenue which passes along the northern edge of Vanderbilt University on the way to Centennial Park and Belle Meade, the home of the Warner Parks.

As you continue along West End, you'll be traveling parallel to Elliston Place, a thoroughfare filled with shops and restaurants like the classic Elliston Place Soda Shop with ice cream treats and meat-and-three combos and Elder's Bookstore which has produced several reprints of historically significant books and has thousands of rare and out-of-print books in stock. Red Hot and Blue, TGI Friday's, Chez Jose, Tower Books and Records, Rotier's, and the Calypso Cafe line Elliston Place as you approach Centennial Park. Jimmy Kelly's is nearby and has served appreciative Nashvillians steaks and seafood since 1932.

The first replica of the Parthenon was made of plaster and wood, but it was reconstructed from concrete in the 1920s. At this writing, the Parthenon was open to the public but undergoing renovation to stabilize the detailed frieze and pediment.

In addition to the Parthenon with its impressive statue of Athena and downstairs art museum,

Centennial Park, on West End Avenue near Vanderbilt, has picnic areas, open green spaces, and lovely landscaping. It hosts excellent craft shows including the TACA spring and fall shows, the American Artisan Show, and free presentations during the summer of Nashville Shakespeare Festival's Shakespeare in the Park.

Hog Heaven on the park's western border serves some of Nashville's best barbecue and an outstanding white barbecue sauce that's downright heavenly if you'd like to picnic in the park.

If none of these choices appeal to you, continue on West End to the Tin Angel, the Way Out West Cafe, Houston's, or our favorite, the Cakewalk Cafe, renamed Zola under Deb Pacquette's watchful eyes and experienced hands.

A graduate of the Culinary Institute more than twenty years ago, Deb was the first female executive chef in Tennessee and has a loyal following in Nashville. Zola is light and airy with a Mediterranean feel and the delicious eclectic menu Nashvillians have come to expect from Pacquette and her staff.

If you continue on West End, it becomes Harding Road as it passes in front of Percy Warner Park. Together the Warner Parks contain 2,665 acres bordered by some of the finest homes in Nashville. One of the largest municipally operated parks in the United States, the parks contain more than twenty-eight miles of roads, two stone bridges, numerous picnic shelters, the steeplechase course, and miles of beautiful dry-stacked stone retaining walls from the late 1930s. Additional amenities in Percy Warner Park include a twenty-seven-hole golf course. The annual Iroquois Steeplechase, part gala and part horse race, is held here each year.

The Belle Meade Mansion on Harding Road was one of Tennessee's greatest plantations. The 1853 Greek Revival Mansion distinguished a 5,400-acre Thoroughbred farm and nursery that began with the purchase of 250 acres and a log cabin along the Natchez Trace at a trading post known as Dunham Station. At onetime Belle Meade was the largest Thoroughbred farm in America. It counted Iroquois, the winner of the English Derby in 1881, among its many great steeds.

At the junction of TN 100 and TN 70, bear left onto TN 100. You'll soon see the sign for Cheekwood—Nashville's Home of Art and Gardens. Once the home of a member of the Cheek family of Maxwell House Coffee fame, the mansion now houses a permanent collection of eighteenth-, nineteenth-, and twentieth-century art in addition to visiting collections. The grounds contain splendid display gardens ranging from the Howe Wildflower Garden to rose gardens and peaceful ponds filled with darting koi. The Pineapple Room restaurant offers delicious lunches overlooking a lush meadow. Continue on Highway 100 to the northern terminus of the Natchez Trace Parkway, a 450-mile scenic drive along the historic route between Natchez and Nashville.

Bear to the right at the Highway 100/70 split to visit the Rose Garden, Jim and Shirley Rupperts homestay accommodations. In addition to a lovely rose garden, the Rupperts invite visitors to enjoy an entire downstairs living area with private entrance, fireplace, seating area, queen and twin beds, and a stocked kitchen. Continue along TN 70 to Bellevue Mall, another shopping mecca for Middle Tennesseans.

Music Row And Vicinity

The area known as Music Row is the heart of Nashville's recording industry. Bound by Demonbreun Avenue on the north and Music Square

The amazing Opryland Hotel is located next to the Grand Ole Opry House. (Photo courtesy of Opryland Hotel Convention Center)

East and West (formerly known as Sixteenth and Seventeenth Avenues), Music Row is the home of more than a dozen major record labels and nearly three hundred music publishing companies.

Of great interest to visitors with a fondness for country music, the Country Music Hall of Fame and Museum at the corner of Music Square East and Demonbreun is open daily except Thanksgiving, Christmas, and New Year's Day. The museum is slated to move to new, expanded quarters beside the Nashville Arena in late 1999.

Included in the price of admission is a twenty-minute Music Row tour on trolleys that depart from the museum every fifteen minutes. A tour guide will point out recording studios, record labels, publishing companies, offices of performers, and performing rights organizations like ASCAP and BMI.

There's also a stop at RCA's historic Studio B for a studio tour and a chance to glimpse a recording session in progress behind the sound-proof glass.

Demonbreun Street near Music Row has a plethora of tourist attractions and souvenir shops. Hank Williams Jr. Museum and Gift Shop has exhibits on both the legendary father and son.

The Shoney's Inn Music Row on Demonbreun

and the Quality Inn Hall of Fame on Division are both quite close to Music Row.

Granite Falls on Broadway is a popular lunch destination for the Music Row and Vandy crowd. In good weather the patio fills up quickly and in winter a heater and plastic windows let you continue dining out of doors. Lunch and dinner are served daily and the Sunday brunch is also very popular.

The menu at the Wild Boar down the street is unparalleled and many Nashvillians think the food, the service, and the wine list are the best in town. Dinner is served every night but Sunday.

Across the street, the Great Escape has an extensive collection of vintage records for sale. Vandy students frequent the San Antonio Taco Company on Twenty-first Avenue across from the campus. A few blocks south, the vegetarian pizza at Pizza Perfect lives up to its name.

Bed and breakfast travelers will want to visit the 1920s Georgian–style Commodore Inn & Guest House at 1614 Nineteenth Avenue South near Music Row and Vanderbilt. Guest rooms with private baths in the main house and a cottage with a living room with a fireplace and equipped kitchen in the back welcome visitors.

In the same vicinity, the Hillsboro House on Twentieth Avenue South is a lovely Victorian cottage with three charming guest rooms with feather beds and private baths. Both the Commodore Inn and the Hillsboro House serve scrumptious breakfasts.

Not far away, the Italianate Belmont Mansion at Belmont College on Wedgewood Avenue was the home of Adelicia Acklen, one of the wealthiest women in the United States during the Civil War. Visitors may tour the mansion and learn more about this remarkable Nashville woman.

Another notable Nashvillian, Judge John

The General Jackson *showboat departs from the dock near Opryland Hotel for a variety of cruises on the Cumberland River. (Donnie Beauchamp photo courtesy of Gaylord Entertainment)*

Overton, lived in the vicinity before 1800. Travellers Rest, the Federal-style two-story frame dwelling with double galleries, was Overton's home from 1789 to 1833. Overton was a lifelong friend of Andrew Jackson and one of the founders of Memphis in 1819. Confederate General John B. Hood headquartered here before the 1864 battle of Nashville.

For those of you visiting the Music Row/Hillsboro Village area, several of Nashville's best restaurants are in walking distance. The Midtown Cafe on Nineteenth Avenue South is quiet and casually elegant.

The Bound'ry on Twentieth Avenue South reigned supreme in the Summerlin household until executive chef Deb Pacquette returned to the Cakewalk. Now it's number two, but still an excellent choice. The decor features colorful murals matching the creations offered on the imaginative menu. If you've arrived without reservations and the Bound'ry's wait is too long, there's always the

South Street Smokehouse & Crab Shack and Authentic Dive Bar next door.

Our favorite lunch choice remains the Sunset Grill on Belcourt. Both the lunch and dinner menus have a good wine list and a wide variety of entrees including delicious vegetarian and low fat dishes, but for many the desserts top the list of delicacies. Since they stay open until 1:30 A.M. except on Sundays, the Sunset Grill is a great stop after concerts, movies, etc.

Hillsboro Village on Twenty-first Avenue South offers variety shops and popular restaurants. The Pancake Pantry is a Nashville tradition. Across the street Provence Breads and Cafe serves wonderful pastries, sandwiches, and cappucino. Grab a snack and head west a couple of blocks to Fannie Mae Dees Park, known locally as Dragon Park, for a picnic.

These restaurants along with Bongo Java, Boscos Nashville Brewing Company, and Jonathon's Village Cafe are casual and popular with Vandy/Music Row folks.

Continue on Twenty-first Avenue to Brown's Diner where the burgers are juicy, the fries are hot, and the beer is cold. What more could you ask for?

Shopping, perhaps? Twenty-first Avenue becomes Hillsboro Road on its way to the Mall at Green Hills, a favorite of Nashvillians with shopping on their minds. In addition to department stores and specialty shops, the area around the mall contains Davis-Kidd Booksellers with its delightful Second Story Cafe; Dad's Old Book Store, which has a good collection of used and rare books as well as authenticated signatures of famous personages; and Green Hills Antique Mall. The Green Hills Grille and Clayton Blackmon are popular dining destinations, as is the meat-and-three Sylvan Park restaurant on Bandywood behind Davis-Kidd.

One of Nashville's most popular musical venues, Amy Kurland's legendary Bluebird Cafe is on your left after you pass Davis-Kidd. The list of greats who have played here since it opened in 1982 range from Vince Gill and Garth Brooks to Mary Chapin-Carpenter and Bonnie Raitt, many of whom were up and coming at the time they performed.

The popular in-the-round format features many of Nashville's best songwriters. Reservations for each week's shows are taken by phone on Monday at noon. It's a good idea to have a phone with a redial button and lots of patience. It's worth the effort.

Continuing along Hillsboro Road for about five miles through the upper income Green Hills and Forest Hills neighborhoods you'll come to Otter Creek Road. A left turn will take you to Radnor Lake State Natural Area. The fourteen-hundred-acre facility has an eighty-five-acre lake and supports wildlife and hundreds of species of wildflowers, ferns, shrubs, and trees. All activities here must be low impact, which means Radnor is best suited to hiking, photography, and contemplation of this incredibly beautiful spot. The visitor center at the western end is a good place to learn about special activities like wildflower hikes and owl hoots.

Opryland and Vicinity

The jewel in Gaylord Entertainment's crown is the fabulous Opryland Hotel, off Briley Parkway east of downtown Nashville. With 2,883 rooms and suites, 600,000 square feet of meeting and exhibit space, massive indoor gardens covering nine acres, three swimming pools, fifteen restaurants and thirty shops, the Opryland Hotel is the largest combined hotel and convention center in the world.

The first of three glass-roofed indoor gardens, the Conservatory, emphasizes tropical plants. The Cascades followed in 1988 with waterfalls ranging from twenty-three to thirty-five feet tumbling from a forty-foot-tall mountain into a 12,500-square-foot lake. The Delta is the largest and newest of the three. Completed in 1996, the glass roof soars to 150 feet above the quarter-mile-long Delta River and its passenger-carrying flat boats. As you would expect, the landscaping is breathtaking. The restaurants are supervised by an award-winning culinary staff.

On Friday night, March 15, 1974, the final performance of the Opry at the Ryman took place. The following night, President Richard Nixon joined Roy Acuff onstage in the six-foot circle of hardwood brought from the Ryman and welcomed the audience to the first performance at the Grand Ole Opry House next to Opryland Hotel.

Built as the world's largest broadcast studio, the Grand Ole Opry House is also used for television productions and concerts. There's seating for two thousand on the orchestra level and twenty-four hundred in the balcony on carpeted wooden benches. All seats have unobstructed sight lines to the stage. The state-of-the-art sound system has nearly one hundred speakers and fifty microphone outputs on stage.

Three museums surround the Grand Ole Opry House. The Roy Acuff Musical Collection and Museum displays more than two hundred stringed instruments in addition to memorabilia acquired throughout his long career. The Minnie Pearl Museum focuses on the "Queen of Country Comedy" and the Grand Ole Opry Museum pays tribute to the world's longest-running radio show and its legendary performers. All three are free and open on Opry performance days.

In 1990 Opryland added the Springhouse Golf Club, an eighteen-hole Scottish links-style course designed by U.S. Open and PGA champion Larry Nelson that is the home of the Bell-South Senior Classic.

The *General Jackson* showboat, named for the first steamboat to arrive in Nashville in 1819, offers daily morning, lunch, and evening cruises for dining, entertainment, and sightseeing on the Cumberland for up to twelve hundred passengers. On a much smaller scale, Opryland river taxis carry up to one hundred passengers between Riverfront Park in downtown Nashville and Opryland.

Packages offered by Opryland include hotel accommodations, tickets to the Opry, one of ten sightseeing tours of Nashville, a cruise on the *General Jackson*, and a round-trip on the Opryland river taxis between downtown Nashville and Opryland. Tours are also offered by Johnny Walker Tours, Gray Line Country and Western Tours, and Civil War Tours of Tennessee. The Opryland theme park closed in 1997.

Other accommodations in the Opryland area include the Ramada Inn and Shoney's Inn on Music Valley Drive, as well as the End O' the Bend Lodge and Landing, a five-room log cabin with a screened porch overlooking the Cumberland River about a mile from Opryland. Guests rent the cabin, which includes two bedrooms with private baths, a fully equipped kitchen, and a great room with a fireplace.

The Holiday Nashville Travel Park, the Opryland KOA, and Two Rivers Campground are on Music Valley Drive. All three are open all year and have swimming pools and full hookups.

Our final Nashville destination is the Hermitage, home of President Andrew Jackson, east of Opryland on TN 45N (exit 221 from Interstate 40). At the Hermitage you'll learn about Jackson's early life and his move to the frontier town of Nashville in 1788 where he met Rachel Donelson Robards who became his wife in 1791 in Natchez, Mississippi, erroneously believing she was divorced from her first husband.

When the Jacksons learned of this mistake two years later, they remarried to legalize the union but were haunted by the scandal until Rachel's death on December 22, 1828, days before the grieving Jackson assumed his duties in the White House following a particularly nasty campaign for the presidency. The story is told that the man called "Old Hickory" cried over the cruel attacks on Rachel in the pro-John Quincy Adams press.

The famous hero of the battle of New Orleans returned to the Hermitage following two controversial terms as president. He settled down to the life of a gentleman farmer in 1837 at the age of seventy and worked off the debt he'd incurred while in office. He died on June 8, 1845, and is buried beside Rachel in a tomb on the southeastern corner of the garden.

Tours of the National Historic Landmark begin with a short film in the visitor center before beginning the tour of the Greek Revival antebellum home, the original cabins where the Jacksons lived from 1804 to 1819, and Tulip Grove, the home of Andrew Jackson Donelson, Rachel's nephew and the president's secretary.

Whether you come for music, history, or a relaxing getaway, Nashville welcomes you with open arms. Several communities within a short drive are explored in a series of loop tours departing from Nashville in the following chapters.

All of the following accommodations are Nashville, and all telephone listings are area code 615, except where noted.

Accommodations:
Clubhouse Inn and Suites, 920 Broadway, 800-258-2466 or 244-0150.
Commodore Bed and Breakfast, 1614 19th Ave. S., 269-3850.
Doubletree Hotel, 315 4th Ave. N., 800-528-0444 or 244-8200.
End O' the Bend Lodge and Landing, 2517 Miami Ave., 883-0997.
Guest Inn and Suites/Medcentre, 1909 Hayes St., 800-777-4904 or 329-1000.
The Hermitage Suite Hotel, 231 6th Ave., 800-251-1908 or 244-3121.
Opryland Hotel, 2800 Opryland Dr., 883-2211 or 889-1000.
Renaissance Nashville Hotel, 611 Commerce St., 800-HOTELS1 or 255-8400.
Shoney's Inn Music Row, 1521 Demonbreun St., 800-222-2222 or 255-9977.
Union Station Hotel, 1001 Broadway, 800-331-2123 or 726-1001.

Attractions:
Belle Meade Plantation, 800-270-3991 or 356-0501.
Belmont Mansion, 460-5459.
Bicentennial Capitol Mall State Park, 888-TNPARKS or 741-5280.
Centennial Park.
Chaffin's Barn Dinner Theatre, 646-9977.
Cheekwood—Nashville's Home of Art and Gardens, 353-2140.
Country Music Hall of Fame and Museum, 800-852-6437 or 256-1639.
Cumberland Science Museum and Sudekum Planetarium, 862-5160.
Douglas Corner Cafe, 298-1688.
Dragon Park.
Fort Nashborough, 862-8400.
Hatch Show Print, 256-2805.
The Hermitage, Hermitage, 889-2941.
Nashville Chamber Orchestra, 292-7815.
Nashville Symphony, 255-5600.
Ryman Auditorium, 889-6611.
Sarratt Performing Arts, 322-2471.
Tennessee Performing Arts Center, 782-4000 or Ticketmaster 737-4849.
Tennessee State Museum, 741-2692.
Travellers Rest Plantation House and Grounds, 832-8197.
The Upper Room Chapel & Museum, 340-7207.
Carl Van Vechten Gallery, Fisk University, 329-8720.
Warner Parks, 370-8051.

Dining:
Arthur's, 255-1494.
The Bound'ry, 321-3043.
Brown's Diner, 269-5509.
Demos' Steak & Spaghetti House, 256-4655.
Elliston Place Soda Shop, 327-1090.
F. Scott's, 259-5861.
Green Hill Grille, 383-6444.
Granite Falls, 327-9250.
Hard Rock Cafe, 742-9900.
Hog Heaven, 329-1234.
Houston's, 269-3481.
Jimmy Kelly's, 329-4349.
Loveless Cafe, 646-9700.
The Mad Platter, 242-2563.
The Melting Pot, 742-4970.
The Merchants, 254-1892.
Midtown Cafe, 320-7176.
Monell's, 248-4747.
Pancake Pantry, 383-9333.
The Pineapple Room, 352-4859.
Planet Hollywood, 313-STAR.
Provence Breads and Cafe, 386-0363.
Second Story Cafe, 385-0043.
South Street Smokehouse & Crab Shack & Authentic Dive Bar, 320-5555.
Sunset Grill, 386-3663.
The Wild Boar, 329-1313.
Wildhorse Saloon, 256-WILD.
Zola's 320-7778.

Shopping:
The American Artisan, 298-4691.
Antique Merchants Mall, 292-7811.
Cannery Antique Mall, 269-4780.
Dad's Old Bookstore, 298-5880.
Davis-Kidd Booksellers, 385-2645.
Downtown Antique Mall, 256-6616.
Elder's Bookstore, 327-1867.
The Great Escape, 327-0646.
Green Hills Antique Mall, 383-4999.
Local Color Gallery, 321-3141.
The Mall at Green Hills, 298-5478.
Old Negro League Sports Shop, 321-3186.
One Hundred Oaks Mall, 383-6002.
Pangea, 269-9665.
Whiteway Antique Mall, 327-1098.

Special Events:
January—Nashville Boat and Sport Show
February—Antiques and Garden Show; Heart of Country Antiques Show
April—Tin Pan South
May–Aug.—Dancin' in the District; TACA Spring Crafts Fair; Iroquois Steeplechase
June—American Artisan Festival; Fan Fair
September—Italian Street Fair
September—African Street Festival; TACA FAll Crafts Fair; Belle Meade Fall Fest
October—Southern Festival of Books; NAIA Pow Wow; Storytelling Festival
November—Americana Christmas Sampler Craft, Folk Art and Antiques Show; Christmas Village
December—Trees of Christmas; Twelfth Night Celebration

Camping:
Holiday Nashville Travel Park, 889-4225.
Two Rivers Campground, 883-8559.

For More Information:
Nashville Area Chamber of Commerce, 161 4th Ave. N., 259-4700.
Nashville Convention and Visitors Bureau, 161 4th Ave. N., 37219; 259-4730.
Tennessee Tourist Development, P.O. Box 23170, 37202; 741-2158.

Loop 7

41 Smyrna and Murfreesboro
Civil War Sites in the
Nashville Basin

Smyrna was a sleepy little community situated a few miles off the I-24 corridor before the arrival of the Nissan manufacturing plant in 1983. Visitors over the age of ten are invited for free tours of the facility on Tuesdays and Thursdays.

In addition to bringing lots of jobs to the area, Nissan has brought economic growth and new highways, strip malls, and subdivisions. Remnants from the past include the Smyrna Airfield, which now is a private airfield hosting a popular annual air show but once was a thriving military base. You'll see the remnants of the base housing as you approach the airport.

The oldest structure of interest to visitors is the 1820 home of the "Boy Hero of the Confederacy," Sam Davis. From a middle class family of nine children, Sam joined the First Tennessee Infantry at the age of nineteen.

In the fall of 1863, Davis was assigned to a group of scouts working behind enemy lines to obtain information about the movement of Union troops maneuvering to relieve the siege at Chattanooga. He was captured near Pulaski on November 9, 1863, by Union troopers while in possession of plans of Federal fortifications and information about the size and position of Federal troops.

Davis was asked repeatedly by Union general Grenville Dodge to name his informant in exchange for his life and was even offered a fresh horse and an escort to the Confederate line. Davis's reply has been quoted variously through the years but the essence became his epitaph, "If I had a thousand lives to live, I would give them all rather than betray a friend."

Dodge continued efforts to discover the identity of a possible traitor in his camp, but Davis remained steadfast. His character and courage won the admiration of the Union commander who was later one of the contributors for the purchase of a statue of Davis that stands on the capitol grounds in Nashville today.

Davis was court-martialed and convicted of spying. The sentence was death by hanging. By all accounts, he faced his death with bravery. After sending a final letter to his mother, he rode to the scaffold on his coffin and was hanged, taking the secret of his informant with him to his grave.

Visitors may tour the museum, home, and grounds daily. The annual Days on the Farm celebration demonstrates various aspects of farm life and the fall Heritage Days event is popular as well.

The upper sections of J. Percy Priest Lake, an impoundment of the U.S. Army Corps of Engineers (USACE) are accessible from Smyrna. The most popular lake in Middle Tennessee, Priest covers 14,200 surface acres during summer pool and is a good place to find crappie, black bass, white bass, and rockfish.

Fate Sanders Marina is a good place for bait and current fishing information. To get there, follow Sam Ridley Road east to Weakley Road and follow the signs. There are several Corps of Engineers Recreation Campgrounds and boat ramps nearby that may be accessed via Sam Ridley Parkway including locations at Fate Sanders, Lamar

The Stones River National Cemetery is the site of a dramatic lantern-light summer presentation.

Hill, and Stewart Creek off Weakley Road and Fall Creek and Jefferson Springs off Gladeville Road on Mona Road.

As you continue along US 41S to Murfreesboro, you'll pass the Omni Hut on your left. Although it's a surprise to find a Polynesian restaurant in the heart of Middle Tennessee, it's even more of a surprise to find such a good one. Check it out for dinner.

Situated in the heart of the Nashville Basin at an altitude of about six hundred feet above sea level and surrounded by cedar barrens, Murfreesboro grew from a small settlement nearby named Jefferson on the navigable portion of the Stones River.

The Stones River was discovered in 1766 by a party of four men and named for one of them, Uriah Stone. Rutherford County was established in 1803, with the first county seat at Jefferson named to honor Thomas Jefferson. Rutherford County was named for Maj. Gen. Griffith Rutherford, a Revolutionary War veteran.

At first, only flatboats and barges made their way upstream from Nashville, but steamboats eventually carried passengers between Jefferson and Nashville. As overland transportation improved, the prosperity of Jefferson waned. In October 1811, a new county seat was established named Cannonsburgh in honor of Minos Cannon, a prominent early settler and the father of Newton Cannon who was a personal and political enemy of Andrew Jackson.

The reconstructed Cannonsburg Village, a living history museum on Front Street, reflects this period in Murfreesboro's history. Included are a log house, blacksmith shop, general store, gristmill, one-room schoolhouse, church, and museum.

The name of the town was later changed to Murfreesboro to honor Col. Hardy Murfree, a Revolutionary War veteran who owned the land on which Oaklands, a historic house museum, now stands. The Italianate mansion, restored to its early 1860s appearance with original and period furnishings, was the site of Confederate Gen. Nathan Bedford Forrest's daring raid on Murfreesboro in July 1862 and the visit of Jefferson Davis in December 1862. Visitors enjoy tours of the home and picnic tables on the ten-acre grounds daily except Mondays.

Murfreesboro was the capital of Tennessee from 1819 to 1825 and fought unsuccessfully to keep the capital from returning to Nashville with its "sources of amusement ... to distract legislators from strict attention to their duty."

Today Murfreesboro is one of the three fastest growing communities in the Southeast and strives to find a balance between its venerable homes and historic landmarks and rapid development.

Rutherford County's lovely antebellum courthouse sits in the middle of Murfreesboro's bustling, old-fashioned town square. The present brick courthouse was originally completed in 1859. One of six antebellum courthouses remaining in the state, it has undergone extensive renovations and alterations.

The City Cafe just off the square on East Main is a local landmark noted for serving delicious country-style cooking for more than fifty years. One street off the square at 114 East College, the Front Porch Cafe delights diners with its lunch menu, Friday night buffet, and its preservation of one of Murfreesboro's few remaining downtown townhouses.

The Kleer-Vu Lunchroom on Highland Avenue attracts diners from laborers to lawyers. The menu changes, but the quality remains the same. Everything, as the owner says, is freshly cooked "from the ground up."

There are several antique dealers in town including the Antique Centers I and II, Keepsake Antique Mall, and Antiques Unlimited on Church Street near I-24. Together these three malls represent more than 250 dealers.

The Stones River National Military Park was established in 1927 to preserve the relics of the battle of Stones River which began December 31, 1862. Union Maj. Gen. William Rosecrans had

Officers from both the Union and Confederate armies sought the hospitality of Oaklands as the surrounding countryside changed hands during the Civil War.

moved his troops out of Nashville the day after Christmas intending to sweep Confederate general Braxton Bragg from the position he'd taken since October with the intent to winter in Murfrees-boro. The two armies camped within sight of each other's flickering campfires. The bands of the opposing forces struck up "Dixie" and "Yankee Doodle Dandy" with bravado.

The Confederates struck at dawn with an intensity that sent the Federals reeling. The fight-ing was fierce all day and drew to a close as dark-ness descended over the now deathly still camps. The next day there was no fighting, but both armies remained in position. On the afternoon of January 2, the Confederates again launched an attack, but this time were stopped by the overpow-ering Union artillery fire.

Both sides claimed victory, although out of 37,000 men the Confederates lost 10,000, while the Federals lost 13,000 from an army of 44,000. At the end of the battle, the Confederate army had blocked the Union advance toward Chattanooga, but they withdrew from the field after pushing on too far against the retreating Union line.

In addition to a visitor center with an excel-lent film about the battle, this 509-acre area includes the Stones River National Cemetery across the road, which is the site of an evening lantern-light presentation. You must arrange reser-vations for these extremely popular events held during the summer season.

The Stones River and Lytle Creek Greenways are trails for pedestrians and bicyclists that con-nect the Stones River Battlefield and Old Fort Park, which was developed around the ruins of Fortress Rosecrans. The remains of the earthen fort and exhibits can be seen along a half-mile trail. The park offers tennis courts, a great play-ground for the kids, a picnic pavilion, a riding

The Rutherford County Courthouse is one of the few remaining antebel-lum courthouses still in use in Tennessee.

ring for horse shows, and an eighteen-hole golf course.

Follow the gracious homes along tree-lined East Main Street to Middle Tennessee State Uni-versity (MTSU), an important part of the local cultural and economic environment.

The third largest university in Tennessee with an enrollment of 17,000, MTSU was founded in 1911. It has two Centers of Excellence established by the Tennessee General Assembly—the Center for Historic Preservation and the Center for Pop-ular Music.

The Children's Discovery House on North Maple sits behind a bright multicolored fence.

Inside children aged two to twelve and their families find opportunities to freeze their shadows, make colored rainbows, and meet live animals including iguanas, birds, and turtles.

There are several national motel franchises including Days Inn, Garden Plaza Hotel, Holiday Inn, Howard Johnson's, and Ramada Inn. Clardy's Guest House on East Main is a massive, twenty-room, three-story Romanesque-style home built in 1898 by a former mayor of Murfreesboro. In operation as a guest house since 1948, it has three guest rooms with private or shared baths. Visitors enjoy the nineteenth-century furnishings, ornate moldings, and carved woodwork. A continental breakfast is served.

Simply Southern Bed and Breakfast is on Tennessee Boulevard across from MTSU. The handsome brick home has three cozy, comfortably furnished guest rooms and one suite with private baths. Guests are invited to relax around the courtyard or in front of a roaring fire depending on the season or play a game of pool in the basement rec room. A full southern-style gourmet breakfast is served. The most unusual accommodations in the area are to be found at Rock Haven Lodge, a nudist campground.

Uncle Dave Macon Days and the International Folk Festival draw increasing numbers of visitors to Murfreesboro each year. Since 1976 Uncle Dave Macon, the "King of the Hillbillies," has been remembered at an old-timey festival that hosts three national championships including old-time banjo playing, for which Uncle Dave was famous, as well as old-time clogging and old-time buckdancing.

What started as a gathering on the courthouse lawn of fans of the claw-hammer style of pickin' brought to millions by Uncle Dave, the first individual featured performer on the Grand Ole Opry,

has grown to a three-day festival of more than thirty thousand held at Cannonsburgh Pioneer Village. As it was in the beginning, admission is free.

Follow TN 96 E to Lascassas. If you take the old Highway 96 off Tennessee Boulevard near MTSU, you'll pass the geographic center of the state of Tennessee, as determined in 1834. The Rutherford County Historical Society marked the spot with an obelisk in 1976.

Continuing on TN 96 past the Stones River, you'll see another local landmark, Brown's Store. Biscuits start rolling out of the oven near sunrise for folks stopping by for a cup of coffee and a ham biscuit to start off their day. If you pass by on Tuesday or Thursday around lunch time, you'll be able to sample their plate lunches; otherwise you can usually find something homemade on the counter or a cold soft drink in the cooler.

Continue on TN 96 to the community of Milton, where a right turn will take you to Manuel's Cajun Country Store. Manuel's is the site of toe-tappin' live Cajun music performed on Friday and Saturday evenings by the Manuel family, Louisiana transplants who have found a loyal following in Middle Tennessee for their easy-going style and their delicious étouffée, red beans and rice, fried alligator tail, and gumbo.

Diners seated at the red-checked tablecloths scan the shelves stocked with Cajun seasonings and potent hot sauces while waiting for the steaming dishes they've ordered to arrive. Call for a reservation before 6:30 for dinner Friday and Saturday or grab some lunch Wednesday through Saturday. Bring your lawn chair if the weather's nice; you'll want to sit outside when the music starts unless you choose to two-step it on the nearest patch of grass.

Continue on TN 96 to Liberty where you'll turn east on US 70 to Smithville.

All of the following accommodations are Murfreesboro with zip code 37130, and all telephone listings are area code 615, except where noted.

Accommodations:
Clardy's Guest House, 435 E. Main St., 893-6030.
Country Inn & Suites, 2262 Old Fort Pkwy., 800-456-4000 or 890-5951.
Simply Southern Bed and Breakfast, 211 N. Tennessee Blvd., 896-4988.

Attractions:
Cannonsburgh Village, 893-6565 (Chamber of Commerce).
Children's Discovery Museum, 890-2300.
Fortress Rosecrans, 893-9501.
Nissan Motor Manufacturing Corporation USA, Smyrna, 459-1444.
Oaklands Historic House Museum, 893-0022.
Rutherford County Chamber of Commerce, 893-6565.
Sam Davis Home, 459-2341.
Stones River National Battlefield, 893-9501.
Tennessee Aviation Days Air Show, Smyrna Airport, 355-0494.

Dining:
City Cafe, 893-1303.
Demo's Steak and Spaghetti House, 895-3701.
The Front Porch Cafe, 896-6771.
Kleer-Vu Lunchroom, 896-0520.
Manuel's Cajun Country Store, 273-2312.
The Omni Hut, Smyrna, 459-4870.
Parthenon Steak House, 895-2665.

Shopping:
Antique Center I, 896-5188.
Antique Center II, 890-4252.
Antiques Unlimited, 895-3183.
Keepsake Antiques Mall, 890-4125.

Special Events:
May—International Folk Festival; Days on the Farm at Sam Davis Home
July—Uncle Dave Macon Days; Civil War Encampment
September—Tennessee Aviation Days Air Show at Smyrna Airport
October—Harvest Day at Cannonsburgh; Heritage Days at Sam Davis Home

For More Information:
Rutherford County Chamber of Commerce, P.O. Box 864, 800-716-7560 or 893-6565.

42 *Smithville, Sparta, Spencer*
The Beauty of the Eastern Highland Rim

Smithville is the county seat of De Kalb County, which was named for Baron Johann De Kalb, a Bavarian who accompanied Lafayette to America in 1777. De Kalb served as major general in the Continental army of the American colonies during the Revolution and died at the battle of Camden in 1780.

Much of this part of the plateau was crossed quickly and only by necessity during Middle Tennessee's early history. Its remoteness made it a haven for outlaws operating on the "western frontier" near Nashville and later the bushwhackers of the Civil War.

Today Smithville is best known to many Tennesseans as the home of the Fiddlers' Jamboree each July. Since 1972 the jamboree has drawn musicians, entertainers, and craftsmen from around the world for two days of bluegrass and folk music, craft displays, and demonstrations.

Crafts are in the limelight at the Joe L. Evins Appalachian Center for Crafts off TN 56 northeast of Smithville on the shores of Center Hill Lake. The center is a professional crafts school with exhibits and sales of fine Tennessee, Appalachian, and contemporary crafts daily.

Smithville is near Center Hill Lake about half the sixty-four-mile distance between the dams at Great Falls southeast of town and Center Hill north of town. One of Middle Tennessee's prettiest lakes, the U.S. Army Corps of Engineers

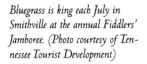

Bluegrass is king each July in Smithville at the annual Fiddlers' Jamboree. (Photo courtesy of Tennessee Tourist Development)

(USACE) Center Hill Reservoir has 18,220 surface acres at summer pool and 415 miles of shoreline. The upper end of the lake is riverine, but it begins to widen near Smithville.

The closest marinas to Smithville are Sligo and Hidden Harbor. Both have cabins for rent. Sligo also has fishing boats and pontoons for rent. The closest USACE recreation areas are east of town at Ragland Bottom on US 70 past Sligo and Holmes Creek off US 70 north of town. Ragland has seventy-eight campsites and Holmes Creek has ninety-six.

Southeast of Smithville on US 70, the area below Great Falls Dam known as Blue Hole is a sixty-foot-deep walleye honey hole. The 883-acre Rock Island State Rustic Park is located near the confluence of the Caney Fork, Collins, and Rocky Rivers. The dramatic falls are created by the rushing waters of the Caney Fork, which now contain the flow from the Collins and Rocky, crashing through a deep gorge, dropping almost one hundred feet in two miles.

The park has ten cabins open year-round, sixty campsites with hookups, a natural sand beach on Center Hill Lake, picnic areas, and hiking trails. It is comprised of lands leased from the TVA, private tracts purchased by the state of Tennessee, and land leased from USACE downstream from the Great Falls Dam.

Smallmouth bass, largemouth bass, Kentucky bass, walleye, stripe, crappie, and bream are taken from the Center Hill Lake. Center Hill Dam is seventeen miles north of Smithville via TN 96. Across the lake above the dam is Edgar Evins State Rustic Park, named for the former mayor of Smithville and a Tennessee state senator. The 6,280-acre park attracts boaters, fishermen, and other water sports enthusiasts who are interested in the marina, campground with sixty campsites, or thirty-four cabin rentals.

The cold water released from the bottom of the dam at Center Hill makes the Caney Fork one of Middle Tennessee's best trout streams.

The Caney Fork River below the dam is one of Middle Tennessee's premier rainbow trout streams. The Tennessee Wildlife Resources Agency stocks 125,000 rainbows and browns in the Caney Fork between March and November so your chances are good whether you're a fly-fisher-man or using salmon eggs and corn on spinning tackle. Be aware of the generation schedule and preplan a quick exit on the same side of the river as your car if you travel very far downstream. We've been caught downstream in a canoe more than once. It's impossible to paddle back upstream until the generation stops and it's a long walk with a canoe and tackle in tow!

The "pond" below the dam has several acres of surface area with easy access for anglers of all types. Boats and canoes troll back and forth, while bank fishermen and waders also try their luck. There are boat ramps on both sides of the dam and Longbranch Recreation Area has a campground with fifty-seven sites on the western side. Big Rock Market on the eastern side is a popular destination for fishing supplies and canoe rentals.

Continue east on US 70 to Sparta. Like Smithville, Sparta is situated on the upland area between the Nashville Basin and the Cumberland Plateau known as the Eastern Highland Rim at an altitude of one thousand feet above sea level. Calfkiller River runs through town.

The seat of White County is named for ancient Sparta. White County is believed to be named for the first settler in the area, John White, a Revolutionary War veteran who settled here illegally while the land was still part of the territory belonging to the Cherokee Nation. The county was formed in 1806 following a treaty with the Cherokee that opened the area for settlement. The town of Sparta was officially laid out in 1809. Today its population is about forty-seven hundred.

Two free concerts each month take place in downtown Sparta at the five-hundred-seat amphitheater in Liberty Square. Liberty Square Antiques and other specialty shops invite visitors to stroll around the White County Courthouse.

Legendary bluegrass musician Lester Flatt grew up near Sparta. He and his future partner, Earl Scruggs, joined Bill Monroe's band in 1944. Four years later, Flatt and Scruggs left the band to form the Foggy Mountain Boys, beginning a collaboration that would last a quarter of a century.

Flatt and Scruggs were already bluegrass icons and long-time regulars on the Grand Ole Opry when they found an international audience playing the theme song for and making cameo appearances on the *Beverly Hillbillies* TV show. Flatt is buried in Sparta and Lester Flatt Days, a bluegrass and gospel festival, is held in his honor at the Foggy Mountain Music Park on US 70 east of Sparta.

If you have time to visit, the Rock House Shrine is also east of Sparta on US 70. Completed around 1839, this was a stage stop and toll house on the Knoxville-Nashville route. Between Sparta and Bon Air, US 70A winds onto the Cumberland Plateau with an ascent of eight hundred feet in three miles on its way to Crossville. On a clear day, there's an overlook known as Sunset Rock nearby with an impressive fifty-mile view across the Highland Rim to the Nashville Basin.

Continue another four miles on US 70 toward Crossville to visit the 317-acre Virgin Falls Pocket Wilderness, a State Natural Area set aside for preservation by the Bowater Paper Company. Turn off US 70 at the community of De Rossett on Mourberry Road. From this point, it's eight miles to the parking area on Scott's Gulf Road and a four-mile hike to the falls.

The intrepid among you will be rewarded with a 110-foot waterfall on the edge of the Cumberland Plateau above the Caney Fork River that emerges from a cave, drops over the cliff, and

goes back into a cave at the base. There's a backpack camping area near the Caney Fork. Otherwise, you should allow six to eight hours for the roundtrip.

To continue this portion of the tour, proceed south from Sparta on TN 111 to Spencer, the closest town to the highest waterfall east of the Rockies at Fall Creek Falls.

Fall Creek Falls is a slender column of water dropping 256 feet into a plunge basin 400 feet in diameter. The free-falling cascade on the Cumberland

Fall Creek Falls is the highest waterfall in the eastern United States.

Plateau is the centerpiece of the twenty-thousand-acre park, which is the largest in the state system.

There are three other falls in the park as well as an inn with seventy-two rooms, a restaurant that seats 120, twenty two-bedroom cabins including ten two-story fisherman cabins with private porches over the lake and two handicapped-accessible landside cabins.

Three campgrounds offer 227 campsites with hookups and bathhouses, an eighteen-hole, par-72 golf course, a wading pool for children, canoe, pedal and fishing boat rentals to enjoy the 375-acre lake, bicycle rentals, horseback riding, miles of hiking trails, and an Olympic-sized pool.

Reservations are taken (and necessary!) for the inn and cabins but the campgrounds are first come, first served. Park fishing permits are required unless you're a registered inn or cabin guest. Then a valid Tennessee fishing license will suffice if you're over sixteen. A nature center at Cane Creek Cascades has exhibits on the natural and cultural history of the park.

Located only a mile or two from the park, the Fall Creek Falls Bed and Breakfast Inn has seven guest rooms and one suite with private baths in a sixty-four-hundred-square-foot "modern" facility set on thirty-five acres. Their hospitality includes a full gourmet breakfast each morning and lunches are available if you make arrangements the night before. Adults and children over twelve are preferred.

Continue on TN 56 to McMinnville.

All of the following accommodations are Smithville with zip code 37166, and all telephone listings are area code 615, except where noted.

Accommodations:
Edgar Evins State Park, Rt. 1, Silver Point, 38582; 800-421-6683 or 931-858-2446.

Fall Creek Falls Bed and Breakfast Inn, Rt. 3, Box 298-B, Pikeville, 37367; 423-881-5494.
Fall Creek Falls State Resort Park, Rt. 3, Pikeville, 37367; 423-881-3297 or 800-250-8610.
Hideaways at Center Hill Lake, 337 Hurricane Ln., Silver Point, 38582; 931-858-3687.
Hidden Harbor Marina at Holmes Creek, 2700 Holmes Creek Rd., 597-8800 or 597-4387.
The Inn at Evins Mill, 1535 Evins Mill Rd., 597-2088.
Rock Island State Rustic Park, Rock Island, 931-686-2471.
Sligo Marina, 597-5245 or 597-5242.

Attractions:
Edgar Evins State Park, Silver Point, 800-421-6683 or 931-858-2446.
Fall Creek Falls, 423-881-3297 or 800-250-8610 (park headquarters).
Joe L. Evins Appalachian Center for Crafts, 597-6801.
Rock House Historic Site, Sparta, 931-836-3552.
Smithville Municipal Golf Course, 597-6648.

Dining:
Candleglow Restaurant, 597-5040.
Sundance, 597-1910.

Shopping:
Country Treasures and Gifts, Sparta, 931-836-3572.
Joe L. Evins Appalachian Center for Crafts, 597-6801.
Jongee's Antiques and Gifts, Sparta, 931-836-2822.

Special Events:
July—Fiddlers' Jamboree
August—Lester Flatt Days, Sparta
September—Kornpone Day Festival, Sparta

Camping:
Edgar Evins State Park, Silver Point, 800-421-6683 or 858-2446.
Fall Creek Falls State Resort Park, Pikeville, 423-881-3297 or 800-250-8610.
Rock Island State Rustic Park, Rock Island, 931-686-2471.
USACE Recreation Areas:
Long Branch, 548-8002.
Floating Mill, 858-4845.
Holmes Creek, 597-7191.
Cove Hollow, 548-8781.
Ragland Bottom, 931-761-3616.

For More Information:
Smithville/DeKalb County Chamber of Commerce, P.O. Box 64, 37166; 597-4163. Open weekdays except Wed.
Sparta/White County Chamber of Commerce, 16 W. Bockman Way, Sparta, 931-836-3552.
Van Buren County Chamber of Commerce, P.O. Box 814, Spencer, 38585, 931-946-7033.

43 McMinnville and Manchester

Landmarks and Nurseries

McMinnville is the seat of Warren County, which was named for Revolutionary War general Joseph Warren who participated in the Boston Tea Party and was killed at the battle of Bunker Hill. McMinnville was on the old Indian war trace known as the Chickamauga Trail between southeastern Tennessee and Kentucky that later was widely used by early settlers.

McMinnville is situated on the Highland Rim at 1,038 feet above sea level, but the elevation in Warren County varies by about 1,000 feet. This range in elevation, along with the variety of soils found in the area, makes Warren County an extremely productive area for nurserymen and there are hundreds of them here.

In fact, Tennessee is nineteenth in the nation in nursery production and Warren County, known as "the nursery capital of the world," produces about 60 percent of Tennessee's nursery stock.

The current Warren County Courthouse was completed in 1897 on College Street. The two-story brick building originally had a four-story clock tower, but in the 1950s it was lowered to three stories and given a pyramid-style roof to match the other three corner pavilions.

In 1830 a McMinnville businessman named Asa Faulkner realized the tremendous potential of the water power in the area. He began to build a cotton mill at the Great Falls of the Caney Fork, but he died before he could complete the task. (see Smithville for more on the Great Falls).

His son, Clay, along with brothers H. L. and Jesse Walling, completed the project in 1892. Next Clay Faulkner built a ten-thousand-square-foot

Historic Falcon Manor is a restored mansion available for bed-and-breakfast accommodations.

Cumberland Caverns is one of the largest cave systems in the world.

Victorian mansion next to a woolen mill he owned that was about 2.5 miles from McMinnville.

In 1989 the McGlothlins purchased the house at auction and began four years of painstaking restoration before opening a bed and breakfast known as Falcon Manor filled with museum-quality antiques. The six guest rooms all have private baths. Their efforts earned a National Trust 1997 Great American Home Award. McMinnville also has Holiday Inn and Scottish Inn franchises.

Seven miles southeast of McMinnville on TN 8, Cumberland Caverns, at twenty-eight miles, is the largest cave in Tennessee, the second largest in the United States, one of the larger caves in the world, and a National Landmark. Locally known as Higginbotham Cave, Cumberland Caverns was discovered in 1810 by Aaron Higginbotham, a surveyor who was mapping the Chickamauga Trail, which runs by one of the two natural entrances.

According to legend, Higginbotham lit a pine torch and entered the small opening he'd discovered, only to find himself in an immense chamber.

About one hundred yards from the entrance, his remaining torch fell to the floor leaving him stranded in the darkness on top of a narrow ledge. Near the end of the third day of his ordeal, his companions found his equipment outside the opening. When they discovered Higginbotham, his hair had turned completely white.

Caves were very important to frontier settlers because they provided a source of saltpeter, a concentrated source of nitrates which, along with charcoal and sulfur, was used to make gunpowder.

During the War of 1812, Britain's blockade shut off any overseas sources of gunpowder and frontiersmen were left to their own devices. A similar situation occurred in the South during the Civil War, so it is not surprising that remains of saltpeter mining have been found here in an area known as Henshaw Cave, which was discovered to be connected to Higginbotham Cave in 1953.

Mining involved the construction of leaching vats, excavation of saltpeter-rich dirt, and saturation of the dirt with water within the vats. A concentrated lye solution was added to the saltpeter solution, producing potassium nitrate, the type of saltpeter needed for gunpowder.

This solution was boiled until crystals of saltpeter remained that could be removed, dried, and shipped to a powder mill where charcoal and sulfur were added.

Cumberland Caverns is open for commercial tours from May through October through grand underground hallways and breathtaking galleries with waterfalls, columns, stalactites, and massive formations. There's even a huge underground ballroom complete with a three-quarter-ton crystal chandelier.

At a similar altitude of 1,069 feet, Manchester also sits on the Highland Rim at the foot of the Cumberland Plateau. It is the seat of Coffee County, which was named for Gen. John Coffee, a close friend and nephew by marriage of Andrew Jackson, who fought alongside him at New Orleans in 1814. Manchester was named for Manchester, England, in hope that it, too, would attract major industries along the Duck River. The area was once known for cotton milling, but the visions of the founding fathers for an industrial center have yet to be recognized.

On a natural plateau where the two forks of the Duck River converge, the enigma known as Old Stone Fort rises from a broad, flat plain with earthen walls sixteen to twenty feet thick at the base partially enclosing fifty-two acres.

Archaeological investigations began to unearth the mystery after the four-hundred-acre site was purchased by the state of Tennessee in 1966. It was determined by radiocarbon dating that the various sections of the wall were built between A.D. 30 and 430 by Middle Woodland Indians who lived in Tennessee shortly after the birth of Christ.

Rather than serving as a fortification, it seems more likely that the low walls at Old Stone Fort were used to define the area as a point of some sort of ceremonial significance, perhaps religious, perhaps social, or even political.

A small museum on the site exhibits artifacts from the area and two miles of even paths wind along the Duck River.

Fifty-one campsites, picnic areas, fishing, and a nine-hole golf course provide additional opportunities to enjoy the beautiful surroundings.

The lovely Italianate Coffee County Courthouse was built in 1871. With its graceful cupola, this historic courthouse has been in jeopardy off and on for the past thirty years as voters tried to decide whether to demolish it and start all over or remodel and restore. So far, it still stands. The building houses the Coffee County Historical Society, which maintains historical and genealogical research materials and information. It is listed in the National Register of Historic Places.

The Old Timers' Day celebration in October features bluegrass music, arts and crafts, and activities for the kids.

Continue on TN 55 past the huge Arnold Engineering Development Center to visit Tullahoma and begin the portion of this tour west of I-24.

All of the following accommodations are McMinnville with zip code 37110, and all telephone listings are area code 931, except where noted.

Accommodations:
Ambassador Inn and Luxury Suites, 925 Interstate Dr., Manchester, 37355; 800-237-9228 or 728-2200.
Falcon Manor Bed and Breakfast, 2645 Faulkner Springs Rd., 668-4444.
Lord's Landing Bed & Breakfast, 375 Lord's Landing Ln., Hillsboro, 37342; 467-3830.
Super 8 Motel, 2430 Hillsboro Blvd., Manchester, 37355; 800-800-8000 or 728-9720.

Attractions:
Arrowheads/Aerospace Museum, Manchester, 723-1323 or
   723-1324.
Coffee County Courthouse, Manchester, 723-5100.
Cumberland Caverns, 668-4396.
Manchester Arts Center, Manchester, 782-3434.
Old Stone Fort Archaeological Park, Manchester, 931-723-
   5073.

Shopping:
The Collection, 473-1666.
Foothills Crafts, Manchester, 728-9236.

Camping:
Manchester KOA, Manchester, 800-562-7785 or 728-9777.
Old Stone Fort Archaeological Park, Manchester, 37355.
Whispering Oaks Campground, Manchester, 728-0225.

For More Information:
Manchester Chamber of Commerce, 110 E. Main St., 37355;
   728-7635.
McMinnville/Warren County Chamber of Commerce, P.O.
   Box 574, 473-6611.

44 Tullahoma and Normandy
Duck River Country

As you drive west along TN 55 from Manchester
toward Tullahoma, you'll notice the Arnold Engineering Development Center (AEDC) to the
south. The forty-thousand-acre reserve was once
part of the army's Camp Forrest. This was one of
several camps in Tennessee to house German
POWs during WWII.

Created in 1951, the AEDC is named for
Gen. Henry "Hap" Arnold who proposed the creation of a center for advancing the design of jet
and rocket engines. Visitors are given free tours by
reservation on weekdays.

According to the *Tennessee Wildlife Viewing Guide*,
AEDC is jointly managed by the U.S. Air Force

and the Tennessee Wildlife Resources Agency.
Songbirds like the prairie warbler, blue grosbeak,
and Acadian flycatcher are seen here, along with
wildflowers including terrestrial orchids and
dwarf iris.

To the north, look for a connecting road to
the Old Tullahoma-Manchester Road which runs
parallel to TN 55, in order to visit another local
landmark, Rutledge Falls, on Short Springs Road.

One of several waterfalls situated on the
Highland Rim in an area known as the Barrens,
Rutledge Falls is privately owned; but a small
parking lot has been provided for visitors who
enjoy the serenity of this quiet, beautiful, cool
spot.

The 420-acre Short Springs Natural Area is
also in this vicinity. Known for its profusion of
wildflowers, it has hiking trails leading to waterfalls and Normandy Lake, another good spot for
wildlife viewing or wetting a line.

You'll also pass the Coca-Cola Bottling Company, not usually the kind of stop we recommend.
If you're a Coke collector, you may be interested
in the retail outlet next door. It offers all kinds of
merchandise with the Coke logo ranging from
glasses to clothing.

As you drive into Tullahoma, you'll notice the
business district closely paralleling the railroad
track. The Nashville and Chattanooga line came
through before the Civil War and was partially
responsible for Tullahoma's early prosperity.

A Confederate force under Gen. Braxton
Bragg took up winter quarters here in January
1863 after the battle of Stones River. According
to Thomas L. Connelly in *Civil War Tennessee*, Bragg
caught wind of criticisms of his retreat from
Murfreesboro and sent off a famous round robin
letter to his generals asking for their "candid"
views on his ability to command. Their replies

were nearly unanimous in advising him to resign. Instead, Bragg launched a destructive campaign against his critics that dragged on for months despite efforts by Jefferson Davis to get things under control.

Meanwhile, on June 24 Union general William Rosecrans began an advance from his winter position in Murfreesboro. Bragg appeared to be near a breakdown and his senior officers, uncertain about their ability to lead the troops into battle without him, could do no better than

The Tullahoma Fine Arts Center sponsors a regional arts and crafts festival.

to organize a retreat to Chattanooga, leaving Middle Tennessee's rich farmland and railroad supply lines to Rosecrans. Tullahoma fell to Union forces on July 3, 1863, and Rosecrans promptly turned his attention toward Chattanooga.

As you enter Tullahoma from the east you'll soon cross Atlantic Street, both of them, on either side of the railroad track. A walking tour of the Historic Depot District is available from the Chamber of Commerce on West Lincoln near Atlantic.

One of the nicest homes in the district is now known as the Hollyberry Inn, a bed and breakfast offering three guest rooms with private baths. The former home of the railroad superintendent, it has an elegant interior matched by the lovely gardens outside.

The Tullahoma Fine Arts Center, in a nicely renovated two-story frame house on Jackson Street has an art gallery featuring works of southern artists for sale and a museum that exhibits traveling collections on loan, in addition to a permanent regional collection. The annual Fine Arts and Craftartists Festival held each May has displays in the center and booths and exhibits on the shady school grounds across the street.

The Walter H. Beech Staggerwing Museum beside the Tullahoma airport has the first Staggerwing Beechcraft ever built, as well as one of every model built between 1932 and 1946. These classic biplanes were the result of a design innovation that staggered the upper wing by moving it farther back than the lower wing, which improved cruising speeds. The museum is open on weekends between April and November and by appointment otherwise.

Ledford Mill, on Shipman's Creek Road, invites guests to an 1884 gristmill that was restored in 1996 to make tasteful accommodations

George Dickel was the distiller of that other fine Tennessee sippin' whiskey.

with stone walls, bathrooms that encircle mill workings, and industrial antiques that serve as room dividers. There's also a large loft apartment with a minikitchen and a second bedroom if you need it. Outside a stone path leads through the garden to two waterfalls. There's a gift shop offering gifts, maps, and books open to the public from noon to 4 P.M., Monday through Thursday. Next door, an eighteenth- and nineteenth-century antique tool museum is open by appointment.

Down the road is Granny Fishes' House which serves trout and catfish dinners and features frog legs weekly.

It's well worth the short drive to two other interesting area restaurants. Cortner Mill Restaurant has a Normandy address, but it's an easy outing from Tullahoma. Take the scenic route by weaving past the George Dickel Distillery nestled on Cascade Hollow Road north of Tullahoma.

George Dickel came to Tullahoma in the 1860s. He set out to find good water to use in making fine sipping whiskey. The limestone water from Cascade Spring did the trick so he purchased some land and opened his distillery in the 1870s. It closed in 1911 with the arrival of prohibition in the state and remained closed until 1958.

If you arrive at the distillery before 3 P.M. on weekdays, you can take a free tour and visit the rustic log General Store and Gift Shop. Continue past the distillery and follow TN 269 to Cortner Mill Restaurant.

With a back porch that overlooks the Duck River, Cortner Mill serves dinner by reservation Tuesday through Saturday or buffet lunch on Sunday. There's even a bar with a glass top so you can view the Duck River below while sipping beer or wine coolers.

Built for flood control by the TVA, Normandy Lake has no marinas but two recreation areas for camping and six available boat ramps along its seventy-two miles of shore line.

The Duck River is popular with flatwater

canoeists looking for an easy, scenic float. You're likely to hear the protest of the occasional blue heron, kingfisher, or wood duck breaking the stillness. The portion of the river below Normandy Dam is good for trout fishing. If the fishing is hot, you'll probably catch your limit before encountering the dam four miles downstream at Cortner Mill, where you'll need to take out or portage.

The Parish Patch Farm and Inn is a little farther up TN 269 toward Wartrace but you won't see much of it from the road. This three-hundred-acre country estate has twenty-one rooms and suites stylishly decorated for personal comfort. There are also a couple of cottages with cozy hammocks inviting you to kick back and enjoy the peaceful surroundings. For summer visitors, a swimming pool is the perfect antidote for the summertime blues. In winter, cozy up to the fireplace with a good book from the library. There are also VCRs, color TVs, and telephones. A full country breakfast is served at the inn. If you're planning a day on the water, you may want to arrange for box lunches ahead of time.

Continuing along TN 269, you'll see the sign for Haley Road (also known as Bugscuffle Road). Take this turn to visit one of the more unusual restaurants we've ever had the pleasure to visit. The first thing you'll notice about the modest-appearing house will be the extensive gardens surrounding it. There's obviously a talented gardener as well as a chef at work here. Once you step through the doors, you'll find a dazzling baby grand piano in the foyer, crisp white linens, and fresh flowers on the tables.

Call Bill Hall for reservations for lunch on Thursday and Sunday or dinner Tuesday through Saturday. Bring your own beverage if you're so inclined since this part of the county is "dry."

Continue the few miles north into Wartrace on TN 269.

All of the following accommodations are Tullahoma with zip code 37388, and all telephone listings are area code 931, except where noted.

Accommodations:
Ledford Mill Bed & Breakfast, Rt. 2, Box 152B, 455-2546.
Parish Patch Farm & Inn, 1100 Cortner Rd., Normandy, 37360; 857-3017.

Attractions:
George A. Dickel Distilling Company, 857-3124.
Walter H. Beech Staggerwing Museum, 455-1974.
Tullahoma Fine Arts Center, 455-1234.

Dining:
Cortner Mill Restaurant, Normandy, 857-3018.
Our House, Haley, 800-876-6616 or 389-6616.

Special Events:
May—Tullahoma Fine Arts and Craftartists Festival
June—Paul Pyle Dulcimer Festival

Camping:
TVA Barton Springs, east of dam on Normandy Rd.
TVA Cedar Point, west of Normandy Dam on Red Hill Rd.

For More Information:
Tullahoma Chamber of Commerce, P.O. Box 1205, 455-5497.

45 *Wartrace and Bell Buckle*
Home of Strolling Jim and Tennessee's Poet Laureate

Wartrace was founded in 1852 when the Nashville, Chattanooga, and Saint Louis Railway came through the area, at the junction of the branch line to Shelbyville and the main line. We were pleased to discover the Walking Horse and Eastern Railroad Excursion Train still running the oldest branch line in Tennessee. The excursion offers one-way and round-trip tickets for the six-teen-mile trip from Shelbyville to Wartrace, from May to November. Dick Abernathy, who has worked with railroads since his high school days, and his wife, Faye, now own the line.

The train boards across the street from the station in Shelbyville departing at 10 A.M. and arriving in Wartrace an hour later. Round trip passengers get a couple of hours to explore Wartrace and enjoy a lunch of salads, sandwiches, pasta, and desserts made daily at the Strolling Jim Restaurant in the Walking Horse Hotel before their 2 P.M. departure. The restaurant serves all three meals every day.

Commerce in Wartrace grew along the rail-road line, with hotels built to house the railroad passengers, many of whom came for the healthful effects of its waters. The demand for Wartrace's water was so great at one point that it was bottled and shipped to other towns.

The brick-and-frame structure proclaiming Wartrace "The Cradle of the Tennessee Walking Horse" is the town's well house. Built in 1909, it was used as the judges' reviewing stand during the first walking horse shows which were held here before they were moved to Shelbyville.

Built in 1917 by Jesse Robert Overall and his wife, Nora, the Overall Hotel became known as Floyd's Walking Horse Hotel in 1930 when it was purchased by Floyd and Olive Carothers.

Carothers was a horse trainer and he set out to train a plow horse he'd bought the even, gentle gait of the Tennessee Walking Horse. The gamble paid off when Floyd rode that same three-year-old, Strolling Jim, to the world's championship at the first Walking Horse Celebration in Shelbyville in 1939. Jim died in 1957 at the ripe old age of twenty-one. He was buried in the grassy meadow

The streets of Bell Buckle are teeming with visitors during the Moon Pie Festival as well as the spring and fall craft fairs.

behind the Walking Horse Hotel and his grave remains undisturbed to this day.

The three-story Walking Horse Hotel has a restaurant on the first floor and shops on the second floor with gift items ranging from weather vanes and preserves to tee shirts. Overnight visitors are welcomed to the third-floor guest rooms with queen-sized beds, claw-foot tubs, and TVs and VCRs. There's a generous-sized front porch complete with rockers.

The Blockade Runner in the old mill building has Civil War costumes, period-style tents, ladies clothing, and antiques. Gallagher and Son has been making acoustic guitars for top musicians around the country for more than thirty years.

The Whistle Stop Cafe serves lunch and dinner and offers a gift area. About three miles out of town, fine dining by reservation only is featured at Our House and it is well worth the short drive (*see* Tullahoma for more information).

Continue on TN 269 to Bell Buckle, one of our favorite small towns in Tennessee (population 500). Settled in the late 1700s, Bell Buckle was a thriving railroad town in the 1880s when the Webb brothers came looking for a place to move their school from Culleoka in Maury County. Bell Buckle residents offered the Webb brothers a deal they couldn't refuse, and the Webb School became one of the most respected boarding schools in the South.

The business section of this tiny village boasts numerous interesting craft and antique shops. The Daffodilly is an antique consignment shop in the town's old drug store. Phillips General Store now has architectural antiques, folk art, dolls, and collectibles. Bell Buckle Crafts displays regional crafts in the old bank building. The Bell Buckle Bookstore has old and new books and steaming cups of cappuccino. There's even a specialty press published by the poet laureate of Tennessee, Margaret "Maggie" Britton Vaughn.

The Bell Buckle Cafe serves barbecue and country-style cooking daily and features live country music Thursday through Saturday nights and Sunday afternoons. On Saturday the live broadcast of the J. Gregory Jamboree Radio Show takes center stage in the cafe from 1 to 3 P.M.

Down the street, the mayor runs Bell Buckle Antique Mall in an old hosiery mill that holds more than fifty dealers. Across the street, more than thirty dealers house their wares at the Livery Stable Antique Mall. The peaceful little town threatens to pop at the seams when the Spring Craft Show and the Webb School Arts and Craft Show are held in April and October respectively. Somehow, it all works out, and although traffic and parking can be a bit of a nightmare, everyone seems to have a good time.

There are no motels in town, so if you're planning on spending the night you'd better call the Bell Buckle Bed and Breakfast on Webb Road to reserve one of their three guest rooms, or the Mingle House Bed and Breakfast on Main Street.

There are even a couple of museums in town. The Junior Room Museum at the Webb School portrays the original one-room school. The Louvin Brothers Museum highlights the long and successful careers of the former Grand Ole Opry stars.

From Bell Buckle, proceed west on TN 82 and south on US 321 to Shelbyville.

All of the following accommodations are Wartrace with zip code 37183, and all telephone listings are area code 931, except where noted.

Accommodations:
Bell Buckle Bed & Breakfast, Bell Buckle, 389-9371.
Mingle House Bed and Breakfast, Bell Buckle, 389-9453.
Walking Horse Hotel, 389-7050.

Attractions:
Walking Horse and Eastern Railroad, 389-7050 (for tickets).

Dining:
Bell Buckle Cafe, 389-9693.
Circle 9 Restaurant, 389-6044.
Our House, 800-876-6616 or 389-6616.
Strolling Jim Restaurant, 389-7050.

Shopping:
Bell Buckle Antique Mall, Bell Buckle, 389-6174.

Bell Buckle Crafts, Bell Buckle, 389-9371.
Bell Buckle Bookstore, Bell Buckle, 389-9328.
Bell Buckle/Iris Press, Bell Buckle, 389-6878.
Blockade Runner, 389-6294.
The Daffodilly, Bell Buckle, 389-9663.
J. W. Gallagher & Son Guitars, 389-6455.
Livery Stable Antique Mall, Bell Buckle, 389-6354.
Miller Studios, 389-6474.
Phillips General Store, Bell Buckle, 389-6547.
Whistle Stop Cafe, 389-9988.

Special Events:
April—Spring Art and Craft Show, Bell Buckle
May—Gallagher Guitar's Birthday Celebration
June—Moon Pie Festival, Bell Buckle
October—Webb School Art & Craft Festival, Bell Buckle

For More Information:
Bell Buckle Chamber of Commerce, 389-9371 or 389-6174.
Shelbyville/Bedford County Chamber of Commerce, 684-3482.

46 *Shelbyville*
The Walking Horse Capital of the World

The seat of Bedford County was named for Isaac Shelby who led a force of Tennessee riflemen at the battle of Kings Mountain against the British (*see* Elizabethton for more on Kings Mountain). Bedford County was named for Thomas Bedford Jr., a veteran of the Revolutionary War who moved to Tennessee around 1795 after he had obtained large tracts of land in Middle Tennessee.

The town was laid out in 1810 with a courthouse in the center of a business district. This is believed to have been the prototype for the town square type of design used throughout the South and Midwest. The collection of Victorian commercial buildings on the square is listed in the National Register of Historic Places. The Duck River almost encircles the town.

According to the *WPA Guide to Tennessee*, the high point in the early days of Shelbyville was Muster Day. This event was held in accordance with congressional militia laws that required every man in the county subject to military service to report here to drill. Some conscientious types turned up in homespun uniforms, but the more lighthearted came in outlandish costumes waving willow switches and corn stalks as weapons. After the technicalities of drilling had been met, the participants turned to whiskey and horse trading, not necessarily in that order.

Horse trading persists to this day, due in no small part to the emergence of the southern plantation walking horse, better known as the Tennessee Walking Horse, from the plantations in Middle Tennessee in the nineteenth century.

Selectively bred for gentle dispositions and trained for a comfortable gait called a running walk, the Tennessee Walking Horse was an all-purpose horse used on farms and plantations where owners and overseers were often in the saddle most of the day.

Beautiful to see in motion, the Tennessee Walking Horse overstrides with its rear feet while lifting its front feet chest high in a one-two-three-four stepping pattern with three feet on the ground at a given moment. This action also gives its head the characteristic nodding motion that gave rise to one of its earlier names, the nodding walking horse.

The Tennessee Walking Horse began to be recognized as an organized breed in the 1930s, with the formation of the Breeder's Association in Lewisburg in 1935. Since that time hundreds of thousands of walking horses have been registered.

The granddaddy of all the walking horse shows in the world is held here in Shelbyville. The annual ten-day Tennessee Walking Horse Celebration crowns the World Champion Walking Horse on the final Saturday night.

It's a ceremony that's been marred by ugly allegations of abuse by trainers since the 1960s. A process called soring to induce the horses to lift their front feet higher, or produce "the big lick" as the high step is called, is the center of the controversy.

The Tennessee Walking Horse Breeders and Exhibitors Association has denounced the practice and the U.S. Department of Agriculture Horse Protection Program has inspectors who examine the horses for more subtle signs of abuse like the application of kerosene or diesel fuel during training, which induces irritation but leaves no visible signs other than tenderness to touch. The hope is that this practice is disappearing, but the controversy continues to rear its ugly head from time to time, sending shudders through the industry.

The Tennessee Walking Horse Museum on the celebration grounds showcases the history of the Tennessee Walking Horse.

Shelbyville was known for its Union sympa-thies during the Civil War and breathed a collective sigh of relief when Federal troops reached the town in June 1863. They didn't arrive in time to save the courthouse, which had been accidentally burned by the Confederates a few months earlier.

Around the turn of the century, the immense cedar forests surrounding town and the availability of water power from the Duck River, gave rise to the pencil industry. There are still several pencil manufacturers in town including Shelbyville Pencil which offers free tours by appointment.

You'll find classic meat-and-three restaurants open for all three meals including Pope's Cafe on the Square and Rebecca's on North Cannon.

Cinnamon Ridge has five guest rooms with private baths in a Colonial-style home. The Olde Gore House has four bedrooms and two suites, all with private baths. The Taylor House, an 1890s home, has been updated with four guest rooms with private baths. National motel franchises include Best Western and Quality Inn.

Outside town, Bottle Hollow Lodge, located between Shelbyville and Lynchburg, sits on a

The World Champion Walking Horse is crowned each year in Shelbyville.

beautiful ridgetop and offers four guest rooms with private baths, along with handicapped access.

Northwest of town near Chapel Hill and the Duck River is Henry Horton State Resort Park (*see* Lewisburg for more).

The Tennessee Walking Horse and Eastern Railroad runs an eight-mile diesel train excursion from Shelbyville to Wartrace on rails dating from 1852 and used by Confederate and Union troops during the Civil War. The locomotives and baggage-passenger coaches date from the 1940s. Board the Volunteer in downtown Shelbyville for a pleasant outing.

From Shelbyville, continue on TN 82 to TN 55 and turn west to Lynchburg.

All of the following accommodations are Shelbyville with zip code 37160, and all telephone listings are area code 931, except where noted.

Accommodations:
Blue Ribbon Inn, 717 N. Main St., 684-3101.
Bottle Hollow Lodge, 111 Gobbler Ridge Rd., 695-5253.
Cinnamon Ridge Bed & Breakfast, 799 Whitthorne St., 685-9200.
Henry Horton State Park, 800-250-8612.
Olde Gore House Bed & Breakfast, 410 Belmont Ave., 685-0636.
Shelbyville Inn, 317 N. Cannon Blvd., 800-622-0466 or 684-6050.
Taylor House, 300 E. Lane St., 800-867-7326 or 684-3894.

Attractions:
Tennessee Walking Horse & Eastern Railroad, 684-6223.
Tennessee Walking Horse Museum, 684-0314.

Dining:
Pope's Cafe, 684-7933.
Prime Steak House, 684-0741.
Rebecca's, 684-6050.
Richard's Cafeteria, 684-7288.

Special Events:
August—Tennessee Walking Horse Celebration

Camping:
Henry Horton State Park, Chapel Hill, 364-2222.

For More Information:
Shelbyville/Bedford County Chamber of Commerce, 684-3482 or 888-662-2525.

47 Lynchburg and Fayetteville
Historic Town Squares

Lynchburg is the county seat of Moore County, which was named for Maj. Gen. William Moore, an early settler who ventured here from Kentucky in 1808. He commanded a company in the Creek War and was a veteran of the War of 1812. According to the *WPA Guide to Tennessee*, the town was named for Tom Lynch, a frail sort of fellow, who it seems was always chosen to deliver the lashes to a man sentenced to the whipping post.

The seat of justice in Moore County since 1885 has been the brick Moore County Courthouse which sits in the middle of the town square. Although of a simple exterior design, elaborate arched door and window lintels and cornice create a pleasing facade topped with a square cupola.

The Historic Jail Museum is located in the jail that was used from 1900 to 1990. The sheriff and his family lived here and the cells were in the back and upstairs with a special section for women.

Down the street about a block, you'll see the trim picket fence and white sign announcing Miss Mary Bobo's Boarding House. Miss Mary ran the boarding house and restaurant from 1908 until her death at the age of 101 in 1983.

Lynne Tolley has taken on the task of providing a bounty of down-home cooking for two midday meal seatings every day but Sunday. You'll have a pretty good chance of getting a seat during the week with reservations, but you'll need to plan way ahead to be counted among the sixty-two diners on Saturdays who come to enjoy southern regional foods and specialty recipes.

Fortunately, if you've not planned far enough ahead for Miss Mary's, On the Square Restaurant is also open for lunch every day but Sunday and stays open for dinner on Friday and Saturday nights.

There are several specialty shops around the square catering to the tourist trade and we were pleased to find at Mary Ruth Fuqua Antiques classic treasures that we couldn't leave town without.

Thanks to the highly successful Jack Daniel's Distillery advertising campaign, Lynchburg may be the most recognized small town in the country. This, as most of America now knows, is where Jack Daniel made his famous Tennessee sour mash whiskey.

Jasper Newton "Jack" Daniel was born near here in 1848 and started working at a distillery owned by a devout Lutheran around 1860. By the

end of the Civil War, the owner had been convinced by his fellow Lutherans to mend his whiskey makin' ways, leaving Jack the sole owner of the enterprise for the princely sum of twenty-five dollars.

Jack discovered that Cave Spring was the perfect source of the iron-free spring water he needed to produce good whiskey, so he bought the spring and five hundred acres surrounding it. In 1866 he moved the operation and registered it, making his distillery the first in the country to receive a federal license.

Although Jack died in 1911, his nephew, Lem Motlow, continued the operation in an otherwise "dry" county and it remained in the Motlow family until it was purchased by a corporation from Kentucky.

More than 280,000 visitors take the free hour-long tour every year, inhaling the odors of the fermenting sour mash while learning about the charcoal mellowing process. Wear comfortable

Miss Mary Bobo's still serves good country cooking to those lucky enough to have reservations for one of two lunch seatings.

shoes because there's a lot of walking and stair climbing involved as you visit warehouses stocked with white oak barrels of aging whiskey and Cave Springs with its constant flow of fifty-six-degree spring water. There's also an elevator for handicapped access to the first building where you get your poker chip and wait for the tour with your color to depart.

In addition to the tour, a Jack Daniel's World Championship Invitational Barbecue Cookoff draws about twenty thousand hungry visitors a year.

If you succumb to Lynchburg's charms, there are classic choices for overnight stays within walking distance of the distillery and the courthouse square including Lynchburg's first bed and breakfast, the 1877 Lynchburg Bed and Breakfast, which has two guest rooms with private baths, and the Cottage Haus, a restored Victorian cottage with two guest suites and private baths.

About three miles from town you'll find the Goose Branch Farm Bed and Breakfast, a secluded

These barrels at the Jack Daniel Distillery contain some of Tennessee's finest sour mash.

1899 farmhouse surrounded by hills and trees with two antique-filled suites and private baths on fifty-seven acres.

Cedar Lane Bed and Breakfast has four guest rooms with private baths in a newly built farmhouse with a big wraparound porch and a country setting.

Six miles south of town on the way to Fayetteville, guests enjoy the historic Gothic-revival home of Wiley Daniel, one of Jack's brothers, which is now Dream Fields Bed and Breakfast. It offers three guest rooms with private baths, creekside picnics, buggy rides, 260 acres of nature trails, and a full country breakfast to send you on your way. In the same vicinity, Mulberry House Bed and Breakfast, a 115-year-old farmhouse, with two guest rooms and private baths also offers buggy rides.

From Lynchburg, follow TN 50 to visit Fayetteville, a charming town with a population of about seven thousand and a square full of interesting shops, and several bed and breakfasts in the vicinity.

The county seat of Lincoln County was named in honor of Fayetteville, North Carolina, the hometown of some early settlers. Lincoln County was established in 1809 and named for Revolutionary War veteran Maj. Gen. Benjamin Lincoln of Massachusetts. He was chosen by George Washington to receive the sword of Lord Cornwallis at the Yorktown surrender.

Lincoln County is the site of Camp Blount where troops assembled in 1813 with Andrew Jackson for a punitive expedition against the Creek Indians after the massacre at Fort Mims and again in 1814 to march to Mobile to oppose the British.

Although Fayetteville is situated along the Elk, the limited navigability of the river because of large gravel bars, islands, and inadequate water

The Old Bagley House Bed and Breakfast offers peaceful accommodations on thirteen acres.

levels limited its usefulness in the early development of the town. Kelso Canteen and Canoe Rental is about seven miles east of Fayetteville on US 64 if you'd like to try your hand at navigating the river on a scenic canoe float trip.

After the Borden Milk Company came to town in the 1920s, dairy farming became an important part of the area's economy. Lincoln County retains a strong agricultural base although the Borden plant closed in 1967 and today houses the Lincoln County Museum.

The thriving town square is surrounded on all sides by interesting shops including the Fayetteville Antique Mall; Magnolia Mall; Mockingbird Antique Mall and Ice Cream Parlor; Earthworks Antiques and Art; and Marbles, a fun shop with bins of marbles and lots of other gift ideas.

Wyatt Antiques wins the vote for most gorgeous antique shop. The lovely Steamboat Gothic-style house was built in 1894 by Hugh and Byrd Douglas. Inside, the walnut-and-maple staircase dominates the entry, and parlors to

either side are trimmed in maple on the one hand and cherry on the other, right down to the original shutters on the windows.

Owner Don Wyatt started collecting antiques in grade school and moved to this house with his parents in 1949 so he's had plenty of time to assemble an impressive array of fine European and American antiques.

There are several dining choices around the square including O'Houlihans and Just Desserts. A couple of restaurants have turned utilitarian structures into fun dining experiences. Mulberry Bay is in the town's rejuvenated car wash; Cahoots serves lunch and dinner in the town's former firehouse and jail.

Several bed and breakfasts greet visitors. One is the Fayetteville Bed and Breakfast, one mile west of the courthouse square, which has one guest room with a private bath. Another is the antebellum Heritage House, with its three guest rooms and private baths that may also be arranged as a two-room suite for families. The Old Bagley

House is across from Motlow State Community College's campus and features three guest rooms with private baths on thirteen lush, landscaped acres. National franchises include Best Western and Days Inn.

The Elk River Plantation on Eldad Road has two guest rooms, along with nature trails, fishing, canoeing, and horseback riding. The Old Cowan Plantation Bed and Breakfast is two miles from the courthouse square and has two comfortable guest rooms with private baths in an 1886 Colonial-style home that also offers a gift shop with antiques and quality crafts

Proceed north on US 431 to Lewisburg and continue on 31A to Triune and Nolensville before returning to Nashville to complete this loop tour.

All of the following accommodations are Lynchburg with zip code 37352, and all telephone listings are area code 931, except where noted.

Accommodations:
Bagley House Bed and Breakfast, 1802 Winchester Hwy., Fayetteville, 37334; 433-3799.
Cedar Lane Bed & Breakfast, Rt. 3, Box 155E, 759-6891.
Dream Fields Bed and Breakfast, 9 Backstreet, Mulberry, 37359; 438-8875.
Fayetteville Bed and Breakfast, 1111 W. Washington, Fayetteville, 37334; 433-9636.
Goose Branch Farm Bed & Breakfast, 140 Goose Branch Rd., 759-5919.
The Heritage House Bed and Breakfast, 315 E. College, Fayetteville, 37334; 433-9238.
Lynchburg Bed & Breakfast, Mechanic St., 759-7158.
Mulberry House Bed & Breakfast, Old Lynchburg Hwy., Mulberry, 37359; 433-8461.
The Old Cowan Plantation, 126 Old Boonshill Rd., Fayetteville, 37334; 433-0225.

Attractions:
Jack Daniel Distillery, 759-6180.
Kelso Canteen and Canoe Rental, Kelso, 800-933-2827 or 438-4402.
Lincoln County Museum, Fayetteville, 438-0339.
Moore County Jail Museum.

Dining:
Cahoots Historic Jail and Firehouse Restaurant, Fayetteville.

Just Desserts, Fayetteville, 438-4313.
Miss Mary Bobo's Boarding House, 759-7394.
O'Houlihans, Fayetteville, 433-0557.
On the Square, 759-5123.

Shopping:
Baker's Antiques and Collectibles, 759-4964.
Country by Nature, 759-6444.
Earthworks Antiques and Art, Fayetteville, 433-4148.
Fayetteville Antique Mall, Fayetteville, 433-1231.
Magnolia Mall, Fayetteville, 433-9987.
Mary Ruth Fuqua Antiques, 759-4476 or 455-4816.
Lynchburg Hardware and General Store, 759-4200.
Mockingbird Antique Mall and Ice Cream Parlor, Fayetteville, 438-0058.
Sir's Fabrics, Fayetteville.
Wyatt Antiques, Fayetteville, 433-4241.

Special Events:
May—Spring in the Hollow
June—Frontier Days
September—Jack Daniel's Birthday Celebration
October—Jack Daniel's World Championship Invitational Barbecue Cook-off
December—Christmas in Lynchburg

For More Information:
Fayetteville/ Lincoln County Chamber of Commerce, 208 S. Elk Ave., Fayetteville, 37334; 433-1235.
Lynchburg Chamber of Commerce, P.O. Box 421, 759-4111.

48 *Lewisburg, Triune, Nolensville*
Home of Henry Horton State Park, Orchards, and Greenhouses

The county court of Marshall County appointed a committee in October 1836 to build a county courthouse and jail, lay out streets, and sell lots at a location in the fertile Nashville Basin. The town was named for Meriwether Lewis, co-commander of the Lewis and Clark Expedition, who died in mysterious circumstances along the Natchez Trace not far from here on October 11,

1809, while governor of the Louisiana Territory.

Marshall County is named for John Marshall of Virginia, who was secretary of state from 1800 to 1801 and chief justice of the Supreme Court from 1801 to 1835. The current courthouse was completed in 1929. Its simple rectangular design of brick and limestone features clock towers incorporated into the facade of the exterior walls above the roof line.

The eleventh president of the United States, James Knox Polk, practiced law here between 1841, when he relinquished the governorship of Tennessee, and 1844, when he was elected president. The building stood on the southeast corner of the public square. If you find yourself looking for a meal while you're in town, mosey over to the Fountain Square Restaurant for meat-and-three-plate lunches or dinners on weekdays. They're open for dinner on Saturday and Sunday for a lunch buffet.

The Tennessee Walking Horse Breeders and Exhibitors Association is on the Ellington Bypass. In addition to housing the Walking Horse Hall of Fame, all registrations, transfers, and other membership services are conducted here (*see* Shelbyville and Wartrace for more on Tennessee Walking Horses). Lewisburg is also home to several pencil manufacturing plants

On your way to Henry Horton State Park on US 31A, you'll pass a couple of antique-junk-flea market stops. The road you're following was once a well-traveled Indian path used by tribes to the south to reach the rich hunting grounds to the north.

The park was part of the farm once owned by Tennessee governor Henry H. Horton. Located on the banks of the Duck River, the park has a seventy-room inn with handicapped access and five cabins with fireplaces. All have TV and telephone. Other facilities include a campground with full hookups as well as primitive and tent sites, picnic areas along the river, an Olympic-size swimming pool, hiking trails, skeet and trap range, and a year-round eighteen-hole, par-72 championship golf course with a full-service pro shop. The Horton Inn Restaurant serves home-style cooking for up to 350 diners and features breakfast, lunch, and dinner buffets daily.

After passing the entrance to Henry Horton and crossing the Duck River, you'll go through the community of Chapel Hill, the birthplace of Nathan Bedford Forrest, the Confederate cavalry officer who was known as the "Wizard of the

The Marshall County Courthouse is a Lewisburg landmark.

Saddle." A former slave trader, Forrest would later be suspected of being the first Grand Wizard of the Ku Klux Klan.

The Depot Station Cafe is open daily for lunch and dinner and has homemade fried peach pies in addition to sandwiches, burgers, steak, and chicken. Crafty People offers handmade gifts. There's also the Duck River Canoe Rental if you have time for a float down this portion of the Duck, which meanders past rock bluffs and forested hillsides. A pretty, easy Class I float, this section is good for beginners and families with children ages five and up.

Continue on US 31A into Williamson County where you'll encounter the Triune Flea Market at the intersection with TN 96. At this point a turn to the east takes you to Murfreesboro, the starting point of this loop tour. A turn to the west takes you past DH Interiors, which has lots of neat garden stuff ranging from garden gates to obelisks, on the way to historic Franklin with its antique shops and Civil War sites.

You may also continue north on US 31A past Fast's Greenhouse, a great source of bedding annuals, perennials, and herbs, to Nolensville, a charming community with a couple of antique shops and a bed and breakfast.

A Homeplace Bed and Breakfast is as delightful as its owners, Alfred and Evelyn Hyde Bennett. Situated in the heart of Nolensville along the old stagecoach road, the antebellum inn is filled with antiques and hospitality. The Parlor Suite has a large half-tester bed, fireplace, private bath, and is wheelchair accessible. There's also a two-room suite on the second floor that shares a bath. The Victorian Cottage out back has a bath and a small kitchen. The gardens are inviting and breakfast in the formal dining room is often cause for Alfred to don his kilt.

Next door at Traditions you'll find a good collection of antique furniture, glassware, and accessories artfully displayed.

Across the street, Mary Ann Scales's Honeysuckle Antiques and Treasures and the Daisy Chain feature antiques and collectibles.

From Nolensville, continue north on US 31A to begin your exploration of Nashville, Music City USA, which was covered in chapter 40. Or get to I-24 and head southeast to Chattanooga, where we go next.

All of the following accommodations are Lewisburg with zip code 37091, and all telephone listings are area code 931, except where noted.

Accommodations:
Celebration Inn, 1234 Nashville Hwy., 359-7490.
Henry Horton State Resort Park, P.O. Box 128, Chapel Hill, 37034; 364-2222.
A Homeplace Bed and Breakfast, 7286 Nolensville Rd., Nolensville, 37135; 776-5181.

Attractions:
Duck River Canoe Rental at Forest Landing, Chapel Hill, 364-7874 or 364-2969.
Hazelburn Golf Course, 293-4653.
Saddle Creek Golf Club, 270-7280.
Tennessee Walking Horse Breeders and Exhibitors Association, 800-359-1574 or 890-9120.

Dining:
Depot Station Cafe, Chapel Hill, 364-2425.
Fountain Square Restaurant, 359-7488.
Horton Inn Restaurant, 364-2222.

Shopping:
Bargain Finders, 359-8131.
Crafty People, Chapel Hill, 364-3282.
The Daisy Chain, Nolensville, 776-3539.
DH Interiors, Arrington, 395-4630.
Honeysuckle Antiques and Treasures, Nolensville, 776-5806.
Lewisburg Flea and Antique Market, 359-5939.
Traditions Antiques, Nolensville, 776-3337.

Camping:
Henry Horton State Park, Chapel Hill, 364-2222.

For More Information:
Marshall County Chamber of Commerce, 227 2nd Ave. N., 359-3863.

❧Chattanooga

49 *Chattanooga*
The Environmental City

"Chattanooga had a heart attack," says city councilman Dave Crockett. "More than twenty years ago we had the worst air in the country." As it is with a person, it often takes a heart attack for a city to stop and take stock of its life and future. Chattanooga took stock and is now the Environmental City. "Today we are one of the cleanest cities in the world," Crockett proudly proclaims.

Early in the 1990s, Mayor Gene Roberts challenged Chattanooga "to maximize its potential by becoming the best mid-sized city in America." As a result, the needed partnerships were formed among city, county, state, and federal governmental agencies, corporations, private businesses, local and national organizations, clubs, and individuals.

They came up with a plan. The timetable included short-range goals, mid-range goals for completion by 2000, and long-range goals to be finished in 2005. By 2005 Chattanooga envisions being both the Environmental City and the Scenic City.

One part of that plan has already been visited by millions of people, the Tennessee Aquarium. It's the largest freshwater ecosystem in the world. The theme of the aquarium, the Tennessee River, is represented for its entire course from its mountain origin to the Gulf of Mexico. It cost $45 million. The twelve-story building houses four hundred thousand gallons of water with four thousand living specimens representing 350 species of fish, birds, mammals, reptiles, and amphibians.

The building's sixty-foot central canyon is an inclined ramp that gives you a sense of immersion as you walk down viewing the tanks on both sides. Illumination comes from inside the tanks from fiber optic strands stretched the length of the ceiling. The aquariums offer excellent opportunities to photograph underwater species in natural settings without getting wet.

Another part of Chattanooga's plan that is coming to fruition is the twenty-two-mile-long Tennessee RiverPark. On the south side of the river below the Chickamauga Dam are the Hubert Fry Center, five fishing piers, trails, playgrounds, picnic tables, a restaurant, and two boat launching ramps.

On the north side of the river is the North Chickamauga Creek Greenway. Presently you can enjoy the riverside beauty from near the Chickamauga Dam upstream to the Spangler Farm. Here you can fish, picnic, hike, and enjoy wildflowers. Eventually a thirty-five-mile trail along the stream will allow you to hike from its mouth to Falling Waters, the source of the North Chickamauga Creek.

Ross's Landing Park and Plaza is where downtown Chattanooga meets the Tennessee River. This environmental art piece reveals the essence of the community's cultural, historical, and geographical heritage through unique landscaping treatments. It is composed of a series of landscaped bands that interweave public art and native plantings to tell the story of Chattanooga. Taken in sequence, the bands chronologically trace area history backwards from the 1992 dedication to early Indian contact with Spanish explorers.

The plaza also serves as a link in the riverwalk connecting the Hunter Museum and the historic Walnut Street Bridge to the aquarium.

Looking south over downtown Chattanooga with Moccasin Bend in the background. (Photo courtesy of Chattanooga Convention and Visitors Bureau)

The Walnut Street Bridge and walkways stretching from Ross's Landing Park and the Bluff View Arts District, home of the Hunter and Houston Museums and the River Gallery. Renovated as the longest pedestrian walkway bridge in the world, the 2,370-foot Walnut Street Bridge in downtown Chattanooga reopened in 1993. Built in 1891, the old truss bridge became the first multiuse structure to span the Tennessee River with the exception of a military bridge constructed during the Civil War.

You should know about Chattanooga's free electric shuttle. It runs to every downtown hotel, the trade center, and all points in between every five minutes. We found the service very convenient for seeing many of the attractions, shopping, and dining. It is also part of the Environmental City's plan to reduce automobile emissions. You can get on at Shuttle Park North (near the Tennessee Aquarium and IMAX theater), at the Shuttle Park South next door to the Chattanooga Choo Choo, or at any of the stops in between on Broad and Market Streets.

Chattanooga is home to the Tivoli Theatre, a historic showplace known as the Jewel Box of the South. The Tivoli opened March 1921 and its interior reflects the baroque style popular for movie palaces of the 1920s. Declining attendance led to its closure in 1961, although a grant in 1963 allowed the Tivoli to reopen after a partial renovation. It was placed in the National Register of Historic Places in 1974 and reopened in 1989.

In keeping with the heyday of stage performances, in 1941 Glenn Miller released a song composed for the film *Sun Valley Serenade*. The song reached number one on the Hit Parade, sold more than a million copies as a single, and Miller was awarded the record industry's first gold record for "The Chattanooga Choo Choo."

In 1909 when the first train departed to Atlanta from the city's new Southern Railroad terminal, Chattanooga's golden age of railroads began, and millions of travelers passed through the city during the sixty-one years the Chattanooga depot was in operation. With the competition from airplanes, the railways were replaced, and the last passenger train left Chattanooga in 1970. The depot fell silent, was boarded up, and left to ruin.

In 1971 a group of investors decided to restore the depot and after a year of renovation, the Chattanooga Choo Choo opened. It contains shops, restaurants, train exhibits, even two hotel suites in original passenger coaches. Centered around the restored terminus is the Holiday Inn Chattanooga containing more than 360 comfortable rooms and suites. Guests are able to play tennis and swim in either outdoor or indoor pools.

The Chattanooga Choo Choo offers a wide selection of food, from southern specialties in the Gardens Restaurant to an elegant Dinner in the Diner. For a unique dining experience, enjoy live entertainment as waiters and waitresses sing and serve steaks and seafood at the Station House Restaurant.

You may walk around in the formal gardens, tour the thirty-acre complex in a 1924 New Orleans trolley, and shop in the fourteen specialty stores. You can see the 174-foot-long model railroad display complete with more than

Fish, walk, and picnic along Chattanooga's Tennessee RiverPark, which will be twenty-two miles long when completed.

"The Chattanooga Choo Choo" became popular in 1941, and today the renovated railway station is known for lodging, dining, and entertainment.

three thousand feet of track, one thousand model freight cars, and model cities along the route through Chattanooga.

We had a grand time sitting and listening to live music among the train cars, gardens, and trees in the old train yard. If you are a people watcher, you'll enjoy sitting in plush chairs in the huge lobby as people check in or walk through. We had a very comfortable stay at the Choo Choo.

Whether you have children or not, you'll have a big time in the Creative Discovery Museum. It brought the child out in us. This is not a stuffy place; it is alive with hands-on fun. The forty-two-thousand-square-foot building promotes discovery through sight, sounds, and exploration. You can dig for dinosaur bones, crank up all sorts of electric gadgets, and play any number of musical instruments. This is a place to experience.

And if you like experiencing things, then the IMAX theater is the place to get close and personal with a movie. We dare you to sit through a movie and not reach out to touch the objects that float by you.

The Chattanooga Regional History Museum at 400 Chestnut Street is housed in a 1910 school building two blocks from the Tennessee River in downtown Chattanooga. The museum presents the history of southeast Tennessee, northwest Georgia, and northeast Alabama, from prehistory to the present. The museum has outstanding collections of artifacts relating to prehistoric Chattanooga, the Civil War, nineteenth- and early twentieth-century business and industry, and the history of tourism in the region. The Houston Museum of Decorative Arts houses the antique glass, china, and furniture collection of Anna Safely Houston, an eccentric woman known as "Antique Annie." The ten-thousand-piece collection is permanently displayed in a turn-of-the-century home. The museum opened in 1961 with collections of eighteenth- and nineteenth-century china, glass, ceramics, textiles, and American furniture. In 1957 a group of concerned citizens organized to establish the museum. In downtown Chattanooga's Bluff View

Art District, it is across the street from the Hunter Museum of American Art.

The Hunter Museum of American Art has a physical presence as arresting as the fine collection of American art housed within its galleries. Situated on a ninety-foot limestone bluff overlooking the Tennessee River on one side and downtown Chattanooga on the other, it is a prominent feature of the cityscape. It operates in two different buildings that function as a unit while retaining their unique visual integrity. An ingeniously designed elliptical stairwell and an outdoor sculpture garden link the 1904 classical revival mansion and a contemporary structure. The Hunter Museum of American Art holds over fifteen hundred works, with approximately 20 percent on view because of limited space. Pieces dating from 1790 to 1950 are housed chronologically in the mansion galleries, while contemporary works are in the 1975 addition.

The Lookout Mountain Incline Railway was built in 1895 for use by residents living on the top of Lookout Mountain. (Photo courtesy of Chattanooga Convention and Visitors Bureau)

This famous site, Lover's Leap in Rock City, allows visitors to see seven states and a bird's-eye view of Chattanooga. (Photo courtesy of Rock City Gardens)

Shifting to another art form, no one would ever have imagined that the Empress of the Blues would have called a one-room shack in the heart of Chattanooga home. Despite her humble beginnings, Bessie Smith became a legendary figure whose unique ability to combine the sounds of blues and jazz secured her place as one of the most important women in American music. She was the highest paid African-American singer, making over two thousand dollars a week. She inspired many musical greats, such as Louis Armstrong, who said, "Bessie used to thrill me at all times. It's the way she could phrase a note in her blues, a certain something in her voice that no other singer could get."

Smith's achievements and contributions are remembered at Chattanooga's annual festival, Riverbend. A crowd of one hundred thousand or more comes to celebrate Smith on Martin Luther King Boulevard, where barbecue and blues are on every street corner. An old warehouse on the corner of Martin Luther King Boulevard and Lindsay Street has been renovated into the Bessie Smith Memorial Hall, a multipurpose facility that acts as an educational, cultural, and entertainment center. The hall boasts a performance hall-cabaret-restaurant area and practice rooms for students.

The Tennessee Aquarium delights many thousands of visitors each year with a fish-eye view of the Tennessee River and other important waterways of the world. (Photo courtesy of Tennessee Aquarium/Lookout Mountain)

All this sightseeing requires energy, and downtown Chattanooga has plenty of good food stops. Tony's Pasta Shop and Trattoria at 212-B High Street is our favorite place to stop while exploring the Bluff View Art District. Freshly made pastas are part of a classical Italian meal that satisfies any hunger.

The Loft across the river on Cherokee Boulevard was our favorite dinner spot. It has been voted Chattanooga's First Choice in Fine Dining twenty years in a row. American and Cajun foods and all the other popular items you would want are on the menu.

A trip to Chattanooga would not be consummated without a meal at the Choo Choo. Dinner in the Diner is its top spot, but for a little more casual place with music, try the Station House. We had a good meal here while the waiters entertained us from a stage. It is an amusing restaurant worth a visit.

There are some bed and breakfast inns in the area. Look at the end of the chapter under accommodations for a list.

If you are interested in Civil War sites, you will want to visit the Chickamauga and Chattanooga National Military Park. In the fall of 1863, two armies clashed in an effort to gain control of a vital transportation hub leading straight into the heart of Dixie. Over a period of nine weeks, the Confederate and Union armies fought two major battles, each side claiming one victory. In the end, the champion would hold the key to the Deep South, Chattanooga.

Cravens House was the site of some of the fiercest fighting on the mountain and also served as headquarters for both sides. Today the restored house is open for a tour of pre–Civil War living.

The Chickamauga Battlefield Visitor Center features a state-of-the-art audio-visual program that explains the battle and its place in the Civil War. Also in the visitor center is the Fuller Collection of American Military Arms, containing the best collection of Springfield long rifles in the world and other rare items and weapons.

The park also features self-guiding tours, monuments, and historical tablets, plus hiking and horse trails. Ranger-guided talks and Civil War-era demonstrations are conducted during the summer.

The Chattanooga National Cemetery was established in December 1863 as a military cemetery by order of George Thomas, the Union general nicknamed "the Rock of Chickamauga." The seventy-five-acre cemetery became a national cemetery in 1867. Three Civil War battle sites can be viewed from here: Missionary Ridge, Lookout Mountain, and Chattanooga. There is no Confederate soldier interred in the cemetery.

To visit these historic sites you can experience the thrill of riding America's most amazing mile on the Lookout Mountain Incline Railway. It gives you wonderful views of Chattanooga and the surrounding mountains and valleys as the trolley-style rail cars travel into the clouds. The breathtaking grade of the track, 72.7 percent near the top, gives the Incline the unique distinction of being the world's steepest passenger railway.

From its mountaintop station, visitors have a panoramic view from the highest overlook on Lookout Mountain. On a clear day they can see two hundred miles to the Great Smoky Mountains. While you are on Lookout Mountain, you shouldn't miss seeing Ruby Falls, a 145-foot underground waterfall with no known beginning. More than three hundred gallons of water are funneled each minute into a crystal-clear, four-foot-deep pool. You'll see stalagmites made from white onyx, rock formations that resemble steak and potatoes, an angel's wing, an elephant's foot, and more. Be prepared for a temperature of fifty-eight degrees that remains steady year-round.

In 1928 engineers led by explorer Leo Lambert began digging an elevator shaft down to the cave within the Lookout Mountain Caverns. After ninety-two days and nights of drilling through 420 feet of solid stone, the crew reached its mark. But some 260 feet down, Lambert felt wind. Searching for the source, he discovered a small crevice eighteen inches high and four feet wide that disappeared into the mountain. Traveling seventeen hours, much of it on his hands and knees, Lambert stumbled upon a spectacular waterfall and breathtaking scenes of rock formations and mineral deposits within a large cavern. When he returned to the group to describe his discovery, it seemed so preposterous that they refused to believe him. He returned to the falls a second time with his wife, Ruby. When she repeated Lambert's story to the engineers, work began on a second shaft and Ruby Falls was opened to the public in 1929. For over six decades, Ruby Falls has been one of the most popular attractions in southeast Tennessee.

Over sixty years ago during the Great Depression, Frieda Carter developed a ten-acre garden. Her husband, Garnet Carter, found inspiration in his wife's work, and he spent two years improving her pine needle path among the huge boulders and natural rock formations. Then Rock City Gardens opened to the public in 1932.

In the 1950s Rock City developed a birdhouse campaign to complement their barn advertising, but the Beautification Act of 1965 brought an end to both campaigns. Barn slogans and birdhouses alike were painted over and only eighty-five barns remain today. The See Rock City slogan can still be seen around the world, in British subways, French country sides, Japanese gardens, and even in the Near East as Desert Storm soldiers erected a Rock City birdhouse in the desert sands of freed Kuwait.

Since the beginning, Rock City has been a natural attraction that provides entertainment for the whole family. There are many natural wonders at Rock City: the towering rock formations, beautiful gardens, and the astounding view from Lover's Leap where you can see seven states. The flag court salutes those states.

For those who have adventure in their blood, Lookout Mountain is an ideal spot to hang-glide. Lookout Mountain Flight Park is open year-round and spectators are welcome to watch the brave at heart fly from the 1,350-foot mountain.

On the western slope of the mountain are Reflection Riding and the Chattanooga Nature Center. The center is an environmental educational facility with nature exhibits and a rehabilitation place for injured wildlife. Reflection Riding is a three-hundred-acre nature preserve that adjoins Lookout Mountain National Park. Maintained as an English landscape, visitors can see a wide variety of trees, shrubs, and wildflowers.

We drove along Lookout Creek delighting in the pastoral setting. It is a serene change from the bustle of the city. The park contains more than one thousand species of plants with more than three hundred wildflowers identified. The Great Indian Warpath that ran from Alabama to New York remains in its original condition within the park. It is thought that de Soto and his men traveled this way in 1540. Also the 1807 Old Federal Road that ran from Augusta, Georgia, to Nashville, the first road through the Cherokee Nation, is preserved here. There are markers throughout the park, such as at Cherokee Chief Walking Stick's log cabin, one of the oldest structures in the state.

Native Americans have been living in this region for at least eight thousand years. The Tafachady Gallery celebrates the spirit of Native-American culture. On display at the gallery are Native American clothing, musical instruments, weaponry, and art.

Let's take a quick tour of some historic buildings and sites.

We've described Ross's Landing Park and Plaza. In 1815 Chief John Ross built a small warehouse-trading post on the south bend of the Tennessee River where the park and plaza surrounding the Tennessee Aquarium are. Ross was chief of the Cherokee when they were forced on the Trail of Tears to the Oklahoma Territory in 1838.

Warehouse Row on Market Street is where eight turn-of-the-century railroad warehouses stood. Today this newly renovated complex is the Southeast's premier fashion outlet center with over thirty designer outlet stores. Warehouse Row was listed in *Woman's Day* magazine as the fifth best outlet center in the nation during 1991. In the National Register of Historic Places, this multi-use facility also includes an upscale office complex. You need to plan spending at last half a day among these fascinating shops.

The Radisson Read House is on the site of the Crutchfield House that was once the political, social, and economic heart of Chattanooga. The present building, constructed in 1926, is a hotel at Broad Street and M. L. King Boulevard that is in the National Register of Historic Places.

The John Ross House is a memorial to the man who was the greatest chief of the Cherokee Nation. Although only one-eighth Indian, Ross was principal chief of the Cherokee Nation for nearly forty years. Built in 1779 by the grandfather of Ross, the house is located on Highway 27 on the way to Chickamauga and Chattanooga National Military Park.

Aptly named Signal Point atop Signal Mountain is the spot where messages were relayed to clear the way for supplies coming down the Tennessee River for Union soldiers during the Civil War. The strategic location provides spectacular views of the Grand Canyon of the Tennessee River, as well as views of Lookout Mountain.

In east Chattanooga are our next two stops, Harrison Bay State Park and Booker T. Washington State Park, then we continue east to Cleveland.

All of the following accommodations are Chattanooga with zip code 37402, and all telephone listings are area code 423, except where noted.

Accommodations:
Chattanooga Choo Choo, 1400 Market St., 800-TRACK29 or 266-5000.
Milton House Bed and Breakfast, 508 Fort Wood Pl., 265-2800.
Radisson Read House, M. L. King and Broad Sts., 800-333-3333 or 266-4121.
Alford House Bed & Breakfast, 5515 Alford Hill Dr. at Lookout Mountain Pkwy., 825-5253 or 821-7625.
Chanticleer Inn Bed & Breakfast, 1300 Mockingbird Ln., 706-820-2015.
McElhattan's Owl Hill Bed & Breakfast, 617 Scenic Hwy., 821-2040.

Attractions:
Bessie Smith Hall, 757-0020.
Chattanooga African-American Museum, 266-8658.
Chattanooga Regional History Museum, 265-3247.
Chattanooga Riverboat Co., 800-766-2784 or 266-4488.
Creative Discovery Museum, 756-2738.
Houston Museum, 267-7176.
Hunter Museum of American Art, 267-0968.
IMAX 3D Theater, 800-262-0695.
International Towing & Recovery Hall of Fame & Museum, 267-3132.
Renaissance Commons, 757-0125.
Tennessee Aquarium, 800-262-0695.
The J. Peterman Company Warehouse Store, 266-3434.
Warehouse Row Factory Shops, 267-1111.
    Lookout Mountain Area Attractions

Battles for Chattanooga Museum, 821-2812.
Chattanooga Nature Center & Reflection Riding Botanical Garden, 821-1160.
Lookout Mountain Hang Gliding, Rising Fawn, GA, 800-688-5637.
Lookout Mountain Incline Railway, 821-4224.
Raccoon Mountain Caverns, 821-9403.
Raccoon Mountain Pumped Storage Project, 706-820-2531.
Ruby Falls, 821-2544.

Dining:
212 Market, 265-1212.
4th Street Cafe, 266-0184.
Adams Hilborne's Porch Cafe, 265-5000.
Big River Grille & Brewing Works, 267-BREW.
The Boiled Frog, 756-3764.
Choo-Choo Cafe Espresso, Chattanooga Choo Choo, 266-5000.
Dinner in the Diner, Chattanooga Choo Choo, 266-5000.
Durty Nelly's Irish Pub, 265-9970.
La Dolce Vita, 267-7141.
Mocha Mambo, 756-2414.
Mudpie Coffeehouse, 267-9043.
Nikki's Forties Restaurant, 265-9015.
Quixote's, 265-4721.
Rembrandt's Coffee House, 265-5033.
Renaissance Commons, 265-5033.
Silver Diner, Chattanooga Choo Choo, 266-5000.
Southern Belle Riverboat, 266-4488.
Station House, Chattanooga Choo Choo, 266-5000.
The Loft, 266-3601.
The Sloppy Greek's Cafe, 752-1946.
Town & Country Restaurant, 267-8544.

Vine Street Market, 267-8165.
    Lookout Mountain Area
Bea's Restaurant, 867-3618.
Big Rock Cafe, 820-2531.
Hot Sauce Charlie, 265-2827.

Shopping:
All Books/Mountain Herbs, 266-0501.
The Galleries at Southside, 267-8101.
The In-Town Gallery, 276-9214.
The J. Peterman Company Warehouse Store, 266-3434.
Moll Hill Pottery, Signal Mountain, 886-5636.
Warehouse Row Factory Shops, 267-1111.

Special Events:
May—Bessie Smith Traditional Jazz Festival; River Roast
June—Riverbend Festival and Bessie Smith Strut
September—Hamilton County Fair
October—Fall Color Cruise and Folk Festival
November–January—Enchanted Garden of Lights
November through February—Winter Day & Lights
December—Christmas on the River

Camping:
Best Holiday Trav-L-Park, 800-323-8899 or 706-891-9766.
Chattanooga North/KOA, Cleveland, 472-8928.
Raccoon Mountain Campgrounds, 821-9403.

For More Information:
Chattanooga Area Convention and Visitors Bureau, 1001 Market St., 37402; 800-322-3344 or 756-8687, fax 265-1630.

ᐁ Loop 8

50 *Booker T. Washington and Harrison Bay State Parks*
Parks on Chickamauga Lake

Booker T. Washington State Park is on the shores of Chickamauga Lake northeast of Chattanooga via TN 58. This 353-acre park is named in honor of the famous leader, Booker Taliaferro Washington. Washington was born a slave at Hale's Ford, Virginia, but with determination he secured an education to become one of our great Americans. He is perhaps best known as a former president of the Tuskegee Institute, a black organization for higher education.

With a capacity of ninety-six persons, this completely equipped camp is available to youth and church groups and family reunions from May through October. A modern group lodge accommodating up to forty-two people is available year-round for weekend or week-long outings.

Situated on Chickamauga Lake, the park offers opportunities for fishing and boating. Boat launching ramps and a day-use-only boat dock with pier are conveniently located and boaters enjoy fishing or pleasure boating. Fishing is good all year and catches include largemouth bass, crappie, sauger, striped bass, and catfish. A longer fishing pier with a sink for cleaning your catch is popular.

The park has a large pool and bathhouse complex open from early summer through Labor Day. Many picnic tables and grills are placed along the shores of the lake, and restrooms and water are available nearby for visitor convenience. Park recreation activities include hiking, field games, playgrounds, basketball, and others. Recreation equipment is available free of charge at the park office.

Harrison Bay State Park is about four miles north of Booker T. Washington State Park via TN 58. The twelve-hundred-acre park contains almost forty miles of Chickamauga Lake shoreline. Its name is derived from a large bay of the main channel of the Tennessee River that covers the old town of Harrison.

The parklands are of historic significance. The waters of Harrison Bay cover the site of the last Cherokee campground that consisted of three villages ruled by Chief Joe Vann, one of the last great Cherokee chieftains. This wooded park is a haven for campers, boaters, and anglers, as well as picnickers.

Harrison Bay has 156 campsites with tables and grills and most have water and electrical hookups. Restrooms and bathhouses are conveniently located in the camping areas. A camp store carrying camping and fishing supplies is open during the summer season.

Harrison Bay's marina, in one of the most protected harbors on Chickamauga Lake, has two major boat-launching ramps with ample parking for boaters. Marine supplies, fuel, fishing tackle, bait, and ski accessories are carried in the marina shop. A restaurant is open from June through September. A number of shady picnic grounds are scattered throughout the park, all with tables and grills, and two picnic pavilions are available for group picnics for thirty to eighty persons.

A swimming pool, kiddy pool, playground, concession stand, bathhouse, and recreation shelter are close together. Horseshoe pits, tennis courts, basketball and volleyball courts, shuffleboard, playgrounds, and ball fields are available. A Jack Nicklaus championship eighteen-hole golf course opened in 1998. The park's recreator provides planned programs and activities including arts and crafts, campfires, organized games, and movies during the summer months.

For More Information:
Booker T. Washington State Park, 5801 Champion Rd., Chattanooga, 37416; 423-894-4955.
Harrison Bay State Park, 8411 Harrison Bay Rd., Harrison 37341; 423-344-6214.

51 *Cleveland*
Growth City of the Southeast

Bradley County had one building in 1836, a small log cabin in the heart of the Cherokee Nation known as the Taylors' Place, where Andrew Taylor and his Indian wife lived. Bradley County was established from land sold by the Cherokees and named for Edward Bradley, a friend of Andrew Jackson and a fellow officer. The city of Cleveland, incorporated in 1838 (1842 by another source), honors Benjamin Cleveland, a Revolutionary War hero. This was the last area evacuated by the Cherokee to leave on the Trail of Tears in 1838.

Cleveland is near the western edge of the Cherokee National Forest (CNF) with the CNF superintendent's office here. The Ocoee River, east of Cleveland in the Cherokee National Forest, is a drawing card for rafters, canoeists, and anglers and was a site for some events of the 1996 Olympics. In addition to fishing and white-water rafting, you can enjoy picnicking, hiking, camping, hunting, wildflowers, and wilderness experiences in the CNF.

There are three tours you may enjoy and you can get brochures from the Cleveland/Bradley County Convention and Visitors Bureau at 2145 Keith Street. The Greenway walking tour directs you by four-inch green spots in the sidewalks to historic sites in town. The day-long Cherokee Scenic Loop Tour takes you to Red Clay, Bald River Falls, the Ocoee River, and Reliance Historic District. The Cherokee Heritage Wildlife Tour is a self-guided auto tour.

There are two fruity trips you may enjoy. Apple Valley Orchard sells apples and many products made from the more than two dozen varieties grown on fifty acres in Cleveland. About eight miles north of town is Morris Winery and Vineyard, which produces six wines including apple and muscadine. You can pick your own fruit (blueberries, grapes and muscadine) from July into October.

The Aquatic Wildlife Company isn't your typical aquarium. It is a twenty-four-thousand-gallon mariculture, the only one in the South. Here are propagated marine organisms to save and to sell. If you want to add some exotics to your tank, you'll want to stop here.

The Primitive Settlement on Kinser Road has restored early American log cabins furnished with household and farm items.

From Cleveland take TN 60 Northwest to Dayton.

All of the following accommodations are Cleveland with zip code 37320, and all telephone listings are area code 423, except where noted.

Accommodations:
Brown Manor Bed and Breakfast, 215 20th St. NE, 37311; 476-8029.

Attractions:
Apple Valley Orchard, 472-3044.

Cherokee National Forest, 476-9700.
Cleveland Creative Arts Guild, 478-3114.
Morris Winery and Vineyard, 479-7311.
Primitive Settlement, 476-5096.
Wildlife Ecosystems, 559-9000.

Dining:
Ciao Restaurant, 476-5003.
Jenkins Deli, 478-1648.
John's Bar-B-Q, 479-7885.
Prime Sirloin of Cleveland, 479-3356.
The Rebel, 472-6525.
Roblyn's Steak House, 476-8808.
The Spot, 423-1615.
Stadfeld's Family Restaurant, 479-3123.

Special Events:
February—Cherokee Heritage Wildlife Weekend
March—Spring Arts and Crafts Fair
April—Spring Arts Festival
May—Pig-Out for PRIDE
June—Riverbend Festival
July—Summerfest; Blue Springs Valley Sing; Scopes Trail and
    Festival
October—Prater's Mill Country Fair
December—Christmas Parade

Camping:
33 Campground, 336-6821.
Chattanooga North KOA, 800-KOA-9039 or 472-8928.

Outfitters:
Adventures Unlimited, 800-662-0667.
Nantahala Outdoor Center, 800-232-7238
Ocoee Outdoors, 800-533-PROS or 423-338-2438.
Quest Expeditions 800-277-4537.
Southeastern Expeditions, 800-868-7238.
Wildwater, 800-251-1475.

For More Information:
Cleveland/Bradley County Convention and Visitors Bureau, P.O.
    Box 2275, 2145 Keith St., 800-472-6588 or 472-6587.

52 *Dayton and Pikeville*
Scopes Trial and Villain Town

W. H. Smith, a schoolmaster from New England, founded Dayton in Rhea County in 1820, but it wasn't until 105 years later that the name of the

town became nationally known as the site of the famous "Monkey Trial."

Dr. George Rappelya, while sitting with a group of men at Robinson's Drug Store in Dayton, persuaded a twenty-four-year-old science teacher at Rhea County High School to join a conspiracy. John T. Scopes agreed to violate a Tennessee statute to provide a court test case. On the surface, this was a publicity stunt, but worldwide publicity quickly resulted and astonished the conspirators. The original drug store table where the decision was made May 15, 1925, is in the Scopes Museum in the basement of the Rhea County Courthouse in Dayton.

The law prohibiting the teaching of evolution had been passed by the Tennessee legislature in March 1925. It stated that it was unlawful for any public teacher "to teach any theory that denies the story of the divine creation of man as taught in the Bible, and to teach instead that man descended from a lower order of animals." The statute further stated that "any teacher violating this section shall be guilty of a misdemeanor and fined not less than one hundred dollars ($100) and not more than five hundred dollars ($500) for each offense." Scopes was charged with violating this law.

William Jennings Bryan and Clarence Darrow faced each other to argue this case, and the trial became a media event as well as a historical event. The media merry-making began as hundreds of reporters came to town for the Monkey Trial. The *Baltimore Sun* sent several writers including H. L. Mencken. The radio, a new invention at the time, was used to report the proceedings. Thousands of visitors swarmed to Dayton daily to see the trial. Revivalists put up tents, biblical warnings were posted throughout the town, and rumors circulated that Darrow must have horns and a tail.

The trial lasted from July 10 to July 21 in one

of the hottest and driest Tennessee summers. Emotions ran as high as the temperatures in the overcrowded courtroom, and this led to moving the trial under the oaks trees on the north side of the courthouse.

The trial was supposed to deal with whether Scopes violated the Tennessee law while acting as a substitute biology teacher. Public interest, however, lay in academic freedom, science, evolution, and religion. Many came also to see the contest between Darrow and Bryan, and they saw it.

Bryan said, "I want the world to know that this man who doesn't believe in God is using a Tennessee court to cast slurs on Him." To which Darrow replied, "I am simply examining you on the fool ideas that no intelligent Christian in the whole world believes." The judge declared that enough fireworks had taken place and the trial was cut short, depriving the audience more anticipated theater.

The jury convicted Scopes, and Judge Raulston fined him one hundred dollars. The Ten-

nessee Supreme Court later overturned the conviction on the technicality that the jury, rather than the judge, should have set the fine.

Bryan died in Dayton five days after the trial, Darrow returned to Chicago, and Scopes attended the University of Chicago to study geology, which led him into Louisiana's oil industry. The anti-evolution law was expunged from Tennessee law in 1967.

The Scopes Trial Play and Festival held in July reenacts the Monkey Trial in the same courtroom, using the court transcripts. This gives you an authentic look at what happened without the layers of distorting time and what the press said happened.

May is Strawberry Festival time—celebrating the sweet red berry with a beauty contest, children's fair, rides, and the world's longest strawberry shortcake.

Bed and breakfasts include Cross Creek Farm, which has two rooms with shared bath; Magnolia House, which has three rooms with shared and

The $100 fine levied against John Scopes for his teaching evolution was overturned on a technicality.

private baths and serves dinner by reservation; and Rose House, which has three rooms with shared and private baths and a charming Victorian Cottage. All serve full breakfasts. Of interest to hikers is the 710-acre Laurel-Snow Pocket Wilderness, named for two waterfalls and located about 2.5 miles northwest of Dayton.

From Dayton, take TN 30 to Pikeville in Bledsoe County. The county was formed from Roane County in 1807 and named for Anthony Bledsoe, a Revolutionary War patriot who came to Tennessee in the late 1700s. Pikeville became the county seat in 1815 and was incorporated in 1830. It is the only incorporated community in the county.

John Murrell, the infamous outlaw, worked as a blacksmith in Pikeville after he was released from prison in 1844. Later he died here of tuberculosis he contracted in prison. Murrell is credited with organizing the Mystic Brotherhood of criminals. The Mystic Brotherhood began as a group of horse and slave thieves, and grew into an organization that was rumored to have buried a million dollars in loot.

Murrell was a slight, dapper man who developed eloquent speech by talking during his travels with book peddlers, unprincipled educated men, and evangelists. He found the finer speech to be more helpful than the one he learned in his mother's tavern and brothel. He became known as Brother Murrell and was frequently asked to preach. There is a story that he attended services wearing his a long-tailed coat and commingled with churchgoers after returning from a brutal raid on some Natchez Trace travelers.

It was at his mother's knee and from her various paramours that he learned the outlaw trade. One of his mother's boyfriends, named Harry Crankshaw, took young Murrell down the Natchez Trace into Alabama to shoot travelers from ambush. They took the victims' goods back to Mom Murrell for her to sell. In 1835 he was captured, tried, and sentenced to ten years in prison.

Bledsoe County has many historic southern homes and scenic beauty and is also the Pumpkin Capital of the World. Pikeville, situated on the Trail of Tears, contains stately homes with listings in the National Register of Historic Places.

Bed and breakfast accommodations include Colonial Bed and Breakfast with three rooms with shared bath and Fall Creek Falls Bed and Breakfast (*see* Spencer for more on Fall Creek Falls), which has eight rooms with private baths. Antiques and collectibles are found at the Attic, the Little Store on Nickel Row, Sapp's Country Store, and the Vaughn House.

Our next stop is Altamont. Take US 127 south from Pikeville to TN 8, turn northwest to Cagle, then turn southwest on TN 399 to the TN 56 junction and turn north to Altamont on TN 56.

All of the following accommodations are Dayton with zip code 37321, and all telephone listings are area code 423, except where noted.

Accommodations:
Cross Creek Farm Bed and Breakfast, Hwy. 30 E., 334-9172.
Magnolia House, 656 Market St., 775-9288.
Rose House, 123 Idaho Ave., 775-3311.

Attractions:
Laurel-Snow Pocket Wilderness, 336-7424.
Scopes Trial Museum, 775-7801.

Dining:
Dayton Coffeeshop, 775-6156.
Frontier House, 775-6353.
Golden Monkey, 775-0707.
Prime Steak Out, 775-0598.

Special Events:
May—Tennessee Strawberry Festival
July—Scopes Trial Festival

Camping:
Armstrong Ferry Campground, 334-4192.
Blue Water Campground, 775-3265.

For More Information:
Dayton Chamber of Commerce, 107 Main St., 775-0361.

All of the following accommodations are Pikeville with zip code 37367, and all telephone listings are area code 423, except where noted.

Accommodations:
Colonial Bed and Breakfast, 303 S. Main, 447-7183.
Coachman Inn (cabins) and Restaurant, P.O. Box 723, 447-2424.
Fall Creek Falls Bed and Breakfast, Rt.3, Box 298 B, 881-5494.

Attractions:
Pikeville Historic District, 447-2791.

Dining:
Campbell's Restaurant, 447-6801.
Genesis Pizza, 447-2669.
Sapp's Country Store and Deli, 447-6336.
The Vaughn House, 447-2678.

Shopping:
The Attic, 447-7041.
The Fabric House, 447-6195.
The Little Store on Nickel Row, 447-7357.
Sapp's Country Store, 447-6336.
The Vaughn House, 447-2678.

Camping:
Fall Creek Falls State Park, 881-5241.

For More Information:
Bledsoe County Chamber of Commerce, P.O. Box 205, 447-2791.
450-Mile Outdoor Sale, P.O. Box 1128, Jamestown, 38556; 800-338-3999 or 931-879-7713.

53 *Altamont, Tracy City, Monteagle*
Highlands of the Southern Cumberland Plateau

At an elevation of nineteen hundred feet, Altamont is one of the oldest towns on the Cumberland Plateau. It is an ideal setting for escaping the summer heat of the lowlands. There are two bed and breakfasts in town, the Woodlee House and the Manor.

The Woodlee House was originally a one-room log cabin that has been enlarged to make it a two-story Colonial home. The last addition was in 1910. The home must always be owned by a lawyer per instructions stated in the will of an owner named Woodlee. It has two bedrooms with a shared bath, antiques, quilts, and law books dating back to 1838 and is in the National Register of Historic Places.

The Manor, also in the national register, has five bedrooms with four baths and a three-room cabin. Guests in the Manor are served a full breakfast but guests in the cabin prepare their own. The Manor was built in 1885. It has many antiques, the rooms have themes such as the Civil War, and the inn has more than three thousand books—one of the largest libraries found in a bed and breakfast.

From Altamont go south on TN 56 to Tracy Cit,y but you may want to swing northeast on TN 56 to look around historic Beersheba Springs first.

Tracy City has a couple of attractions worth visiting. The Dutch Maid Bakery is Tennessee's oldest family-operated bakery. Swiss immigrant, John Baggenstoss, established it in 1902. Old World breads and famous applesauce fruitcakes

The 115-year-old Manor boasts one of the largest libraries housed in a bed and breakfast.

are baked year-round and the bakery is as much a museum as a bakery. Many appliances were new during the 1920s and now the parts have to be made to repair them. If you're wondering why a Swiss called his bakery Dutch, it was a mistake. The name *Swiss Bakery* was being used, so Baggenstoss applied for *Deutsche Bakery,* and a bureaucratic mistake spelled it *Dutch.*

The other notable spot to visit in Tracy City is Mountain Lake Glassworks on Lake Road. Here you can see hand-blown glassware, pottery, bronze castings, and fine crafts.

From Tracy City stay on TN 56 and head west to Monteagle. South Cumberland Recreation Area, between Tracy City and Monteagle, is headquarters for seven parks, of which five are natural areas. South Cumberland Recreation Area is a large expanse of land that contains dense forests, rivers, creeks, mountains, caves, natural bridges, lakes, and hiking trails. The visitor center

at South Cumberland Recreation Area is the place to learn about the outdoor opportunities in the area: Grundy Lake State Park, Grundy Forest Natural Area, Foster Falls Small Wild Area, Sewanee Natural Bridge State Natural Area, Carter State Natural Area, Hawkins Cove Natural Area, and the well-known Savage Gulf Natural Area. Also there is a good museum here.

Monteagle is seven miles west of Tracy City on TN 56. The Monteagle Assembly was founded in 1882 as a Chautauqua, a nineteenth-century system that brought religious, educational, and cultural opportunities to towns throughout the country. Monteagle became a refuge for people escaping summer heat and yellow fever and cholera epidemics in the South in the late 1800s. The centerpiece of this community is the Queen Anne–style Adams Edgeworth Inn, built in 1896. A National Register property, the rambling antique-filled structure has twelve guest rooms with private baths. Dinner is available by reservation and breakfast is served to all guests.

The North Gate Inn, also on the Assembly grounds, has seven bright, comfortable guest rooms with private baths and serves a full breakfast. During the summer season, daily admittance is charged to the Assembly grounds. This entitles you to attend all programs and use all the facilities. The Monteagle Inn, across the road from the Assembly, has sixteen suites with private baths.

Wonder Cave, discovered in 1897 by college students, offers hour-long tours. It is lightly commercialized; no lights to shine on your path other than the one you carry. You are taken along a river and your guide points out the interesting rock formations. The cave is ranked as one of the top ten in the country. Wonder Cave Bed and Breakfast, in a log home on the property, is roomy, private, and quiet.

From Monteagle go west for our next stops of Sewanee and Winchester.

All of the following accommodations are Altamont with zip code 37301, and all telephone listings are area code 931, except where noted.

Accommodations:
The Manor, 1885 Main St., 692-3153.
The Woodlee House, 10 Cumberland St., 692-2368.

Dining:
Cumberland Cafe, 692-9998.
The Ridge Inn, 692-9973.
Zak's Pizza & Grill, 692-2132.

For More Information:
Grundy County Chamber of Commerce, HCR 76, Box 578, Gruetli-Laager, 37339; 779-3238.

All of the following accommodations are Tracy City with zip code 37387, and all telephone listings are area code 423, except where noted.

Built in 1896, the famous Adams Edgeworth Inn satisfies travelers with fine dining and comfortable accommodations.

Attractions:
Dutch Maid Bakery, 592-3171.

Camping:
South Cumberland Recreation Area, Monteagle, 924-2980.
Foster Falls, east of town about five miles on Hwy. 150.

For More Information:
Grundy County Chamber of Commerce, Box 578, Gruetli-
   Laager, 37339; 779-3462.

*All of the following accommodations are Monteagle with zip
code 37356, and all telephone listings are area code 931,
except where noted.*

Accommodations:
Adams Edgeworth Inn, Monteagle Assembly, 924-4000.
North Gate Inn, 103 Monteagle Assembly, 924-2799.
Wonder Cave Bed and Breakfast, Rt. 1, Box 446, 467-3060.

Attractions:
Monteagle Wine Cellars, 800-556-WINE or 924-2120.
South Cumberland Recreation Area, 924-2980.
Wonder Cave, 467-3060.

Dining:
Adams Edgeworth Inn, 924-4000.
Jim Oliver's Smokehouse Restaurant and Lodge, 800-489-
   2091 or 924-2268.

Camping:
Jim Oliver's Smokehouse Campground, 800-489-2091 or
   924-2091.
Laurel Trails Campground, 924-2738.
Post Cottage, 924-2758.

For More Information:
City of Monteagle; 924-2265, Grundy County Chamber of
   Commerce, HCR 76, Box 578, Gruetli-Laager, 37339; 779-
   3462.

54 *Sewanee and Winchester*
The Chapel and the Jail

Franklin County, named for Benjamin Franklin,
was formed in 1807, and its county seat, Winchester, was named for Indian and Revolutionary
War fighter Gen. James Winchester. Franklin
County was home to four Tennessee governors:
Isham G. Harris, Albert S. Marks, Peter Turney,
and Henry Horton.

   The county is probably best known for the
University of the South at Sewanee and Tims
Ford Lake. Sewanee, founded in 1857 by Episcopal Bishops Leonidas Polk and James Otey, is
owned by twenty-eight Episcopal dioceses in
twelve states. It has an impressive record of producing twenty-two Rhodes Scholars. More than
70 percent of the college's students pursue graduate studies.

   In Sewanee, on US 64 at the western edge of
the southern Cumberland Plateau, the University
of the South's campus is a most impressive feature. Built of Tennessee sandstone quarried from
the property, it looks like an English village.

   The village of Sewanee offers Shenanigans, a
casual restaurant with great sandwiches and cold
beer, City Cafe, and gift and specialty shops like
the Lemon Fair and the Treasure Hunt Shop.

   Winchester is west of Sewanee on US 64.
First you go through Cowan and you may want to
stop to see the Cowan Railroad Museum in the
middle of town. It has a collection of artifacts, a
caboose, and a model railroad.

   Dinah Shore came from Winchester and you
can see some mementos of her on the second
floor of the Old Jail Museum, listed in the Register of Historic Places. Other exhibits include
Indian artifacts, Civil War uniforms and other
relics, and items used during the operation of the
jail, which was built in 1897. While in town you
can visit some of the fifteen antique shops, many
of them on Rainbow Row, the 100 block of Second Avenue Northwest.

   Winchester is at the eastern end of the
10,700-acre Tims Ford Lake. Stripers, largemouth

Sewanee, University of the South, has its roots in the mid-nineteenth century and rests on the edge of the Cumberland Plateau with the largest campus area in the United States.

bass, smallmouth bass, crappie, stripe, catfish, and bream are the most sought game fish species in the lake. Rainbow and brown trout thrive below Tims Ford Dam in the Elk River. There is easy bank fishing or wading along the Elk River.

Tims Ford State Park (413 acres) offers cabins, camping, hiking and biking trails, swimming, boating and marina. The park caters mostly to anglers and water sports. A Jack Nicklaus golf course should be completed in 1999.

Southwest of Winchester via US 64 is the grave of David Crockett's first wife, Polly Finley Crockett. She died in 1815, two years after they settled near the present community of Maxwell. Look for the historic marker.

There is only one way to get back to our loop and that's US 64E. You may take either I-24 at Monteagle or US 41 at Tracy City south to Chattanooga, completing this loop tour.

All of the following accommodations are Sewanee with zip code 37375, and all telephone listings are area code 931, except where noted.

Accommodations:
Cloud's Rise Farm, 166 Rattlesnake Springs Ln., 598-0993.
Highland Myst, 166 Rattlesnake Springs Ln., 598-0770.

Attraction:
University of the South, 598-1286.

Dining:
Pearl's Café, 598-9568.
Quidnunc Café, 598-1595.
Shenanigans, 598-5671.

Shopping:
Elvin King, 598-5867.
Hallelujah Pottery Gallery, 598-0141.

Camping:
Wild Heart Ranch, 837-0849.

For More Information:
Franklin County Chamber of Commerce, P.O. Box 280, Winchester, 37398; 967-6788.

All of the following accommodations are Winchester with zip code 37398, and all telephone listings are area code 931, except where noted.

Accommodations:
Antebellum Inn, 974 Lynchburg Rd., 967-5550.
Country Manor Bed and Breakfast, 765 Pine Bluff Rd., 962-0541.
Green Pasture, 114 Sharp Springs Rd., 967-9509.
Tims Ford State Park and Lake, 570 Tims Ford Dr., 967-4457.

Attractions:
Old Jail Museum, 967-0524.
Tims Ford State Park and Lake, 967-4457.

Dining:
Green Pasture Restaurant, 967-9509.

Shopping:
Southland Antiques, 967-9569.
T's Antiques, 967-5170.
Wenger's, 967-8764.
Winchester Antique Mall, 967-9930.

Special Events:
May—Crimson Clover Ball
September—Art, Crafts, and Antiques Showcase

Camping:
Tims Ford State Park, 967-4457.

For More Information:
Franklin County Chamber of Commerce, P.O. Box 280, Winchester, 37398; 967-6788.

✒ Loop 9

55 *Goodlettsville*
Longhunter History

(To get to Goodlettsville from Nashville take I-65 north and then go west on TN 174.)

Longhunter Kasper Mansker came to the Goodlettsville area in 1769. Ten years later he and others built a fort on Mansker Creek. Mansker's Station was abandoned within a year because Indians raids became too close and too dangerous. Returning to ashes in 1783, Kasper and his wife, Elizabeth, built another station on the east bank of Mansker Creek. This station became the hub of a thriving community, where Mansker lived until his death in 1821. Today partial reproduction of the station features interpreters in period costumes carrying on the daily activities of the time.

On the same site is the Bowen Plantation House. In 1785 Capt. William Bowen began this two-story Federal-style mansion of handmade bricks. The elegant twin front-doored, twin-chimneyed building contrasted with the rough log structures of the station. It was completed in 1787 and became the first brick building in the region. Captain Bowen's grandson, William Bowen Campbell, became governor of Tennessee. The estate home is a good example of what settlers aspired to. The house, restored and furnished with period antiques, is open to the public.

Over time, the name Mansker's Station was dropped, and the name Goodlettsville was adopted for the community when it was incorpo-rated in 1857. Moss-Wright Park, where Mansker's Station and the Bowen House stand, has 147 acres with lighted walking trails winding along Mansker Creek, which flows into the headwaters of Cheatham Lake, a large playground, picnic shelters, and volleyball courts.

The Path of the Longhunter is a self-guided automobile tour beginning at Mansker's Station and Bowen House and including Rock Castle, Wynnewood, and Cragfont, thus following the progression of the settlement of the area. The seventeen-mile trek takes you through parts of the historic Avery Trace, the original trail that connected Fort Nashborough with the wilderness outpost at Castalian Springs.

Main Street is fertile territory for antique collectors. Several of the antique malls are clustered in the 100 and 200 blocks of North Main Street. Although it doesn't look like it from the outside, the Goodlettsville Antique Mall is the granddaddy of the shops in town with twenty thousand square feet and more than one hundred booths. After you walk through the smaller front space, the building opens up to a huge room filled with good furniture finds ranging from American primitive to 1950s retro pieces. There are also lots of collectibles reasonably priced and an additional twenty or so craft booths.

The Rare Bird Antique Mall sits alone a few blocks away on South Main. When you walk through the old-fashioned screen doors, you'll find seventy booths with a good assortment of collectibles. This mall doesn't have as extensive a furniture collection as you will usually find at the Goodlettsville Antique Mall, but it is a very interesting and worthwhile stop with several outstanding booths.

Open since 1940, Mason's Restaurant on

This unusual Bowen Plantation House, built in 1785, is situated next to Mansker's Station, the first settlement in the area of what was to become Goodlettsville.

South Main Street a few blocks from the Rare Bird has homemade plate lunches daily. Bob's Cafe also specializes in country classics for lunch and dinner daily.

If you're heading north from Goodlettsville to Portland for the Strawberry Festival in May, you may want to stop at the White House Inn. Established in 1796, the inn housed travelers along the Louisville and Nashville Pike. Today it is the home of the White House Inn Library and Historical Museum. The museum includes old photos and antiques provided by residents of the community.

All of the following accommodations are Goodlettsville with zip code 37072, and all telephone listings are area code 615, except where noted.

Accommodations:
Terrawin Bed and Breakfast, 304 Highland Heights Dr., 859-0041.

Attractions:
Bowen House, 859-FORT.
Historic Mansker's Station Frontier Life Center, 859-3678.
Museum of Beverage Containers and Advertising, 859-5236.

Dining:
Autry's Bar-B-Que, 859-9071.
Bailey's Sports Grill, 851-9509.
Goodlettsville Cafe, 859-5166.
Mason's Restaurant, 859-7653.
Pen Anelo's Italian Kitchen, 859-2125.

Shopping:
Antique Corner Mall, 859-7673.
Antiques on Main, 851-9155.
Goodlettsville Antique Mall, 859-7002.
Main Street Antique/Craft Mall, 851-1704.
Quilters Attic, 859-5603.
Rare Bird Antique Mall, 851-2635.
Rivergate Mall, 859-3456.
Magnolia Station Antique Mall, 851-1704.
Sweet Memories, 851-9922.

Special Events:
February—Rook Tournament, 851-2253
March, May, July, September, October, December—Mansker's Station Living History Camp
May—Mansker's Station 18th Century Colonial Fair
August—Bowen Campbell Annual Auto Expo

September—Fall Music Festival
October—Pumpkinfest
November—Portland Highland Harvest Craft Show
December—Christmas Tour of Historic Sites

Camping:
Holiday Rest Campground, Millersville.
April–October—KOA Nashville North, 859-0075.

For More Information:
Goodlettsville Chamber of Commerce, 100 S. Main, Suite D,
    859-7979.

56 *Adams*
Haunted by the Bell Witch

From Goodlettsville take US 41 to Adams and
Port Royal State Historic Area.

No other apparition has been as well docu-
mented as John Bell's witch. Bell, a well-to-do
man, moved from North Carolina to Adams in
the early 1800s, where he bought land and
began farming. He was considered a pious man
with a large family and many slaves. After he
purchased some land from a neighbor, Kate
Batts, she began bemoaning that Bell had
cheated her. This supposed injustice festered in
Batts, and on her deathbed she swore she would
come back and "hant John Bell and all his kith
and kin to their graves."

She was true to her word, and the Bell family
suffered the wrath of a female specter named
Kate. Beginning with noises at night, Kate grew
more rambunctious and began tossing furniture.
She got along with Mrs. Bell but was especially
belligerent toward John and their daughter Betsy.
The witch became so widely known that Andrew
Jackson and some friends went to see John Bell
and his witch. As Jackson's group entered the Bell
property, Kate locked their wagon wheels. Finally

Kate let the wagon go saying, "All right, General,
the wagon can move." The next day as Jackson was
leaving, he was reported to have said, "I would
rather fight the British again than have any more
dealings with that torment."

Stories of the witch are kept alive in Adams
though all the Bells are gone. If you want to try
your luck at seeing Kate, visit the Bell Witch
Cave that is on the former Bell property. Tourists
going through the cave have reported strange vis-
itations on their persons. Maybe these are strong
imaginings suggested by the tour guide's outlandish tales.

For the complete story read *An Authenticated
History of the Famous Bell Witch of Tennessee* by M. V.
Ingram. This book is based on interviews and eye-
witness accounts. It makes fascinating reading.

Bell Witch Opry occurs every Saturday night
at the Old Bell School. It's picking and grinning,
and anyone may join in. In August the Bell Witch
Bluegrass Festival and Arts and Crafts Show
cranks up.

Another special event is the Tennessee-
Kentucky Threshermen's Association annual July
wheat threshing and steam engine show. There are
displays of antique threshers, tractors, and steam
engines, as well as music, square dancing, storytelling, tractor-pulls, mule-pulls, and a lot of
other fun in conjunction with the festival.

Port Royal State Historical Area is about six
miles west of Adams on TN 76. Port Royal was
one of Tennessee's earliest communities and trading centers.

At Port Royal you can see one of the few covered bridges in the state and a museum that
recounts the community's history. A twenty-six-
acre park around the covered bridge that spans the
Red River offers visitors interpretive walks, with
talks available on request.

All of the following accommodations are Adams with zip code 37172, and all telephone listings are area code 931, except where noted.

Attractions:
Bell Witch Cave, 696-3055.
Bell Witch Opry in Old Bell School.
Port Royal State Historical Area (near Adams), 358-9696.

Dining:
Catfish House.

Shopping:
Bell School Antique Mall, 696-8179.

Special Events:
July—Threshermen's Steam Show
August—Bell Witch Bluegrass Festival; Arts and Crafts Show; Competition Antique Car Show

For More Information:
Springfield Chamber of Commerce, 100 5th Ave. W., Springfield 37172; 384-3800.

57 *Clarksville*
Fifth-Largest City in Tennessee

Montgomery County was formed in 1796 from Robertson County that was formerly Tennessee County before that name was selected for the state's name. It was named after Col. John Montgomery, who had explored the Cumberland country in 1777.

Clarksville, named for Gen. George Rogers Clark, was established in 1784. The Clarksville-Montgomery County Museum at 200 South Second Street is in an ornamental building built in 1898, whose architecture is a blend of styles to create an entertaining look. It is a good place to pick up two tour guides, one for a walking tour of twenty-five downtown sites and the other

for a driving tour of about fifty county sites. One of the highlights of the driving tour is the Smith-Trahern Mansion built in 1858 by wealthy tobacco merchant Christopher Smith. This is a New Orleans-style home with a widow's walk   so Smith could watch the barge traffic on the Cumberland River. Another stop on the tour is Sevier Station, oldest structure in Montgomery County, built in 1792 by one of the first settlers, Valentine Sevier. Fort Defiance, near Sevier Station, is a well-preserved Civil War post used by the Confederates overlooking the Cumberland and Red Rivers. Fort Defiance was not very defiant. It was surrendered to the Federals without a shot being fired. The Post House, built in 1830 on the north of town, was a stagecoach stop between Clarksville and Hopkinsville, Kentucky.

Dunbar Cave State Natural Area is a 110-acre site with many caves and sinkholes. Dunbar Cave was used ten thousand years ago by Indians and later by whites as a mineral spring resort. The former bathhouse serves as a museum and trailhead for a guided tour of the cave. The large room at the entrance has been used as a dance hall and concert hall.

Within the city the River Walk has an amphitheater, a permanent wharf/stage, courtesy docks, and the *Queen of Clarksville* riverboat, which runs daily trips in the Cumberland River and dinner-dance cruises. The Cumberland River Interpretive Center, River Bend Stage, and a pedestrian overpass link the river to the downtown historic district. The River Bend Stage holds ten thousand people for major performances and the seats follow the contour of the river.

Bed and breakfasts in the area include the Hachland Hill Inn, which has seven rooms with

Clarksville's Montgomery County Museum's exceptional architecture hints at its contents.

All of the following accommodations are Clarksville with zip code 37043, and all telephone listings are area code 931, except where noted.

Accommodations:
Hachland Hill Inn, 1601 Madison St., 647-4084.
Southern Pines Bed and Breakfast, 52 Taylor Rd., 647-0399.

Attractions:
Beachaven Vineyards and Winery, 645-8867.
Clarksville-Montgomery County Museum, 648-5780.
Cumberland Riverwalk, 645-7476.
Downtown Architectural Historic District, 647-9670.
Dunbar Cave, 648-5526.
Historic Post House, 431-5605.
Queen of Clarksville, 647-5500.
Smith-Trahern Mansion, 648-9998.

Dining:
Blackhorse Brewery, 552-9499.
Buffalo Brady's Wooden Nickel Pub, 552-1401.
Catfish House, 648-2121.
Daddy's Bar-B-Que, 553-0927.
Franklin Street Pub, 552-3726.
G's Pancake House, 648-4939.
Hananoki Japanese Steakhouse, 647-0999.
Lil Gasthaus, 431-5630.
Loco Lupes, 645-8333.
Magoo's, 647-7775.
Wilson's Catfish, 552-2342.

Shopping:
The Mill, 645-6450.

Special Events:
March—Old Time Fiddlers' Championship
August—Rodeo
September—Riverfest

Camping:
Clarksville Campground, 648-8638.

For More Information:
Clarksville-Montgomery County Tourism Commission, 180 Holiday Rd., 648-0001.

private baths as well as three log cabins. There's also Southern Pines, one of the area's oldest homes. Both bed and breakfasts serve full breakfasts. National franchises include Comfort Inn, Days Inn, Hampton Inn, Howard Johnson's, Holiday Inn, Ramada Inn, Super 8, and Travelodge.

Our next stop is Cumberland Furnace and Dickson, south of Clarksville on TN 48. You may want to go west on US 79 to Dover (*see* loop 11 in the Jackson loop in the West Tennessee section).

58 Dickson

Antique Shops Galore

Dickson County was formed in 1803 and the county seat is Charlotte, named for Charlotte Robertson, wife of James Robertson. Charlotte retains its small-town atmosphere, whereas nearby Dickson has grown considerably, helped by easier access to I-40.

Cumberland Furnace is north of Dickson about fifteen miles on TN 48. James Robertson, cofounder of Nashville, built the Cumberland furnace here in 1793. Most of the iron was made into implements and utensils, and some was sent to New Orleans. Cannonballs made here under the supervision of Montgomery Bell, who had taken over the operation, were used by Andrew Jackson during the battle of New Orleans.

It operated during the early part of the War Between the States and became a refuge for Confederate soldiers after the fall of Fort Donelson in February 1862. It was active after the war, but by 1924 the price of iron was so low it ceased operation again and reopened for the last time in 1937.

Nicks Hardware at 100 South Main Street in Dickson is half-hardware store and half-museum. Samuel Clay Nick, the owner, has an extensive collection of arrow points running the length of the store high on the wall. We were shown an old pair of shoes with a note sealed in plastic. The huge shoes were custom made for a farmer who lived in Dickson County named Harley Deal. He was seven feet tall and weighed 564 pounds. The shoes cost $175. There is a picture of Harley in the plastic.

Just a few doors down from Nicks is the Inn on Main Street built about 1900, owned by Brett and Misha Lashlee. Accommodations include the

Nicks Hardware in Dickson is as much a museum as it is a hardware store. Try these on for size!

Walker Suite with an Eastlake bedroom suite, Noah's Ark Room (everything comes in twos), the Victorian Gran C Room, and the Family Attic that sleeps six people. The Lashlees offer a gourmet breakfast and special packages including mystery weekends.

The Deerfield Country Inn is situated on fifty acres, while East Hills Bed and Breakfast has four bedrooms with private baths. Both serve full breakfasts. Shopping opportunities range from sewing supplies and collectibles at the Antique Thimble to the forty-eight specialty shops at Hamilton Place. Antique malls and shops are plentiful, too.

From Dickson go east on US 70 to Montgomery Bell State Park.

All of the following accommodations are Dickson with zip code 37055, and all telephone listings are area code 615, except where noted.

Accommodations:
Deerfield Country Inn, 170 Woodcrest Close, 446-3325.

East Hills Bed and Breakfast, 100 East Hills Terrace, 441-9428.
The Inn on Main Street, 112 S. Main, 441-6879 or 441-1514.

Attractions:
Cumberland Furnace Historic District, Cumberland Furnace, 446-2346.
Grand Old Hatchery, 446-2575.
Nicks Hardware, 446-2869.
Dickson County Square Dance, 446-6351.

Dining:
Catfish Kitchen, 446-4480.
East Hills Restaurant, 446-6922.

Shopping:
Antique Thimble, 797-2993.
Hamilton Place, 446-5255.
Haynie's Corner, 446-2993.
Main Street Antiques, 441-3633.
Nana's Attic, 441-6032.
Old Timer's Antique Mall, 446-2387.
Ox Yoke Antiques & Gifts, 446-6979.
Pepper Patch Antique Mall, 740-0904.
Reeder House Gallery, 446-2603.

Special Events:
May—Old Timers Day. Parade, crafts, arts, flea market

Camping:
Dickson KOA, 446-9925.

For More Information:
Dickson Chamber of Commerce, P.O. Box 399, 446-2349.

59 *Montgomery Bell State Park and Narrows of the Harpeth*
From Iron Works to State Park

Montgomery Bell State Park is located seven miles east of Dickson on US 70. In 1795 Gen. James Robertson established the Cumberland Iron Works, a first for this area of the state. Seven years after the Cumberland Furnace went into

Recently renovated, Montgomery Bell State Park offers fishing, boating, swimming, and other outdoor activities, as well as lodging and dining.

operation, a young Pennsylvanian, Montgomery Bell, came to Tennessee. Bell operated Robertson's furnace until he purchased it in 1804.

Beginning with this single furnace, Bell rapidly built a Dickson County industrial empire. He is remembered for his Narrows of the Harpeth, a 290-foot tunnel cut through a rock bluff to supply water power for his iron forge on the Harpeth River. He earned his place in Tennessee's history as the first capitalist and industrialist and the South's greatest iron magnate. The Narrows of the Harpeth is preserved and managed by Montgomery Bell State Park. An inn and restaurant (renovated in 1998) overlooks thirty-five-acre Lake Acorn, with a swimming pool for inn and cabin guests. The Frank G. Clement eighteen-hole golf course has a modern pro shop complete with golf accessories and equipment, rental carts, and concession stand.

Campers will find 120 campsites in a wooded valley, each with table and grill; 95 of the sites have water and electrical hookups. The park has three fishing lakes: Acorn, Woodhaven, and Creech Hollow. John boats, paddleboats, and canoes are available for rent at Lake Acorn. A typical catch includes bass, bream, and catfish.

You reach the Narrows of the Harpeth by going east from the park on US 70 and turning left (north) on Cedar Hill Road after you cross the Harpeth River. There is a canoe-launching site that lets you paddle the loop around Bells Bend for about six miles and take out very close to where you put in. This makes a nice outing on the river where you can see the historic tunnel. Two-hour to five-day canoe trips and canoe rentals are available at Tip-A-Canoe.

From the Narrows of the Harpeth we head to Ashland City by going back to US 70, turning left (east), continuing to the junction of TN 249,

and turning left (north). Stay on TN 249 until it joins TN 251 and turn left. This is River Road; it runs along the Cumberland River to TN 49. Turn right (east) on TN 49 and cross the river into Ashland City.

If you are more adventuresome, take Lockert Road northeast from the Narrows of the Harpeth through the Cheatham Wildlife Management Area to join TN 249 about a mile before it intersects with TN 251.

Canoeing
Tip-A-Canoe, 800-550-5810 or 615-646-7124.

For More Information:
Montgomery Bell State Park, P.O. Box 39, Burns, 37029; 800-250-8613 or 615-797-9052.

60 *Ashland City*
Former Chitlin Capital of Tennessee

First known as Ashland, Ashland City was almost incorporated in 1859 to become the county seat three years after Cheatham County was formed from Davidson, Dickson, Montgomery, and Robertson Counties. However, the county officials dropped the ball and had to forfeit the incorporation charter, but it was restored a few years later. Ashland City was the third county seat, the first two being Sycamore Powder Mills (1856) and Forest Hills (1858).

Historic Birdsong Lodge Bed and Breakfast was built in the early 1900s by Leslie and Mabel Cheek of Maxwell House Coffee fame and served as their vacation cabin for approximately ten years.

Today Birdsong Lodge is listed in the National Register of Historic Places. The original part of the home (great room with a stone fireplace and four other rooms) was constructed of red cedar logs cut on the property. The four guest rooms are individually decorated and furnished with many antiques from the 1800s.

You can hike the Cumberland River Bicentennial Trail or the challenging nature trails in the wildlife area and canoe down the Harpeth River. Binoculars are provided for those who want a closer look at the many birds. Sycamore Golf Course is located nearby. Tee times can be arranged with advance notice.

Stratton's Restaurant and Soda Shop is the coolest place in Ashland City. Step back into the 1950s for a burger, fries, and shake. We recommend stopping by to look at the '50s stuff and putting a coin in the old jukebox for a taste of the past.

One taste from the past that is no longer served is chitterlings—"chitlins" to old-timers. In case you want to whip up a batch, here's what you do: Clean the small intestines of a pig, soak in salt water overnight, cut into bite-sized bits, cover with meal, and deep fat fry. Umm good!

Take TN 12 southwest into Nashville to complete the loop tour.

All of the following accommodations are Ashland City with zip code 37015, and all telephone listings are area code 931, except where noted.

Accommodations:
Birdsong Country Inn Bed and Breakfast, 1306 Hwy. 49E., 792-4005.

Attractions:
Historic County Courthouse, 792-4316.
Tip-A-Canoe, Kingston Springs, 952-2674.

Dining:
El Ray Azteca Mexican Restaurant, 792-1330.
Bill's Catfish, 792-9177.
Brantley's Restaurant, 792-4703.
Farley's Bar-B-Q, 792-1353.
Stratton's Restaurant and Soda Shop, 792-9177.
River View Restaurant and Marina, 792-7358.

Shopping:
B. J.'s Attic, 792-7208.
Magnolia Shop, 792-1144.

Special Events:
June—Ashland City's Summer Fest
August—Cheatham County Fair
December—Christmas Parade

Camping:
Harpeth River Bridge Campground, 792-4195.
Lock A Campground, 792-3715 or 792-5697.

For More Information:
Cheatham County Chamber of Commerce, 792-6722.

✺ Loop 10

61 *Leipers Fork*
First Town on the
Natchez Trace Parkway

This is the Natchez Trace Parkway loop that
begins southwest of Nashville where TN 100
joins the Natchez Trace Parkway. We will loop
southwest of Nashville to the Tennessee River and
get back to Nashville along some of the roads
General Hood took on his way to the battle of
Franklin.

From the northern terminus of the Natchez
Trace Parkway going southwest toward Leipers
Fork you cross the largest pre-stressed, pre-
formed bridge (see Franklin chapter for details)
in the United States. You'll see several parking
areas before you get to the bridge and these offer
viewing points and short hikes. The parking area
on the western side of the Trace just before you
reach the bridge allows you to get out and walk
along the bridge. There you get a grand panorama
of the valley.

The next intersection is just south of the
bridge where you can take TN 96 east into
Franklin. Continue to the next intersection at the
junction with TN 46 and turn right into the
nearby community of Leipers Fork, our hometown.

The rural community of Leipers Fork and its
surrounding area have become the place to live in
Middle Tennessee—just ask all the country music

stars who have moved here. The community has
welcomed them quietly for the most part, respect-
ing the universal need for privacy.

South of town on Leipers Creek Road is
Namaste Acres Bed and Breakfast, a modern
Dutch Colonial home. Its facilities include an
outdoor swimming pool and hot tub, queen-sized
rope bunk beds, a claw-foot tub, an indoor outhouse in an Old West-style Tennessee bunkhouse,
and private entrance to a large suite with private
bath.

One of the most unusual features about
Namaste is its proximity to a twenty-seven-mile
bridle and hiking trail on the Natchez Trace. Your
hosts have facilities for horses, and about 40 percent of their visitors bring their four-legged
friends along for the ride. A full breakfast is
served (often out by the pool in good weather)
and ranges from French toast and sausage to
breakfast casseroles and fresh fruit.

Marty Hunt's Leipers Fork Antiques not only
has an interesting and varied collection, she's a
wealth of information about the community as
well. She and her husband, Bruce, host the annual
community flea market each fall in their pasture
down the road. Inside her shop you'll find a variety of antiques and collectibles.

The Country Boy Restaurant is pleased to
serve you breakfast, lunch, and dinner, if you can
find a parking spot among all the pickup trucks.
Its breakfast of country ham, eggs, biscuits and
gravy, or the western omelet with country ham,
grilled onions, peppers, and cheese are such crowd
pleasers that they're served all day.

At Leipers Fork Market you can buy snacks,
cold beverages, and homemade sandwiches for a
picnic on the Natchez Trace.

The West Fork of the Harpeth River flows

A few miles north of Leipers Fork on the Natchez Trace Parkway is the world's longest pre-cast bridge, spanning 1,160 feet across a scenic valley.

through the valley and may be of interest to fishermen and canoeists. The put-in on Southall Road is six river miles from the takeout on TN 96 west of Franklin. The river is shallow in spots, Class I throughout its length, and is best run November through early June.

Let's get back on the Natchez Trace Parkway and head southwest to Centerville. You may want to get a copy of our book *Traveling the Trace* for more details about the parkway and what lies along it from Nashville to Natchez, Mississippi. From Leipers Fork take the Natchez Trace Park-

way southwest to TN 7 and turn right (west) to TN 100 where you go left (west) to Centerville via Lyles.

Leipers Fork has a Franklin address and all of the following accommodations are zip code 37064, and all telephone listings are area code 615, except where noted.

Accommodations:
Namaste Acres Bed and Breakfast, 5436 Leipers Creek Rd., 791-0333.

Dining:
Country Boy Restaurant, 794-7680.

Namaste Acres in Leipers Fork welcomes horses as well as humans and offers access to the Natchez Trace Parkway's twenty-seven-mile equestrian trail.

Leipers Fork Market, 794-0985.
Puckett's Grocery, 794-1308.

Shopping:
Marty Hunt's Leipers Fork Antiques, 790-9963.

For More Information:
Williamson County/Franklin Chamber of Commerce, P.O. Box 156 (City Hall), Franklin, 37065; 800-356-3445 or 794-1225.

62 *Centerville*
Cousin Minnie's Backyard

The Natchez Trace Parkway, 450 miles long running from Nashville to Natchez, Mississippi, is the historic road that Kaintucks used when traveling home. Kaintucks were men who loaded their wares on barges, floated down the Cumberland, Tennessee, Ohio, and Mississippi Rivers to sell in Vicksburg, Natchez, and New Orleans. With their earnings, they had to walk home along the Natchez Trace, and highwaymen often preyed on them.

Today the modern Natchez Trace is certainly worth traveling. The Gordon House (1817–1818), one of the oldest in Hickman County, is at the edge of the Duck River. It has interpretive trails beyond the house along the river. Jackson Falls is a historic rest stop near Shady Grove. A large spring with waterfalls was a camping place named for Andrew Jackson who used the Natchez Trace during 1813–1814. Bakers Bluff is also nearby and provides a scenic view of the Duck River valley. You will see these attractions if you stay on the Trace until you reach TN 50 that goes west into Centerville. If you got off on TN 7 and took TN 100 into Centerville, you may want to go back to visit these sites.

Turn west off TN 7 onto TN 100 and you

are in Lyles. Norma Crow owns and operates Silver Leaf Country Inn, one of the oldest log homes in Middle Tennessee dating back to 1815. Norma offers you fine dining in a wooded setting. She serves lunch and dinner in addition to breakfast for her bed and breakfast guests. You need to make reservations.

Also in Lyles is Rocking Horse Antiques and Collectibles across from the old Lyles Post Office.

Less than twelve miles southwest on TN 100 is Centerville.

Centerville, the county seat of Hickman County, holds to tradition and maintains its small town homeyness. Hickman County, named for Edwin Hickman who was killed by Indians near the mouth of Defeated Creek, was formed in 1807. Hickman was with a party of surveyors camped at the creek, and he alone died from the attack.

The community of Vernon at the junction of Pretty Creek and Piney River was the county seat from 1808 until 1823 when Hickman County included Lewis and Lawrence Counties, and parts of Perry, Humphreys, and Wayne Counties. The county seat was moved to Centerville in 1823 and David Crockett represented Hickman County in the House of Representatives when the seat was moved. Hickman County was a leading producer of iron in the Western Iron Region. The remains of Napier Mine and Metal Ford can be seen on the Natchez Trace Parkway and Lee's Furnace near Bucksnort off I-40.

In Centerville we found Breece's to be the favorite place to eat by locals and tourists alike. Its special is a very tasty meat-and-four that hardly leaves room for the wonderful desserts. Almost all its produce is home grown.

You've heard Cousin Minnie Pearl talk about her home in Grinder's Switch; it's just a stone's throw northwest from Centerville. Sarah Ophelia Colley Cannon, AKA Minnie Pearl, was born in Centerville and incorporated Grinder's Switch into her act. The railroad switching area got its name from the man who owned Grinder's Stand (an inn) in Meriwether Lewis Park on the Natchez Trace where Lewis died. Hickman County records show the name Grinder was originally Griner and he operated a railroad-switching yard before running the stand, hence Grinder's Switch.

Centerville was established on the banks of the Duck River, which is known for its smallmouth bass fishing.

You may return to the Natchez Trace via TN 50 and go down the Trace to TN 20 and then west into Hohenwald; or you can take TN 100 south from Centerville to TN 48 and turn left (south) on TN 48 to go into Hohenwald. The Trace route is longer but far more scenic.

All of the following accommodations are Centerville with zip code 37033, and all telephone listings are area code 931, except where noted.

Accommodations:
Grinder's Switch Inn, 107 N. Central Ave., 729-5195.
Silver Leaf Country Inn, Rt. 1, Box 122 (Mill Creek Rd.), Lyles, 37098; 670-3048.
Trace Reservation Service (Kay Jones), P.O. Box 193, Hampshire, 38461; 800-377-2770 or 285-2777.

Attractions:
Natchez Trace Parkway 13 miles east on TN 50.

Dining:
Beacon Light Tea Room, Lyles, 670-3880.
Breece's Cafe, 729-3481.
Fishcamp Restaurant, 729-4401.
Manley's Restaurant, 729-2948.
Silver Leaf 1815 Country Inn, Lyles, 670-3048.

Shopping:
Breece's Variety Store.
Broken Kettle Antiques.
Highway 100 Antique Mall.
Rocking Horse Antiques, Lyles, 670-3817.
Tarkington General Store, 729-2767.
Nash Antiques, 729-9210.

Special Events:
May—Arts and Crafts Fair
August—Gem and Mineral Show
September—Duck River Music and Arts Fair on the Square
December—Christmas at Silver Leaf

Camping:
Lehman's Lake and Campground, 729-9136.

For More Information:
Hickman County Chamber of Commerce, P.O. Box 126, 729-5774.

63 *Hohenwald*
High Forest

In 1806 settlers began building homes and raising families in the area that became Lewis County. In 1843 the Tennessee legislature created Lewis County from the region surrounding the grave of Meriwether Lewis, who died a mysterious death about seven miles east of Hohenwald in 1809. The county is named to honor the explorer.

German immigrants created a town named Hohenwald (meaning "high forest") in 1878 and developed a thriving lumber industry. Hohenwald is the highest town between New Orleans and Chicago at an elevation near one thousand feet above sea level. Sixteen years later Swiss immigrants built their New Switzerland just south of Hohenwald. In time the two towns merged under the name Hohenwald. Unlike many frontier towns, Hohenwald was highly cultured with a broad assortment of artisans and craftsmen. Since the 1890s Lewis County has continued to attract a high percentage of artists and craftsmen.

The Museum of Natural History is not something you would expect to find in this small southern town. It contains an unusually large collection of exotic animals taken from Europe, Asia, Africa, and South America. Also there are exhibits of the early settlers and artifacts of Meriwether Lewis. This is a worthwhile stop.

The Blackburn Farmstead and Pioneer Museum features log buildings and is in the National Register of Historic Places. Gemstone mining gets under way at Indian Creek using original or enriched materials.

The Hohenwald Depot, built in 1896, is listed in the National Register of Historic Places and contains displays and photographs of the history of the county, including German prisoners of war in WW II. The depot also serves as the tourist information center.

Hohenwald's original jail has been converted into Armstrong's Bakery Bed and Breakfast, which has three guest rooms with private and shared baths. A full breakfast is served. Ridgetop Bed and Breakfast has a choice of guest room, cottage, or cabin.

From town, go east on TN 20 to the Natchez Trace Parkway and to Meriwether Lewis Park. You can hike and bicycle at Meriwether Lewis, and it has thirty-two campsites with grills and picnic tables. A telephone is available at the ranger station. There is a monument and exhibits, an old log house, and Pioneer Cemetery that contains only the grave of Lewis.

This is the site of Grinder's Stand (*see* Centerville chapter) where Meriwether Lewis, of the Lewis and Clark expedition, former governor of the Louisiana Territory, and good friend and personal secretary to Thomas Jefferson, met his death. No satisfactory resolution has ever been reached whether it was murder or suicide. The top half of the Meriwether Lewis monument was left unfinished to commemorate the half-spent life of Lewis.

Inside the reconstruction of Grinder's old stand is a museum with the chronology of the Natchez Trace beginning in 1765.

From Hohenwald take TN 48 southwest to the junction with TN 13, and take TN 13 south to Waynesboro, a scenic but curvy road running along the Green River.

All of the following accommodations are Hohenwald with zip code 38462, and all telephone listings are area code 931, except where noted.

Accommodations:
Armstrong's Bakery Bed and Breakfast, 309 Park Ave. S., 796-7591.

Ridgetop Bed and Breakfast, Hwy. 412, 800-377-2770 or 285-2777.

Attractions:
Historic Blackburn Farmstead and Pioneer Museum, 796-7264.
Indian Creek Gemstone Mining, 796-4745.
Lewis County Museum, 796-1550.
Meriwether Lewis Park, Grave, and Monument, 601-680-4025 (Natchez Trace information).

Dining:
Big John's Bar-B-Que, 796-2244.
E. W. James and Sons Deli, 796-2480.
Highlander Restaurant, 796-5988.
Swan View Restaurant, 796-4745.

Shopping:
Lawson's, 796-4380.

Special Events:
May—Maifest
October—Meriwether Lewis Arts & Crafts Fair; Volksmarch; Crafts Festival/High Forest Jamboree; Oktoberfest

Camping:
Meriwether Lewis Park on the Natchez Trace Parkway. 32 sites, no hookups. Open year-round.

For More Information:
Hohenwald Chamber of Commerce, P.O. Box 819, 796-2731.
Tennessee Natchez Trace Corridor Association/Lewis County Chamber of Commerce/The Lewis County Historical Society, 112 E. Main St., 796-4084.

64 *Waynesboro*
In Tennessee's Second-Largest County

Revolutionary War major general "Mad" Anthony Wayne was honored by having Wayne County named for him in 1819. The first Wayne County was formed in 1785 where present-day Carter and Johnson Counties are in East Tennessee but was abolished in 1788. The modern Wayne County was formed from Hickman and

Humphreys Counties and is the second-largest county in the state. Waynesboro became the county seat in 1822.

The first courthouse, like many during that time, was a log building with a dirt floor, board roof, and wide openings on the side for windows. That building served for five years. Today the sixth courthouse stands in Waynesboro's square.

Waynesboro is where David Crockett gave his first political address, and it was the historical hideout for Natchez Trace bandits.

We found good dining at Emerald's on the corner of the square. It specializes in pizza, has a very nice atmosphere, and serves a broad menu—steak, chicken, burgers, and fries. Behind Emerald's at 128 High Street you will find Williams and Walker's Something Old Shop. Besides a nice selection of antique furniture and reproduction Tiffany lamps, they have gifts, dolls and custom framing.

All of the following accommodations are Waynesboro with zip code 38485, and all telephone listings are area code 931, except where noted.

Accommodations:
Waynesboro Inn, 406 S. Main, 722-7321.

Attractions:
Buffalo River Trail Ride, 722-9170.

Dining:
Emerald's, Waynesboro, 615-722-5611.

Shopping:
Williams and Walker, Something Old Shop, 722-7118 or 722-5560.

Special Events:
July—Horse Shoe Bend Festival; Mule & Horse Frolic
September—Old Timers' Day
October—Pumpkin Harvest Festival

Camping:
Crazy Horse Canoe and RV Park, 800-722-5213 or 722-5213.

For More Information
Waynesboro/Wayne County Chamber of Commerce, P.O. Box 675; 722-3418.

65 *Lawrenceburg*
Home of David Crockett

Hickman and Maury Counties gave portions of themselves to form Lawrence County in 1817. It is named for Capt. James Lawrence, skipper of the *Chesapeake* during the War of 1812. He is credited with having said, "Don't give up the ship."

Lawrenceburg was established in 1821 and conducted business in a two-story brick courthouse now known as the David Crockett Courthouse. A life-sized bronze statue of Crockett graces the town square. Lawrenceburg was Crockett's home from 1817 to 1822. The flood of 1821 washed away his gristmill, powder mill, and distillery, leaving him financially ruined. He moved to West Tennessee where he was elected to Congress. David Crockett State Park, located on 950 acres just west of Lawrenceburg toward the Trace on Highway 64, was dedicated in his honor in 1959. Here you can visit his reconstructed distillery, grist, and powder mills. There is a park restaurant with a seating capacity of 240 on a hill overlooking Crockett Lake. The forty-acre lake has year-round fishing with a permit. You can fish from a rowboat or the bank, or even rent a pedal boat at the dock. There is also a swimming pool with bathhouse, concession stand, bike trails, hiking trails, tennis courts, amphitheater, and an interpretive center.

Another monument in Lawrenceburg is one of only two in the United State dedicated to the

David Crockett State Park west of Lawrenceburg honors one of the city's famous residents.

Mexican War. It was erected in 1849 to perpetuate the memory of the Lawrenceburg Blues and Capt. William B. Allen.

The Old Jail Museum on Waterloo Street is headquartered in the 1800s jail, a National Register of Historic Places property.

Around the public square and historic district you will find restaurants and antiques shops. The Golden Panda came highly recommended as the place to eat. David Crockett Park Restaurant, Rick's Barbeque, and Kuntry Kitchen were runners-up.

Victorian Manor Bed and Breakfast offers three guest rooms with shared baths, while Granville House Bed and Breakfast has five guest rooms with private bath. There's also a Best Western franchise in town.

The Amish have roadside stands with their hand-crafted and homemade goods in Ethridge, north of Lawrenceburg about five miles on US 43. At the junction of US 43 and Red Hill Road, turn left (west) and Ethridge is less than a mile.

More than two hundred Amish families live in the area offering baskets, quilts, canned vegetables, bread, candy, fresh vegetables, furniture, and other items for sale in their yards, homes, and outbuildings. Many of these farming families are also craftspeople. There are five shops under one roof offering Amish quilts, woodwork, rockers, over one hundred different kinds and colors of baskets, an art gallery featuring local artists, and much more at Amish Country Galleries on US 43 in Ethridge.

The Amish first came to the United States in 1727. Today they live only in rural areas so they can continue their simple and religious lifestyle. Please, do not photograph the Amish because their religious beliefs don't allow it. However, wagon tours are available.

From Lawrenceburg go to Pulaski via US 64E.

All of the following accommodations are Lawrenceburg with zip code 38464, and all telephone listings are area code 931, except where noted.

Accommodations:
Victorian Manor Bed and Breakfast, 213 Pulaski St., 766-1241.
Granville House Bed and Breakfast, 229 Pulaski St., 762-3129.

Attractions:
David Crockett Cabin and Museum, 762-4911.
Old Jail Museum, 762-4911.

Dining:
Bernie's Tea Room, 762-9229.
Big John's Bar-B-Que, 762-9596.
The Brass Lantern, 762-0474.
The Golden Panda, 762-5888.
Kuntry Kitchen, 766-0260.
Rick's Barbeque, 762-2296.

Shopping:
Flea Market Shop, 762-1441.
Heirlooms, 762-5570.
Gibbs Antiques, 762-1619.
Carriage House, 766-0428.

Special Events:
May—Heritage Festival; Tractor Pull
June—Fishing Derby; Summertown Bluegrass Festival
July—Rodeo
August—David Crockett Days; Crossroads of Dixie Antique
    Tractor Show
September—Sacred Heart Barbecue
October—Octoberfest
November—Veterans Day Parade
December—Christmas Pops

Camping:
David Crockett State Park, 762-9408.

*All of the following accommodations are Ethridge with zip
code 38456, and all telephone listings are area code 931,
except where noted.*

Accommodations:
Amish Country Bed and Kitchen, 4011 Hwy. 43 N., 829-
    2065.

Attractions:
Amish Community, 829-2147.
Amish Country Galleries, 829-2126.

Dining:
Dutch Country Deli and Bakery.

Shopping:
Amish Country Galleries, 829-2126.

For More Information:
Lawrence County Chamber of Commerce, 1609 Locust St.;
    762-4911.

66 *Pulaski*
Shuns the KKK

Giles County was formed from Maury County in
1809. The stately brick courthouse built in 1909
with a large central cupola housing a bell cast in
1858 is the fifth courthouse in the county's history. The French Renaissance-style design building
is worth a tour. Count Casmir Pulaski of Poland,
who helped the colonies during the Revolutionary
War, is honored by having the county seat named
for him.

The Sam Davis Museum here honors the boy
hero of the Confederacy, who was hanged as a spy
(*see* the Smyrna chapter). It contains many Civil
War artifacts, including Davis's leg irons and the
stands where he was hanged.

Although this part of Pulaski's history is
ignored or reluctantly acknowledged, the Ku Klux
Klan was organized here Christmas Eve 1865 by
Judge T. M. Jones and his son Calvin. Originally
the KKK was a social club, and Calvin and his
young friends sought to make it interesting by
issuing fanciful initiations, wearing flowing white
robes and comical conical hats, and meeting in a
"haunted" house. Excesses of the once-social club
became impossible to direct, and in 1869 the
original organizers and the Grand Wizard, Nathan
Bedford Forrest, disbanded the Ku Klux Klan.

The KKK didn't die but evolved into the hate-
filled organization it is today. Pulaski's citizens
stood firm in 1989 when the Klan came to town

to stage a rally. They organized a boycott, and the KKK arrived to a deserted town, with businesses closed and the streets deserted. The Klan knows it is no longer welcome in Pulaski.

Frank Mars, founder of Mars Candy Company, built a Tudor mansion in 1932 north of Pulaski. Originally his twenty-eight-hundred-acre estate, known as Milky Way Farms, raised prize cattle and horses and even had its own railroad. It was like a small town with many buildings, including thirty-eight barns. You can spend the night in one of the twenty-one bedrooms. The dining table is twenty-eight feet long, twelve feet wide, and seats forty people; it is the largest privately owned dining table in Tennessee. You can reserve a place for lunch or dinner.

There are a number of tours available through the Chamber of Commerce to see Pulaski's historic sites. The Pulaski Historical Home Tour is a two-and-one-half-hour drive through three neighborhoods, the Old Graveyard Memorial Park, and Sam Davis Museum. Another tour covers downtown and a third takes you through the county. There's also a brochure to antique, collectible, and gift shops in the area. Be sure to stop by the chamber to get details about this historic county. The 1855 Brown-Daly-Horne House is an excellent example of Queen Anne-style architecture. Built in 1909, the Giles County Courthouse is a neoclassical design.

Our next destination is Columbia, north on US 31.

All of the following accommodations are Pulaski, with zip code 38478, and all telephone listings are area code 931, except where noted.

Accommodations:
Milky Way Farms Bed and Breakfast, 1864 Milky Way Rd., 800-869-9788 or 363-9769.

Attractions:
Giles County Historic Site Tour, 363-3789.
Giles County Historical Museum, 363-2720.
Sam Davis Museum, 363-3789.
Sam Davis Trail, 363-3789.

Dining:
Heritage House, 363-2313.
Hickory House, 363-0231.
Lawler's BBQ, 363-3515.

Shopping:
Kevin Walker Antiques, 424-1825.

With reluctance, the Union Army hanged Sam Davis near Pulaski for refusing to divulge his network of Rebel spies.

Lone Wolf Galleries, 424-6263.
Mama J's Cabin, 762-0678.
Special Events:
January—Gospel Sing (monthly)
February—Black History Program
March—Lawn and Garden Show
May—Summertime Festival
June—Clean up the Elk River
July—An Old-Fashioned 4th
November—Main Street Masked Ball
December—Trees of Christmas

Camping:
Valley KOA, 363-4600.

For More Information:
Giles County Chamber of Commerce, 100 S. 2nd St., 363-
   3789.

67 *Columbia*
Mule Town

Maury County was formed from Williamson
County in 1807 and named for Abram Maury, a
surveyor who lived in Williamson County. Columbia, the county seat, was established in 1808.

   Steeped in Civil War history, Columbia and
Spring Hill offer tours of many outstanding
antebellum homes and other sites, such as the
modern Saturn plant. For example, General
Hood slept in the Rippa Villa mansion as the
Union army walked by the front door up the
road to Franklin, and he held his last council
meeting there before the disastrous battle of
Franklin (*see* Franklin chapter).

   Maj. Nathaniel Cheairs and his family lived in
the earliest structure that later became the kitchen
while Rippa Villa was being built. The walls were
erected and dismantled three time before they
were perfect. It is this mindset toward perfection
that made Rippa Villa such a magnificent home

*Columbia's James K. Polk home, built in 1816 by his father, is where the
eleventh president of the United States lived briefly before entering college
and then politics.*

when it was completed in 1855. Rippa Villa has
changed hands several times since then and is now
owned by the Saturn Corporation.

   President James K. Polk's home at 310 West
Seventh Street was built in 1816 by his father,
Samuel Polk, while young James was attending the
University of North Carolina. He returned home
to begin his law career and in 1824 was elected to
the state legislature, then to the U.S. House of
Representatives. After seven terms in Washington,
he returned to Tennessee to become governor for a

two-year term. In 1845 Polk moved into the White House as the eleventh president of the United States and returned to Columbia four years later.

During your tour of the home you will see many furnishings that were used by Polk in Tennessee and in the White House. Of interest is the Bible used by Polk at his inauguration.

Also to be seen are Greenway Farm, Saint John's Church, Hamilton Place, Scott-Matthews-Wendt Home, Persimmon Ridge, and Rattle and Snap. Built in 1845, Rattle and Snap is a Greek Revival-style historic landmark offering a delightful dining experience and gift shop for visitors. Contact the Maury County Convention and Visitors Bureau for a brochure for the historic driving tour and be sure to ask about Mule Day.

Mule Day is more than a half century old and the grandest celebration in Columbia. In the 1840s the town became a crossroads for mule traders and by 1934 Columbia's market day was an official festival. It was touted as "1,000 girls and 1,000 mules." A liars contest, mule sale, flea market, fiddlers' contest, and the world famous mule parade are held the first weekend in April, unless it's Easter, when it is held the next weekend.

Plan a whole day to allow time for seeing all the sights in Columbia and touring the Saturn plant. You won't want to miss the Mount Pleasant/Maury Phosphate Museum's fossils, Indian artifacts, and Civil War relics. The Southport Saltpeter Cave is a wild cave open by reservation. Monsanto Ponds comprise 5,345 acres of precious wetlands offering wildlife viewing. TWRA's Williamsport lakes offer excellent largemouth bass, bluegill, and catfish opportunities for anglers. There are Days Inn, Holiday Inn, Ramada Inn, and Scottish Inn franchises in Columbia.

Franklin is our next stop. Go north on US 31 for about twenty-three miles.

Rippa Villa, a nearly perfect antebellum home in Spring Hill, played an important role in the war of Northern Aggression.

Athenaeum was established in 1835 and was later used to teach living and social skills for young women.

All of the following accommodations are Columbia with zip code 38402, and all telephone listings are area code 931, except where noted.

Accommodations:
Locust Hill Bed and Breakfast, 1185 Mooresville Pk., 800-577-8264 or 388-8531.
McEwen Farm Log Cabin Bed and Breakfast, P.O. Box 97, Duck River, 38454; 583-2378.

Attractions:
The Athenaeum Rectory, 381-4822.
Columbia Historic Driving Tour, 381-7176.
James K. Polk Home, 388-2354.
Mount Pleasant/Maury Phosphate Museum, 379-9511.
Rattle and Snap, 379-5861.
Rippa Villa, 800-381-1865 or 486-9037.
Southport Saltpeter Cave, 379-4404.
Tennessee Wildlife Observation Area-Monsanto Ponds, 388-2155.

Dining:
Albert's, 381-3463.
Back Porch Barbecue, 381-3463.
Buckey's Family Restaurant, 381-2834.
Catfish Campus, 380-8439.
Chinese Panda Restaurant, 381-7733.
Lucille's Restaurant, 383-3005.
Nolen's Bar-B-Que, 381-4322.

Sarge's Shack, 381-2268.
Sam Hill's, 388-5555.

Shopping:
Birds & Bygones, 380-8444.
Franklin's Old Book Shop, 540-0520.
High Attic Antiques, 381-2819.
Luna's Antiques, 388-7101.
Mule Town Antiques, 381-2514.
Sewell's Antiques, 388-3973.
Uptown Antiques, 388-4061.

Special Events:
February—Mule and Draft Horse Sale
April—Mule Day
May—Walking Horse Spring Jubilee
June—Maury County Charity Horse Show
July—Fireworks at Rippa Villa Plantation
August—Rodeo; Scenic Century Bike Ride
September—County Fair; Majestic Middle Tennessee Fall Tour
October—Meriwether Lewis Craft Fair, Natchez Trace; Chili Cook-off
November—Arts Guild Craft Show
December—Trees of Christmas; Christmas Parade

Outfitters
River Rat Canoe Rental, 381-2278.

For More Information:
Maury County Convention and Visitors Bureau, 8 Public Square, 800-381-1865 or 381-7176.

68 *Franklin*

The Essence of Middle Tennessee

Williamson County was formed from Davidson County in 1799 and named for Dr. Hugh Williamson, a member of the Continental Congress. The county seat, Franklin, was named for his friend Benjamin Franklin. The first courthouse was a log cabin built in the center of the square in 1809. The present courthouse was built in 1859 with renovations in 1937, 1964, and 1976. During the Civil War it was used as a hospital and Union headquarters.

On November 30, 1864, Franklin was the site of one of the Civil War's bloodiest and most decisive battles. Five hours of fighting resulted in the death, wounding, or capture of six thousand Confederates and two thousand Union soldiers. Among the mortally wounded were five Confederate generals.

The area prospered as an agricultural community after the war with a slow but steady growth. In the 1970s, Williamson County became the fastest-growing county in the state, with the highest per capita income.

Franklin's historic downtown has undergone an impressive restoration and revitalization. The fifteen-block downtown area is listed in the National Register of Historic Places. Several historic sites are on tour year-round, and special tours of private homes are conducted by the Heritage Foundation in May and during the Candlelight Tour each December.

Franklin retains its small-town charm but due to its proximity to Nashville, offers specialty and antique shopping usually associated with larger communities. Antique shops and malls offer a wide variety of collections for antique enthusiasts.

Specialty shops line both sides of Main Street and several restaurants accommodate a range of palates.

Franklin is situated around a courthouse square and Main Street divides the numbered streets into northern and southern portions. Follow the signs to historic downtown Franklin at the intersection of TN 96 and Hillsboro Road. You may also proceed straight ahead on Bridge Street to visit Winchester Antique Mall where Kim

The focal point of downtown Franklin is the square with the monument honoring Confederates who died defending the South.

Tuzzio will be happy to help you with a wide selection of antiques and collectibles. After you've visited this mall, drive along Bridge Street to the First Avenue Antique Mall, which specializes in furniture and accessories.

The next traffic light is the intersection with Main Street, and two Franklin landmarks are located side by side after you make a left turn. Dotson's Restaurant may not look like much from the outside, but inside you'll find delicious country-style cooking. The vegetable plates are excellent and the coconut pie defies description. Next door Mr. Earl at Earl's Fruit Stand has been providing Franklin with fresh produce and live plants for years, but his most loyal patrons are the children (with no age restrictions) who come in droves every year to see Pumpkinland. He creates corridors through the middle of his shop with pumpkins decorated and dressed to resemble prominent personages. Each year a new cast of characters appears around October 1. The pumpkin personalities are visited by thousands before Halloween.

The historic Carter House survived being in the middle of the Battle of Franklin but Todd Carter, son of the owners, did not.

First Avenue turns into Margin Street and Rebel's Rest at 212 South Margin offers the largest selection of Civil War artifacts for sale and display in the area. There's a nominal fee to tour the museum that is applied toward any purchase you make.

If you turn west at First Avenue onto Main Street you'll want to visit the Williamson County Visitor Information Center in the 1839 brick building that was once the office of Dr. Daniel McPhail. This building served as Gen. John M. Schofield's command headquarters prior to the battle of Franklin. They will happily supply you with maps, brochures, and directions. Additional information is available at the Chamber of Commerce in the City Hall building on the square. If the Civil War is of special interest, be sure to request the self-guided driving tour for the battle of Franklin.

According to Virginia Bowman's *Historic Williamson County*, the Carter House was built by Fountain B. Carter between 1829 and 1830 and was severely damaged during the Civil War. It was the scene of several skirmishes but the major damage was sustained during the battle of Franklin.

Union Gen. John Schofield had managed to slip his troops past Gen. John B. Hood's Confederates during the night of November 29, 1864. Schofield attempted to reach the Union fortifications at Nashville but was unable to cross the Harpeth River speedily. Schofield continued preparations to cross the Harpeth near the northern edge of town and left Gen. Jacob Cox to hold Hood at the southern end of town until the army could cross the river to the safety of Nashville. General Cox established his communication center near the Carter House and dispelled the Carter family's fears for their safety throughout the early part of the day by his belief that a battle was not imminent. Later that afternoon when Hood's intention to attack became apparent, it was too late to escape, so Carter's seventeen servants and family members and five members of the Lotz family hid in the basement. Above and around them, the battle raged.

South of town on Winstead Hill, Capt. Todd Carter looked anxiously toward Franklin and home. It was his family who huddled in the basement with the sounds of running feet, bullets, and cannons echoing above.

Gen. Thomas Benton Smith rode to the house and asked that Fountain Carter be informed that his son lay grievously wounded upon the battlefield. The young captain's father and sisters followed the general a short distance southwest of the smokehouse where they found him by lantern light face down by his horse but still alive. His wounds were dressed and he was placed in bed. He lived only forty-eight hours after finally returning home. With daybreak, unbelievable scenes lay before the horrified citizens of Franklin. Thousands of dead and wounded men and horses lay there.

To visit historic Carnton Plantation, proceed from the Winstead Hill Overlook north toward Franklin. Turn right before you reach the bottom of Winstead Hill onto the Mack Hatcher bypass. Turn left at the Lewisburg Pike intersection and watch for signs for Carnton on your left.

Carnton was designed to be a place of elegance and grace, but was forced into service as a hospital following the battle of Franklin. Virginia Bowman tells us in *Historic Williamson County* over three hundred wounded filled the house to overflowing. Every piece of white linen, damask, and cotton in the house was torn for bandages. Even family members' clothes were utilized. The columned back gallery contained the silent bodies

Beyond the largest private cemetery containing the remains of fifteen hundred Confederate dead is the elegant Carnton Plantation built by John McGavock.

of four generals: Patrick Cleburne, John Adams, Hiram Granbury, and Otho Strahl.

Bodies of soldiers hastily buried in shallow graves were reinterred in a two-acre cemetery donated in 1866 by the owner, John McGavock. With fifteen hundred graves, this is the largest private Confederate cemetery in existence. Tours of Carnton are available daily. Admission is charged.

On your way back to Franklin on Lewisburg

Pike watch for the Country Charm Antique Mall on your right. A right turn on Margin Street and a right turn at the traffic light on Murfreesboro Road (also known as Third Avenue South) will take you to two excellent antique malls and a Mexican restaurant. Harpeth Antique Mall and Heritage Antique Gallery are in Alexander Plaza, a shopping center on your left before you reach the I-65 access.

Harpeth Antique Mall has more than eighty dealers and an excellent selection of furniture, art, pottery, books, prints, linens, and depression glass. Heritage Antique Gallery specializes in English, French, and American antiques and occasionally has some very unusual pieces. The two together make the short drive worthwhile. The Camino Real restaurant offers Mexican food at very reasonable prices. It is small and simple, the servings are generous, and the service is prompt.

There are a number of bed and breakfasts in and around Franklin. The Magnolia House Bed and Breakfast is a few blocks south of the Carter House at 1317 Columbia Avenue and within walking distance of downtown Franklin. The house was built in 1905 on property that once was part of the Carter farm. It features four upstairs guest rooms with queen- or twin-sized beds, private baths, and ceiling fans. Breakfast fare frequently includes specialty dishes and home-made breads.

Blueberry Hill offers two guest rooms with private baths and serves a full breakfast. Carothers House Cottage has two guest rooms with private baths. The Old Marshall House has three guest rooms with private baths and serves a full breakfast, while Sweet Annie's in Fairview has two guest rooms with shared baths. National franchises include Best Western, Comfort Inn, Days Inn, Holiday Inn, and Hampton Inn.

On the Natchez Trace Parkway west of Franklin is a unique bridge over TN 96. This bridge is 1,610 feet long, 33 feet wide, and 160 feet above the valley below. It was made of precast concrete sections. There are stairwells in the two main piers for inspecting the piers, the arches, and the road support structures. It has been written about extensively and has been featured in *National Geographic Magazine.* Visitors may walk or drive across the bridge to the viewing station on the north side of the bridge. The northern terminus of the Natchez Trace Parkway is five miles north on TN 100. Namaste Acres Bed and Breakfast is near the Leiper's Fork exit.

Franklin is the last stop on this loop tour. You can take I-65 or US 31 north to Nashville.

All of the following accommodations are Franklin with zip code 37064, and all telephone listings are area code 615, except where noted.

Accommodations:
Blueberry Hill, 4391 Peytonsville Rd., 791-9947.
Carothers House Cottage, 4301 S. Carothers Rd., 800-327-8492 or 794-4437.
Magnolia House, 1317 Columbia Ave., 794-8178.
Old Marshall House, 1030 John Williams Rd., 800-863-5808 or 591-4121.
Namaste Acres, 5436 Leipers Creek Rd., 791-0333.
Sweet Annie's Bed & Breakfast, 7201 Crow Cut Rd., SW, Fairview, 37062; 799-8833.

Attractions:
Carnton Plantation, 794-0903.
Carter House, 791-1861.
Fort Granger, 791-3217.
Lotz House Museum, 791-6533.
Rebel's Rest, 790-7199.

Dining:
The Bunganut Pig, 794-4777.
Camino Real, 790-3104.
Dotson's Restaurant, 794-2805.
H R H Dumplin's, 791-4651.
Hunan Chinese Restaurant, 790-6868.
Magnolia's, 791-9992.
Merridee's Breadbasket, 790-3755.
One Stop Market, 794-3881.

Shopping:

Antiques Britain, 791-9070.
Battleground Antique Mall, 794-9444.
Country Charm Mall, 790-8908.
First Avenue Antiques, 791-8866.
Franklin Antique Mall, 790-8593
Harpeth Antique Mall, 790-7965.
Heirloom Antiques, 791-0847.
Heritage Antique Gallery, 790-8115.
Hood's Retreat Antiques, 591-7819.
Magic Memories, 794-2848.
Patchwork Palace, 790-1382.
Peggy's Place, 790-6408.
Rebel's Rest, 790-7199.
Sparkman Jewelers, 794-5284.
Watson's Antique & Estate Jewelry, 790-0244.
Winchester Antique Mall, 791-5846.

Special Events:

April—Main Street Festival
May—Heritage Foundation Town and Country Tour; Franklin
    Rodeo
August—Franklin Jazz Festival
October—Pumpkin Fest
December—Christmas at Fox Hollow; Carter House Candle-
    light Tour of Homes; Dickens of a Christmas.

For More Information:

Downtown Franklin Association, 231 2nd Ave., 37065; 790-
    7094.
Heritage Foundation, P.O. Box 723, 37065; 591-8500.
Williamson County/Franklin Chamber of Commerce and
    Tourism, P.O. Box 156 (City Hall), 37065; 800-356-3445
    or 794-1225. Ask for self-guided tour of Historic Down-
    town Franklin, driving tour of the battle of Franklin, driv-
    ing tour of Brentwood and Franklin, and Scenic Parkway
    through Williamson County.
Williamson County Visitor Information Center, 209 E. Main,
    591-8514. This should be your first stop in Franklin.

The authors paddle at dawn on Reelfoot Lake to enjoy its beauty and to fish for largemouth bass, crappie, and bluegill.

WEST TENNESSEE

❧

West Tennessee is less densely populated than the remainder of the state even though it contains Memphis, Tennessee's largest city. Memphis embodies enough appeal, charm, and temptations to keep you busy for a string of days and nights. Memphis covers a large area and is chock full of sites and things to do. When you visit, allow an extra day or three to see and do some of the special things that will present themselves that you didn't plan on. We tried to see the city in four days and left many sites unseen.

A wide variety of museums display Egyptian and Indian artifacts, botanical gardens, great paintings and sculptures, dinosaurs, gemstones, and the list is more voluminous than pages in this book. We give you enough samplings of the museums to encourage you to see it all for yourself. Music is perhaps the main attraction in Memphis, closely followed by its diversity of cuisine. Blues and rock 'n' roll grew up in Memphis. You can follow their histories downtown and on Beale Street, from W. C. Handy to Elvis.

Memphis is the hub for two of our loop tours. While visiting Memphis you may choose to venture north or east on these loops to see other sites.

If you prefer the quiet of the countryside, the land west of Kentucky Lake to the Mississippi River offers scenic splendors quite unlike the high plateaus and mountains farther east. The two loop tours from Memphis and one from Jackson will give you an excellent sampling of attractions, bed and breakfasts, dining, and historic sites, as well as give you a sense of West Tennessee's wide open spaces.

For a sense of history, visit sites along the Mississippi and Tennessee Rivers. These were the first avenues open to settlers. From these rivers, the pioneers moved along the tributaries to settle new areas unencumbered by mountains.

Each town on the loop tours offers something unique. Whether it is a stolen courthouse, Olympic games, teapots, bald eagles, champion bird dogs, log cabins, fishing holes, antique guns and cars, local and international art, Art Deco, and any number of treasures, you'll be glad you took the time to visit.

ᔅᔆLoop 11

69 Jackson
Home of Casey Jones

In 1821 Madison County was formed in the Western District and was named for President James Madison. Jackson, named for Andrew Jackson because many of his wife's relatives lived in the area, became the county seat in 1822.

Engineer Casey Jones called Jackson home when he took the throttle of "Old 382" on the night of April 30, 1900. Just outside of Vaughan, Mississippi, Casey and his fireman came upon a stalled train on the same track. Realizing that it was too late to come to a complete stop, Casey told the fireman to jump, but he remained aboard, trying to stop the train. Casey had slowed down the train enough so that he was the only casualty of the wreck. He immediately became a folk hero and his experience has been recounted for nearly a century in story and song.

The house he was living in at the time of his death is now the Casey Jones Home and Railroad Museum. It is located within the Casey Jones Village complex at exit 80A off I-40 in Jackson. Visitors get a chance to learn about the man through exhibits and a fifteen-minute video. There is also a model train exhibit in an 1890s railcar, and there's a full-size steam locomotive outside. Children are welcome to climb aboard, ring the bell, and sing out the ballad of Casey Jones.

In addition to the museum, the Casey Jones Village offers the five-hundred-seat Old Country Store Restaurant, which features three family-style buffets each day. If you like hearty country breakfasts, you've come to the right place. You can enjoy the buffet or order from a menu that features everything from Tennessee country ham to homemade biscuits. Breakfast ordered from the menu is always available, even if the breakfast buffet has already closed down.

Inside the Old Country Store Restaurant, there are more than 15,000 turn-of-the-century antiques; a 6,000-square-foot gift, confectionery, and souvenir shop; and an 1890s ice cream parlor. The village also contains several other shops, including the Wildlife in Wood shop, which features a life-size carved eagle that took more than twenty-three thousand hours to create. There's also the Cheese Factory, where you can watch cheese being made.

Families can stay at the Casey Jones Station Inn and can sleep in one of the two original red cabooses or an 1890s railcar suite. Highland Place

Casey Jones became a hero for staying on board, keeping pressure on the brakes, and minimizing an accident; but he had a reputation for being a reckless engineer.

A tourist industry has grown around the Casey Jones legend in Jackson.

Bed and Breakfast has four rooms with private baths and special romantic packages that include a tub for two. Full breakfast is served. National franchises include Best Western, Comfort Inn, Garden Plaza Hotel, Hampton Inn, Holiday Inn, Quality Inn, and Sheraton Inn.

Cypress Grove Nature Park is an outdoor family adventure. You begin your tour at the visitor center, and at the new Raptor Center you get a close-up view of the flora and fauna of this part of the state as you walk through the 165-acre cypress forest on a two-mile-long elevated boardwalk. Along the path you'll pass bald cypress and water tupelo trees and acres of colorful wildflowers. There's also a very good chance you'll see hawks, the barred owl, muskrats, great egrets, white-tailed deer, and many other animals that call the park home. In the spring this is a good place to view migratory wetland songbirds. The Nature Park is located west of Jackson off Highway 70 and is free.

Rich in history, Jackson has a strong sense of historic preservation, from the East Main Street

homes and Carnegie Library to the Britton Lane Civil War battlefield.

The next stop, Pinson Mounds, is southwest of the city via US 45.

All of the following accommodations are Jackson with zip code 38305, and all telephone listings are area code 901, except where noted.

Accommodations:
Casey Jones Station Inn, 1943 Hwy. 45 bypass, 800-628-2812 or 668-3636.
Highland Place Bed and Breakfast, 519 N. Highland Ave., 427-1472.

Attractions:
Britton Lane Battlefield Park, Medon, 935-2209.
Casey Jones Home and Museum, 668-1222.
Cypress Grove Nature Park, 425-8364.
East Main Homes Tour, 422-7738.
Electro Chalybeate Well, 422-7500.
Old Country Store, 668-1223.

Dining:
Asia Garden, 661-9950.
Baudo's Restaurant, 668-1447.
Barnhill's Country Buffet, 664-5163.
Catfish Galley, 668-7555.
Davis-Kidd Booksellers, 661-9595.
Old Country Store, 668-1223.
Suede's, 664-1956.
Zeto's, 424-9001.

Shopping:
Friendly Frank's Flea Market.
Native American Legacy, 668-0400.

Special Events:
May—Mrs. Tennessee Pageant
June—Shannon Street Blues Festival
July—Fireworks, Jackson Fairgrounds
September—Rally in the Alley; African Street Festival
October—Rocktober Fest
December—Christmas Parade

Camping:
Jackson Mobile Village and RV Park, 668-2487.

For More Information:
Jackson/Madison County Convention and Visitors Bureau, 400 S. Highland, 800-498-4748 or 425-8333.

70 *Pinson Mounds State Archaeological Area*
Woodland Indian Interment

Pinson Mounds is located ten miles south of Jackson off US 45 at Pinson. Follow the signs from US 45 along Ozier Road to the mounds.

Pinson Mounds, discovered in 1820 by surveyors, is named for surveyor Joe Pinson. J. G. Cisco, a Jackson journalist, began publicizing the mound in 1880; but it wasn't until the early 1900s that William E. Meyer, a Smithsonian Institution archaeologist, began to work on the mounds.

The site consists of at least twelve mounds, an earthen geometric enclosure, and habitation areas that cover approximately four hundred acres. This site was built during what archaeologists term the Middle Woodland period, which ranges from about 200 B.C. to A.D. 500. The archaeologi-

cal evidence recovered so far suggests that the site was occupied during the first three centuries A.D. This was the largest mound center in the southeastern United States during the Middle Woodland period. Sauls Mound is seventy-two feet in height, which makes it the second tallest earthen mound in North America. Pinson Mounds is listed in the National Register of Historic Places.

The Visitor Center and Museum was designed to replicate an Indian mound and houses. It has forty-five hundred feet of exhibit areas, an eighty-seat theater, the West Tennessee Regional Archaeology office, an archaeological library, and the park offices.

Two large picnic shelters are situated in the park, with additional picnic sites equipped with tables and grills. There are approximately six miles of trails, including a nature trail and a boardwalk near the Forked Deer River. Most of the trails are accessible to bicycles and wheelchairs.

The annual Archeofest, held the third week-

Pinson Mounds is off the main highways, but it is worth the trip through scenic farmland of West Tennessee to visit the museum and Woodland Indian mounds.

end in September, celebrates the Native-American culture. Crafts, foods, native dances, and tours are just a few of the things you will find at this culturally rich event.

Our next stop is Lexington via TN 197 northeast, TN 200 east, and TN 22 north into town.

For More Information:
Pinson Mounds, 460 Ozier Road, Pinson, 38366; 901-988-5614.

71 Lexington and Parsons
Dragboats and Coon Dogs

Henderson County grew out of the Western District in 1821 and was named for Col. James Henderson who commanded the Tennessee troops at the battle of New Orleans. Lexington, the county seat, was named after a city of the same name in Massachusetts.

Henderson County is a sportsman's paradise, as outdoor recreation abounds. The county features seven major lakes with more than one hundred miles of beautiful shoreline, Tennessee's largest state park, and the world's third largest pecan tree.

Area lakes play host to hundreds of fishermen each year. Beech Lake, located in Lexington, is the site of the National Drag Boat Races and the annual Freedom Day Lake Festival. The latter is held annually in July on the shore of Beech Lake and features a Bar-B-Que Cook-off, beauty pageants, arts and crafts, talent show, and lots of live entertainment.

Beech Lake also boasts one of the most complete camping facilities in the area. Beech, Pine,

and Pin Oak Lakes all offer white sand beaches, swimming, and water skiing; and all the lakes have excellent fishing, including bass and crappie.

Parsons is east of Lexington about sixteen miles on US 412 in Decatur County. No guns are allowed, but here is where you'll find the world's largest coon hunt in April. Hundreds of hunters from all over the United States converge on the fairgrounds to show their dogs' stuff. Tracking and treeing are the parameters for judging the best coon dog in the world. Country music keeps the hunters company as they sit around the fire at night jawing about their dogs. The money raised from the festivities goes to Saint Jude's Children's Research Hospital in Memphis. Contact Decatur Chamber of Commerce at 901-847-4202 for more information

From Lexington go northeast on TN 114 to Natchez Trace State Park.

All of the following accommodations are Lexington with zip code 38351, and all telephone listings are area code 901, except where noted.

Accommodations:
West Shores Lodge, 732 Church St., 968-0171.

Attractions:
Beech River Lakes, 968-6191.

Special Events:
April—West Tennessee Fiddlers Contest, Sardis; World's Largest Coon Hunt, Parsons
July—Drag Boat Races and Freedom Day Lake Festival

Camping:
Beech Lake Family Camping Resort, 968-9542.

For More Information:
Henderson County Chamber of Commerce, P.O. Box 737, 968-2126.

*North of downtown Lexington is
Beech Lake, where National Drag
Boat races are held.*

*North of downtown Lexington is
Beech Lake, where National Drag
Boat races are held.*

72 Natchez Trace State Park and Parker's Crossroads
The Wilderness Spur and the Grave Facing South

Natchez Trace State Park is in Carroll, Henderson, and Benton Counties in West Tennessee. The park was named for the famous Natchez to Nashville wilderness road, an important trace during the late eighteenth and early nineteenth centuries. A western spur of the Natchez Trace ran through a portion of what is now the park.

Pin Oak Lodge, situated on the wooded shores of Pin Oak Lake, contains twenty rooms and the restaurant serves southern cuisine. Support facilities include a recreation room, playground, tennis courts, and adult and children's swimming pools.

Cabins are on Cub Lake, which has a beach and day-use area. The park's three campgrounds feature 145 campsites. Most sites are equipped with a table, grill, water and electrical hookups.

There is a campground specifically for campers who bring their horses and there are miles of equestrian trails.

Many miles of hiking trails meander through the forest and fields and along lakeshores and streams. There is a twenty-eight-mile, long-distance, overnight hiking trail for the backpacking enthusiast. Many miles of fire roads and back-country trails are also open to motorcycles and other off-road vehicles.

The park has four lakes for boating and fishing. Cub Lake is a small lake where only park rental boats are allowed. Pin Oak Lake with its 690 acres, 90-acre Maple Creek Lake, and 167-acre Brown's Creek Lake permit private boats and motors. Fishing is a popular activity with catches of bluegill, catfish, crappie, largemouth bass, rock bass, and hybrids.

Recreation activities include softball, archery, basketball, volleyball, lighted tennis court, shuffleboard, Ping-Pong, field games, and a recreation building. Organized recreational and nature interpretation programs are provided during the summer season, and there is an environmental learning center in the park.

Now for some Civil War sites. Take I-40 west to Parker's Crossroads. The Civil War Reenactment and Living History demonstration is held biannually on even-numbered years at Parker's Crossroads. A self-driving tour of the battlefield is open year-round.

The battle of Parker's Crossroads took place in December 1863. The self-guided driving tour is designed to provide a complete view of the battlefield, with stops at important points of interest. Except for the city park, north of Interstate 40, all of the battlefield and points of interest are located on private property, and you must therefore use state and county roads on the tour.

Space doesn't allow for us to describe all the sites but here are two examples.

Stop 1: The city of Parker's Crossroads's city park. The historical marker tells about the battle of Parker's Crossroads where Union Col. Cyrus L. Dunham met Confederate Gen. Nathan Bedford Forrest.

Stop 4: Jones Cemetery. Here you will find the graves of the Rev. John A. Parker and his wife, Rebecca. At the time of the battle, Parker was a Republican and a Union sympathizer. However, when the Union placed a cannon in his front yard during the battle, Parker demanded that the artillery be removed, fearing Confederate counterfire. The Union officer loftily asked Parker, "What is more important, the Union cause or your house?" Parker emphatically stated, "My house!" When the Reverend Mr. Parker died in

1864, his last wish was that he be buried with his feet to the north and his head to the south, so that when the Angel Gabriel sounded his trumpet, Parker could rise and "kick the Yankees back north!" You can see that the Parker graves face north and south, while everyone else in the cemetery is buried east and west.

Our next stop is Camden. You can go through Huntingdon via TN 22 and turn east on US 70, or go east on I-40 and turn north on US 641.

All of the following accommodations are Lexington with zip code 38351, and all telephone listings are area code 901, except where noted.

Attractions:
Parker's Crossroads Battlefield, 968-5533.

Camping:
Parker's Crossroads Campground, Yuma, 968-9939.
Natchez Trace State Park, Wildersville, 800-250-8616.

For More Information:
Natchez Trace State Park, 24845 Natchez Trace Rd., Wildersville, 38388; office 901-968-3742, inn 901-968-8176, reservations 800-250-8616.
Parker's Crossroads, Henderson County Chamber of Commerce, P.O. Box 737, Lexington, 38351; 968-6191.

Pin Oak Lodge on the shores of Pin Oak Lake in the Natchez Trace State Park provides lodging and food for visitors looking for the outdoor experience.

73 *Camden*
Home of Folklife and Pearls

Benton County was formed from Henry and Humphreys Counties in 1835, and its county seat is Camden. The county was first named for Missouri senator Thomas Hart Benton, a friend of Andrew Jackson and former resident of Tennessee. Later the populace claimed it was named for David Benton, an early settler. Benton County was known for its peanuts and sorghum in the 1800s; today its sorghum production ranks twelfth in the nation.

Camden is at an elevation of about 450 feet. About ten miles east, on the highest point in the western part of the state is Pilot Knob within the Nathan Bedford Forrest State Park. Here you'll find the Tennessee River Folklife Center, a tribute to the people who lived and worked on the Tennessee River. The interpretive center is located on Pilot Knob, an ancient landmark for fishermen

and pilots who traversed the river far below. The view of the river from up here is superb.

Most of the exhibits in the Folklife Center incorporate segments of oral histories taken from the locals who lived along the river. The audio segments recall the early industries, music, religion, and community events of the area.

Maggie Sayre lived on a houseboat on the river for more than fifty years, capturing her life by using a Brownie camera. The center has her collection on display. The museum allows the people to tell their own stories through audio, written word, and photographs. Children will be engrossed by some of the stories and some of the early music that was specially recorded for the exhibits.

The entrance to the state historical area and the Folklife Center is at the end of TN 191, about ten miles east of Camden. Nathan Bedford Forrest State Park is located on the western bank of Kentucky Lake eight miles north of Camden in Benton County. In 1929 the park was dedicated to

From Pilot Knob and the Tennessee River Folklife Center you get a grand view of the Kentucky Lake and remains of old Johnsonville.

Nathan Bedford Forrest, one of the greatest military tacticians and cavalry leaders of the Civil War.

The park has two campgrounds. The Happy Hollow camping area has thirty-eight sites equipped with table, grill, and water and electrical hookups. This area is served by a playground, bathhouse with hot showers, and restroom facilities. A dumping station is provided. The second campground is more primitive, but located on the shoreline with fifteen campsites. Water is available, but not at each site and there is a central restroom.

More than twenty miles of hiking trails meander through the park providing excellent views of woods, water, and wildlife. There is also a long-distance backpacking trail available for the more adventuresome.

Boating, skiing, and fishing are very popular activities on two-hundred-thousand-acre Kentucky Lake. Boat launching ramps are available at the park. Commercial marinas and public boat docks are located nearby. Catches of smallmouth and largemouth bass, striped bass, sauger, crappie, bream, and catfish are common.

Recreational activities at the park include softball, volleyball, badminton, horseshoes, and more. There are two playgrounds and a large play field with a softball diamond. A swimming beach is in the park, but no lifeguards are on duty.

The battle of Johnsonville, fought when Confederate General Forrest sought to destroy the supply lines for Union General Sherman's March to the Sea, took place across the river from the park. Forrest had long been a terror to the Union army, appearing at unpredictable spots and times with a marked faculty for creating impressions of having forces tremendously larger than he ever actually possessed.

In the 1960s, John Latendresse developed a technique for creating freshwater pearls in mollusks, and in 1985 he harvested his first crop of Tennessee-produced pearls. He learned to implant a small piece of shell inside the mollusk. In response the mussel excretes a protective coating around the foreign substance to relieve the irritation. That coating is what forms the pearl. You can take a tour of a mussel farm at Birdsong Marina on Kentucky Lake. A Pearl of a Tour operates from May to October and lasts for about three hours. You climb aboard a pontoon boat that takes you out to where you will be able to see divers working the mollusk fields. Tours include dinner and other attractions of the area. An on-site jewelry store and museum feature the local pearls. Birdsong Resort and Marina offers cabins, boat rentals, a pool, restaurant, and lounge.

Just north of Camden on March 3, 1965,

At Birdsong Marina and Resort on Kentucky Lake south of Camden you can see the fruits of freshwater mussel farming.

Patsy Cline, Cowboy Copas, Hawkshaw Hawkins, and pilot Randy Hughes crashed. There is a commemorative monument 2.8 miles east of US 641 on Mount Carmel Road.

From Camden go east on US 70 to Waverly, then north on TN 13 to Erin. From Erin take TN 49 to Dover.

All of the following accommodations are Camden with zip code 38320, and all telephone listings are area code 901, except where noted.

Accommodations:
Birdsong Resort & Marina, 255 Marina Rd., 800-225-7469 or 584-7880.

Attractions:
Birdsong Resort and Marina/Pearl of a Tour, 800-225-7469 or 584-7880.
Nathan Bedford Forrest State Park, Eva, 584-6356.
Tennessee River Folk Life Center, 584-6356.

Dining:
1850 Log House, 584-7814.
Jack Bar-B-Q, 584-8334.
The Catfish Place, 584-3504.

Special Events:
April—Fiddler's Bluegrass Championship
June—Merchants Street Fair
July—Summer Song Festival, N. B. F. State Park
August—Benton County Fair; Tennessee River Folklife Festival, N. B. F. State Park
November—Lioness Craft Fair
December—Christmas Parade

Camping:
Beaverdam Resort, 584-3963.
Birdsong Marina and Campground, 800-225-7469 or 584-7880.

For More Information:
Camden/Benton County Chamber of Commerce, 202 W. Main, 584-8395.
Johnsonville State Historic Area, 200 Museum Ln., New Johnsonville, 37134; 535-2789.

74 *Dover*
Small Historic River Town

Duncan Stewart was a Revolutionary War soldier and an early settler in the Dover area from whom the county takes its name. Dover, originally named Monroe, became Stewart County's county seat in 1805, two years after the county was formed from part of Montgomery County.

Dover was prosperous for the fifty years before the War Between the States. Dover and Stewart County led Middle Tennessee's iron production with fourteen furnaces. But Dover suffered mightily at the hands of the Union army.

By 1862, after the fall of Fort Donelson, only four houses remained. One of these structures became known as the Surrender House. It was here that Gen. Simon Buckner was headquartered and surrendered to Gen. U. S. Grant, his old friend. The first major victory for the Union earned Grant his nickname "Unconditional Surrender." Buckner, in spite of spending the war in Yankee prisons, retained his friendship with Grant and was one of his pallbearers in 1885. Today the Dover Hotel, built between 1851 and 1853, has been remodeled to reflect that period. One account says it was the old Dover Tavern built in 1826 that housed Buckner and was where he surrendered.

Capturing Fort Donelson opened the Cumberland River—and Nashville—to the Yankees. It also signaled to the Confederacy that the war was going be longer and more onerous than expected after the win at Manassas.

Fort Donelson National Battlefield located a mile west of Dover is a fifteen-acre site with river batteries, outer defense earthworks, and the Surrender House. You can drive the six-mile tour of the area and walk interpretive trails. A ten-minute slide presentation will give you a better understanding of the taking of Fort Donelson if you watch it before the tour. The Fort Donelson National Cemetery with 655 interred Union soldiers, 504 unknown, is on West Church Street. Confederate dead were buried at the Dover Cemetery at the corner of Forrest and Church Streets.

Dover is at the mouth of the Land Between the Lakes: Kentucky Lake on the Tennessee River and Lake Barkley on the Cumberland River, west and east of the land, respectively. TVA condemned this 270-square mile area, displacing about eight hundred families, to establish an educational and recreational reserve in 1959.

LBL, as it has become known, is about one-third in Tennessee and offers many recreational opportunities, with more then two hundred marked hiking trails, a sixty-five-mile long trek along the Trace (the road that traverses the peninsula north to south), bicycle trail, off-road vehicle trails, horse trails, and hunting and fishing.

The Home Place 1850, just south of the Tennessee-Kentucky state line, is a living history site. From costumes to chores, the compound looks like an old farm with log cabins, corrals, and fields. You can take part in the activities of farm life during a two-day June Folk Festival and again in the Apple Festival in October.

Bison and elk have a home behind fences, and the Tennessee Wildlife Resources Agency is considering reintroducing free-ranging elk here. You are free to explore over one hundred miles of roads and walk through the woods.

Golden Pond Visitor Center in Golden Pond, Kentucky, will provide you with information about LBL. If you're there Wednesday through Saturday, go to the planetarium for special programs (502-924-5602).

Cross Creeks National Wildlife Refuge is a nine-thousand-acre waterfowl and eagle sanctuary.

The Riverfront Plantation Inn has five guest rooms with private baths and serves a full breakfast.

Paris Landing and Paris are west of Dover on US 79.

All of the following accommodations are Dover with zip code 37058, and all telephone listings are area code 931, except where noted.

Accommodations:
The Riverfront Plantation Inn, 190 Crow Lane, 232-9492.

Attractions:
Cross Creeks National Wildlife Refuge, 232-7477.
Dover Cemetery.
Fort Donelson National Battlefield, 232-5706.
Fort Donelson National Cemetery.
Land Between the Lakes National Recreation Area, Golden Pond, KY, 502-924-2000.
Gourd Museum and Historic Rice House, 232-4098.

Dining:
The Dover Grill, 232-7919.
P.J.'s Restaurant and Resort, 232-8954.
Town and Country Restaurant, 232-6930.

Shopping:
Old Town Dover Shops, Church St.
Yesterday's Memories, Antiques & Crafts, 232-8960.

Special Events:
April—Earth Week, LBL 232-7956
June—Folk Festival, LBL
September—River Days Festival
October—Apple Festival, LBL

Camping:
Elk Harbor Lake Side Campground and RV Park, 827-2384.
LBL Big Pine Campground, 232-4570.
Leatherwood Resort and Marina, 232-5137.
P. J.'s Restaurant and Resort, 232-8954.
Piney Campground, 232-5331 or 502-924-5602.

For More Information:
Stewart County Chamber of Commerce, P.O. Box 147, 232-5400.

75 *Paris Landing, Buchanan, Paris*
The Fishing Hole

Paris Landing got its name from a steamboat and freight landing on the Tennessee River dating back to the mid-1800s. From here and other landings on the Tennessee and Big Sandy Rivers supplies were transported to surrounding towns and communities by oxcart.

The 841-acre Paris Landing State Park is situated on the western shore of Kentucky Lake, one of the largest man-made lakes in the world. Paris Landing Inn, remodeled in 1998, provides a commanding view of picturesque Kentucky Lake and has one hundred guest rooms. The spacious restaurant is noted throughout the region, especially among the local fishing guides, for its fine

southern foods, including catfish. We stayed in one of the ten new cabins built in the woods overlooking Kentucky Lake. These deluxe villas are fully equipped for housekeeping with three bedrooms (five double beds), two baths, a full-size kitchen, stone fireplace, telephone, and cable TV. All villas have central heat and air conditioning. Guests have easy access to the lake

Paris Landing has a par-72, 6,689-yard, eighteen-hole golf course. The park pro shop provides a snack bar, rental clubs, gasoline golf carts as well as pull carts, and a line of golf accessories. The campground has a total of sixty-six campsites, all with tables and grills, and forty-six sites have water and electrical hookups. Two centrally located bathhouses provide hot showers, and there is a dumping station and launderette. A playground is in the campground and the swimming pool is nearby.

The park's marina is in a protected harbor off

Paris Landing State Park on the western shores of the Tennessee River has been renovated and offers a wide variety of outdoor opportunities.

the main channel north and west of the bridge. It is fully equipped to handle crafts of all sizes and types. Transportation is provided from the marina to the inn and restaurant for transit boaters wishing to spend the night and dine at the restaurant. A free launching ramp is provided, and rental fishing boats and motors are available. The park store is located at the marina.

The two-hundred-thousand-acre Kentucky Lake is a popular place for yachts, sailboats, cruisers, and runabouts. Water-skiing and fishing are by far the most popular activities. Rewarding stringers of largemouth, smallmouth, and white bass, crappie, bluegill, catfish, and sauger are not uncommon.

West of Paris Landing is Buchanan, the main resort area at the northern end of the lake; about twelve miles farther on US 79 is the town of Paris.

Patrick Henry had Henry County named for him in 1821, and two years later, Paris, the county seat, honored the popular Revolutionary War hero Lafayette.

Centered around one of the oldest Tennessee courthouses still in use is a walking tour of Paris. It includes the Crete Opera House built in 1899, the longest continuous row of courthouse square buildings existing from before the turn of the century, antique shops, the City Cemetery, and five churches with examples of stained glass. Market Street Antique Mall at 414 Market Street, the largest in West Tennessee, contains more than sixty thousand square feet of shopping space. Also go by to see the sixty-foot replica of the Eiffel Tower in Memorial Park.

The biggest event in Paris is the World's Biggest Fish Fry held each April for the last forty-four years. Mounds of coleslaw, hushpuppies, white beans, and fried catfish (eighty-five hundred

Any city named Paris needs an Eiffel Tower. This sixty-foot replica rises from a mound in Memorial Park.

pounds) feed all comers. Begun as Mule Day in the 1950s, it has dropped the mules and grown into a weeklong shindig. A bed race, rodeo, carnival, arts and crafts, small-fry parade, and catfish race are among some of the events held that week at the Henry County Fairgrounds.

From Paris continue on US 79 to McKenzie.

All of the following accommodations are Paris with zip code 38242, and all telephone listings are area code 901, except where noted.

Accommodations:
Paris Landing State Park, 116055 Hwy. 79, Buchanan, 38222; 800-250-8614 or 642-4311.
Sunset View Inn Bed and Breakfast, 1330 Shady Grove Rd., 642-4778.

Attractions:
Eiffel Tower, 642-1212.
Paris-Henry County Heritage Center, 642-1030.
Tennessee National Wildlife Refuge, 642-2091.
Walking Tour of Historic Downtown. Contact Chamber of Commerce for brochure.

Dining:
Knott's Landing Restaurant, 642-4718.
Redmon's Bar-B-Que, 642-9381.
Old Oak Tree Restaurant, Springville, 800-225-6302 or 642-8810.

Shopping:
Market Street Antique Mall, 642-6996.
Sally Lane's Homemade Candies, 642-5801.

Special Events:
April—World's Biggest Fish Fry

Camping:
Britton Ford Campground, 593-3458.
Buchanan Resort, Springville, 800-225-6302 or 642-8810.
Country Junction USA, 593-3662.
Hill Top Lodge, 644-2049.
Howell's Resort, 642-7442.
Mansard Island Resort and Marina, 800-533-5590 ext. 120 or 642-5590.
Oak Haven Resort, Buchanan, 642-1550.
Paris Landing KOA Kampground, Buchanan, 800-KOA-2815 or 642-6895.

For More Information:
Northwest Tennessee Tourism Council, P.O. Box 963, Martin, 38237; 587-4213.
Paris/Henry County Chamber of Commerce, P.O. Box 8, 800-345-1103 or 642-3431.

76 *Milan*
Bullet Town

You've probably not given much thought to what the early driver's licenses looked like but, if it starts bothering you, you can see the first one issued in 1938, at the Gordon Browning Museum in McKenzie. Browning was governor three times and it has been said he didn't throw anything away.

South of McKenzie is the small community of McLemoresville, home of actress Dixie Carter.

Farther south is Milan with two attractions, the ammunition plant and the West Tennessee Agricultural Museum. The plant occupies twenty-two thousand acres and has been producing cartridges and artillery shells since World War II. The Bullet Town Celebration held each September honors the ammunition industry by having a community get-together to enjoy sporting events, entertainment, arts and crafts, and a general good time.

The Agricultural Museum is considered one of the best museums in West Tennessee. One of its exhibits is a time line from the early agricultural inhabitants of West Tennessee to the present, including Indians, settlers, farmers, and planters. These and other exhibits of an early schoolhouse, blacksmith shop, and old farm tools are, appropriately, in a large barn.

Held in July, No-Till Day is a fun and educational time. People from about forty states and thirteen foreign countries come to spend a week learning more about no-till farming. It isn't all work. There are fashion shows, trap shooting, golf tournaments, concerts, softball, tennis, horse show, car show, and the selection of Miss No-Till.

The Agricultural Museum is a must-see for those interested in the evolution of farming and its implements.

From Milan take US 45E back to Jackson to complete the loop tour.

Attractions:
Gordon Browning Museum-Carroll County Historical Society, McKenzie, 352-3510.
U.T. West Tennessee Agricultural Museum, Milan, 686-8067.

Dining:
Catfish Restaurant, McKenzie, 352-5855.
Hig's Restaurant, 352-7532.

Hig's Restaurant, Milan, 686-9901.
Los Caballeros, Milan, 686-3700.

Special Events:
July—No-Till Field Day, Milan
September—Bullet Town Celebration, Milan

For More Information:
Carroll County Chamber of Commerce, P.O. Box 726, Huntingdon, 38344; 986-4664.
Milan Chamber of Commerce, 1061 S. Main, Milan, 38358; 686-7495.

⚘ Memphis

77 *Memphis*
Crown Jewel of the Delta

"Blues ain't nothing but a good man feeling bad," so the saying goes. And Memphis has the blues but it certainly ain't bad. It's Good—with a capital *G!* From the blues to blue suede shoes, Memphis means music. B. B. King, Jerry Lee Lewis, Albert King, Muddy Waters, Roy Orbison, Howlin' Wolf, Little Milton, Ray Perkins, and Elvis. If you want it proven to you, just head on down to Memphis.

We spent a week discovering this town but that wasn't long enough to get saturated; in fact we didn't get damp looking at the advertised sights such as Mud Island on the Mississippi River, Beale Street, and Graceland. Let us get your feet wet with a little background on this Crown Jewel of the Delta.

Chickasaw Bluffs, formed during the last ice age from rock powder blown and deposited in a layer about one hundred feet thick, was first settled about a thousand years ago and remained inhabited for more than five hundred years by Indians. The Spaniard Hernando de Soto is thought to have been the first European to arrive in the 1540s, followed by French explorers, who claimed the region for France.

The French built the first permanent structure, Fort Assumption, there in 1739 but it was rarely manned. In 1795 Manuel Gayoso constructed Fort San Fernando de las Barrancas on the same site, but within two years the new U.S. government claimed that Gayoso's fort was an invasion of its territory. Isaac Guion was sent to the area, only to find the fort dismantled and moved across the river. Guion then built Fort Adams upon the Spanish fort's ruins on the old site. The fort was later renamed Fort Pike for Capt. Zebulon Pike of Pikes Peak fame.

As early as 1794 the United States had a trading post here under the authority of Judge John Overton, who was also temporary agent of Indian affairs. Tennessee was admitted to the Union two years later. In 1801, Capt. Pike found a better location for Fort Pike, about two miles downstream just above the Indian Mounds in what is now DeSoto Park. Here Pike built Fort Pickering, named for Thomas Pickering, secretary of state to President George Washington. The fort was later under the command of Zachary Taylor, who became the twelfth president.

Memphis, the city on the fourth and southernmost of four bluffs, was laid out with wide streets and four public squares in 1819 and took its name from the city on the Nile River that means a "place of good abode." Shelby County was formed in 1819 from Hardin County, and the river town began to grow, becoming a lawless town rife with gamblers, Indians trading for liquid spirits, and Kaintucks stopping to sell upriver-goods and buying trouble. This was part of the West during the early 1800s, and within twenty years Memphis would be the one of the busiest ports on the Mississippi River. Life was good with wonderful potential; the town grew from sixty-four hundred people in 1850 to thirty-three thousand in the next ten years.

With the coming of the Civil War, river towns and forts were important strategic places: Nashville and Fort Donelson on the Cumberland

Memphis grew on the banks of the Chickasaw Bluffs near where De Soto first saw the Mississippi River.

River, and Fort Pillow, Memphis, Vicksburg, and Natchez on the Mississippi River.

Fort Pillow fell to the Union after a month's engagement during April 1862. The fort was on the riverbank at the time but the river has moved since then (*see* Fort Pillow). Confederate Capt. James Montgomery retreated from Fort Pillow with eight cotton-clad steam rams to protect Memphis.

The Battle of Memphis began on June 6, 1862, at dawn when the Union fleet of five ironclads and four ram boats steamed to engage Montgomery's boats. Crowds watched from the bluff for ninety minutes. The close-quarter fighting and boat ramming resulted in the loss of seven Confederate boats with about one hundred dead and nearly that many captured. The Union lost four men. The city was spared siege, such as Vicksburg later experienced, and the burning that Atlanta suffered.

Fort Pickering, mostly abandoned since 1810 and weathered away, was revived and rebuilt by the Union army to a much larger fort. F. M. White of Memphis had planned to build a one-hundred-room house with the materials that were diverted to the fort's construction. Some of those buildings of the 1860s now house the U.S. Army Reserve on West California Avenue across from DeSoto Park.

When Tennessee rejoined the Union on July 24, 1866, Memphis was financially strapped. While the war did not inflict destruction on the city, deadly horror came in 1867 in the form of yellow fever, and it returned in 1873 and 1878. More than thirty thousand fled in 1878, the worst epidemic. Fewer than twenty thousand remained in Memphis, fourteen thousand of whom were African Americans, and fewer than one thousand of them died. Among the six thou-

You know you're on Beale Street when you see B.B. King's Blues Club and hear the blues emanating from within.

sand remaining whites, more than four thousand died.

The city of Memphis ceased to exist. It surrendered its charter. Memphis then installed a sewer system, dug drainage ditches to remove the threat of mosquitoes, and dug wells to supply clean water rather than taking water from the river. By 1890 Memphis was again a boom (non)town with a population of nearly sixty-five thousand. It regained its charter in 1893. It became the largest hardwood center in the world and timber rivaled cotton as an export.

Robert Church, a former slave, was one of the first citizens to invest in the new Memphis. He came to Memphis before the war and worked as a cabin boy, cook, and ship's clerk on steamboats as a free man. During the yellow fever epidemic, Church bought real estate at a bargain from those leaving the city. Later he founded the Solvent Bank and Trust and became the South's first black millionaire.

During this time Beale Street, covering fifteen city blocks, became the black Mecca. Beale was probably the name of a Revolutionary War soldier who settled the area in the early 1800s, according to a Memphis Music Hall of Fame display. Beale extends 1.5 miles east from the riverfront and was laid out in the 1830s. During the years before the Civil War and yellow fever epidemics, Beale Avenue (its official name) was an exclusive residential area with majestic homes of wealthy whites. In the 1870s, these affluent families moved east of town.

Farmers, loggers, musicians, gamblers, streetwalkers, lawyers, doctors, other professionals, and educated blacks flocked to Beale early in the 1900s. It contained some rough elements that would remind us of Memphis's early lawless days. There were a lot of gambling and associated fights those living in South Memphis Sodomites, the reference coming from the "wicked" side of town nicknamed Sodom. Street fights broke out between the two because of these names.

During this period of the early 1900s, one man was developing into a major political force: Edward Hull Crump, known as "Boss Crump." In 1909 W. C. Handy wrote a catchy tune for Crump's mayoral campaign called "Mr. Crump." This tune later became known as "Memphis Blues," the first blues song ever published, and Handy became the "Father of the Blues," and, by extension, father of jazz, ragtime, soul, and rock 'n' roll.

In the late 1940s a young man from Indianola, Mississippi, came to Memphis to join the music scene. Known back then as Riley King, he soon traded that name for a new moniker, B. B. (for Blues Boy) King. Others who made Beale Street home are Bobby "Blue" Bland, Albert King, Furry Lewis, Alberta Hunter, and Memphis Minnie McCoy.

Meanwhile, Clarence Saunders opened a grocery store called Piggly Wiggly in 1916. It was the first self-service market, and Saunders patented his store's design and equipment. Then he began selling franchises. By 1923 he had 1,267 Piggly Wiggly stores in operation. You'll read more about his Pink Palace later.

Another success story came in 1952 when Kemmons Wilson franchised motels. He decided on the motel chain's name after seeing a Bing Crosby movie called *Holiday Inn*.

Two years later, the best-known Memphis success story made his first recording at Sun Studios. The song's refrain was "That's all right, Mama," and the singer did all right, too!

Alabamian Sam Phillips took out a ten-year lease in January 1950 and opened Memphis

The early history of rock 'n' roll was created in Sam Phillips's Sun Studio in the 1950s.

for real or imagined cheating. For crap shooting, Judge David P. Hadden devised his "Hadden horn"—a stiff leather bell-shaped device—to keep the peace. Dice were put in the narrow end and they were turned twice by two leather screens before falling onto the table.

The Pinch was a poor section of town. The *WPA Guide to Tennessee* recounts that this area in north Memphis got its name from the poor people who lived on Catfish Bay. "Pinch guts" were the skinny, malnourished people who pinched their guts with their belts. The Pinchites called

The Center of Southern Folklore features blues musicians like ninety-plus-year-old Mose from Holly Springs, Mississippi, who has seen the blues move from front porches and fields into the cities.

Recording Services. Two songs could be recorded on an acetate disc for $2.99. Howlin' Wolf recorded his first blues cut, "Moaning at Midnight" here in 1950. In 1951 Phillips recorded Jackie Brenston and the Delta Cats, with bandleader Ike Turner. That year he also recorded the first rock 'n' roll song, "Rocket '88," featuring Jackie Brenston, and the distorted guitar and back beat became a hallmark for Chess Records.

Elvis came in to record the song "That's When Your Heartaches Begin" for his mom's birthday. The secretary at Sun Studio, Marion Keisker, did the recording, asked Sam listen to it, and then nagged him for a year before Elvis was asked to come back for a professional recording session.

In 1952 Rufus Thomas recorded "Bear Cat," which sounded a lot like another tune you've heard. Does the line "You ain't nothing but a bear cat" sound familiar? In 1954 Dewey Phillips's WHBQ Red, Hot and Blue radio show introduced Elvis's "That's All Right, Mama," the product of Elvis's first professional recording session. It played fourteen times in three hours, and Phillips signed Elvis to a three-year contract. He recorded five songs before leaving in 1955. The microphone Elvis used is still in Sun Studio. You can hear the original recording, including all the goofs and Sam telling Elvis not to make it "too damn complicated" in the middle and not to get too close to the mike. Carl Perkins was outside the glass clowning around distracting everyone including Elvis.

Phillips sold Elvis's contract for forty thousand dollars to keep Sun from going bankrupt and gave Elvis five thousand dollars in royalty fees. Carl Perkins recorded "Blue Suede Shoes" here. Johnny Cash sold Marion Keisker a vacuum cleaner before being signed and recording "I Walk the Line." Cash had fastened a dollar bill to the neck of his guitar and made a scratchy sound by rubbing his fingertips back and forth across it rhythmically. Roy Orbison, who came in 1956 and stayed one year, had one hit—"ObeeDoobee." There's a famous photo in the studio of the "Million-Dollar Quartet"—Carl Perkins, Jerry Lee Lewis, Johnny Cash, and Elvis (who had only stopped by to visit).

In 1991 B. B. King returned to Beale Street to open his restaurant, B. B. King's Blues Club. In 1997 the first Elvis restaurant opened on Beale a little closer to the river.

Today the metropolitan area centered in Memphis has about 1.1 million people. We didn't have to travel as much in any other Tennessee city but no other city has so much to see. Keep in mind we can only mention main highlights; you can discover much more.

Your first stop should be the Memphis Convention and Visitors Bureau in the old Woolen Building at 47 Union Street, just up the hill from the river. It's the oldest commercial building in the city but it has all the up-to-date info about getting around Memphis.

Downtown

Blues drift up and down Beale Street, in the park, in the bars, and in one special, unpretentious spot that claims stewardship of the toe-tapping rhythms of the South, the Center for Southern Folklore. Judy Peiser, founder of the center, told us she started making films in the early 1970s about the South and the center has grown from that. "Its mission," she says, "is to preserve, defend, and protect the music, culture, arts, and rhythms of the South." Among the signs on her wall is one stating, "No black, no white, just the blues."

Experience the sights and sounds of Memphis through the seasoned eyes and ears of the Center for Southern Folklore, a private, nonprofit organization that documents the people and traditions of the South. Located in the heart of the Beale Street Historic District, the center is well known for its entertaining films and exhibits on Memphis music as well as books, recordings, and tours.

Schwab's Dry Goods Store at 163 Beale Street has such an assortment of items difficult to describe. Since 1876 this historic business has kept the people of Memphis supplied with everything from voodoo potions to suspenders. Its motto is "If you can't find it at Schwab's, you're better off without it." The store has been at this location since 1912 and is still owned by the same family. It's the only original business still on Beale Street. Take a step back in time and enjoy the blend of yesterday's dry goods with today's products.

King's Palace Cafe on Beale Street has a dark, cool interior (very important in Memphis in the summer) with soothing strains of blues and jazz

When you step into the Hunt-Phelan Home, you step into the well-preserved 1800s, and you won't want to leave.

The Woodruff-Fontaine House exhibits excellent wood craftsmanship, mannequins in period dress, and 1800s furnishings.

The Hunt-Phelan House, built in the 1800s, is east of the Blues District on Beale Street. The current heir, William B. Day Jr., lives upstairs. This house has been in the same family for more than 160 years. Downstairs, a wall mural depicts a view down the Mississippi from Memphis and most furnishings are original. There is a hidden tunnel under the hall, a place where the family hid during raids by the Chickasaw. Later the tunnel was lengthened to connect to another house on Beale Street so messages could be carried during the Civil War. Fireplace screens are interesting; they served to protect the ladies' wax-based make-up. Gasolier chandeliers were installed in 1832 and the estate had its own gas plant using resins and cottonseed.

During the Yankee occupation, U. S. Grant used the parlor as his receiving room and the library as his office. Grant planned the battle of Vicksburg on the mahogany table in the library. Another famous visitor to the house was Jefferson Davis.

The dining table can serve up to twenty people and is made of carved pieces of Cuban mahogany (now extinct). Many sterling silver pieces were part of a collection commissioned by King George III. The hand-carved four-poster bed stayed in a packing crate in the attic from 1880 until 1993 when restoration began. It was a one-hundred-year-old antique when purchased in 1880. In another bedroom, the bed traveled in the boxcar of furniture the lady of the house carried around the South during the war.

The Woodruff-Fontaine House, at 680 Adams Avenue, was built in 1870 by Amos Woodruff in a Second Empire-style. Woodruff, his wife and four children lived here from 1871 until 1883. The yellow fever is responsible for him selling the home to Noland Fontaine, who

in the background, photos on the walls of blues legends, cold beer on tap, crab cakes and gumbo to die for. Its signature breakfast is Creole-style shrimp and grits. The taproom has more than one hundred different beers. Across the street are the two faces of Silky O'Sullivan's—inside kind of crazy and wild, with the outside a quieter garden setting with live music.

lived here 46 years. He and his wife raised eight children here.

The house was used as part of the James Lee Art Academy for a while, then left vacant to be vandalized. In 1964 the home was restored and opened to the public.

If you enjoy seeing fine old craftsmanship, you will certainly find this home worthwhile. The two doors in the hall are solid mahogany from France and one of the doors opens into a blank wall. It was put there for a cosmetic purpose, to balance the door on the other side of the central hall. Inside the blind door are the signatures of the craftsmen. We weren't sensitive enough to feel the presence of the resident ghost who resides in Molly Woodruff's bedroom. We were told it is a female and has been heard crying.

Across from DeSoto Park is the National Ornamental Metal Museum, the only museum in the United States dedicated to preserving the art and craftsmanship of metalworking. Changing exhibitions range from jewelry and hollowware in precious metals, to architectural wrought iron. It has a working blacksmith shop on the grounds overlooking the Mississippi River. It holds Repair Days during October for the public to bring in items for estimates and repairs.

Be sure to study the ornamental iron gates as you enter the property; there are many surprises on them. These are the Anniversary Gates made in scroll and rosette components to represent more than 180 metalsmiths from eighteen nations. They were designed in Surrey, England, to commemorate the museum's tenth anniversary.

In the 1930s the Peabody Hotel general manager, Frank Schutt, placed his live hunting decoys in the lobby fountain and started a tradition. Today the Peabody ducks have become a world-famous symbol for the hotel and for Memphis

hospitality. Every day at precisely 11 A.M., the ducks arrive, marching on their own red carpet to John Philip Sousa's "King Cotton March." The fanfare repeats at 5 P.M. when they retire to their penthouse pond. Throngs of spectators gather daily in the mornings and evenings to witness this charming tradition in the spectacular Grand Lobby of the Peabody Hotel in downtown Memphis. Don't miss it, but get there early for a good view.

The Memphis Music Hall of Fame at 97 Second Street was collected by John Montague, a Memphis attorney. Don't be surprised by the unpretentious facade. It's a wonderful place to immerse yourself in the music of Memphis. The Memphis Music Hall of Fame has more than seven thousand square feet of exhibits containing thousands of photos, rare recordings, and twenty video and six continuous audio presentations. Biographies of all Memphis legends are displayed with original instruments and personal effects. It has the largest collection of W. C. Handy memorabilia in the world, the largest collection of Elvis Presley memorabilia outside of Graceland, the complete collection of personal memorabilia of Charlie Rich, and an extensive exhibit of STAX and HI record-label memorabilia, including very rare video tapes by major STAX and HI artists. The museum houses artists and artifacts in large glass cases that you walk among to look and listen.

Now let's go to the Sun Studio at 706 Union Avenue. The birthplace of rock 'n' roll was opened by Sam Phillips in 1950. Today the studio is open to the public for tours daily while still operating as a studio by night.

Next to Sun Studio is Sun Studio Cafe and the third table is where Sam Phillips signed contracts. The cafe serves beer, milkshakes, freshly squeezed lemonade, burgers, fries, grilled cheese, and in honor of the King, a grilled peanut butter and banana sandwich. Above the cafe is a new museum/gallery featuring hundreds of rare recordings, memorabilia, photographs, and vintage recording equipment. The Gallery is complementary to the studio tour.

Just west and one street north of the Sun Studio area is the Overton Park District. Overton Park, built in the 1930s is a 355-acre park with 100 acres of old-growth forest, a memorial to John Overton, a golf course, the Brooks Museum, and the zoo.

The Memphis Brooks Museum of Art was erected in 1926 and given to the city by Mrs. Samuel Brooks in memory of her husband. It has one of the most comprehensive collections of Western art in the South. This is Tennessee's oldest and largest museum of fine and decorative arts, and it includes sculptures, prints, drawings, and photographs from antiquity to the present. There is no admission to the Brooks collections but there are occasional charges for special exhibitions. Signing for the deaf is provided with advance notice.

Mississippi River Area

Mud Island, now owned by the city of Memphis, grew from sediment settling at the stern of a boat anchored in place for about seven months during low water. The boat departed, leaving a small sand bar. During a succession of high-water periods, the island grew, and the flood of 1913 caused it to add twenty-five feet of elevation. River shanties and river "gypsies," inhabited the island off and on. In 1919 Memphis became the owner of the island.

Today you can ride the overhead tram from Memphis to Mud Island and back. On the island you can walk in the concrete reconstruction of the river. The thousand-mile journey of the lower Mississippi is reproduced in a half-mile-long con-

crete sculpture with a scale of thirty inches to one mile. The vertical scale is one inch to eight feet. The river system is made of 1,746 precast concrete panels, each weighing five tons. Mud Island has picnic tables, benches, fountains, and an outdoor swimming pool.

Also on Mud Island is a pavilion sheltering the *Memphis Belle,* a World War II B-17 bomber that was the first U.S. bomber to complete twenty-five missions against Nazi targets without a casualty.

Mud Island also has an excellent museum with eighteen galleries covering ten thousand years of history. Among its displays are Indian canoes, log rafts from 1780, flatboats of the 1800s, keelboats from 1815, and steam-powered side-wheelers.

The Memphis Queen Line at 45 South Riverside Drive has paddle wheelers for sightseeing cruises that last 1.5 hours on the Mississippi River. The pilot provides commentaries on the city and its history. All vessels are inspected and certified by the U.S. Coast Guard. There is limited wheelchair access and complimentary information booklets for those who are hearing impaired.

Adjacent to the Pyramids, the Pinch Historic District runs on North Main Street from the Memphis Cook Convention Center to North Parkway. It has become the newest entertainment area in downtown Memphis, with restaurants/bars featuring live entertainment every weekend. The restaurants have great menus serving luncheon specials, a wide selection of sandwiches, and unbeatable desserts. You can find the largest selection of bottled and draft imported beers in Memphis on "the Pinch." Visit one of these great places: High Point Pinch, the North End, the Pizza Place, T. J. Mulligan's, 78 Overton, the Pinch Station, and Pig 'n' the Pinch. The Pinch District also has an antique area.

The National Civil Rights Museum at 450

The scale model of the Mississippi River runs along Mud Island, emptying into a large swimming pool.

Mulberry Street is the world's first museum dedicated to the lessons of the American civil rights movement. It is housed at the site of the Lorraine Motel, where Dr. Martin Luther King Jr. was assassinated. Exhibits and interactive displays trace the history of civil rights activity and of its leaders.

The Children's Museum of Memphis at 2525 Central Avenue is a discovery museum for children and their families. It provides interactive exhibits and programs within a child-sized city. Climb aboard a real police motorcycle. Become a dentist as you work on a puppet's teeth. Shop for groceries in a miniature grocery store. The museum is adjacent to Liberty Bowl Memorial Stadium.

Midtown

Located in historic Midtown is the revitalized Cooper-Young neighborhood, one of the city's most diverse areas. The district features shops,

boutiques, and galleries with a collection of unique art, gift items, clothing, and memorabilia. Popular restaurants and coffeehouses offer a variety of international cuisines. Child-care services are available also. While you're in Cooper-Young, be sure to check out the First Church of the Elvis Impersonator.

South

Operated by the University of Memphis Department of Anthropology, Chucalissa (meaning "abandoned house") is a reconstruction of a prehistoric Native-American village dating to the fifteenth century A.D. and includes a museum, earthworks, and village. Choctaw staff members provide guided tours and demonstrate crafts. The entrance to Chucalissa is a museum that contains many artifacts, giving you an idea of the time period the village was alive.

Graceland is a long way from Elvis's first shotgun home in Tupelo, Mississippi.

This long-abandoned site, called *Chucalissa* by the Choctaw, was rediscovered by the Civilian Conservation Corps in the 1930s. Initial archaeological testing by the University of Tennessee took place in the 1940s; it was established as a state park in 1955 and is now operated by Memphis State University.

The town was occupied and abandoned several times between A.D. 1000 and 1500. During its last occupation it may have had fifteen hundred inhabitants. They left no written records and disappeared before Europeans arrived.

What has been determined through archaeology is that the people were farmers, built permanent houses, held religious and political ceremonies, and had skilled craftsmen. The community had four social levels. The Chief and his family and the craftsmen were top of the order, secondary chiefs and priests were next, ordinary citizens were the third order, and captives taken in warfare who were adopted into the community made up the fourth class.

There are displays on weaving, herbal medicines, and Chucalissa pottery including incised bowls and jars, as well as hunchback human effigy bottles. Outside at the top of the largest mound there is a diorama of a peace ceremony that is a composite of historic accounts and archaeological record. You can walk the Chickasaw Bluff Interpretive Trail behind the largest mound.

Also south of Memphis is Elvis Presley's Graceland. It was once in the middle of horse country but now is in the midst of urban sprawl. Evidence of Elvis's timeless appeal is seen in the children visiting Graceland who were born after Elvis died in 1977. He moved here in the spring of 1957 but the southern Colonial-style residence was originally built in 1939. Elvis bought the house and 13.8 acres for one hundred thousand dollars. Graceland is a long way from the shotgun house where he lived as a child in Tupelo, Mississippi.

The house is handicapped accessible except for the basement portions. There are self-guided audio tours in Dutch, French, German, Italian, Japanese, Portuguese, Spanish, and English. You stand in lines across the street waiting for shuttles to the mansion.

East

Clarence Saunders, who made a fortune conceiving the forerunner of today's supermarkets, began building a mansion but went bankrupt. The city of Memphis ended up with what is called the Pink Palace. At 3050 Central Avenue, it is a multifaceted facility that includes award-winning natural and cultural history exhibits, a planetarium, and an IMAX theater.

The Piggly Wiggly exhibit in the Pink Palace is a full-scale replica of the self-serve grocery that opened September 11, 1916, in downtown Memphis. Shelves have authentic cans of products by manufacturers that still are household names, such as Libby, Campbell, Lipton, Crisco, Quaker, Kellogg, Aunt Jemima, Jell-O, and Hershey. The idea caught on and Piggly Wiggly expanded to 1,241 stores by 1922 but a battle for control of Piggly Wiggly stock with Wall Street businessmen

resulted in Saunders's bankruptcy. Saunders was building the pink Georgian marble structure at the time. A realty company purchased it and donated it to the city in 1926. It was converted to the Museum of Arts and Industry in 1930. The Pink Palace Mansion, built in 1923 is the site of the original museum that reopened in the spring of 1996.

As you walk through the museum you will find a medical history exhibit, Civil War artifacts, and a Triceratops dinosaur. The natural history exhibits include skulls and skeletons of birds, reptiles, mammals, and snakes. There are interactive exhibits on human cells and a quarter brings the dinosaur to life (it moves, eats, and looks around). You'll see fossils from 700 to 485 million years ago, when the mid-South was covered by water. The museum traces twelve thousand years of man's activities in the region. You shouldn't go to

The most interesting museum in Memphis is the Pink Palace, built by Clarence Saunders, founder of Piggly Wiggly.

Memphis without spending time in the Pink Palace to learn about the history of the city.

The Memphis Botanic Garden at 750 Cherry Road has ninety-six acres of outdoor gardens. The Goldsmith Civic Garden Center features a Boehm porcelain collection, art exhibitions, horticultural shows, and a plant information library.

Lichterman Nature Center at 5992 Quince Road is a sixty-five-acre environmental education facility and wildlife sanctuary. It is the first accredited nature center in the United States and is listed in the National Register of Historic Places.

The Dixon Gallery and Gardens at 4339 Park Avenue is one of the country's finest small museums. It features a collection of eighteenth- and nineteenth-century British paintings, French and American Impressionist art, and Meissen porcelain. The gardens are gorgeous year-round.

Main Street Trolley is the way to visit sites in the downtown area from the Pyramid to Central Station. Riding the refurbished antique trolley cars costs fifty cents one way and saves your energy for sightseeing rather than walking.

For all these places and things we've mentioned to see and do, there are many more waiting for you to discover in Memphis.

All of the following accommodations are Memphis with zip code 38103, and all telephone listings are area code 901, except where noted.

Accommodations:
Peabody Hotel, 149 Union Ave, 800-PEABODY or 529-4000.
Talbort Heirs Guesthouse, 99 S. Second St., 527-9772.

Attractions:
A. Schwab Dry Goods Store, 523-9782.
Art Museum of the University of Memphis, 678-2224.
Beale Street Historic District, 526-0110.
Center for Southern Folklore, 525-3655.
Children's Museum of Memphis, 458-2678.

Chucalissa Archaeological Museum, 785-3160.
The Dixon Gallery and Gardens, 761-5250.
Elmwood Cemetery, 774-3212.
Graceland, 800-238-2000 or 332-3322.
Hunt-Phelan home, 800-350-9009 or 344-3166.
IMAX theater, Pink Palace Museum, 320-6320 or 320-6362.
Institute of Egyptian Art and Archaeology, 678-2555.
Lichterman Nature Center, 767-7322.
Main Street Trolley, 577-2640.
Mallory-Neely House, 523-1484.
Magevney House, 523-1484.
Memphis Belle Pavilion, 800-507-6507 or 576-7241.
Memphis Botanic Garden, 38117-4699; 685-1566.
Memphis Brooks Museum of Art, 722-3500.
Memphis Music Hall of Fame, 525-4007.
Memphis Queen Line, 800-221-6197 or 527-5694.
Memphis Zoo and Aquarium, 800-288-8763 or 276-WILD.
Mud Island, 800-507-6507.
National Civil Rights Museum, 521-9699.
National Ornamental Metal Museum, 374 Metal Museum Dr.; 774-6380.
Orpheum Theatre, 525-7800.
Overton Square, 272-1495.
Peabody Hotel, 529-4000.
Pinch Historic District, 525-4444.
The Pyramid, 521-9675, 526-5177.
Slave Haven-Burkle Estate, 527-3427.
Sun Studio, 521-0664.
W. C. Handy House Museum, 522-1556.
Woodruff-Fontaine House, 526-1469.

Dining:
Anderton's Steak and Seafood Restaurant, 726-4010.
Automatic Slims Tonga Club, 525-7948.
B. B. King's Blues Club, 800-443-8959 or 524-5464.
The Bar-B-Q Shop, 272-1277.
Bayou Bar and Grill, 278-8626.
Blues City Cafe, 526-3637.
Boscos Pizza Kitchen and Brewery, 756-7310.
Chez Philippe, Peabody Hotel, 800-PEABODY or 529-4000.
Ciao Baby Cucina, 529-0560. 529-0406 for bakery.
The Cupboard Two, 527-9111.
Elvis Presley's Memphis, 800-238-2000.
Rendezvous, 523-2746.
Run Boogie Cafe, 528-0150.
78 Overton, 526-4038.
Silky O'Sullivan's, 522-9596.

Special Events:
This is a partial list of hundreds of events. Call 543-5333 for a booklet of all this year's special events.
January—Elvis Presley Birthday Bash
February—Martin Luther King Jr. Day; Black History Month
March—Memphis Flea Market (the BIG one); Emerald Isle Shenanigans, St. Patrick's Day at Magevney House; St.

Patrick's Day in the Pinch, High Point Pinch; Spring Tour for Seniors. Brooks Museum

April—Dr. Martin Luther King Jr. Memorial March; Big (Vintage) Car Show, Cooper-Young District; Africa in April Cultural Awareness Festival

May—Memphis in May

First weekend: Beale Street Music Festival

Second weekend: More music and related cultural events, arts and crafts

Third weekend: Barbecue contest

Fourth weekend: Sunset Symphony and fireworks in Tom Lee Park; Memphis Cotton Makers Jubilee; Victorian May Pole Day Festivities at Woodruff-Fontaine House

May—W. C. Handy Blues Awards

June—Ducks Unlimited Great Outdoor Sporting & Wildlife Festival; Carnival Memphis Crown and Sceptre Coronation Ball; Perennial Symposium at Memphis Botanical Gardens; Native American Pow Wow at Shelby Farms; Zoo Arts Festival at the zoo

July—Independence Day Fireworks Dinner Cruise on Memphis Queen riverboats; Hollywood Flea Market; Summer Nights at Lichterman Nature Center; Memphis Music and Heritage Festival at Center for Southern Folklore

August—Choctaw Cultural Festival, Chucalissa Archaeological Village; Elvis Week at Graceland; Labor Day Fest in Beale Street District; Memphis Blues Festival

September—Labor Day Festival; Mid-South Fair; Southern Heritage Classic; Goat Days Family Festival; Cordova Arts & Crafts Festival

October—Pink Palace Crafts Fair; Arts in the Park; Zoo Boo, kids in the Memphis Zoo

November—Christmas at Graceland until January; Starry Nights at Shelby Farms

December—St. Jude Liberty Bowl; Beale Street New Year Eve's Bash

Camping:

Elvis Presley Boulevard RV Park, 3971 Elvis Presley Blvd., 38116; 332-3633. 85 sites, electricity, dumping station, showers, phone. Open year-round.

Leahy's RV Park, 3070 Summer Ave., 38112; 452-7456. 50 sites, electricity, toilets, dumping station, pool, shower, groceries, phone. Open year-round.

Memphis Graceland KOA, 3691 Elvis Presley Blvd., 38116; 800-562-9386 or 396-7125. 72 sites, 4 cabins, electricity, showers, toilets, dumping station, pool, groceries, grills, phone.

Mississippi River RV Park, 870 Cotton Gin Pl., 38106; 800-827-1714 or 946-1993. 31 sites, electricity, shower, dumping station, groceries.

For More Information:

Memphis Convention and Visitors Bureau, 47 Union Ave., 543-5300.

Visitor Information Center, 340 Beale St., 543-5333.

 # Loop 12

78 T.O. Fuller State Park
Fun South of Memphis

One of the first four state parks of the Tennessee Department of Conservation, in 1937 T. O. Fuller was the first state park east of the Mississippi River open to blacks and only the second in the nation. The 384-acre park was named to honor Dr. Thomas Oscar Fuller (1867-1942), a prominent clergyman, educator, and exponent of interracial cooperation.

During the excavation for a proposed swimming pool in 1940, CCC workers unearthed evidence of a prehistoric village, opening the door to a lost and forgotten civilization. As the magnitude of the discovery became apparent, an ambitious project to reconstruct the village was launched. The site has since been developed as Chucalissa Indian Village and is under the management of the University of Memphis.

The park is situated just inside the city limits in the southwest sector of the city. It is on Mitchell Road, three miles west of US 61 (or Third Street), ten miles south of the downtown area. T. O. Fuller is near Interstates 40, 55, and 240 and is in close proximity to the many Memphis attractions.

For overnight use, the park offers fifty-three campsites, which are open all year. This is a popular campground due to the park's proximity to metropolitan Memphis. Each site has a table, grill, electrical and water hookups.

The swimming pool is centrally located in the main recreation area of the park and is served by a bathhouse and concession stand. It is open from early summer to Labor Day, and lifeguards are on duty during swimming hours.

For More Information:
T. O. Fuller State Park, 1500 Mitchell Rd. W., 38109; 901-543-7581.

79 Covington
North of the Delta

From Memphis take US 51 north for about thirty-five miles to the third-largest city in western Tennessee, Covington in Tipton County.

West Tennessee was part of the Chickasaw Nation until 1818, when the territory was opened to settlement under treaties with the Indians. The area was divided into five districts by the legislature in 1819. The first county in the Western District was Shelby, which was organized as the Village of Chickasaw Bluff in 1819.

Tipton County, formed from Shelby County in 1823, was named for Capt. Jacob Tipton who was killed while leading his men against Indians near Fort Wayne in 1791.

Due west of Covington via TN 59 on the bluff was Randolph. On April 23, 1861, Gov. Isham Harris ordered Lt. Col. Marcus Wright, stationed in Memphis, to go north of Randolph to take a defensive position on the Mississippi River. The next day Colonel Wright arrived at Randolph with a battalion of men with artillery. During the next four months five thousand Confederate forces gathered in the Fort Wright-

Tipton County Courthouse, on the square in Covington's Historic District.

Randolph area. Their mission was to fortify the Chickasaw Bluffs with artillery batteries and earthen field defenses to guard against the expected Union naval-military invasion.

From late April through July of 1861, Fort Wright served as the forwardmost defensive position on the Mississippi River that represented the left flank of the Provisional Army of Tennessee. If the Union had come down that corridor as expected, the battle would have taken place there (*see* Memphis for battle of Memphis).

A training place, Fort Wright was one of Tennessee's first attempts to build fortifications. The Confederates set up river batteries and heavy artillery to defend the Mississippi but they didn't have time to sharpen their skills. The process of military discipline began here to produce soldiers from raw recruits who were farm boys, students, and young men from the streets of Memphis. The

process succeeded. Some of the recruits would make the Army of Tennessee famous at Shiloh, Belmont, Murfreesboro, Chickamauga, Franklin, and Bentonville. Fort Wright formed the future of two lieutenant generals, Alexander P. Stewart and Nathan Bedford Forrest.

By 1862 Confederate infantry forces had evacuated the Randolph area. Southern naval and cavalry forces occupied the site on an irregular basis. In the fall of 1862, a squad of irregular Confederate soldiers fired into the steamer *Belle of St. Louis* that was docked at the landing. No damage was done but Gen. William T. Sherman retaliated by having Randolph burned except for an old church and one dwelling. The Union soldiers carried a sick elderly lady out into her yard on her bed and set her house on fire. The two remaining buildings in Randolph were destroyed by fire in 1865.

All that remains of Randolph today is the powder magazine dug by the Confederates at Fort Wright. It is the only remaining Civil War powder magazine in Tennessee. The brick magazine was built underground to keep fire away from it. The state is trying to buy the land around it so it can be affiliated with Fort Pillow State Historic Site about six miles to the north.

Covington is a growing, prosperous town. It has four parks ranging from eighty acres with developed areas to a one-acre garden park with gazebo rentals for wedding or picnics. The Tipton County Bar-B-Que Festival is held each year in Cobb-Parr Park. More than twenty-five thousand people swarm into Covington for a three-day event that produces the best 'que in the South. Each July the event features music, games, arts and crafts, a truck pull, demolition derby, and barbecue.

The Art Deco Ruffin Theatre is used for community plays, Germantown Symphony Orchestra, the Memphis Ballet Troupe, and other cultural performances. Originally this was the Palace Theatre built in 1927. In 1934 W. F. Ruffin converted it into West Tennessee's most modern playhouse.

The theater was very popular in the 1940s and 1950s, but it lost its luster when television boomed. In 1980 the Tipton Fine Arts Council bought the theater and restored it.

South Main Historic District consists of fifty-two homes and other structures, including the Ruffin Theater, the Tipton County Courthouse, and Hotel Lindo, to total seventy-five sites built in the late 1800s and early 1900s. The area is listed in the National Register of Historic Places. The public may tour many of the homes during the Annual Heritage Day Festival on the last Sunday in September.

Fort Pillow is northwest of Covington via US 51, then turn west on TN 87.

All of the following accommodations are Covington with zip code 38019, and all telephone listings are area code 901, except where noted.

Accommodations:
Havenhall Farm Bed and Breakfast, Inc., 183 Houston Gordon Rd., 476-7226.

Attractions:
Ruffin Theater, 476-9727.
South Main Historic District, 476-1619.
Tipton County Veterans Museum, 476-1107.

Dining:
51 Steak House, 476-3108.
Anne Cooks for You, 476-2663.
Country Kitchen, 476-1591.
Craig's Bar-B-Que, 476-2897.
Hazel's Restaurant, 476-4481.
Little Porky's Pit B-B-Q, 476-7165.
Isacc Elam Cafe, 476-1323.
Miss Tiny's Restaurant, 476-4662.
Papa's Country Catfish, 475-1405.
Side Street Pizza, 476-8167.
Veanos Italian Restaurant, 475-2110.

Shopping:
Gift Gallery, 476-4438.
The Rose Garden, 476-2662.

Special Events:
May—Spring Fling Golf Tournament
June—Frazier Park Fun Festival
July—BBQ Festival
September—Tipton County Fair; Heritage Day Festival
October—Great Pumpkin Patch Halloween Festival

For More Information:
Covington/Tipton County Chamber of Commerce, P.O. Box 683; 476-9727.

80 *Meeman-Shelby Forest State Park*
On the Third Chickasaw Bluff

Meeman-Shelby Forest State Park is located thirteen miles north of Memphis near Millington in Shelby County. From Memphis go north on US 51 to TN 388 and follow the signs.

The Mississippi River flows along the western boundary, and the developed sections of the park sit atop the Chickasaw Bluffs. They were formed from wind-blown silt and dust, called loess, deposited in ancient times. The bluffs and the river bottoms below are rich in Indian lore and one of the finest arrays of plant and animal life in the state. The park includes two fishing lakes, both with boat launch areas. Scenic drives along the third Chickasaw Bluff reveal upland hardwood and bottomland forests.

The late Edward J. Meeman, for whom the park was named, was a Memphis newspaper editor and an avid conservationist who was also helpful in establishing this site as well as the Great Smoky Mountains National Park in East Tennessee. The park has six two-bedroom cabins along the shore of Poplar Tree Lake in a heavily wooded section. The campground contains fifty campsites, each equipped with a table, grill, and electric and water hookups. A bathhouse provides hot showers, restroom facilities, and dumping station. Scattered throughout the park are three hundred picnic tables and grills.

Johnboats are available for rent at the park's boat dock on Poplar Tree Lake, but many enjoy fishing from the bank or the fishing pier. Personally owned boats with electric motors are allowed on the lake for a small launching fee, but gasoline motors are not allowed. Some outstanding largemouth bass have been caught. Other species include bream and catfish. A park fishing permit

Meeman-Shelby Forest State Park swimming area, on Poplar Tree Lake.

is required as well as a state license or permit.

There are more than twenty miles of hiking and horseback trails weaving through the park and some run along the Mississippi River. Horses are available for rent at the park stables, or you can bring your own mount and ride the established bridle paths. Horses are permitted only on trails specifically marked for equestrian use.

A nature center containing many natural history exhibits and displays is open during the summer months, and at other times by appointment. The center features woodland and wetland exhibits as well as historical displays.

Go back to US 51 and head for Covington.

For More Information:
Meeman-Shelby Forest State Park, Box 10, Grassey Lake Road, Millington, 38053-5099; 901-876-5215.

81 *Fort Pillow State Historic Park*
Controversy on Chickasaw Bluff Number One

Fort Pillow was occupied throughout most of the War Between the States by Union or Confederate forces. The fortification was named after Gen. Gideon J. Pillow, a Mexican War hero from Maury County. Early during the war, the Confederacy saw the need for defending against a Union invasion of the south by way of the Mississippi River. Fort Pillow was one of several fortifications constructed as part of a river defense system.

The fort was built on Chickasaw Bluff No. 1 overlooking the river. Batteries of cannons were constructed facing the river. An extensive system of breastworks was dug for the protection of the river batteries in case of land attack. During the war the fort's river batteries were close to the river, but since the war the river has moved a mile west.

The Union navy did launch an invasion on the river. Following the fall of Island No. 10 and other Confederate losses to the north and east of Fort Pillow, the main U.S. Navy flotilla on the Mississippi River proceeded to work its way downriver. On May 10, 1862, they met the Confederate River Defense Fleet in the naval battle of

Fort Pillow was named for a Mexican War hero.

Plum Point Bend, within sight of Fort Pillow. The Confederate gunboats were victorious, but the Union gunboats were soon able to proceed downriver and attack Memphis a month later.

During the spring and early summer of 1862 the Union navy bombarded Fort Pillow from its mortar boats. Few casualties resulted, but with the increasing danger of being cut off from the main army, the Confederate army evacuated Fort Pillow in June 1862. Union forces immediately occupied the fort and held it for almost two years.

On April 12, 1864, Confederate Gen. Nathan Bedford Forrest and approximately 1,500 Confederate soldiers attacked Fort Pillow. The Union garrison, commanded by Maj. Lionel F. Booth, was manned by approximately 550 soldiers, almost half being black troops. The Confederates were able to gain a commanding position on the field of battle, and General Forrest asked for surrender, which Major Bradford refused. The Confederates then stormed the fort and overran it. After April 12, 1864, neither Union nor Confederate forces occupied Fort Pillow. Because of high Union casualties and the presence of black Union troops, controversy surrounding this battle still exists today. It has been charged that the black soldiers were unnecessarily killed. Fort Pillow State Historic Park is located approximately sixty miles north of Memphis overlooking the Mississippi River. This 1,646-acre park is rich in historical and archaeological significance.

The Frank Gardner Memorial Interpretive Center contains displays of Civil War artifacts and interpretive materials relating to Fort Pillow's role in the Civil War. This location on the First Chickasaw Bluff is one of West Tennessee's most beautiful sites. From this point, one may observe a panoramic view of the Mississippi River with its river traffic. A five-hundred-acre oxbow lake shows how the river has changed course , and Osceola, Arkansas, can be seen across the river. The overlook is accessible by automobile, and picnic tables are available.

The rustic campground has forty sites and is designed primarily for tent camping, although pop-ups, pickups, small trailers, and RVs are accommodated. Two modern bathhouses with hot showers and restroom facilities and a laundry are centrally located. Water faucets are available, but there are no electrical hookups. A small camping area on the Chickasaw Bluff State Scenic Trail can only be reached by hiking. It overlooks the Mississippi River with a panoramic view for miles up and down the river. The site provides campers with water, fire rings, and an old-fashioned outhouse.

Fort Pillow Lake's twenty-five acres are stocked with bass, bream, catfish, and crappie. A boat ramp is available but there are no rental boats. Visitors may launch their own boats and may use an electric trolling motor, but no gasoline motors.

Go back to US 51 and go east to Henning on TN 87.

For More Information:
Fort Pillow State Historic Park, Rt. 2, Box 109 A, Henning, 38041; 901-738-5581.

82 *Henning, Ripley, Dyersburg*
Rich Farm Lands

Henning is seven miles north of Covington just off US 51. Turn right on TN 209 past the rest area. After visiting the Alex Haley home, continue seven miles north on TN 209 to Ripley. From Ripley take TN 208 to US 51 and go twenty miles to Dyersburg.

Dyer County grew into a county from the Western District in 1823 and was named in honor of Andrew Jackson's friend Col. Henry Dyer. Dyer served with Jackson in several military campaigns.

Henning became a known spot on Tennessee's map after Alex Haley's book *Roots* reached television as a miniseries. Haley first heard the story of his ancestors from his grandmother, while sitting on her front porch. Kunte Kinte, Chicken George, and Kizzy made interesting stories to young Haley but his retelling captured millions of readers' and viewers' attention.

From TN 209 in Henning turn left (west) on Haley Avenue at the sign for the home, and go a few blocks to the corner of Haley Avenue and Church Street. The ten-room house, built in 1918 by Haley's grandfather, Will Palmer, is now a museum. Haley's books are for sale and you can see how the house looked when he was a child and look at some of his personal items. Alex Haley is buried in front of the home.

The Choctaw Indian Festival is held in Henning each October to demonstrate dances, songs, games, culture, skills, and traditions. It is sponsored by American Indian Affairs.

Ripley, home of the Tomato War, was founded in 1835. The Chickasaw Indians called the area "nearer heaven" because the land is higher here than most of the surrounding area. But Ripley's first charter of 1838 was repealed in 1901 to outline the town better. The new charter stated, "...thence 85 degrees east to a black gum marked with a cross and with mistletoe in the top, and with a blue bird sitting on a limb, which is a short distance east of Ed Johnson's horse lot...."

Each year this agricultural community takes

This is Lauderdale County Court-house in Ripley, which is the home of the annual Tomato War.

Alex Haley, the author of Roots, *spent many hours listening to stories about his ancestors at his grandparents' home in Henning.*

pride in holding the annual Lauderdale County Tomato Festival to honor a major agricultural product of the county. This three-day affair held the first weekend in July offers music, entertainment, barbecue, shooting contests, and a tomato war. Juice and seeds elsewhere on the body are just wounds. A limited number of tomatoes are allowed so things don't get out of hand. It's a lot of fun!

Dyersburg was established in 1826 as the county seat and the first courthouse was a two-story log building. It was replaced in 1836 by a wood frame courthouse. The third courthouse, built of brick in 1850, was burned by the Union army in 1864. The present, and fifth courthouse, was built in 1912 and is in the National Register of Historic Places. Dyersburg is one of the largest cities in northwest Tennessee, set amid rich farm lands.

At Dyersburg State Community College is the Dr. Walter E. David Wildlife Museum. It contains a species of every kind of duck on the Mississippi Flyway. Also there are displays of kodiak and polar bears, African animals, and animals from other areas. Dyersburg Army Air Base at Halls was active from 1942 to 1945. Once a World War II B-17 training facility, it now is a ninety-five-acre apron, one hangar, and an active runway.

From Dyersburg take TN 78 for about twenty-three miles to Tiptonville.

All of the following accommodations are Dyersburg with zip code 38025, and all telephone listings are area code 901, except where noted.

Accommodations:
Aunt Ginny's Bed and Breakfast, 520 Sampson Ave., 285-2028.

Attractions:
Dr. Walter E. David Wildlife Museum, Dyersburg State Community College, 285-3200.
Haley House Museum, Henning, 738-2240.
Lauderdale Cellars, Ripley, 635-4321.

Dining:
Abe's Rib Eye Barn, 285-4648.

Blue & White Cafe, Ripley, 635-1471.
Broadway Pizza, Ripley, 635-5300.
Catfish Plus, Ripley, 635-7570.
City Cafe, Henning, 738-1112.
Grecian Steak House, 285-6842.
Mary Lou's Airport Restaurant, 285-1598.
Neil's Barbecue & Grill, 285-2628.
Taco Casa, 286-2272.

Shopping:
Antiques and Things.
Candlewick Antiques, 285-2329.
Dyersburg Antique Gallery, 285-0999.
Dyersburg Flea Market, 286-6739.
Mike's Antiques, 287-8663.
Walton's Antiques, 287-7086.

Special Events:
February—Black History Month, Henning
April—Dogwood Festival, Dyersburg
July—Tomato Festival, Ripley; Jimmy Dean Foods Barbecue
   Festival, Dyersburg
September—County Fair, Dyersburg
October—Choctaw Indian Festival, Henning
December—Annual Christmas Parade, Dyersburg

For More Information:
Dyersburg/Dyer County Chamber of Commerce, P.O. Box
   906, 285-3433.
Lauderdale County Chamber of Commerce, 103 E. Jackson
   Ave., Ripley, 38063; 635-9541.

83 *Reelfoot Lake, Tiptonville, Samburg*
Earthquake Lake

Tiptonville, chosen as the county seat of Lake County in 1870, was dubbed the Town on Wheels because it was destroyed twice: once by Union gunboats that fired on the town during the War Between the States and the second time by the Mississippi River, which flooded the town. Tiptonville was rebuilt on higher ground after the flood. William Tipton built the first store in the original town of Tiptonville in 1857.

Thirty-five years after the Declaration of Independence was signed reports circulated that a catastrophe had occurred in the Mississippi Valley and a great lake had been formed in the Indian country. The New Madrid earthquake, we now believe, rivaled the strongest quakes in history.

A walkway lets you stroll among Reelfoot Lake's cypress trees and is a good way to watch wildlife.

When its shockwaves rocked North and South America late in 1811, the force was centered in the Reelfoot Lake area, which was then a huge cypress forest. On December 16 the earth's surface rose and sank, and the bottom of the nearby Mississippi River went wild. The river flowed backward and poured into the open fault. Land and forests slid down the bluffs, and more than fifteen thousand acres of forest land sank beneath the river to a depth of twenty feet.

Cypress trees and willow flourished, but other trees died. Today nearly two-century-old trunks remain in one of the world's greatest natural fish hatcheries.

The lake is named for a clubfooted Indian chief of the Chickasaw Tribe. In the legend, the chief is blamed for the earthquake. Chief Reelfoot was in love with an Indian maiden who lived south along the Mississippi River. She repulsed his offer of marriage because of Reelfoot's clubfoot. In revenge, he set out with some of his braves in canoes, raided her father's camp at night, and kidnapped the girl. Medicine men disapproved of Reelfoot's act and predicted it would bring disaster to his people. The earthquake that wiped out the tribe and formed the lake fulfilled their predictions, it was said.

The Reelfoot area is rich in Civil War history. Battles raged across fields now under cultivation. Minié balls, cannon balls, and similar items are still plowed up from time to time. Upriver, at Columbus, Kentucky, a huge chain was forged and placed across the river to block the Union fleet, a futile effort. Ten thousand soldiers of the Confederate army surrendered at Tiptonville. The important battle of Island No. 10 was fought eight miles north of Tiptonville and cleared the way for the Union takeover of Memphis and, ultimately,

Sweet Dreams Cottage in Tiptonville is convenient to Reelfoot Lake.

the entire river.

Reelfoot Lake State Park, in the northwest corner of Tennessee, is one of the greatest hunting and fishing preserves in the nation. The park encompasses twenty-five thousand acres (fifteen thousand are water) and harbors almost every kind of shore and wading bird, as well as the golden and American bald eagles. Other animals are also diverse and abundant here. Its many species of flowering and nonflowering plants attract botany enthusiasts from all over the country. Cypress dominates the margins of the lake, but many other trees and shrubs are also present.

Reelfoot Lake State Park has two hundred eighty acres broken into ten segments located along twenty-two miles of the Reelfoot Lake shoreline. The Airpark Inn resort complex is located on State Highway 78, ten miles north of Tiptonville. The other sections of the park include the visitor and interpretive center with an auditorium, and picnic and camping areas located along TN 21 and TN 22.

Reelfoot's twenty-unit Airpark Inn and Restaurant, open on a seasonal basis, are situated over the lake among cypress trees. For those who wish to fly in, Reelfoot offers a thirty-five-hundred-foot, lighted, all-weather landing strip adjacent to the inn. The park also provides a five-unit motel at the Reelfoot Lake Spillway.

Reelfoot features two campgrounds with a total of 102 campsites. One campground is located at the airfield, with the main campground at the south end of Reelfoot Lake. Bathhouses are centrally located at both areas, and dumping stations are provided. There is a playground and Laundromat at the southern campground.

Boating and fishing are popular at Reelfoot, with catches of crappie, bream, and largemouth bass. Both bank and boat fishing are available. Rental boats are at the park dock. Privately owned boats and motors are permitted.

You may ride on one of the Reelfoot scenic cruise boats operated daily from May through September (weather permitting).

One of the main attractions at Reelfoot is its wintering population of bald eagles. From December through March, park naturalists conduct daily eagle tours. Special weekend programs include slide shows, guest lectures, and bus tours. Reservations for the tours should be made in advance by contacting the park office. During the summer months seasonal naturalists conduct a variety of interpretive programs, with special pro-

grams arranged by contacting the park naturalist. There are many resorts on the lake for anglers and families.

From Tiptonville take TN 21 east along the southern shore, then TN 22 north to Samburg, and on to Union City.

All of the following accommodations are Tiptonville with zip code 38079, and all telephone listings are area code 901, except where noted.

Accommodations:
Backyard Birds Bed and Breakfast, Rt. 1, Box 2300, Air Park Rd., 253-9064.
Sweet Dreams Cottage Bed and Breakfast, 431 Wynn St., 253-7653 or 253-7203.
Reelfoot Lake State Park, Air Park Dr., 253-7756.

Dining:
Blue Bank Cypress Point Resort and Restaurant, 253-6878.

Shopping:
Eagle Tree Gallery, 253-8652.
Hillbilly Junction Gift Shop, 253-3099.

Special Events:
January–February—Peak Eagle Watching, Reelfoot Lake
July—Fireworks Annual Display, Reelfoot Lake
August—Waterfowl Festival, Samburg-Reelfoot Lake
November—Reelfoot Lake Arts and Crafts Festival, Tiptonville

Camping:
Bo's Landing, Rt. 1, Box 18, 253-7809. 30 sites, electricity, water, shower, boating, fishing, grills. Open Jan. 15–Nov. 30.
Bill's Spillway Campground, Rt. 1, Box 146A, 38079; 538-3411. 36 sites, electricity, water, shower, sanitary facilities, dump station, fishing, swimming area. Open Mar. 1–Oct. 30.
Gooch's Resort, Rt. 1, Hwys. 21 and 22, 253-8955. 16 sites, electricity, water, shower, sanitary facilities, dump station, boating, fishing, grills. Open year-round.
Ray's Camp, Rt. 1, Box 5B-D, 38079; 253-7765. 37 sites, electricity, water, shower, sanitary facilities, dump station, boating, fishing, grills. Open Mar.–Nov.
Reelfoot Lake State Park, Air Park Dr., 253-7756.

For More Information:
Northwest Tennessee Tourist Council, P.O. Box 963, Martin, 38237; 587-4213.

Reelfoot Lake Chamber of Commerce, Rt. 1, Box 140B,
    38079; 253-8144.
Reelfoot Lake Tourist Council, 6622 W. Hwy. 22, Hornbeak,
    38232; 538-2666.
Samburg Obion County Chamber of Commerce, P.O. Box 70,
    Union City, 38261; 885-0211.

84 *Union City*
The Stolen Courthouse

Once part of the Western District, Obion County was formed in 1823 and named for the river running through it. Union City became the county seat in 1890 after having been in Troy County since 1823. There is a story in James Ewing's book *It Happened in Tennessee* called "The Night They Moved the Courthouse."

David Crockett, taking time out from hunting, helped lay out the county seat of Troy. Troy was a thriving community before and after the Civil War. About twelve miles northeast of the community was another town beginning to grow, Union City, founded in 1854.

A railroad offered to come through Troy if some incentive was offered. The people of Troy considered that being the county seat was inducement enough and the railroad would come anyway. It must have been an arrogant stand by the Trojans because when the railroad changed its plans to run the line through Union City, the leaders of Troy pleaded for the railroad to run as originally planned. The rail officials stated there were only two places they would not go, Hell and Troy.

With the new railroad running through Union City bringing produce and goods to that city, Troy felt the pinch of trade leaving town. Also the people of Union City grew to resent

having to spend all day going twelve miles to Troy to conduct county business. In 1870 Charles Gibbs, son of the founder of Union City, went to Nashville as a delegate to the Constitutional Convention where he asked for an amendment to the new constitution exempting Obion and Cocke Counties from requiring two-thirds of the voters to approve change of county seat. He asked and received approval for a simple majority to make

Union City "stole" the courthouse from nearby Troy on July 9, 1890, at 3 A.M.

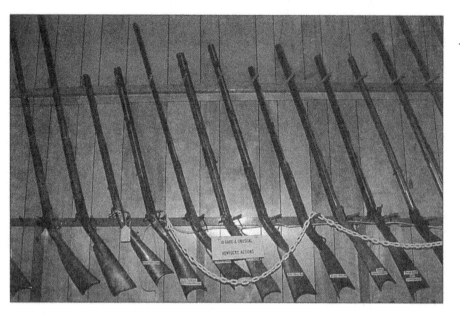

In addition to antique and replica firearms, Dixie Gun Works also displays antique automobiles, trucks, and outboard engines.

the change. However, the new law went unused for years in Obion County.

In July 1888, construction began on a new courthouse in Union City after raising funds by selling bonds. On January 1, 1890, the building was ready but the county seat was still in Troy. The mayor and aldermen moved into the new building and invited the branch law and chancery to take offices there also. Union City presented a petition in the county court calling for an election to settle where the county seat would be by employing the simple majority vote approved by the state's new constitution.

The court voted, 22–11, to call for an election, and it was a bitter campaign. Union City offered Troy its own law court if it would agree to the change. Troy went on the attack. Battles took place in many meetings and in the press until voting day, May 18, 1889. Union City won the county seat by 3,455 votes to 1,906, about 100

votes shy of a two-thirds majority, but only a simple majority was needed.

Troy complained that many of those voting in the election had been dead since the Civil War and went to court to get an injunction to prevent the election from being presented to the court. The suit was dismissed in October. Then it was taken to Tennessee's Supreme Court. Again it was dismissed. On July 7, 1890, the election results were presented to the Obion County Court and were approved by a vote of 21 to 12. Records were to be taken as soon as practical to the new courthouse in Union City. Troy immediately filed an injunction to prevent removal of the records but it was too late. The court was dissolved but a note was inserted in the proceedings that the injunction was asked for.

On July 9, at 3 A.M., shotgun blasts were heard in Union City. It was a signal for two hundred citizens to meet, bringing their guns and wagons. They were going to Troy to bring back all the county records to the new courthouse. As they traveled to Troy, they prevented anyone they met from going ahead of them to Troy to warn them that Union City citizens were coming. Just before reaching Troy a man climbed a telephone pole and placed a call to the officials in Troy telling them they were coming for the records. The officials in Troy thought the call originated in Union City twelve miles away. The Union City group moved quickly into Troy, into the open courthouse. The records were locked in a room. After a brief conversation it was decided they would break open the door. A Mr. Johnson volunteered to do the criminal deed. He borrowed a horse for the job, then escaped into Kentucky where he could not be prosecuted. The records were loaded onto the wagons and taken to the new Union City courthouse. By all accounts, the act was concluded peacefully.

When the Chancery Court met, it had to deal with the injunction that had been filed at the last court meeting. The injunction stated that the records "should remain where they are," and, because there was no contest by the Union City officials to letting the records stay in Union City, the injunction was rendered void.

That happened a long time ago and none taking part in the night they moved the courthouse are alive. But it makes a good story worth the retelling more than a century later.

For more Obion County history, go to the Obion County Museum at 1004 Edwards Street. It features Indian and Civil War artifacts, photography from 1915 to 1923, and Main Street Yesterday, an exhibit including buildings as they were back then: barber shop, print shop, general store, and others. A two-room log cabin with exhibits is next door.

A block away on Edwards Street is the first monument erected to honor unknown Confederate soldiers. It is a forty-foot white granite monolith dedicated in 1869.

Dixie Gun Works on Gun Powder Lane began in an old coal shed in the 1950s. Turner Kirkland collected guns as a child, and during his adulthood he returned to that love by collecting and selling antique guns, most being made before 1898. In 1954 Kirkland began having machine-made versions of the old muzzleloaders built for him to sell. The Hawkins and Kentucky long rifles became hits among collectors and black powder hunters. Guns sold faster than a .50 caliber ball could fly.

From selling guns, the business added lines of reenactment costumes and period guns. Dixie Gun Works supplied the guns used in *Glory* and *The Last of the Mohicans*.

The Old Car Museum housed in the Dixie Gun Works building has thirty-six cars dating back to a 1908 Maxwell two-passenger. They are completely restored and in good running order. Also there are more than two thousand antique automobile accessories, and a collection of farm engines, steam engines, and whistles.

Big Cypress Tree Natural Area and Humboldt are our next stops via US 45W going south.

All of the following accommodations are Union City with zip code 38261, and all telephone listings are area code 901, except where noted.

Attractions:
Dixie Gun Works/Old Car Museum, 885-0700.
Obion County Museum, 885-6774.
Parks Covered Bridge, 536-6242.

Dining:
Dixie Barn Restaurant, 885-3663.
Corner Bar-B-Que, 885-9924.
Catfish Galley, 885-0060.

Flippen's Hillbilly Barn, Troy, 538-2933.
Olympia Steak House, 885-3611.

For More Information:
Obion County Chamber of Commerce, P.O. Box 70; 885-
    0211.

Go back to US 45W and head south to
Humboldt.

For More Information:
Big Cypress Tree State Natural Area, 297 Big Cypress Rd.,
    Greenfield, 38230; 901-235-2700.

85 *Big Cypress Tree State Natural Area*

Oldest Cypress Tree Now a Stump

Big Cypress Tree State Natural Area, west of Ken-
ton (US 45W), is a day-use only natural area and
has no overnight facilities.

The 330-acre natural area lies in the flood
plain of the Middle Fork of the Obion River, and
it consists of bottomland hardwood forests. The
natural area is named for a champion bald cypress
tree that once grew in the area. It was the largest
and oldest bald cypress tree in the United States
and the largest tree of any species east of the Mississippi River. However, a severe thunderstorm in
July 1976 produced a lightning bolt that killed
the tree.

The tree was 175 feet tall, with a circumfer-
ence at the base of forty feet. The diameter meas-
ured thirteen feet. It was 1,350 years old when the
lightning struck.

Big Cypress Tree has a picnic area with tables
and grills, rest rooms, playground equipment, and
a ball field.

The Big Cypress Tree Fall Festival is held
annually, usually in September, and features
arts and crafts, nature programs, Civil War
reenactments, great food, and live musical
entertainment.

86 *Humboldt*

Our Hometown, Your Hometown

When you drive south on US 45W through Ken-
ton you may see white squirrels. These albino gray
squirrels are protected by local laws so their numbers continue to increase.

Trenton is about ten miles north of Humboldt and if you would like to see a collection of
more than five hundred rare antique lighted porcelain teapots from around the world, go by the
Trenton Teapot Museum in City Hall.

Humboldt, the trade center of Gibson
County, promotes strawberries and since 1934 has
held the West Tennessee Strawberry Festival. More
than one hundred thousand people attend the festivities that include two large parades (claimed to
be the longest nonmotorized parades in the United
States), a Tennessee Walking Horse Show, storytelling, checkers tournament, carnival, children's
events, street dance, and more is added each year.

Continuing the tribute to the strawberry is
the Strawberry Festival Museum that includes
memorabilia of past festivals. There are also displays from early city governments, local culture,
and artifacts.

At the same address is the West Tennessee
Regional Art Center. This old City Hall, renovated in 1994, was constructed in 1912 in the
neoclassic style. The downstairs gallery displays

The Strawberry Museum of Humboldt resides in the old City Hall with the West Tennessee Regional Art Center.

traveling exhibits, the lobby shows regional works of art, and the upper floor contains the Caldwell collection of sculptures, watercolor paintings, drawings, prints, and silkscreens. This collection of nearly two hundred pieces is the pride of the museum.

Take US 70A/79 southwest to Brownsville.

All of the following accommodations are Humboldt with zip code 38343, and all telephone listings are area code 901, except where noted.

Attractions:
Humboldt Strawberry Festival, 784-1842.
Trenton Teapot Museum, Trenton, 855-2013.
West Tennessee Regional Art Center, 784-1842 (Chamber of Commerce).

Dining:
Armour's Restaurant/Motel, 784-9938.
China Cafe, 784-7531.
Dough Boys, 784-5555.
Gordon's Restaurant, 784-4465.
Kappis Steak House, 784-2077.

Sam's Barbecue, 784-9850.
The Wall Street Grill, 784-1214.

Special Events:
May—West Tennessee Strawberry Festival; Teapot Festival, Trenton

For More Information:
City of Humboldt, 1421 Osborne; 784-2511.
Humboldt Chamber of Commerce, 1200 Main St.; 748-1842.

87 *Brownsville and Nutbush*
Home of Sleepy John Estes and the Mind Field

Haywood County was formed in 1823 from the Western District and Brownsville was selected as the county seat the next year.

One of the main attractions in Brownsville is the College Hill District. It was placed in the

Brownsville has two notable monuments, with this one representing the traditional memorial to the Confederate States of America.

National Register of Historic Places in 1979. The District consists of about eighty homes and the Oakwood Cemetery. In the College Hill Center you'll find the Haywood County Museum, which houses artifacts and the large Felsenthal Lincoln Collection, a private collection of Abraham Lincoln books, pictures, artifacts, documents, and memorabilia. The Lincoln collection is the second largest in the state (*see* Harrogate chapter). Here you also look at the heritage and history of the

county and its people, beginning with the Indians and ending at the present.

The chamber of commerce offers a book with two walking tours in town and several driving tours. The first walking tour (one and one-half miles long) begins at the chamber of commerce, originally the Carnegie Library, to cover downtown. You will see homes and churches dating back to the early 1800s. The homes are privately owned and are open to the public. Temple Adas Israel, originally built in 1882, is the oldest temple of continuous service in Tennessee, and at one time was the largest synagogue between Memphis and Nashville.

The second walking tour (two miles long) begins at College Hill Center to see well-kept homes built since the mid-1800s. Markers with the names of the homes and their dates are in the front yards. This is the historic district.

The Tennessee Peach Festival held the last of June promotes the peach growers with a walking horse show, Miss Tennessee Peach pageant, tractor pull, arts and crafts, hot air balloon rides, a pilgrimage of homes, petting zoo, pet show, and entertainment. Coinciding with the festival is a fishing rodeo held on O'Neal Lake.

One special event held on Brownsville's Court Square has strong appeal to us. It's the Brownsville Blues Fall Fest held the last Friday and Saturday in September. Most events are free except for the music at night. It wouldn't be a fest in West Tennessee if it didn't have barbecue and, of course, it does. There's also a scarecrow contest, BMX bike race, and a three-on-three basketball tournament.

At this writing, the Blues Heritage is restoring the Sleepy John Estes home, the last house he lived in. Sleepy John, a noted blues singer of the early 1900s, was born in Brownsville. The home should be moved to a new location and restored for public viewing by Blues Fest time, 1998.

While you are downtown, just a few blocks from the chamber of commerce, go by to see *The Mind Field.* It is a seventy-five-foot steel sculpture covering a city lot created by Billy Tripp, telling his life's story symbolically.

If abstract steel isn't for you, then you should treat yourself to a scenic drive through the Hatchie National Wildlife Refuge three miles

This is Brownsville's Billy Tripp's untraditional monument to imagination that he calls the Mind Field.

south of Brownsville. The 11,556-acre refuge borders twenty-four miles of the Hatchie Scenic River, the single remaining river in the Lower Mississippi Valley that has not been channeled. Three miles south of Brownsville on TN 76, it offers nature at its best with nine natural oxbow lakes as well as a man-made lake for fishing, more than two hundred species of birds, fifty mammals, and a myriad of reptiles, amphibians, fish, and invertebrates. You might spot a bald eagle during winter.

One of the new offerings at the refuge is Project Fish, fishing opportunities for anglers with disabilities. At O'Neal Lake, a 130-acre man-made lake has special facilities that allow people who use wheelchairs, are mobility or visually impaired, or who have muscular or mental impairments to fish. The complex includes piers, loading docks, boat ramps, shore fishing pads, benches, sun shelters, screens, and other fishing facilities. Largemouth bass, bluegill and catfish are present in the lake.

Anna Mae Bullock was born on November 26, 1939, to sharecropper parents in the small community of Nutbush, which is northwest of Brownsville on TN 19. As a young girl she was surrounded by cotton fields and dreams that were realized after she became Tina Turner, Queen of Rock and Roll. The shack in which she was born has disappeared, but a sign marks the site, located in Nutbush on Highway 19 adjacent to the cotton gin. The Nutbush Grocery Store that she visited is still standing and is now being developed into a small restaurant featuring southern foods.

Sharon Norris, another Nutbush native, has created a business centered around Tina Turner. If you give her a call at Wild Onion Ridge House, she'll invite you over, show you a small exhibit she has in her home, and then load you up in her car and take you on a trip through the area, telling you fascinating stories about the superstar. She also organizes the Tina Turner Day Celebration, which takes place each year during mid-August.

This concludes the loop tour and you can go back to Brownsville and to I-40 to return to Memphis, or go to Ripley to get on US 51 to Memphis.

All of the following accommodations are Brownsville with zip code 38012, and all telephone listings are area code 901, except where noted.

Attractions:
Lincoln Museum/Haywood County Museum, College Hill Center, 772-4883 or 772-2193.

Hatchie National Wildlife Refuge and Project Fish, 772-0501.
Wild Onion Ridge House, 772-4265.

Dining:
Back Yard, 772-1121.
Hickory Pit Bar-B-Q, 772-9926.
Lovelace's General Store, 772-0343.
Rebachi, 772-3184.
Olympic Steak House, 772-5555.
Z.Z.'s Kreme Kastle, 772-3132.

Special Events:
June—Tennessee Peach Festival and Fishing Rodeo
August—Tina Turner Celebration
September—Brownsville Blues Fall Fest

For More Information:
Brownsville-Haywood County Chamber of Commerce, 121 W. Main; 772-2193.

✒ Loop 13

88 Somerville and Fayette County
Still the Genteel South

About forty miles east of Memphis via US 64 is Somerville, first stop on our loop tour. We'll go east on US 64 to Savannah, south to Pickwick Dam, then west on TN 57 back to Memphis.

Fayette County, formed from parts of Shelby and Hardeman Counties, was named in honor of the Marquis de Lafayette, the French general who served on Washington's staff in the Revolutionary War. The county was established in 1824, the same year Somerville was selected as its county seat.

The legislature named the town in 1824 for Lt. Robert M. Somervill, who had been killed in 1814 while leading a charge for Gen. Andrew Jackson in the battle of Horseshoe Bend in Alabama. The town was originally spelled with two M's, but in 1853 it was pointed out that the family spelled the name with one M and used various spellings: Somervell, Somervill, and Somerville. In 1829 Somerville's Masonic Lodge Number 73 was granted a charter. The Worshipful Master, Richard Cleere, operated a tailor shop in Somerville and had learned his trade with the future president, Andrew Johnson, in the same shop.

During the four years of the Civil War, the doors of the lodge were never locked. On the altar were the Three Lights of Masonry and the silver jewels of the lodge, which were never touched. Not until the yellow fever epidemic of 1878 did the lodge temporarily cease conducting business.

You can visit antique shops on the square and take a free, self-guided tour of the Somerville area. A countywide fall homes tour is offered each year. Also available is a free Fayette County tour called This Trip is a Day of its Own! The county provides a step-on tour guide anytime. There are many old beautiful homes and buildings to give you the feeling that this was a stylish community in the mid-to-late 1800s.

In the center of Somerville is the Fayette County Courthouse, and the county has many beautiful homes built in the 1800s worth seeing.

The pretty but tiny community of Williston flourished in the 1800s with this Crawford building in the heart of town.

About seven miles south of Somerville on TN 76 is the small pre-Civil War community of Williston. Turn right (east) at the water tank on TN 193. Your first right is Hotel Street and it leads to Pleasant Retreat Bed and Breakfast. You may want to go straight to see the 1860 Crawford General Store in the heart of the tiny business district. From there, turn north on Railroad Street, which leads into the drive of the Pleasant Retreat Bed and Breakfast, a restored antebellum home in the National Register of Historic Places.

As you go up the drive, you'll see a small building on your left. It was a doctor's office in the 1800s but now is a playhouse for children. The Pleasant Retreat, complete with gardens and stables, rents three rooms with private baths and serves a full breakfast. Owners Judith and Jim Freeland offer a wide variety of services to guests, including use of the stables, jumping facilities, and miles of trails.

Judith and Jim have a great deal of local his-

tory to share. Most of the land in and around Williston once belonged to T. A. Crawford who died in 1939. Experimenting with plants for better production, he produced the big boll cotton plant, which yielded twice the amount of cotton of a normal plant.

After Crawford died, the place that is now Pleasant Retreat Bed and Breakfast was abandoned off and on until the Freelands bought it in 1989 and began restoration. The bed and breakfast is known by two names, the Crawford Experiment Farm, the primary name, and Pleasant Retreat. They have added a barn to become a horse bed and breakfast too.

The following is a letter to Miss Sophia Davis, Pleasant Retreat, Mississippi, from John Russell:

Dear Miss Sophia,
I take the present opportunity as propitious to pen you a few lines, which I fondly hope will be received with as much pleas-

ure as it gives me to write them. Love is said to be a holy, a
happy passion. To love and to know that one is loved in return
is surely happiness, but to love without knowing one is loved
in return is wretchedness in the extreme. The latter is my case.
From the first moment that I saw you I felt that you were
that being that was to make me happy, or miserable. Sleeping
or waking, your image has been ever before me, since our first
meeting; yes, you are the very ideal of my heart, the only being
that I ever saw, that I could love with my whole heart. I love
you as I never loved another. I feel to have you for a compan-
ion life would be no flowery path. I promise you eternal love.
I offer you a character unstained, a name unblemished, and as
true a heart as ever beat a response to the love of a woman.
Suspense is cruel, therefore let me know whether I can see you
on this subject the last Saturday in January, next, or not as I
start in the morning for Fayette County, Tennessee. I must
ask you to give me an answer by the person that brings this to
you, this you cannot deny me. So detain the bearer until you
can send your response by him. I remain ever yours,

John. A. Russell

*Romance gave this bed and breakfast one of its names, Pleasant Retreat,
and its history is fascinating.*

John and Sophia are the great-grandparents of
Jim Freeland.

Go back to Somerville and turn east on US
643 to Bolivar.

*All of the following accommodations are Somerville with zip
code 38068, and all telephone listings are area code 901,
except where noted.*

Accommodations:
Mebane-Nuckolls House, 1055 Nuckolls Rd., Rossville, 38066;
465-5662.
Pleasant Retreat Bed and Breakfast, 420 Hotel Street, Williston, 38076; 465-4599 or 465-3916.

Attractions:
Crawford General Store, Williston, 465-8646.

Dining:
The Hut, 465-3458.

Special Events:
May—Vic Rhodes Traditional Music Fest, Williston
September—Fayette County Fair and Rodeo
October—Annual Architectural Treasures of Fayette County
and Peddler's Bazaar
December—Christmas Tour of Homes, Williston

For More Information:
Somerville/Fayette County Chamber of Commerce, P.O. Box
411; 465-8690.

89 *Bolivar*
Hatchie Town

About ten miles east of Somerville on US 64 is
the city first known as Hatchie Town. Established
in 1823 on the banks of the Hatchie River, the
town received its new name to honor Gen. Simon
Bolívar, a South American patriot and liberator. It
was the first town in the United States to be
named for the general. In 1825 a permanent site

was selected for Bolivar, downriver from Hatchie
Town, which was maintained as a river port for
keelboats, flatboats, and steamships that traded
along the river.

Bolivar is the county seat of Hardeman
County, a county named for Col. Thomas Jones
Hardeman, who served with Andrew Jackson during the War of 1812. A courthouse was built in
1824 in Hatchie Town. The second courthouse
was ordered burned in 1864 by Union Gen.
Samuel Sturgis, as was most of the town. The present Corinthian courthouse rests on the site of the
previous one and was constructed in 1868. Three-
story wings were added to the building in 1955.

During the first week of May, the city offers a
tour of homes with an emphasis on the history of
the area. More than one hundred buildings are in
the National Register of Historic Places. The
Bills-McNeal District has some of the oldest and
most historically significant structures dating back
to the early 1800s, including the McNeal House,
Polk Cemetery, the Pillars, the Columns, a Confederate monument, and Magnolia Manor. Judge
Austin Miller purchased the land for Magnolia
Manor in 1844, drew the plans, and supervised
the construction of his English country home, an
excellent example of Georgian architecture. Built
by slaves, it has two stories, thirteen-inch-thick
walls of handmade, sun-dried, red brick, and a
bronze eagle on the corner giving the building
date as 1849.

Miller served as a county commissioner, and
he and John D. Graham of Shelby County are
given credit for setting the southern boundary of
Tennessee, which put Memphis in Tennessee
instead of Mississippi.

The manor was built as a symmetrical rectan-
gle, with halls through the full depth of the house
separating rooms on each side. A long porch origi-

*Bolivar was the first city in the United States to be named for the South
American leader Simon Bolívar.*

nally extended across the back. Here, on Sunday
afternoons, Mrs. Miller assembled the slaves.
Long benches were arranged and, as mistress of
the house, she taught the Sunday school lesson of
the day.

Tradition tells that Mrs. Miller drew from her
inner strength and acted as a gracious southern
hostess. However, during a meal one day, General
Sherman, who was known to be less than tactful,

expressed his opinion that all southern women and children should be exterminated. Mrs. Miller abruptly left the room. General Grant, who had not heard the comment, followed her to determine her reason for leaving the table and found her seated on the back porch crying. She explained and Grant, infuriated by the remark, ordered Sherman to apologize. It is said that Sherman apologized but was so incensed by the order that he struck out in anger with his saber, slashing the solid walnut stairway. The mark is still visible.

The home is presently owned by Mr. and Mrs. James C. Cox and serves as a bed and breakfast. It has two suites and two guest rooms. The suites have private baths and the guest rooms share a bath.

The Pillars, former plantation home of John Houston Bills, was built before 1826 and was visited by David Crockett, Sam Houston, James K. Polk, and General Grant. The brick home has a long front porch with eight white Doric columns placed upside down.

The Little Courthouse, built in 1824 of logs, was sold and moved to its present site in 1827 and additions were made to convert it into a Federal-style residence. Today it is a museum.

Return to US 64 and go east to Crump and Savannah but first take a side trip to Chickasaw State Park. Take TN 18 north and turn right (east) on TN 100 to the park.

All of the following accommodations are Bolivar with zip code 38008, and all telephone listings are area code 901, except where noted.

Accommodations:
Magnolia Manor, 418 N. Main St., 658-6700.

Attractions:
Bills-McNeal District. Contact Hardeman County Chamber of Commerce, 658-6554.

The Little Courthouse, 658-3390 (for appointment).
The Pillars, 658-3390 (for appointment).

Dining:
The Grecian Steakhouse, 658-7512.
Joe's Restaurant, 658-7255.
Richard's Barbeque, 658-7652.

Shopping:
Wren's Nest Antiques, 658-3235.
Your Kind of Store, 658-4913.

Special Events:
August—Local Fair
September—Tennessee Forest Festival Tree-judging contest, music, beauty pageant, arts and crafts, walking horse show, loggers breakfast
December—Christmas lights, Chickasaw and Big Hill Pond State Parks

For More Information:
Hardeman County Chamber of Commerce, 500 W. Market St., 658-6554.

90 *Chickasaw State Park*
Serenity in West Tennessee

Chickasaw State Park is on some of the highest terrain in West Tennessee. This 14,400-acre park and forest was once part of a vast area belonging to the Chickasaw Nation prior to the Jackson purchase of 1818. The main part of the park is among tall pines on Lake Placid. Chickasaw has housekeeping cabins, complete with fireplaces and firewood, with easy access to Lake Placid. The restaurant, which offers southern cuisine, is open year-round. The main campground has fifty campsites, and there are another thirty sites at the Wrangler Campground. All park sites have picnic tables and grills; fifty-four have electric and water hookups. Bathhouses provide hot showers and restroom facilities. There is a playground in the campground, and a lodge to accommodate up to forty persons is operated all year.

Rowboats and paddleboats are available for rent on Lake Placid. No personally owned boats or motors are allowed. The park features four miles of hiking trails, and there are seventy-five miles of trails in the forest for mountain bikes, horses, and off-road vehicles.

A recreation director on duty during the summer months conducts group games, arts and crafts, evening movies, campfire programs, and hayrides. One of the park's more popular events is Frontier Days usually held in June with country music and dancing.

Go back to Bolivar to US 64 and go east to Adamsville.

For More Information:
Chickasaw State Park, 901-989-5141.

91 *Adamsville*
Walking Tall

We're sure you have heard of Sheriff Buford "Walking Tall" Pusser. Three movies have been made about him. Pusser grew up in Adamsville, played football here, and then joined the marines. He became a professional wrestler in Chicago before returning home to join the Adamsville police. He became sheriff in 1964. His fame grew the Old West way, getting rid of outlaws with a flourish.

But his fame came at a fatal price. While cleaning up McNairy County between 1964 and 1970 he made enemies of many outlaws. His imposing six-foot, six-inch frame carried 240 pounds, adding to his larger-than-life image. His

being shot eight times, knifed seven times, having his wife killed while she was sitting beside him in his car, and to finally die in an automobile crash that is not believed to have been accidental, all had the makings of an action movie based on his life.

Today his home is a museum with original furnishings, memorabilia, and film interviews with Buford and his daughter Dwana. His mother reportedly said at his death that nothing in the home was to be moved. You can see how his life as a threatened lawman changed the way he lived. He slept in an underground room.

The Buford Pusser Festival, held on Memorial Day weekend, includes softball games, a car show, a 5K run, musical entertainment, a carnival, arts and crafts, and food booths. Also a Bluegrass Music Show is held monthly at Adamsville Community Center.

There is no celebration for another Adamsville native son, Ray Blanton. Once governor of Tennessee, he spent time in prison for illegally selling liquor licenses and pardons.

From Adamsville stay on US 64 west to Crump and Savannah.

All of the following accommodations are Adamsville with zip code 38310, and all telephone listings are area code 901, except where noted.

Attractions:
Buford Pusser Home and Museum, 632-4080.

Dining:
Biggest Little Diner, 632-1333.
Dylan's Restaurant, 632-9373.
Granny's Kountry Kitchen, 632-3030.
Iron Eagle Cafe, 632-3777.
Mike's Cafe, 632-0362.
Neal's Little Fish House, 632-1221.
Price's Bar-B-Que, 632-3036.
Vicki's, 632-1550.

Special Events:
May—Buford Pusser Festival

For More Information:
McNairy County Chamber of Commerce, 114 Cypress St.,
    Selmer, 38375; 645-6360.

92 *Savannah, Crump, Shiloh, Pickwick Dam*

Antiques, Cannonballs, and Catfish

Coming from the west on US 64, Savannah is across the Tennessee River from Crump. Shiloh National Military Park, south of Crump on TN 22, is a must see for Civil War buffs. Visiting the park was one of the most somber experiences we had in our travels. If you love shopping at flea markets and shops for antiques and collectibles, you'll love Crump. It's a small community with a lot of shops.

Peggy Sweats Antiques is open every day except Sunday but you can make an appointment for then. It is typical of the many antique shops along this strip. The flea markets do most of their business on Friday evening and the weekend.

Just beyond Crump's antique district, turn south on Highway 22 to go to Shiloh National Military Park and follow the signs.

Savannah bills itself as "the Catfish Capital of the World." The Tennessee River Museum is in Savannah and also houses the Hardin County Chamber of Commerce.

Inside the museum there are displays of more than two hundred fossils from the Paleozoic and Cretaceous periods, a large display of Indian arrowheads, one of the finest stone effigy pipes of a kneeling human ever recovered, a partial reproduction of the USS Cairo (the original is in Vicksburg), many artifacts of the War Between the States, and an especially impressive display of field artillery projectiles including 132 types of rifle bullets. Some of the bullets are merged with other

The 1908 Ross House in Savannah became a bed and breakfast in 1990.

bullets or other materials, and one has the impression of a button from a uniform.

Among the projectiles exhibited is a canister composed of twenty-seven iron balls. These were fired from cannon and the balls separated when they came out, like shotgun pellets. The display gives us an idea of what it was like to have been in the Hornets Nest at Shiloh during the battle.

When charging Confederate troops got within three hundred yards, Yankee batteries began firing double loads of canister. A well-trained cannon crew could fire a six-gun battery twice per minute. In a fifteen-minute charge, like the Rebels endured, how many iron balls would one battery fire? A calculator is part of the display for computations. Lift the lid that is marked "Answer" to find the correct number. Imagine running toward cannon firing 9,720 balls at you!

A new exhibit about mussel harvesting shows how it was done and how buttons were made from the shells, an industry no longer in existence. At another new exhibit, about the Trail of Tears, an audio narration in English and Cherokee describes the history of the removal of the Indians to Oklahoma. Details about American Indian history and the battle of Shiloh are also available.

It is said that for every two Confederate soldiers enlisting from Savannah, there was also one Union soldier. Tennessee may have been a southern state, but not everyone was for the southern cause. When Grant took command of the Union army, Shiloh, a training ground for raw recruits from the North, became the second-largest city in America.

A living history demonstration takes place at Shiloh on the weekend closest to April 6, the anniversary of the battle. Between five hundred and one thousand Confederate reenactors come, set up camps on the battlefield, demonstrate cannon and rifles, play Confederate music, and produce plays for the public. On Sunday a memorial service is held. This is free except for the regular fee for entrance into the park.

Shiloh went through hell and the hornet's nest before attaining the meaning of its name, Place of Peace.

The Civil War Headquarters Monument, in Savannah, is often referred to as Grant's Monument, where two cannons and a pyramid of cannon balls mark the location of General Grant's headquarters for the battle of Shiloh. The monument is on a traffic island in the street one block west of the museum.

Queen Haley, the subject of the miniseries *Queen*, is buried in Savannah. She was the grandmother of Alex Haley, the author of *Roots*. Her husband, also named Alex Haley, was a ferryman of the Cherry ferry, and she worked at the Cherry mansion as a young woman.

There are two bed and breakfasts in Savannah. E. W. Ross built the Ross House, of neoclassical design, in 1908. A second floor was added in the 1930s. The first-floor interior remains in original condition while the second floor reflects its 1930s origin. Many of the antique furnishings had been stored in the attic.

The house was made into a bed and breakfast in 1990, accommodating guests on the second floor. Situated on Main Street, the Ross House has a library with early-twentieth-century books, gardens shaded by bur oaks, and a dense wooded area behind the house with watchable wildlife. John and Harriet Ross are the innkeepers.

The Victorian-style White Elephant Bed and Breakfast Inn, owned by Sharon and Ken Hansgen, was built at the turn of the century and is in the National Register of Historic Places. It has a circular tower with a conical roof and parlors with curved-glass bay windows for viewing birds and squirrels.

The inn rents three guest rooms, and each has a theme taken from the period in which the house was built. The rooms are furnished with antiques and queen-sized beds. Guests may prevail upon Ken to share his extensive knowledge of the Civil War and the nearby Shiloh Battlefield.

It was from Savannah that General Grant went to work each day before the battle of Shiloh. Grant did not stay with his army of thirty-three thousand men at Pittsburg Landing on the other side of the Tennessee River. He took a river steamer back and forth to work and felt so comfortable with the war situation that he could sleep cozily in a warm house nine miles from his troops.

Five miles north of Pittsburg Landing, Gen. Lew Wallace, later the author of *Ben Hur*, commanded five thousand men on the west bank. Why did Grant leave Wallace vulnerable at Crump's Landing? No answer to this behavior has been given. It has been surmised that Grant was off guard as any of us are at times, in a slump. Grant's slump became costly.

Twenty miles southwest of Pittsburg Landing in Corinth, Mississippi, Confederate Gen. Albert Sidney Johnston had forty-one thousand troops. Johnston had been in Corinth since March 17, 1862, when Grant took command of the troops at Pittsburg Landing.

On April 6 he surprised the Union troops. Reports indicate that the Federals, camping about two miles from Shiloh Church, should have been alerted to the Rebels in the woods on the evening of April 5 because hundreds of rabbits and deer came out of the woods and ran through the Union lines. Johnston's army was only two miles from Grant's.

A small skirmish occurred that evening and a Confederate hostage was taken for interrogation. General Sherman was given the intelligence that Johnston had moved his troops to the area. Sherman concluded that there would be no attack while Grant had gone to Savannah for the night.

Acres of headstones of more than twenty-three thousand Confederate and Union soldiers, many unknown, rest on the hills overlooking the battle-ground and the Tennessee River.

That evening Grant telegraphed Gen. Henry W. Halleck stating he had "scarcely the faintest idea of attack being made upon us, but will be prepared should such a thing take place."

Early on the morning of April 6, more birds were stirring than Union soldiers. It may have sounded like a woodpecker after a tree grub at first but the sounds were not mistaken for long. Rebels poured out of the woods like water though a ruptured levee and gunpowder smoke filled the air like fog.

The Yankees, many caught asleep in their tents, were disorganized and went running toward the river. Other divisions farthest away from the ambush organized and withstood the coming attack. Union soldiers fled through their own standing line. Eventually the Union army yielded and pulled back.

Grant was having breakfast when the cannon's thunder reached his ears and rattled the windows in the house where he was staying.

Grant and his staff took the river steamer to Crump's Landing to join Lew Wallace. Grant told Wallace to head toward the fighting but Wallace either took the wrong road or got lost. He arrived at the battlefield that evening after the fighting was over and contended he took the road he was ordered to take.

Grant was at the battle by midmorning and Gen. D. C. Buell arrived about 1 P.M., but his troops did not arrive from Nashville until the next day. Most of the Union Army was atop the bluff over the Tennessee River with not enough boats to get them across.

Intelligence came to Grant that Confederate General Johnston had been killed. It was true. Johnston was hit in the thigh but, having sent his surgeon back to help other wounded, bled to death because those helping him did not know how to stop the bleeding. Simple first-aid treatment would have saved him.

Without Johnston in command, leadership

fell to Gen. P. G. T. Beauregard, who was not the man for the job at that time. With victory in his grasp, he ordered the troops to fall back. That night in pouring rain, Buell's and Wallace's twenty-five thousand fresh troops arrived. By the evening of April 7 the Confederates were retreating back to Corinth.

The battle of Shiloh was the bloodiest battle to that date, with 13,047 Union men lost, wounded, or dead, and 10,699 Confederate losses. Shiloh in Hebrew means "place of peace."

When we walked the grounds of Shiloh among the thousands of graves, we felt a terrible sadness. Although the park is pretty with well-kept lawns, roads, monuments, and woods, the sense of all those who died here remains.

In the rows and rows of graves, many head-stones have the name of the person who died, but many others have only a number to identify the interred. As you arrive at the farthest edge of the cemetery, you come to a steep slope that goes down to the Tennessee River. The view with your back to the river is a panorama of the memorial.

There is a nine and one-half-mile self-guided tour of the battlefield. Pick up a map and brochure at the visitor center. The drive takes about an hour. You may prefer more detail offered by renting a cassette tape for a two-hour tour. Another option is to view a twenty-five-minute movie called *Shiloh—Portrait of a Battle* that traces events leading up to the battle and presents a description of the fight.

Every other December in an even year, a service called Grand Illumination is held at Shiloh. A candle for every wounded, dead, and missing soldier is lit. More than twenty-three thousand are placed throughout the park and are concentrated in areas where men were wounded. The commem-oration begins at dark and the public drives though the battleground. It lasts until all who wish to go through the park have done so, often until 11 P.M.

To leave Savannah for Pickwick Dam, the shortest route, TN 128, is twelve miles. At Pickwick Dam is the Tennessee River Waterway Museum with Indian and Civil War artifacts, photographs, drawings and charts of the Tennessee River. Included is the history and development of Pickwick Dam. You can also watch boats lock through the dam. This is the place to be for water sports. Pickwick Lake above the dam is known for wonderful smallmouth bass fishing. Below the dam in Kentucky Lake there are smallmouth, sauger, and plenty of catfish.

Return to Memphis via TN 57 to complete the loop tour with our first stop at Big Hill Pond Scenic Natural Area.

All of the following accommodations are Savannah with zip code 38372, and all telephone listings are area code 901, except where noted.

Accommodations:
The Ross House, 504 Main St., 800-647-3174 or 925-3974 or 925-5452.
White Elephant Bed and Breakfast Inn, 304 Church St., 925-6410.
Pickwick Landing State Park, P.O. Box 15, Pickwick Dam, 38365; 800-250-8615 or 689-3135.
Bellis Botel, Hwy. 128 and Botel Rd., 925-4787.

Attractions:
Shiloh Indian Mounds, Shiloh, 689-5696.
Shiloh Military Park, Shiloh, 689-5696.
Savannah Historic District, 925-2364.
Tennessee River Museum, 800-552-3866 or 925-2363.

Dining:
Battlefield Cafe, Shiloh, 689-5570.
Cherry's Restaurant, 925-4297.
Christopher's Restaurant, 925-9285.
D & D Steakhouse, 925-9128.

Jon's Pier at Pickwick, 689-3575.
Hagy's Catfish Hotel, Shiloh, 689-3327.
Happy China, 925-1474.
The Rib Cage, 689-3637.
Toll House Restaurant, 925-5128.
The Wharf Restaurant, 925-9469.

Shopping:
Antiques and More, Crump, 632-1351.
Crump Flea Market.
Ed Shaw's Gift Shop, Shiloh, 689-5080.
Henry D. Strickland, 925-2911.
Peggy Sweat's Antiques, Crump, 632-0106.
Savannah Art Gallery, 925-7529.
Shaw's Antiques, 925-7147.
Steppin into Country, 925-3373.

Special Events:
January—Pickwick Sauger Festival, Pickwick Dam
March—Snow White and the Seven Dwarfs; Hee-Haw and
     Howdy; USA Sportsman's Big Bassarama
April—Savannah Art Guild Civil War Art Display, Shiloh; 125th
     Anniversary Battle of Shiloh Reenactment; Shiloh (an origi-
     nal play), Savannah Theater; Third Annual St. Peter Home
     for Children Bass Classic
May—Moby Rick: The Killer Catfish, Savannah Theater
June—Peach Festival

Camping:
Battlefield Campground, Shiloh, 689-5570.
Bellis Botel, 925-4787.
Savannah R.V. Park, 925-8767.
The Wharf Restaurant, 925-9469.

For More Information:
Hardin County Tourism, 507 Main St., 800-552-3866 or 925-
     2364. Ask for Group Travel Planner.

93 *Big Hill Pond State Park*
Fishing Under the Hill

After leaving Pickwick Dam heading west on TN
57, you come to Big Hill Pond State Park in the
southwestern corner of McNairy County at the
junction of the Tuscumbia and Hatchie State
Scenic Rivers. The 4,218-acre park includes

McNatt Lake, a pond, and a three-quarter-mile-
long boardwalk across Dismal Swamp, a southern
bottomland forest.

Tributaries of Cypress Creek and the Tuscumbia River, with numerous oxbows and sloughs,
influence the park. It takes its name from a thirty-
five-acre pond created by a barren area used for
dirt to help construct a railroad levee across the
Cypress and Tuscumbia Bottoms for the Memphis
and Charleston Railroad in 1853. Today bald
cypress trees surround the pond.

The park has thirty-two camping sites with a
bathhouse. Water is available in the campground,
but not at each site. A playground is within walking distance of the campground. Fishing and
boating are convenient on the Travis McNatt
Lake, which is stocked with bass, bluegill, and catfish. A public launch ramp is available for private
boats, but motors are restricted to electric motors
only on the lake.

The park has six trails that range from a
half-mile to seven miles, for a total of thirty-five
miles. These trails take you along boardwalks
through the Dismal Swamp. There are many vistas and overlooks along the trail system. One
such overlook is an eighty-foot-tall observation
tower that provides a 360-degree view of the
entire park. Wildlife abounds within Big Hill
Pond State Park and there are twenty-two picnic
sites there.

Our next destination is Grand Junction, west
on TN 57.

For More Information:
McNairy County Chamber of Commerce, 114 Cypress St.,
     P.O. Box 7, Selmer, 38375; 901-645-6360.
Big Hill Pond State Park, Rt. 1, Box 150B, Pocahontas, 38061;
     901-645-7967.

94 Grand Junction, LaGrange, Moscow
A Grand Trio

Leaving Big Hill Pond State Park going west via TN 57, you go through three small towns with notable attractions. The first town is Grand Junction. Here is the Ames Plantation where the National Field Trial Championship for bird dogs is held each February. In 1901 Hobart Ames moved south from Massachusetts and bought a plantation called Cedar Grove. Over the next few years, he accumulated thousands of acres for his crops and cattle.

Game was plentiful on his plantation and he took advantage of it, leading him to breed top field dogs. The first field trials had been held in West Point, Mississippi, in 1896. From Ames's love of hunting and dogs, the National Field Tri-

als grew and were moved to his plantation a few years later. He became president of the organization and remained in the position for forty-three years. Today the trials last eight to ten days; when the testing is over, one dog reigns as World Champion Bird Dog.

Today the University of Tennessee operates the plantation. On the 18,600 acres are several log outbuildings and Cedar Grove, the manor house, which gives you the feeling of an early American farm.

Also, the National Bird Dog Museum, the Field Trial Hall of Fame, and the Wildlife Heritage Center are on TN 57 a few miles away. Recognizing more than forty breeds of bird dogs, including retrievers, pointers, and spaniel breeds, the museum features numerous exhibits, sporting dog art, wildlife murals, artifacts, historical objects, and a collection of game birds and wildlife specimens.

LaGrange is the next town along TN 57. This

These bronze statues hold their hunting positions in front of the National Bird Dog Museum in Grand Junction.

area was first an Indian trading post in 1819, then was laid out in 1822 and chartered in 1829. During the Civil War Union troops were quartered in the town and burned and destroyed much of it. Then yellow fever visited its destruction in 1878.

Cogbills' Store and Museum in LaGrange, which began business in 1868 and was rebuilt after a tornado hit it in 1900, has antiques, crafts, collectibles, and old tools. It's at the junction of TN 57 and LaGrange Road at the blinking light. Across the road is a building erected in 1892, the LaGrange General Store, and a little farther down the block is Trading Post Antiques, in a shop built in the 1800s.

When we visited in April, the home next door to Cogbill's Store was ablaze with more than one hundred azaleas. More than a hundred shrubs capture not only your eye but also imagination as to how to care for so many plants. This is an impressive community for its beautiful old homes, a must-see place for those who enjoy looking at grand 1800s architecture.

A Fayette County history written in 1878 states that our next community, Moscow, was named for "the former capital of Russia, the burning of which in 1812 led to the signal defeat of the first Napoleon." But this is not the only root for the name of the town. An old Indian trail, the Mossac, came through here and the name Moscow may have derived from it. Or it may be that it came from an Indian word meaning "between two rivers." Also the French called the Wolf River Margot, pronounced Mar-go, and Moscow may have been corrupted from it. The bottom line is that no one knows for sure where the name came from.

In 1853 Moscow was a register station on the Memphis and Charleston Railroad. This meant that all trains stopped here to register and receive orders. It was also a telegraph office. The railroad was a blessing to the thriving community but became a liability during the Civil War. The Union army had to capture it from the Confederates, thereby creating the first skirmish in the area. The battle of Moscow occurred December 3, 1863. Later the town was devastated by fire as the Union army left.

In 1980 when Moscow, Russia, was to host the Olympics but was boycotted by the United States and others because of Russian aggression in Afghanistan, Moscow, Tennessee, picked up the slack. The mayor jokingly said that Moscow should hold the Olympic Games, and the offhand remark became reality.

The swimming hole in the Wolf River became the Olympic pool, a cow pasture became the shot-put range, and a raccoon was selected as the mascot. The Olympic flame came from Athens (Tennessee) via a coon hunter's lantern.

In June of 1980 competition began in Moscow. Skillet throwing, tobacco spitting, basketball throwing, and a bicycle race were top events. Medallions of pewter, brass, and bronze were awarded. Spectators came from as far away as Australia.

Collierville is our next stop on TN 57.

All of the following telephone listings are area code 901, except where noted.

Attractions:
Cogbill's Store and Museum, LaGrange, 878-1235.
Ames Plantation, Grand Junction, 878-1067.
National Bird Dog Museum, Field Trial Hall of Fame and Wildlife Heritage Center, Grand Junction, 878-1168 or 764-2058.

Dining:
Ann's Country Kitchen, Grand Junction.
Gurkins #4, Moscow.

Tea for Two, Moscow, 877-3883.
Wolf River BBQ Co., Moscow, 877-1000.

Shopping:
LaGrange General Store.
Village Trading Post Antiques, LaGrange.

Special Events:
February—National Field Trial Championship, Grand Junction

For More Information:
Fayette County Chamber of Commerce, P.O. Box 411,
    Somerville, 38068; 456-8690.

95 Collierville
Once Hot, Now a Cool City

Collierville is the last stop along TN 57 before getting back to Memphis. The big city is reaching out to touch this town but Collierville's city fathers are acting to preserve its small town atmosphere.

This was a stagecoach stop in the 1820s and first boosted the town's growth. The railroad came to add another boost, but then came the Civil War and General Sherman, who torched Collierville before he burned Atlanta. Yellow fever did not spare Collierville while it was making its rounds in West Tennessee; but after the yellow plague departed, the town began growing again.

When the burned town was rebuilt in the 1870s, a square was created. Most towns in the South put a courthouse in their square, but Collierville ended up with a bandstand there. Its Main Street, that runs along the square, has been designated a National Main Street, thanks to the control of growth with the right mix of historic preservation and planning. Collierville has the only National Main Street designation in Tennessee.

The bandstand jumps in July with the city's Sunset on the Square concert series. A variety of music entertains the community on hot summer evenings. If no breeze stirs, then you can hire a

Vigorous downtown Collierville has much to offer visitors, including the Heritage Railroad and Memphis Transportation Museum.

horse-drawn carriage for a cool tour of the town. At other times the Harrell Performing Arts Theatre offers a full season of theatre, music, and dance.

The Heritage Railroad and Memphis Transportation Museum displays historically significant train cars, including a 1912 steam engine, a 1915 executive's car, a 1920s caboose, and several cars dating from the 1930s and 1940s.

A site that appeals to all family members is the Saint Nick Farms and Zoological Park. Here you can see the mascot of the University of Memphis, Tom, a Bengal tiger. There are other critters to please your wildlife viewing, such as leopards and lions.

All of the following accommodations are Collierville with zip code 38017, and all telephone listings are area code 901, except where noted.

Accommodations:
Azalea Ridge Bed and Breakfast, 342 Peterson Lake Rd., 853-3421.

Attractions:
The Collierville Carriage Company, 853-6771 (reservations).
Harrell Performing Arts Theatre, 853-3228.

Heritage Railroad and Memphis Transportation Museum, 800-850-5514 or 853-5034.
Historic Town Square, 853-1666.
Saint Nick Farms and Zoological Park, 853-3942.

Dining:
Anna's Steakhouse, 853-1006.
Barnhills' Country Buffet, 854-5660.
Bella Italia Ristorante, 854-7362.
Brangus Feed Lot, 854-7886.
Lamm's Restaurant, 853-1233.
The Silver Caboose, 853-0010.

Shopping:
Abbington Antique Mall, 854-3568.
English Country Antiques, 853-3170.
Not Forgotten Antiques, 854-2189.
Town Square Antique Mall, 854-9839.
White Church Antiques, 854-6433.

Special Events:
February—Valentine's Day at the Memphis Transportation Museum
May—Fair on the Square Arts and Crafts Show; Annual Studebaker Vintage Car Show
July—Sunset on the Square Concert Series
August—Preservation Party and Gourmet Event
November—Antiques Show and Sale
December—Dickens on the Square

For More Information:
Collierville Area Chamber of Commerce, 125 N. Rowlett, 38017; 853-1949.

Index

Suggested Reading

Arnow, Harriette Simpson. *Seedtime on the Cumberland*. New York: The Macmillan Company, 1960.

Bradley, Jeff. *Tennessee Handbook*. Chico, California: Moon Publications, 1997.

Brandt, Robert. *Touring the Middle Tennessee Backroads*. Winston-Salem, North Carolina: John F. Blair, 1995.

Brooks, Maurice. *The Appalachians*. Boston: Houghton Mifflin, 1965.

Caldwell, Mary French. Tennessee: *The Dangerous Example Watauga to 1849*. Nashville: Aurora Publishers, Inc., 1974.

Carpenter, John W. and Michael Emrick. *Tennessee Courthouses*. London, Kentucky: John W. Carpenter, 1996.

Chapman, Jefferson. *Tellico Archaeology*. Knoxville: Tennessee Valley Authority (distributed by University of Tennessee Press), 1985.

Coleman, Brenda D. and Jo Anna Smith. *Hiking the Big South Fork*. Knoxville: University of Tennessee Press, 1993.

Connelly, Thomas. *Civil War, Tennessee, Battles and Leaders*. Knoxville: University of Tennessee Press, 1979.

DeLaughter, Jerry. *Mountain Roads and Quiet Places*. Gatlinburg, Tennessee: Great Smoky Mountains Natural History Association, 1986.

Dixon, Max. *The Wataugans*. Nashville: Tennessee American Revolution Bicentennial Commission, 1976.

Dykeman, Wilma. *Tennessee*. Newport, Tennessee: Wakestone Books, 1975.

Etnier, David A. and Wayne C. Starnes. *The Fishes of Tennessee*. Knoxville: University of Tennessee Press, 1993.

Ewing, James. *It Happened in Tennessee*. Nashville: Rutledge Hill Press, 1986.

Faulkner, Charles H. *The Old Stone Fort*. Knoxville: The University of Tennessee Press, 1968.

Goodspeed, Weston A. *Goodspeed's History of Tennessee*. Nashville: The Goodspeed Publishing Company, 1887. Reprint Charles and Randy Elder, Nashville, Tennessee, 1973.

Houk, Rose. *Great Smoky Mountains*. New York: Houghton Mifflin Company, 1993.

Luther, Edward T. *Our Restless Earth*. Knoxville: University of Tennessee Press, 1977.

Manning, Russ. *The Historic Cumberland Plateau*. Knoxville: University of Tennessee Press, 1993.

Markham, Doug. *Boxes, Rockets, and Pens*. Knoxville: University of Tennessee Press, 1997.

Matthews, Larry E. *Cumberland Caverns*. Huntsville, Alabama: National Speleological Society, Inc., 1989.

McDonald, Michael J. and William Bruce Wheeler. *Knoxville, Tennessee*. Knoxville; University of Tennessee Press.

McPherson, James M., Editor. *The Atlas of the Civil War*. New York: Macmillan, 1994.

Means, Evan. *Hiking Tennessee Trails*. Old Saybrook, Connecticut: The Globe Pequot Press, 1979.

Neely, Jack. *Knoxville's Secret History*. Knoxville: Scruffy City Publishing, 1995.

Rozema, Vicki. *Footsteps of the Cherokee*. Winston-Salem, North Carolina: John F. Blair, 1995.

Sakowski, Carolyn. *Touring the East Tennessee Backroads*. Winston-Salem, North Carolina: John F. Blair, 1993.

Satz, Ronald N. *Tennessee's Indian People*. Knoxville: University of Tennessee Press, 1979.

Sherwin, Holly. *Canoeing in Tennessee*. Franklin, Tennessee: Cool Springs Press, 1996.

Schmidt, Ronald G. and William S. Hooks. *Whistle Over the Mountain*. Yellow Springs, Ohio: Graphicom Press, 1994.

Wise, Kenneth. *Hiking Trails of the Great Smoky Mountains*. Knoxville: University of Tennessee Press, 1996.

WPA Guide to Tennessee. Knoxville: University of Tennessee Press, 1986. Reprint of 1939 guide written and compiled by the Federal Writers' Project of the Works Projects Administration for the State of Tennessee.

Printed in the USA
CPSIA information can be obtained
at www.ICGtesting.com
LVHW080749050824
787165LV00006B/11